Scala Reactive Programming

Build scalable, functional reactive microservices with Akka, Play, and Lagom

Rambabu Posa

BIRMINGHAM - MUMBAI

Scala Reactive Programming

Commissioning Editor: Merint Mathew
Acquisition Editor: Karan Sadawana
Content Development Editor: Akshada Iyer
Technical Editor: Abhishek Sharma
Copy Editor: Pranjali Chury, Safis Editing
Project Coordinator: Prajakta Naik
Proofreader: Safis Editing
Indexer: Priyanka Dhadke
Graphics: Jisha Chirayil
Production Coordinator: Nilesh Mohite

First published: February 2018

Production reference: 1270218

Published by Packt Publishing Ltd.
Livery Place
35 Livery Street
Birmingham
B3 2PB, UK.

ISBN 978-1-78728-864-5

www.packtpub.com

To my lovely wife, Bhargs, for all her help and encouragement during this book and to my beautiful little princess, Sai Aashika.

`mapt.io`

Mapt is an online digital library that gives you full access to over 5,000 books and videos, as well as industry leading tools to help you plan your personal development and advance your career. For more information, please visit our website.

Why subscribe?

- Spend less time learning and more time coding with practical eBooks and Videos from over 4,000 industry professionals

- Improve your learning with Skill Plans built especially for you

- Get a free eBook or video every month

- Mapt is fully searchable

- Copy and paste, print, and bookmark content

PacktPub.com

Did you know that Packt offers eBook versions of every book published, with PDF and ePub files available? You can upgrade to the eBook version at `www.PacktPub.com` and as a print book customer, you are entitled to a discount on the eBook copy. Get in touch with us at `service@packtpub.com` for more details.

At `www.PacktPub.com`, you can also read a collection of free technical articles, sign up for a range of free newsletters, and receive exclusive discounts and offers on Packt books and eBooks.

Contributors

About the author

Rambabu Posa has been working as Java developer since 2004 and a Scala developer since mid-2015. He loves Functional Programming in the Test-Driven Development way to develop Reactive microservices. He loves teaching and has been giving online training and writing tutorials on both the Java and Scala ecosystems. He loves developing Reactive systems using Lightbend's Reactive Platform Technology stack like Lagom Framework, ConductR, Scala, Akka Toolkit, Akka Streams, Play Framework, and others.

I would like to thank my wife, Bhargs, who helped me to draw some of the images, taking paper drawn pictures and photos, and sharing them with me. Without her efforts and encouragement, it would not have been possible to write this book.

About the reviewers

Pavlo Lysak is a seasoned developer with 10 years of experience in JVM and languages that run on it. He has previously worked on Java, that is, JavaEE and Spring, however, since the past 5 years, he has been working mostly with Scala, that is, Play, Akka, and Spark. After working with companies such as Jaspersoft, Kreditech, and more, he became an independent consultant. His daily work includes the development of Reactive Web Applications and RESTful services, taking care of their stability, maintainability, and transparency.

Dave Wentzel is the Chief Technology Officer (CTO) of Capax Global, a premier Microsoft consulting partner. He is responsible for setting the strategy and defining service offerings and capabilities for the data platform and Azure practice at Capax. Dave also works directly with clients to help them with their big data journey. He is a frequent blogger and speaker on big data and data science topics.

Packt is searching for authors like you

If you're interested in becoming an author for Packt, please visit authors.packtpub.com and apply today. We have worked with thousands of developers and tech professionals, just like you, to help them share their insight with the global tech community. You can make a general application, apply for a specific hot topic that we are recruiting an author for, or submit your own idea.

Table of Contents

Preface

This book is all about how to develop Reactive systems using the Functional Reactive Programming (FRP) style. It is a combination of both Functional Programming (FP) and Reactive Programming(RP) styles.

Scala is a multi-paradigm language that supports both FP and RP very well. It also has an AP (Asynchronous Programming) API. It supports Concurrency and true Parallelism using the Future API and Akka's Actor Model.

We will develop a couple of Reactive microservices using Lightbend's Reactive Platform, that is, Scala, Akka, Akka Streams, Play Framework, and Lagom Framework. We will deploy and test our Reactive system into Lightbend's ConductR sandbox environment.

Who this book is for

This book is for Scala developers who have knowledge of the basics of Scala, SBT, and the IntelliJ IDEA and want to update their skills to develop Reactive microservices using Lightbend's Reactive Platform.

What this book covers

Chapter 1, *Getting started With Reactive and Functional Programming*, covers the FP, RP, and FRP paradigm in detail. It covers the Reactive Manifesto and explains how it solves most of the current systems' issues. It also discusses the Actor Model and the Shared-State Concurrency model. This chapter ends with Marble diagrams.

Chapter 2, *Functional Scala*, explains some of Scala's important Functional Programming features at a high level with some simple and useful examples.

Chapter 3, *Asynchronous Programming with Scala*, explains Scala's Future API, how it solves Concurrency issues, and how it supports asynchronous programming.

Chapter 4, *Building Reactive Applications with Akka*, explains about the Actor Model and Akka Toolkit concepts. It demonstrates how to develop Reactive applications using Akka's Actor Model and how it solves shared-state concurrency issues.

Chapter 5, *Adding Reactiveness with RxScala*, explains some basics of Reactive Extensions for Scala, that is, RxScala. Even though RxScala does not support full-fledged FRP functionality, it supports RP using Observables.

Chapter 6, *Extending Applications with Play*, introduces you to Play Framework, a full-stack web application framework. Even though Play Framework supports two separate APIs—one for Scala and another for Java, we will develop Reactive Web Applications using Play and Scala technologies.

Chapter 7, *Working with Reactive Streams*, explains the Akka Streams API, Akka's Reactive Streams implementations. It is a separate module or library from Akka Toolkit for developing streaming data applications using Akka's Actor model under the hood. We will develop a graph-based Streaming data application using Akka Streams Graph DSL.

Chapter 8, *Integrating Akka Streams to Play Application*, focuses on how to integrate the Akka Streams API into the Play web application and develop a multi-user chat application. It introduces you to Akka Stream's dynamic streaming components.

Chapter 9, *Reactive Microservices With Lagom*, introduces Lightbend's new Reactive microservices framework, Lagom. It supports developing Reactive systems easily using Play, Akka, and Scala under the hood.

Chapter 10, *Testing Reactive Microservices*, explains what TDD is and its benefits. It's a good Agile practice to develop our application components by following the unit testing approach.

Chapter 11, *Managing Microservices in ConductR*, focuses on how to set up, deploy, and test our Reactive microservices locally using Lightbend's sandbox environment, ConductR.

Chapter 12, *Reactive Design Patterns and Best Practices*, explains Reactive design patterns and Reactive principles and best practices to develop Reactive systems easily.

Appendix A, *Scala Plugin for IntelliJ IDEA*, demonstrates how to install Scala Plugin for IntelliJ IDE and use it.

Appendix B, *Installing Robomongo*, shows a sequence of steps on how to setup and use Robo 3T or Robomongo tool to access our local MongoDB collections.

To get the most out of this book

1. Readers are expected to have some knowledge of Scala, SBT, and the IntelliJ IDEA or any IDE usage. Familiarity with at least one web application development framework will make learning another web framework easy.
2. Readers should have Java 8, SBT, IntelliJ IDEA, and Scala in their local systems.

Download the example code files

You can download the example code files for this book from your account at www.packtpub.com. If you purchased this book elsewhere, you can visit www.packtpub.com/support and register to have the files emailed directly to you.

You can download the code files by following these steps:

1. Log in or register at www.packtpub.com.
2. Select the **SUPPORT** tab.
3. Click on **Code Downloads & Errata**.
4. Enter the name of the book in the **Search** box and follow the onscreen instructions.

Once the file is downloaded, please make sure that you unzip or extract the folder using the latest version of:

- WinRAR/7-Zip for Windows
- Zipeg/iZip/UnRarX for Mac
- 7-Zip/PeaZip for Linux

The code bundle for the book is also hosted on GitHub at https://github.com/PacktPublishing/Scala-Reactive-Programming. In case there's an update to the code, it will be updated on the existing GitHub repository.

For more useful information and examples you can visit the following repository:

- https://github.com/rposa-srp-book/srp-book-examples

We also have other code bundles from our rich catalog of books and videos available at https://github.com/PacktPublishing/. Check them out!

Download the color images

We also provide a PDF file that has color images of the screenshots/diagrams used in this book. You can download it here: https://www.packtpub.com/sites/default/files/downloads/ScalaReactiveProgramming_ColorImages.pdf.

Conventions used

There are a number of text conventions used throughout this book.

CodeInText: Indicates code words in text, database table names, folder names, filenames, file extensions, pathnames, dummy URLs, user input, and Twitter handles. Here is an example: " The map() function does not give us the expected results, so we only use flatMap() function."

A block of code is set as follows:

```
object HelloWorldApp extends App{
  println("Hello Scala World!")
}
```

Any command-line input or output is written as follows:

```
For comprehension addition output: Some(Success(30))
Scala Future API addition output: Some(Success(30))
Scala Async API addition output: Some(Success(30))
```

Bold: Indicates a new term, an important word, or words that you see onscreen. For example, words in menus or dialog boxes appear in the text like this. Here is an example: "Go to **Configure** at the bottom right and click on the **Plugins** option available in the drop-down."

Warnings or important notes appear like this.

Tips and tricks appear like this.

Get in touch

Feedback from our readers is always welcome.

General feedback: Email `feedback@packtpub.com` and mention the book title in the subject of your message. If you have questions about any aspect of this book, please email us at `questions@packtpub.com`.

Errata: Although we have taken every care to ensure the accuracy of our content, mistakes do happen. If you have found a mistake in this book, we would be grateful if you would report this to us. Please visit `www.packtpub.com/submit-errata`, selecting your book, clicking on the Errata Submission Form link, and entering the details.

Piracy: If you come across any illegal copies of our works in any form on the Internet, we would be grateful if you would provide us with the location address or website name. Please contact us at `copyright@packtpub.com` with a link to the material.

If you are interested in becoming an author: If there is a topic that you have expertise in and you are interested in either writing or contributing to a book, please visit `authors.packtpub.com`.

Reviews

Please leave a review. Once you have read and used this book, why not leave a review on the site that you purchased it from? Potential readers can then see and use your unbiased opinion to make purchase decisions, we at Packt can understand what you think about our products, and our authors can see your feedback on their book. Thank you!

For more information about Packt, please visit `packtpub.com`.

1

Getting Started with Reactive and Functional Programming

In recent times, the word **Reactive** has gained popularity far and wide. We can see this word in all IT books, magazines, blogs, tutorials, videos on YouTube, and so on.

Almost all programming languages, tools, IDEs, and platforms already support the Reactive architecture and the rest will move to it soon.

Here are some terms that are commonly heard in the Reactive world:

- Reactive, Reactiveness, Reactive Manifesto, and Reactive Streams
- **Reactive programming (RP)**, **Function Reactive Programming (FRP)**, OOP RP, Imperative RP, and Reactive Engine
- Reactive system, Reactive applications, Reactive microservices, and Reactive Web Applications
- Reactive Architecture, Reactive Design Patterns, and Reactive principles
- Reactive tools, Reactive Platform, and Lightbend Reactive Platform
- **Reactive Extensions (Rx)**—Rx Scala, Rx Java, Scala, Akka, Play Framework
- Java Reactive API and Spring Reactor project

Are you really curious to know what Reactive is? Do you have the following questions and more in your mind—What is Reactive programming? Why do we need it? How do we write RP? Why is FP good for RP? What are the benefits of RP?

If yes, this book is for you. I'll introduce you to the **Reactive World** in a simple and easy way. I like a Diagram/Example-driven approach to learn new concepts and I feel you will like it too.

We can develop Reactive applications using a wide variety of languages or technologies. However, we will use Lightbend Reactive Platform in this book to develop our Reactive microservices.

Welcome to the Reactive World! Let's understand the Reactive World now. In this chapter, we will discuss the following topics:

- What is Reactive? What is RP and FRP? What are the benefits of RP?
- What is the Reactive Manifesto and what are its main goals?
- Why is FP the best fit for RP?
- What is the Java Reactive Streams API?
- A discussion on the Flow API
- What are Reactive Extensions?
- What is the difference between Reactive and Observer Design Patterns?
- What are RP Operators?
- Marble diagrams for RP Operators

Introduction to Reactive

Before diving into the Reactive Manifesto, Reactive Streams Specification, or Java 9 Flow API, and **Functional Reactive Programming** (**FRP**), we will first understand the meaning of Reactive and Reactive programming in this section.

What is Reactive?

Reactive means *reacting to changes in a timely manner* or *responding to changes in a timely manner*.

Here, in the Reactive World, we can represent a change as an **event**. So we can also define Reactive as *reacting to events in a timely manner*. This change can occur on data or data elements.

Whenever a change occurs in our system, the system should react to those changes immediately in a timely manner. In the current world, users expect a response from an application (website, web application, mobile application, and so on) quickly and in a timely manner. If the system or application does not respond to the user (or customer) in a timely manner, the user will look for some other option and our application will lose its users.

In the Merriam Webster dictionary, Reactive means being *readily responsive to a stimulus* (check out `https://www.merriam-webster.com/dictionary/Reactive`).

 In the Reactive World, a change is an event. In Reactive systems, we represent that event as a message. We will discuss *why we need to represent an event as a message* in detail in subsequent sections.

What is Reactive programming?

Unlike **imperative programming** (**IP**) or (**Object-Oriented Programming**) **OOP**, where we write our code in terms of the order of lines or statements, in **Reactive programming** (**RP**), we write the code or programs in terms of events.

In simpler words, RP means writing programs using events, or RP means writing programs that define how to react to events. As we discussed, events are changes in the state of the program or application. So we can also define RP as follows:

Reactive programming is a kind of programming paradigm to that propagates changes.

Let's discuss one of the important and frequently used RP examples (almost all books or tutorials use the same scenario). Consider the following example of a spreadsheet application:

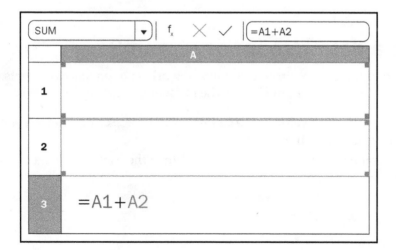

Observe that the *A3* cell has a formula *=A1+A2*, that is, *A3* is the sum of the values of the cells *A1* and *A2*.

Initially, *A3* has a value of *0*. When we change the value of cell *A1* or *A2*, or both, the spreadsheet updates the value of *A3*:

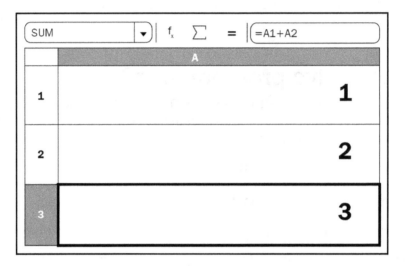

We can observe that the cell *A3* is updated with **3** automatically; this is Reactive programming.

What is a data stream or stream?

In Reactive programming, we write programs to work on a sequence of events. For instance, in a spreadsheet, we can observe the following events in a sequence:

1. The user enters a value 1 into cell *A1*. When the user inputs data into cell *A1*, the value in cell *A3* is updated to 1.
2. The user enters a value 2 into cell *A2*. When the user inputs data to cell *A2*, *A3* is updated to 3.

In the Reactive World, this sequence of events happening over time is known as a stream, events stream, or data stream. The following diagram shows how a sequence of events forms an events stream. It also shows how a **Publisher** sends events to an event stream and how a Subscriber receives events from that event stream:

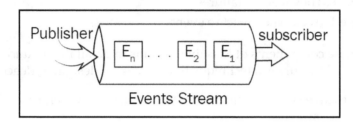

A stream or data stream is a sequence of ongoing events ordered in time.

In RP, the **Publisher** sends events to a **Stream**, and the **Subscriber** consumes those events from the **Stream**.

To react to events, we should monitor them. In RP, the process of monitoring events is known as listening to events or subscribing to events.

We can also define RP using this data stream:

RP is a programming paradigm to do programming with asynchronous data streams.

 Event stream = A sequence of events

RP versus Reactive systems versus Reactive architecture

A Reactive system is a set of components that communicate with each other reactively. By combining those individual components into one, we can form a modern distributed system. We can develop a Reactive system by following a set of architectural design principles.

Reactive system components work as a single system and they react to changes in a timely manner.

Reactive systems or Reactive applications have the following features:

- **Responsiveness**: They react to users in a timely manner
- **Elasticity**: They react to load
- **Resilience**: They react to failures
- **Message-Driven**: They react to events or messages

We will discuss these components of Reactive Streams in detail in the *Reactive Manifesto* section. Reactive Architecture is a technique or a process of designing Reactive systems.

We can develop Reactive systems using many techniques. However, RP or FRP are the best tools to build Reactive systems.

The core principle of a Reactive system is *developing its components using a Message-Driven approach*, whereas RP is all about writing programs using events, which means it follows an Event-Driven approach.

As we said, a Reactive system is a set of components. We use RP at the component level, which means that we develop each component using RP. We use a Reactive system at the system level.

Event-Driven versus Message-Driven

The core principle of RP is the Event-Driven approach, whereas the core principle of a Reactive system is the Message-Driven approach.

RP gives us the benefits at component level only because events are emitted and processed locally. They cannot work across the network in a distributed system.

Reactive systems give us the benefits at the system level, because messages are processed and communicated across the network in a distributed system.

We cannot get the full benefits just with RP; we should use the combination of RP and the Reactive system.

In a Reactive system with RP, generated events are represented as messages under-the-hood, and they are processed as messages.

Benefits of Reactive systems with RP

We will get more benefits when we use RP as a programming paradigm to develop the components of a Reactive system. The combination of RP and Reactive systems gives us the following benefits:

- **Self-healing**: As per the Reactive Streams specification, RP should support Resilience. This means we can write Reactive systems in a way that they have some technique to recover from failure and continue working to give responses to the clients. This is known as self-healing. A client will not know about this, and they will never see those failures.
- **Highly available systems**: As per the Reactive Streams specification, RP should support Elasticity (scale up/down and scale out/in). This means we can write Reactive systems in a way that they are always available. They support 100% up time.
- Highly Scalable to support heavy loads.
- Loose coupling.
- Utilizes system resources (both hardware and software) efficiently.
- Provides better responsiveness.
- Provides real-time behavior or data streaming.
- Easy to perform distributed data processing.
- Supports Location Transparency.
- Low latency.
- Better performance.
- Ease of maintainability.
- No need to use anonymous callbacks (so no more callback hell).
- Easy to address and handle failures.
- Easy to reason about failures.

We should also understand the things that are forcing us to develop and use Reactive systems:

- **IoT (Internet of Things)**
- Cloud environment or services
- Big data systems

- Real-time fast data streaming
- Mobile architectures
- Communication between heterogeneous systems
- Multicore hardware architecture

 Here, Reactive systems means Reactive Web Applications, Reactive applications, and Reactive microservices. In my point of view, all have the same meaning.

So far, we have discussed Reactive World, that is, RP. Now, it's time to enter the Functional World, that is, functional programming.

Functional programming

So far, we have discussed RP. Now it's time to move to **FP** (**Functional Programming**). Before discussing FRP, we should understand what FP is. We will discuss what FP is, its principles, and its benefits in this section.

What is functional programming?

Like **OOP** (**Object-Oriented Programming**), FP is a kind of programming paradigm.

It is a programming style in which we write programs in terms of pure functions and immutable data. It treats its programs as function evaluation.

As we use pure functions and immutable data to write our applications, we will get lots of benefits for free. For instance, with immutable data, we do not need to worry about shared-mutable states, side effects, and thread-safety.

It follows a Declarative programming style, which means programming is done in terms of expressions, not statements.

For instance, in OOP or imperative programming paradigms, we use statements to write programs where FP uses everything as expressions.

Principles of functional programming

FP has the following principles:

- Pure functions
- Immutable data
- No side effects
- **Referential transparency (RT)**
- Functions are first-class citizens
- Functions that include anonymous functions, higher order functions, combinators, partial functions, partially-applied functions, function currying, closures
- Tail recursion
- Functions composability

We will discuss these principles or properties of FP in brief here because we have a dedicated chapter on these concepts. Refer to `Chapter 2`, *Functional Scala*, to understand these concepts in-depth with some simple examples.

A pure function is a function that always returns the same results for the same inputs irrespective of how many times and where you run this function.

We will get lots of benefits with immutable data. For instance, no shared data, no side effects, thread safety for free, and so on.

Like an object is a first-class citizen in OOP, in FP, a function is a first-class citizen. This means that we can use a function as any of these:

- An object
- A value
- A data
- A data type
- An operation

In simple words, in FP, we treat both functions and data as the same.

We can compose functions that are in sequential order so that we can solve even complex problems easily. **Higher-Order Functions (HOF)** are functions that take one or more functions as their parameters or return a function as their result or do both.

For instance, `map()`, `flatMap()`, `filter()`, and so on are some of the important and frequently used higher-order functions. Consider the following example:

```
map(x => x*x)
```

Here, the `map()` function is an example of Higher-Order Function because it takes an anonymous function as its parameter. This anonymous function `x => x *x` is of type `Int => Int`, which takes an `Int` as input and returns `Int` as its result.

An anonymous function is a function without any name.

Refer to `Chapter 2`, *Functional Scala*, to understand these concepts very well. I have provided a useful description and also some simple and easy-to-understand examples.

Benefits of functional programming

FP provides us with many benefits:

- Thread-safe code
- Easy-to-write concurrency and parallel code
- We can write simple, readable, and elegant code
- Type safety
- Composability
- Supports Declarative programming

As we use pure functions and immutability in FP, we will get thread-safety for free.

One of the greatest benefits of FP is function composability. We can compose multiple functions one by one and execute them either sequentially or parentally. It gives us a great approach to solve complex problems easily.

Functional Reactive programming

The combination of FP and RP is known as function Reactive programming or, for short, FRP. It is a multiparadigm and combines the benefits and best features of two of the most popular programming paradigms, which are, FP and RP.

FRP is a new programming paradigm or a new style of programming that uses the RP paradigm to support asynchronous non-blocking data streaming with backpressure and also uses the FP paradigm to utilize its features (such as pure functions, immutability, no side effects, RT, and more) and its HOF or combinators (such as map, flatMap, filter, reduce, fold, and zip).

 Refer to `Chapter 7`, *Working with Reactive Streams*, to know more about backpressure.

In simple words, FRP is a new programming paradigm to support RP using FP features and its building blocks.

FRP = FP + RP, as shown here:

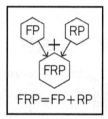

Today, we have many FRP solutions, frameworks, tools, or technologies. Here's a list of a few FRP technologies:

- Scala, Play Framework, and Akka Toolkit
- RxJS
- Reactive-banana
- Reactive
- Sodium
- Haskell

This book is dedicated toward discussing Lightbend's FRP technology stack—Lagom Framework, Scala, Play Framework, and Akka Toolkit (Akka Streams).

FRP technologies are mainly useful in developing interactive programs, such as rich **GUI** (**graphical user interfaces**), animations, multiplayer games, computer music, or robot controllers.

Types of RP

Even though most of the projects or companies use FP Paradigm to develop their Reactive systems or solutions, there are a couple of ways to use RP. They are known as *types of RP*:

- **FRP (Functional Reactive Programming)**
- **OORP (Object-Oriented Reactive Programming)**

However, FP is the best programming paradigm to conflate with RP. We will get all the benefits of FP for free.

Why FP is the best fit for RP

When we conflate RP with FP, we will get the following benefits:

- Composability—we can compose multiple data streams using functional operations so that we can solve even complex problems easily
- Thread safety
- Readability
- Simple, concise, clear, and easy-to-understand code
- Easy-to-write asynchronous, concurrent, and parallel code
- Supports very flexible and easy-to-use operations
- Supports Declarative programming
- Easy to write, more Scalable, highly available, and robust code

In FP, we concentrate on *what to do* to fulfill a job, whereas in other programming paradigms, such as OOP or **imperative programming (IP)**, we concentrate on *how to do*.

Declarative programming gives us the following benefits:

- No side effects
- Enforces to use immutability
- Easy to write concise and understandable code

The main property of RP is *real-time data streaming*, and the main property of FP is *composability*. If we combine these two paradigms, we will get more benefits and can develop better solutions easily.

In RP, everything is a stream, while everything is a function in FP. We can use these functions to perform operations on data streams.

Reactive Manifesto

Reactive Manifesto is a manifesto that describes how to design and architect Reactive systems according to your needs. It describes the four traits of Reactive systems. As of now, we are using Reactive Manifest v.2.0, which was initially published on September 16, 2014.

As per Reactive Manifest 1.0 (initial and old version), Reactive systems are Responsive, Scalable, Resilient, and Event-Driven.

As per Reactive Manifest 2.0, Reactive systems are Responsive, Scalable, Resilient, and Message-Driven.

We can find the manifesto on GitHub as a repository, available at `https://github.com/reactivemanifesto/reactivemanifesto`.

Need of Reactive Manifesto

We need to understand *what the main need of Reactive Manifesto is*, so that we will get clear picture about it.

The main needs or goals of Reactive Manifesto are as follows:

- Users or customers need responses in a timely manner. They don't like slow responses and they don't use slow systems. If they don't get quick responses as needed, they will look for other options.
- We should have an API to support asynchronous streaming data with non-blocking backpressure.
- API for Reactive Technology (frameworks, tools, languages, IDEs, and so on) implementors.
- Heterogeneous Reactive systems should work in an interoperable way.
- We should have a better approach for consumers to avoid buffer overflow issues.

Principles of Reactive systems

In this section, we will discuss what the four traits or principles of Reactive systems are that we should follow to develop Reliable, Flexible, Scalable, Distributable, and Resilient applications.

Reactive Manifesto defines the following four principles:

- Message-Driven
- Elastic
- Resilient
- Responsive

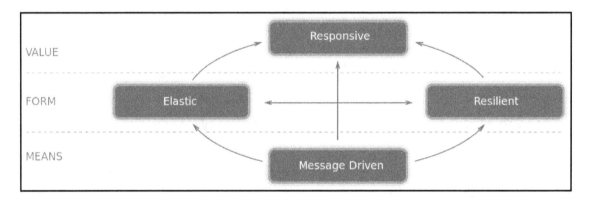

This preceding diagram is copied from Reactive Manifesto. These are design and architectural principles. They are also known as the *Four tenants of Reactive Streams* or *Four core building blocks of Reactive Streams*.

We will pick up each trait one-by-one and discuss it in detail in subsequent sections.

Message-Driven

The core or base principle of the Reactive systems is Message-Driven architecture. It is the foundation principle or method for the rest of the three principles—Elasticity, Resilience, and Responsiveness.

This means a Reactive system depends on asynchronous message-passing between its components to use the benefits of Message-Driven architecture for free.

In simple words, *Message-Driven = React to messages*.

Even though RP represents the system's changes in terms of events, a Reactive system converts them into messages under the hood.

One more important point to note is that in a Reactive system, even failures are represented as messages, so it's easy to perform failure handling.

So, in a Reactive system, all of its components communicate with each other by sending messages. The Message-Driven approach gives us the following benefits:

- Messages are immutable by design
- They share nothing, so are thread-safe by design
- They provide loose coupling between system components
- They can work across the network, so they support Location Transparency
- They support scalability
- They support Resilience because they avoid single-point-of-failure using partitioning and replication techniques
- They support better throughput
- They provide easy-to-apply backpressure

So in RP, we write code in a stream of events, and then Reactive systems convert them into a stream of messages.

Elasticity

Elasticity means scalability. Our system should support scale up/scale down and scale out/ scale in. Our Reactive system should support scale up/scale out so that it responds to the users in a timely manner. It should also support scale down/scale in order to save our organization cost.

In simple words, *Elastic = React to load*.

This means our system should respond to users in a timely manner even at a heavy load.

With this property, a Reactive system can allocate and/or deallocate resources for every component dynamically and automatically to match demands.

If our Reactive system follows the Message-Driven approach, it supports Elasticity easily:

Elasticity = Scale up/down + Scaleout/in

Scale up: When the load increases, a Reactive system should be able to easily upgrade it with more and more powerful resources (for instance, more CPU Cores) automatically, based on the demand:

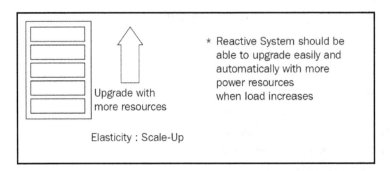

Scale down: When the load decreases, a Reactive system should be able to easily degrade it by removing some resources (for instance, CPU Cores) automatically, based on demand:

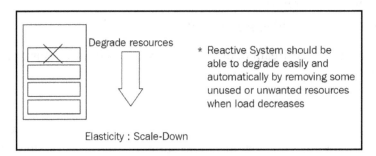

Scale out: When the load increases, a Reactive system should be able to easily extend it by adding some new nodes or servers automatically, based on the demand:

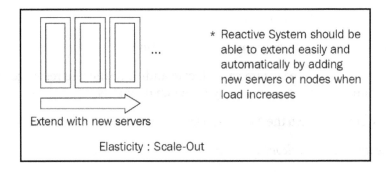

Scale in: When the load decreases, a Reactive system should be able to easily sink it by removing some nodes or servers automatically, based on the demand:

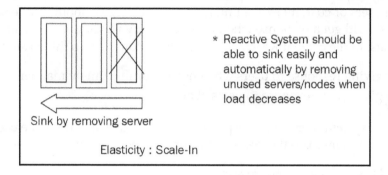

Sink by removing server

Elasticity : Scale-In

Resilience

Resilience is not just fault-tolerance, it's beyond fault-tolerance. A Reactive system should fully recover from failure; this is known as self-healing.

In simple words, *Resilient = React to failure*.

Resilience means a Reactive system should respond to users even in the event of failures, by recovering itself. This is possible by isolating the failure handling to a different component. In a Reactive system, all failures are converted into messages and then processed.

For instance, in Akka Toolkit, Akka Streams (one of the popular Reactive Streams implementations) uses the **supervision** technique to do this failure handling.

Refer to Chapter 4, *Building Reactive Applications with Akka*, to understand this Supervision technique.

In a Reactive system:

- Failures are messages
- Events are messages

Responsiveness

The last but very important trait is responsiveness. In Reactive systems, Responsive means reacting to the users or customers in a timely manner. Here, we should understand this point—a user should get a response when needed, otherwise they will lose interest and go for other options. In the current Reactive World, the following two things are the same:

- Not giving response to users when needed or in a timely manner
- Not giving any response to users at all

Even though our system does give a response to the user at a *later* time, the user does not need it then. Our system loses the users and ultimately, we lose our business.

In simple words, *Responsive = React to users*.

After going through these four traits of a Reactive system, we should understand the following things:

- The main goal of a Reactive system is responsiveness
- The core method that a Reactive system should follow is Message-Driven
- The core principles of a Reactive system are Elasticity and Resilience:

```
┌─────────────────────────────────────┐
│  ┌───────────────────────────────┐  │
│  │                               │  │
│  │        Message - Driven       │  │
│  │                               │  │
│  └───────────────────────────────┘  │
│   Core Method of a Reactive System   │
└─────────────────────────────────────┘
```

The core method of a Reactive system, that is, the Message-Driven approach, will give us Elasticity and Resilience for free:

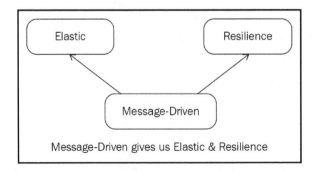

These three traits of a Reactive system (that is, Message-Driven, Elasticity, and Resilience) give us the main goal or value of that Reactive system—responsiveness.

After going through the Reactive Manifesto, we can represent it in a pictorial form, as shown here:

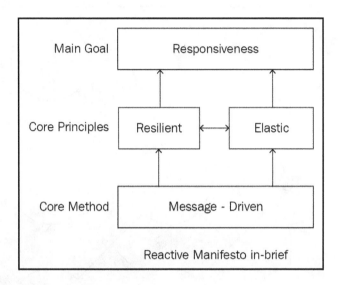

These three traits of a Reactive system (that is, Message-Driven, Elasticity, and Resilience) give us the main goal or value of that Reactive system—responsiveness.

Why Reactive Streams specification?

In this section, we will understand, first of all, *why we really need the Reactive Streams specification*. We will also answer a few more questions, like—*What is the use of this specification or standard*, and *who really needs this specification*?

RSS (**Reactive Streams Specification**) is a standard or specification. It explains how to develop frameworks, tools, toolkits, languages, libraries, IDEs, data stores, servers, and so on, which work in Reactive.

Are we getting any benefits by following this specification? Yes. That's why we need this specification.

The main goals or benefits of this specification are as follows:

- To support reactiveness
- To support interoperability:

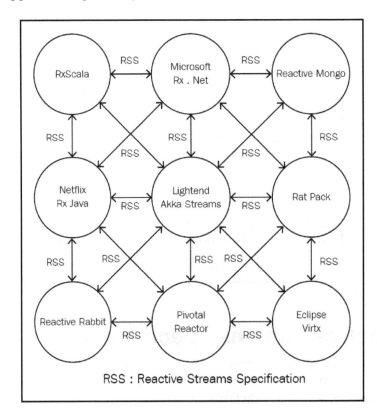

If we observe the preceding diagram, we can understand that many applications are using many Reactive technologies. If they follow their own approach to develop their Reactive systems, then it is a bit tough for them to talk to or work with each other. It is possible to implement some kind of adapters or interfaces to fill the gap and make them work with each other. However, it is not only an old and tedious approach, but also outdated and obsolete.

If we have a specification or standard or API similar to the Reactive Streams Specification and everybody develops their tools, frameworks, and so on, by following this, then there will be no need for extra tools, such as adapters. They can work with each other without using any adapters and without any issues.

This means it enables heterogeneous Reactive systems to work with each other, that is, work in an interoperable way.

As a Java or Scala developer, we know what the use of an API is, why we need it, and who needs it. So, we need a Reactive API or standard or specification to implement or develop Reactive libraries, Reactive servers, Reactive languages, Reactive databases, Reactive tools, Reactive applications, or systems.

Initially, a set of developers from top companies such as Lightbend, Netflix, Pivotal, Redhot, and Oracle Corporation worked together on this area and prepared a specification to develop Reactive systems (or applications) easily. This is known as **RSS** (**Reactive Streams Specification**). They requested Oracle Corporation introduce an API to develop Reactive systems easily in a way that they should work interoperably. Finally, Oracle Corporation introduced a Reactive Streams API as part of JEP-266 in JDK 9 (Java SE 9). This API is known as the Flow API.

In the next section, we will discuss this Flow API in detail.

 From my point of view, specification, standard, API, interface, abstract, and blue-print are all the same. They have the same meaning.

Why is Play Framework the best for Reactive systems?

Play Framework is the best full-stack web framework available in the current market to develop Reactive Web Applications, Reactive systems, Reactive architecture, Reactive microservices, or Reactive libraries using both FP and RP paradigms, that is, FRP.

The following are the reasons to clarify why Play is good for RP:

- Play Framework is built on top of the Akka Toolkit
- By design, the Akka Toolkit supports Reactive Architecture using an Actor Model and Akka Streams
- Akka Streams is the best Reactive API to develop Reactive data streaming
- Play Framework has an integrated module for the Akka Streams API
- Play Framework is written in Scala (a JVM language) and supports both Scala and Java programming languages
- Both Scala and Java run on JVM

- Scala supports FP very well
- FP is the best programming paradigm for RP
- The latest Play Framework has moved from Iteratees to Reactive Streams
- It is a full-stack web framework for Reactive programming

Reactive systems versus traditional systems

In this section, we will see the main differences between a Reactive system and non-Reactive system, that is, a traditional system.

The first and foremost difference is that a Reactive system takes a user or customer request as an event or message, and then reacts to those events in a timely manner. Once it's done, it continuously looks for the next event, as illustrated here:

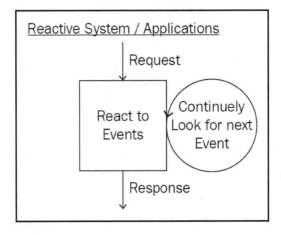

On the other hand, a traditional system takes input(s) from a user, performs an operation based on inputs, and sends an output or response to the user; that's it:

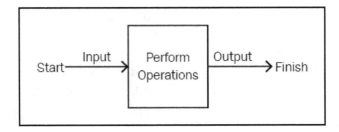

In a Reactive system, the RP model eases the development. As a Reactive system supports abstraction at a very high level, it is easy to develop the applications because we need to concentrate on only our application business logic. Meanwhile, in a traditional system, we need to take care of the application business logic while writing some low-level logic, as it docs not support high-level abstraction.

In a Reactive system, changes are propagated automatically. For instance, in a spreadsheet, we have a formula at cell A3, A3 =*A1+A2*. When we change the value of A1 or A2 or both, then all their references will be updated automatically. This means A3 will be updated automatically. It is not possible in a traditional system or non-Reactive system.

In Reactive systems, we concentrate on the flow of control, whereas in traditional systems, we concentrate on the flow of data.

The Java 9 Flow API

Oracle Corporation has introduced a new API for library or API developers to develop Reactive systems, Reactive libraries, Reactive data stores, Reactive servers, and so on. This API is also known as the Flow API.

It defines a set of interfaces to support developing Reactive systems, so it is also known as the Reactive Streams API. This API is defined under the `java.util.concurrent` package name.

The Java 9 Flow API mainly contains the following components:

- **Publisher**
- **Subscriber**
- **Subscription**
- **Processor**
- **Flow**

The following diagram shows the main five components of the Java 9 Flow API:

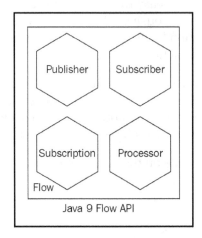

Let's discuss these components of the Flow API one by one in detail in the following sections.

Flow API – Publisher

As its name suggests, **Publisher** is a component that works as a **Producer** of data, which means it emits the data. It acts as a **source** of data, so it is also known as **Producer**, **Source** of data, or emitter:

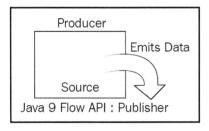

In the Java 9 Flow API, this `Publisher` is an interface with the `subscribe` method and is defined with the following signature:

```
public interface Publisher<T> {
  public void subscribe(Subscriber<? super T> subscriber);
}
```

Here, the `subscribe()` method is taking a single parameter of type `Subscriber`, which is another component of the Flow API. One publisher can subscribe one or more subscribers to it. It is defined within another class as a static component. We will see it in the following section.

Publisher uses this `subscribe()` method to subscribe or register its subscribers, as shown here.

Go through the following pseudo-code for `Subscriber.subscribe()` function usage:

```
Subscriber sub = Receive a Request from a Subscriber
Publisher pub = ...
pub.subscribe(sub)
```

Publisher receives a request from a subscriber and executes `pub.subscribe(sub)` to register that subscriber with it. Once that subscription is created, the publisher sends data to those registered parties.

For instance, we can use a data store, file, collection, server, and more, as a source of data to emit data for subscribers.

Flow API – Subscriber

As its name says, the **Subscriber** is a component that works as a consumer of data. This means it consumes the data from a producer. It acts as a **destination** of data. So, it is also known as a consumer or destination of data:

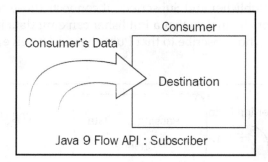

In the Java 9 Flow API, this `Subscriber` is an interface with a set of methods and is defined as follows:

```
public static interface Subscriber<T> {
    public void    onSubscribe(Subscription subscription);
```

```
    public void    onNext(T item);
    public void    onError(Throwable throwable);
    public void    onComplete();
}
```

It has a set of methods:

- `onSubscribe()`: This creates a new subscription. It is invoked prior to invoking any other `Subscriber` methods for the given Subscription.
- `onNext()`: Once a Subscription is created, this is invoked to receive the next data, item, or element from the Publisher.
- `onError()`: This is invoked upon an unrecoverable error encountered by a Publisher or Subscription, after which no other `Subscriber` methods are invoked by the Subscription.
- `onComplete()`: This is invoked when there is no requirement to invoke any further `Subscriber` methods on that Subscription that is not already terminated in error, after which no other `Subscriber` methods are invoked by that Subscription.

It is also defined within another class as a static component. We will see it in the next section.

Flow API – Subscription

In the Flow API, a **Subscription** works as a mediator or interface between two other important components, Publisher and Subscriber. It connects those components and works as a message controller or channel so that a Publisher can emit data into a Subscription and one or more subscribers who subscribe to that Publisher and receive data from that Subscription:

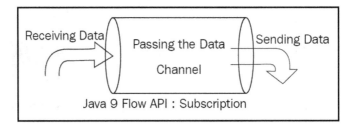

In the Java 9 Flow API, this Subscription is an interface with a set of methods and is defined as follows:

```
public static interface Subscription {
  public void      request(long n);
  public void      cancel() ;
}
```

It contains the following two methods to control the messaging between Publisher and Subscriber(s):

- request(): This is used to add the given *n* number of items to the current active Subscription between Publisher and Subscriber(s)
- cancel(): This is used to cancel or stop the current Subscription between Publisher and Subscriber(s) so that there is no communication happening between them

One Subscription is dedicated between a Publisher and a single Subscriber or a set of Subscribers. Once it's stopped by making a call to the cancel() method, Publisher cannot send data to it or Subscriber cannot receive any messages from it.

It is also defined within another class as a static component. We will see it in the next section.

Flow API – Processor

In the Flow API, Processor is a special kind of component. It works as both a Subscriber and Publisher. We can use it as a source of data, that is, a Publisher, or a destination of data, that is, a Subscriber.

In the Java 9 Flow API, this Processor is an interface with no methods and is defined like this:

```
public interface Processor<T,R> extends Subscriber<T>, Publisher<R> {
}
```

It is also defined within another class as a static component. We will see it in the next section.

Flow API – Flow

In the previous sections, we discussed the components of the Flow API one by one in depth. They are all interfaces and are defined as static components within another component of the Flow API. This component is `Flow`.

In the Java 9 Flow API, this `Flow` component contains the rest of the four components' static components, as shown here:

Flow.java:

```java
package java.util.concurrent;

public final class Flow {

    private Flow() {}
    @FunctionalInterface
    public static interface Publisher<T> {
        public void subscribe(Subscriber<? super T> subscriber);
    }

    public static interface Subscriber<T> {

        public void onSubscribe(Subscription subscription);

        public void onNext(T item);

        public void onError(Throwable throwable);

        public void onComplete();
    }

    public static interface Subscription {

        public void request(long n);

        public void cancel();
    }

    public static interface Processor<T,R> extends Subscriber<T>,
     Publisher<R> {
     }

    static final int DEFAULT_BUFFER_SIZE = 256;

    public static int defaultBufferSize() {
        return DEFAULT_BUFFER_SIZE;
```

```
    }

}
```

This is so that we can access other components as `Flow.xxxx`, which means if we want to access a Publisher, we should use it like `Flow.Publisher`.

When we combine or connect all these components in a working system, we will see them as follows:

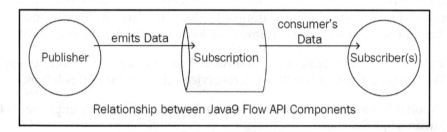

Relationship between Java9 Flow API Components

When we connect the Flow API components in this way, we can observe that a flow is going from source to destination. That's why they have named this API as the Flow API.

We can represent the Java 9 Flow API's **Publisher/Subscriber** complete communication as shown in the following diagram. This communication can end either successfully or in failure:

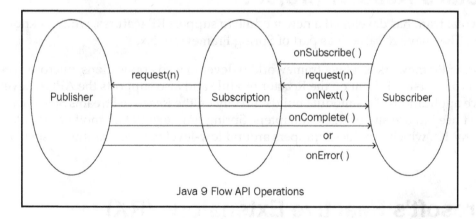

Java 9 Flow API Operations

Implementations of Reactive Streams

In this section, we will discuss the most important and popular Reactive Streams Specification implementations, Reactive Technologies, and so on.

Lightbend's Reactive Platform

Lightbend's Reactive Platform is one of the popular technology stacks that support the FRP paradigm. Lightbend is one of the initiators of the Reactive Streams Specification. This platform has a Reactive microservice framework known as the Lagom framework.

The Lagom framework uses Scala, Play, and Akka Toolkit to develop Reactive systems, Reactive Web Applications, or Reactive microservices. It is a pure FRP Solution.

The Akka Toolkit has an API known as the **Akka Streams API**, which implements the Reactive Streams Specification.

In this book, we will use this technology stack to develop our Reactive system. Go through subsequent chapters to understand how to easily develop data streaming applications using Akka Streams and how to develop Reactive microservices using the Lagom framework.

Pivotal's Reactor project

The Pivotal team has developed a new module to support RP features, which is known as Reactor. They have released it as part of Spring Framework 5.x.

The Spring Framework is a Java framework to develop web applications, microserivces, and more. Its 5.x version is built on the Reactor module and also supports the API to develop Reactive applications. This module builds directly on the Reactive Streams Specification, so we don't need to use any bridge or adapters. Spring Framework has another module known as **Reactor IO**, which provides wrappers around low-level network runtimes, such as Netty and Aeron.

Microsoft's Reactive Extensions (RX)

Microsoft has implemented one Reactive Solution for C# (.Net platform) known as Reactive Extensions. It supports Reactive programming very well.

Reactive Extensions, Rx, or ReactiveX is a library to support asynchronous event-based programming, which has become a base library for other Rx libraries.

Netflix's RxJava

By following Microsoft's Rx library, Netflix has developed their own Rx library for the Java programming language, that is, RxJava.

RxJava stands for Reactive Extensions for Java. It became a base library for other **JVM (Java Virtual Machine**) languages. Many people have developed some adapters on top of this library.

For instance, RxScala is an Rx library for the Scala programming language. We will discuss Rx and the RxScala framework further in `Chapter 5`, *Adding Reactiveness with RxScala*.

Eclipse's Vert.x

Vert.x is an Eclipse Foundation project to support an Event-Driven paradigm on the JVM. Reactive support in Vert.x is similar to Ratpack. Vert.x allows us to use either RxJava or Eclipse native implementation of the Reactive Streams API to develop Reactive systems.

The Eclipse Vert.X website can be found at `http://vertx.io/`.

We can find its source code at `https://github.com/eclipse/vert.x`.

Ratpack

Ratpack is a set of Java libraries for building modern high-performance HTTP applications. It provides a basic implementation of the Reactive Streams specification. However, it is not designed to be a fully-featured RP Framework or toolkit.

We can get more information about Ratpack at `https://ratpack.io/`.

How are Reactive Streams born?

So far, we have discussed many things, such as Reactive programming, Reactive Manifest, the Reactive Streams API, the Java 9 Flow API, and finally, Reactive implementations, in detail in the previous sections.

It is useful to understand how they are all related and why they are required. I prefer a simple diagram to explain it instead of a lengthy description.

Take a look at the following diagram:

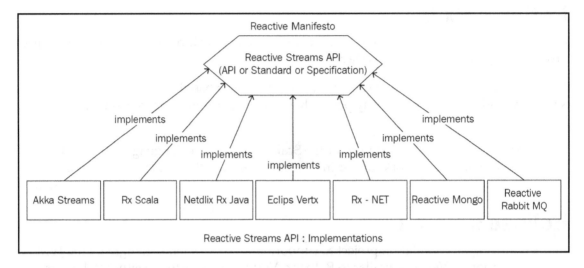

I hope you understood well how the Reactive Streams API was born. In my point of view, there are four phases or stages of the Reactive Streams API.

Marble diagrams

In this section, you will learn what Marble diagrams are, why we really need them or what their benefits are, and the rules we need to follow to draw these Marble diagrams?

We will also discuss some of the important FP operators using Marble diagrams in the following sections.

What is a Marble diagram?

A Marble diagram is a diagram used to visualize an FRP Data Transformation in a very nice and easy-to-understand form. (Refer to the next section to understand what an FRP Data Transformation is.)

Using these diagrams, we can understand the following things very well about an FRP Data Transformation:

- A data element or a set of data elements are emitted or produced from a source (Producer, Publisher, or a data stream)
- A data element or a set of data elements flow in that data stream, that is, they are produced from the source and flow through that data stream
- What data transformation is happening in that data stream?
- How that data stream is picking each element and how it is performing that data transformation for each and every element or only a set of elements
- The way it is preparing the final results after performing that data transformation
- How that data stream is sending the final results to the destination (another Producer, Publisher or a data stream, or maybe a Consumer or Subscriber)

Before starting the discussion about some sample Marble diagrams, I feel it's good to know what an FRP Data Transformation is. Let's define it now.

Data transformation

A data transformation is an operation (or operator), which is applied on a set of source data elements or all data elements in a data stream and produces resultant data elements to send to another data stream:

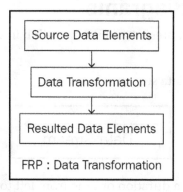

As we use this data transformation to represent a functional operation, Reactive operation, or both, we also call this as an FP operator or RP operator, or FRP operator. It is also known as a Reactive Stream operator, Functional Reactive operator, or Data Flow operator.

Some of the FP operators are map, flatMap, reduce, fold, and filter. They are also known as combinators in the Scala World. Refer to `Chapter 2`, *Functional Scala*, to understand what a Scala combinator is.

We will pick up some of the important and useful FRP operators and discuss them with Marble diagrams in subsequent sections.

Benefits of Marble diagrams

The following are the benefits of Marble diagrams in the Functional and Reactive World:

- They represent a simple or complex FRP operation in a simple and easy-to-understand way
- Pictorial representation of an FRP operation explains better than a text description
- They help us in understanding and solving complex problems in Functional and Reactive ways
- Even FRP beginners can understand those FRP operations easily
- It is easy to design source, data streams, and destinations
- It is easy to understand how to compose and use multiple FRP operations

Rules of Marble diagrams

To draw a Marble diagram to represent an FRP operation in a pictorial form, we should follow these rules:

A horizontal line represents a data stream:

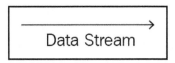

That horizontal line represents a duration or time from left to right to perform that data transformation operation.

Some symbols (such as circles, diamonds, and rectangles) on top of that horizontal line are used to represent the data elements coming from a source data stream or resulting data elements on the destination data stream:

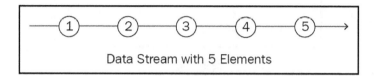

We can use any symbol to represent the data elements in a Marble diagram:

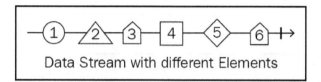

The big rectangular box in the center of a Marble diagram represents the actual data transformation (or functional operation, Reactive operation, or FRP operation) logic:

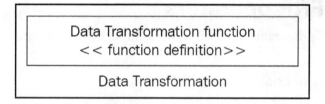

The top horizontal line represents the **Source Data Stream**, and the bottom horizontal line represents the **Destination Data Stream** (or resulting data stream):

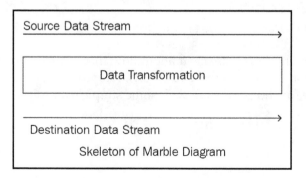

The vertical line (|) on top of the horizontal line represents the data stream completing successfully:

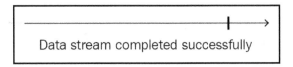

A cross mark (**X**) on top of the horizontal line represents that the data stream is completed with errors:

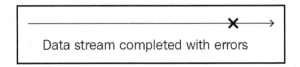

We can say that these are the *properties of a Marble diagram*. We will explore these rules with some useful examples in subsequent sections.

Important FRP operators

We will draw Marble diagrams for the following important and frequently used FPP operations:

- The map() function
- The flatMap() function
- The merge() function
- The filter() function
- The reduce() function
- The concat() and sorted() functions

As a Scala developer, I hope you are clear about how these functions (or operations or operators) work. If you are new to these functions, refer to Chapter 2, *Functional Scala*, which explains these functions in detail with some simple examples.

Let's start with the map() function first.

FRP – the map() function Marble diagram

In Scala, the map() function performs the following steps one by one:

1. Take each element from the source container.
2. Apply the given function.
3. Create a new container of the same type as the destination container. Here, container means any data structure that can hold more than one element; for instance, a Collection, Option, Either, and so on.

In the Reactive World, we can call this container a data stream, as it emits or consumes the data (or data elements).

Here's the Scala sample code for the map() function:

```
scala> val numList = List(1,2,3,4,5)
numList: List[Int] = List(1, 2, 3, 4, 5)

scala> val squaredNumList = numList.map( x => x*x )
squaredNumList: List[Int] = List(1, 4, 9, 16, 25)
```

Here, the map() function picks up each element from a number list, squares it, and creates a new list with the resultant numbers. Let's represent this map() functional operation in a pictorial form using a Marble diagram:

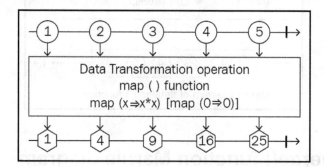

Here, the source data stream is a List (1,2,3,4,5) and the destination or resulting data stream is also a list with the squared value, that is, List (1, 4, 9, 16, 25).

The data transformation or functional operator is map(x => x*x).

FRP – the flatMap() function Marble diagram

We use the `flatMap()` function when we want to map a data stream of data stream elements into a plain data stream element.

For instance, `List[List[Int]]` to `List[Int]`, as illustrated here:

```
scala> val numList = List(List(1,2,3),List(4,5),List(6))
numList: List[List[Int]] = List(List(1, 2, 3), List(4, 5), List(6))

scala> numList.map(x => x)
res9: List[List[Int]] = List(List(1, 2, 3), List(4, 5), List(6))

scala> numList.flatMap(x => x)
res10: List[Int] = List(1, 2, 3, 4, 5, 6)
```

In this case, the `map()` function does not give us the expected results, so we only use `flatMap()`. We can represent this `flatMap()` function in a Marble diagram as follows:

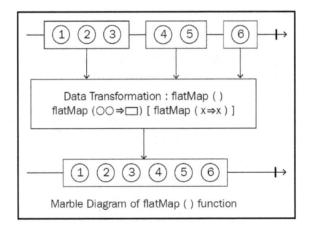

Marble Diagram of flatMap ( ) function

FRP – the merge() function Marble diagram

Suppose we have a code like this to merge two data streams of the same type:

```
scala> val list1 = List(1,24)
list1: List[Int] = List(1, 24)

scala> val list1 = List(1,2,4)
list1: List[Int] = List(1, 2, 4)

scala> val list2 = List(3,5)
```

```
list2: List[Int] = List(3, 5)

scala> list1 ++ list2
res0: List[Int] = List(1, 2, 4, 3, 5)
```

Alternatively, we have a user-defined function, merge(), as shown here:

```
scala> def merge[A](list1:List[A], list2:List[A]): List[A] = list1 ++ list2
merge: [A](list1: List[A], list2: List[A])List[A]
scala> merge(list1,list2)
res1: List[Int] = List(1, 2, 4, 3, 5)
```

If we want to represent this merge() function's Marble diagram, we can do so as follows:

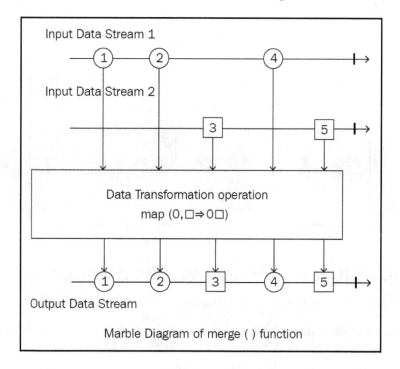

Here, **Input Data Stream1** is list1 and **Input Data Stream2** is list2. When we make a call to the merge() function with them, we will get the resulting (or output) data stream.

FRP – the filter() function Marble diagram

In FP, a `filter()` function is used to filter a data stream (or a set of elements—containers) with a condition (this condition is known as a predicate). For instance, we have a list of numbers and want to filter and return only even numbers, as demonstrated here:

```scala
scala> val numList = List(1,2,3,4,5,6)
numList: List[Int] = List(1, 2, 3, 4, 5, 6)
scala> numList.filter(x => x%2 == 0)
res8: List[Int] = List(2, 4, 6)
```

We can represent this `filter()` function as shown here:

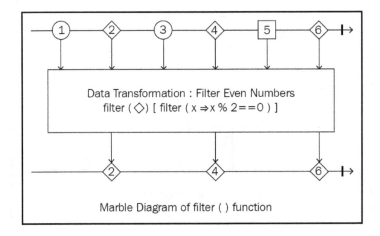

Marble Diagram of filter ( ) function

FRP – the reduce() function Marble diagram

Now we will see another important and frequently used functional HOF, that is, `reduce()`.

It takes each element from the data stream (or container) and applies the given function. Let's do it with `List` (almost all containers have this function):

```scala
scala> val numList = List(1,2,3,4,5,6)
numList: List[Int] = List(1, 2, 3, 4, 5, 6)

scala> numList.reduce((x,y) => x +y )
res22: Int = 21

scala> numList.reduce(_ + _)
res21: Int = 21
```

The following diagram shows the Marble diagram for the `reduce()` function:

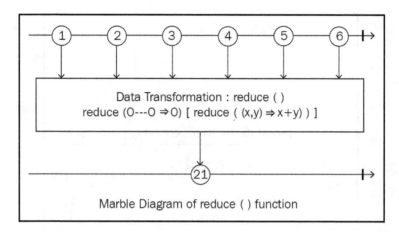

Marble Diagram of reduce ( ) function

 If you are new to HOF, refer to `Chapter 2`, *Functional Scala,* for more information.

FRP – the concat() and sorted() functions Marble diagram

So far, we did simple Marble diagrams, which apply only one function at a time. However, we can compose functions one by one in a sequential order to solve some complex problems easily and in an elegant way.

Now, we will draw Marble diagram for the `concat()` and `sorted()` functions. Let's consider some Scala code using these two functions:

```scala
scala> val hello = "Hello"
hello: String = Hello

scala> val world = "World"
world: String = World

scala> hello.concat(world)
res17: String = HelloWorld

scala> hello.concat(world).sorted
res19: String = Hwdellloor
```

We can represent them as a Marble diagram, as follows:

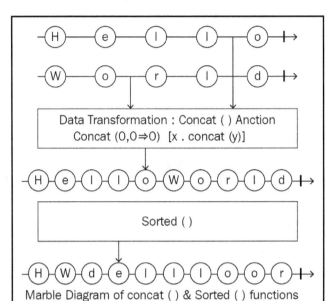

Marble Diagram of concat ( ) & Sorted ( ) functions

In the same way, we can represent any Functional or Reactive or FRP function as a Marble diagram to understand it well.

Observer pattern versus Reactive pattern

In this section, we will try to differentiate between the Observer pattern and Reactive pattern. As we have already discussed, the Reactive pattern gives a lot of benefits to our systems or applications.

The Observer pattern is a widely used OOP design pattern to solve some of the problems, and it mainly has two kinds of components—Subject and Object (where Subject is Observable and Object is Observer).

It gives us the following benefits:

- Separation of concerns into two distinct components—Subject and Object
- Clear abstraction and encapsulation between these two components
- Loose coupling between the Subject and Object components
- We can change a component without affecting others
- We can add more Objects or Observers at any time

Even though the Observer pattern solves most of the problems, it still has the following drawbacks or issues:

- It is not thread-safe
- It may cause leaking if we forget to unregister any Observers
- It does not support the backpressure technique
- It does not support composability, which means we cannot compose multiple small components to solve large or complex problems
- It does not support asynchronous non-blocking communication with backpressure

To solve all these problems, we should go for the Reactive Streams Specification.

The Reactive pattern is more than the Observer pattern. It is the combination of positive points from the Observer pattern, Iterator pattern, and FP.

 Reactive pattern = Observer pattern + Iterator pattern + FP

The Reactive pattern or programming is not a single pattern; it is an **architecture** and gives us a new set of design patterns to develop new kinds of systems or applications (that is, Reactive systems or Reactive applications). We will discuss it in `Chapter 12`, *Reactive Design Patterns and Best Practices*.

By design, the Reactive pattern supports asynchronous non-blocking communication with backpressure. If we use Akka Reactive Streams or Play Framework with FP, we will get composability, thread-safety, concurrency, and parallelism for free.

Check out the *Benefits of Reactive programming* section for more details, which are also the same for the Reactive pattern.

Take a look at `Chapter 7`, *Working with Reactive Streams*, to understand backpressure.

 Going forward, I hope my readers start *thinking functional reactively*.

Summary

In this chapter, we discussed what Reactive programming is, why we need it, its benefits, and its architecture.

Like Imperative and OOP, RP is a kind of programming paradigm.

We also covered the Reactive Manifesto and the Reactive Streams Specification and why we need RSS. You learned the four principles or tenants of Reactive Streams.

We also explored the Java 9 Flow API and its components in depth. It is defined as an API by Oracle Corporation as part of JEP-266. This API is also known as the Reactive Streams API.

Then we introduced another popular programming paradigm known as FP, and discussed why FP is a better fit for RP. Finally, we combined FP and RP into FRP.

We focused on some of the Reactive Streams API implementations, such as Akka Streams, Reactive Extensions (RxJava, Rx Scala), Vert.x, the Spring Reactor module, Reactive Mongo, and more.

I hope you have understood all about what the importance of FRP is in developing Reactive systems.

In this book, we will use the Lightbend Reactive Platform to develop our Reactive applications. The Lightbend Reactive Platform is a set of components, such as Scala, Play Framework, Akka Toolkit, Lagom, and ConductR. So let's start learning about each component one by one in the subsequent chapters.

Once you learn each component, at the end of the book, we will develop our final Reactive systems by following the Reactive Architecture.

2

Functional Scala

In this chapter, we will discuss some of the important and useful **FP (Functional Programming)** principles of the Scala programming language. I assume that you are already familiar with Scala basics such as Scala REPL, Scala OOPs concepts, and more. If you are really new to the Scala world, it'll be helpful if you read some Scala basics first and come to us later.

In this chapter, you will learn the following topics:

- Scala App
- How to use Scala REPL
- Scala FP features
- Scala Functional Design Patterns
- Scala plug-in for IntelliJ IDEA
- The Scala Collections API
- Trait and its linearization rules

Introduction to Scala

Scala stands for Scalable language. Scala is a multi-paradigm programming language built on JVM by the Lightbend (formerly known as Typesafe) team. In Scala, it is easy to write concurrent parallel, distributed, and Reactive applications in a concise, elegant, and type-safe way.

Unlike Java, Scala is a pure OOP and FP language. Java is not a pure OOP language because of the following:

- It supports static members
- It supports primitive data types

Scala does not support static members. Then how do we define utility methods in Scala? We will explore those in the upcoming sections. In Scala, everything is an **object** only. There are no primitive types in Scala.

Both Scala and Java programming languages run on JVM:

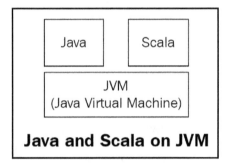

Java and Scala on JVM

From Java 8 onward, we can write functional-style programming in Java. However, it does not support all FP features.

Scala's latest stable version is 2.12.3. We will use this version to develop our applications.

 We can find the Scala Language API at
http://www.scala-lang.org/api/current/index.html.

Scala supports strongly-typed systems, that is, it supports type-safety. Scala is a hybrid programming language that supports both OOP and FP.

The following diagram shows that Scala supports hybrid programming paradigms:

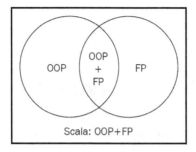

The Scala ecosystem

Hello, readers! Let's see what the Scala ecosystem is.

In my view, the Scala ecosystem means Scala plus its tools, technologies, APIs, frameworks, toolkits, and so on. It contains the Scala language, Play Framework, Akka Toolkit, build tools (SBT, Maven), IntelliJ IDEA (other IDEs, too, that support Scala), Scala testing frameworks such as ScalaTest, Spec2, AkkaTestKit, coverage, ScalaStyle, and more. The following diagram shows the technology stack of the Scala ecosystem:

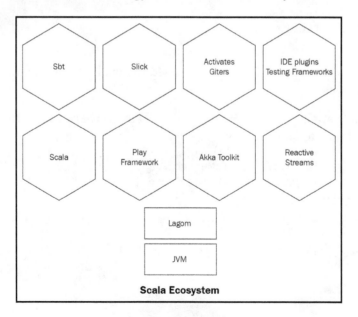

Similarly, Java also has its own ecosystem.

Understanding the Scala Application

Before discussing Scala Functional Programming features, we will discuss the Scala app. As a Java developer, initially everybody starts with some **HelloWorld** example, using the `main()` method. We can do the same thing in Scala using its app (or application).

The Scala app is defined in the `scala` package as `scala.App`. Let's develop a HelloWorld example, using IntelliJ IDEA:

1. Create a Scala SBT project:

    ```
    Project Name: scala-helloworld-app
    ```

2. Create the following Scala app:

HelloWorldApp.scala:

```
object HelloWorldApp extends App{
  println("Hello Scala World!")
}
```

Here, `scala.App` is a trait, which is used to develop Scala standalone applications.

3. Like Java applications with the `main()` method, we can write the same Scala Application, as shown here:

```
object HelloWorldApp_MainMethod_App {
  def main(args: Array[String]) = {
    println("Hello Scala World!")
  }
}
```

Here, we are using a Java-like `main()` method.

4. When we run both programs, we will get the same output as shown here:

```
Hello Scala World!
```

5. By observing both programs, we can understand that `scala.App` provides the following `main()` for free. We don't need to use it again:

```
def main(args: Array[String]) = {
}
```

Scala REPL

The Scala programming language has a command-line shell known as REPL to execute simple Scala expressions, programs, and more to experiment and learn Scala Basics quickly without using any IDEs such as Eclipse and IntelliJ IDE.

REPL stands for **Read-Eval-Print Loop**. In Scala, REPL is an interactive tool and acts a Scala interpreter.

Once we install Scala and set up the environment variables such as PATH, we can access REPL, as shown in the following screenshot:

```
rambabuposa@ram: ~
rambabuposa@ram:~$ scala
Welcome to Scala 2.12.3 (Java HotSpot(TM) 64-Bit Server VM, Java 1.8.0_121).
Type in expressions for evaluation. Or try :help.

scala>
```

Here, we can execute any Scala expression. When I started learning Scala basics a few years ago, initially I was using REPL to experiment with my programs. It's very easy to use.

In this book, we will use Scala REPL in a couple of places without using the IDE.

 For more information about Scala REPL, go through the documentation at https://docs.scala-lang.org/overviews/repl/overview.html.

Principles of Scala FP

Scala supports all FP features. However, it is not easy to cover them in a single chapter. So we will discuss only the following few important FP features in this chapter:

- Pure functions
- Immutability (Immutable data)
- Referential transparency
- Functions are first-class citizens
- Anonymous functions
- **Higher-Order Functions** (HOF)
- Currying
- Tail recursion
- Implicit
- Typeclasses

FP Design Patterns

The following three are the most important and frequently used Functional Design Patterns.

- Monoid
- Monad
- Functor (Applicative functor)

 If you are new to Scala FP features and want to learn them in depth, I recommend that you refer to any Scala Basics books before picking this one.

Consider the following Scala FP features:

Scala FP Main Features
✓ Immutability
✓ Functions as First-class Citizens
✓ No side effects
✓ Pure Functions
✓ RT (Referential Transparency)

In the sections that follow, we will pick these features, one by one and discuss them in depth with some examples.

Scala FP features in action

I assume that you are already familiar with Scala Basics, Scala OOP features, and more. If you are new to them, go through some Scala basics books. In this section, we will pick up each Scala FP feature one by one and discuss it in detail with some simple examples in the coming subsections.

Now, it's time to get our hands dirty and experiment with Scala FP features.

Immutability

Immutable data is data that we can't change once it's created. In Scala, we can mark immutable data using the val keyword:

```
scala> val data = "Result"
data: String = Result

scala> data = "New Value"
<console>:12: error: reassignment to val
       data = "New Value"
```

Not only the Scala ecosystem (API, frameworks, tools, and more), but also most Scala-based applications use immutable data to represent their **models**.

In Scala, function arguments are val by default. In most Scala-based applications, we use **case classes** to represent models as they are immutable by design. We will discuss case classes in the next section.

The following are the benefits of immutability:

- No side effects
- Easy to reason about and test
- Thread safety
- Easy to write concurrent and parallel programs

In Scala, function arguments are `val` by default.

Scala functions

In general, a **function** is an operation that takes some inputs, processes them, and returns results. It is the same for the Scala language too. Take a look at the following diagram:

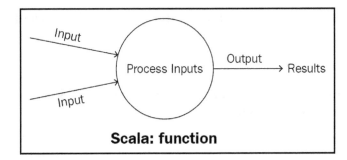

Scala: function

Sometimes, a function is also known as an operation, routine, procedure, or method, depending on the context in which we use it.

In Scala, we can define a function using `def`, as shown here:

```
def add (a: Int, b: Int) : Int = a + b
```

Here, the `add` function has two inputs, a and b, of the same type, `Int`, and returns `Int` as a result.

Scala supports some syntactic sugar to write the same function in different ways:

```
def add (a: Int, b: Int) : Int = {
  a + b
}
```

If our function has one and only one expression, then we can omit the curly braces; they are optional:

```
def add (a: Int, b: Int)  = a + b
```

We can omit the result type of `Int` here. The Scala compiler will guess or infer the return type as follows:

```
scala> def add (a: Int, b: Int)  = a + b
add: (a: Int, b: Int)Int
```

This is known as **type inference**. This is the beauty of the Scala language feature.

Functions always return only one value.

In Scala, avoid using `return` to return a function result, as shown here:

```
scala> def add (a: Int, b: Int)  = return a + b
<console>:10: error: method add has return statement; needs result type
       def add (a: Int, b: Int)  = return a + b
                                       ^
```

If we use the preceding result type, then the Scala compiler cannot infer its return type. We should manually specify its return type, as shown here:

```
scala> def add (a: Int, b: Int):Int  = return a + b
add: (a: Int, b: Int)Int
```

In Scala, if a function has more than one expression in its body, then we should use curly braces. In this case, curly braces are mandatory:

```
scala> def add (a: Int, b: Int)  = {
     |    val result = a + b
     |    result
     | }
add: (a: Int, b: Int)Int
```

Here, the `add()` function is using curly braces because its body has more than one expression. When we don't use `return` in a function body, the Scala compiler will take the last expression from a function body, evaluate it, and infer that function result type, based on that last expression value.

In the preceding `add()` function, the Scala compiler evaluates `result` (the last expression from the function body) and infers its result type as `Int`.

Scala pure functions

Pure functions are one of the important features or principles of FP.

Pure functions are functions whose result (or return value) depends only on its inputs (function parameters). Irrespective of how many times we call that function with the same inputs, we will receive the same result. Take a look at the following diagram:

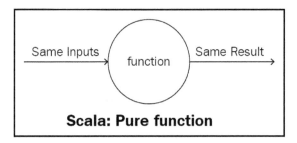

Scala: Pure function

Pattern matching

In Scala, pattern matching is one of the powerful FP constructs, which is not available in many other languages, such as Java. It is used to match an expression with a sequence of alternatives and get the required results.

It is something similar to Java's `Switch` statement, but it does more. One of the greatest benefits of this FP construct is that we can do matching on almost everything, such as values, objects, Case classes, user-defined classes, and more.

The following syntax defines how to use Scala's match statement to do **pattern matching**:

```
[Expression] match {
  case [Pattern1] => [A block of code-1] or [Result-1]
  case [Pattern2] => [A block of code-1] or [Results2]
  ...
  case [Pattern-n] => [A block of code-1] or [Results-n]
}
```

As shown in the preceding code snippet, a pattern matching construct starts with an expression E, followed by the `match` keyword and a set of `case` blocks. A `case` consists of the `case` keyword followed by a pattern, then followed by the => symbol, and finally expression(s) (or a block of code) to be executed, if this pattern matches.

Here, the => symbol separates the pattern from the result, as shown in this example:

```
scala> val num:Int = 10
num: Int = 10
```

```
scala> num match {
    | case 1 => println("one")
    | case 10 => println("ten")
    | }
ten
```

Here, `num` is an expression and has two `case` blocks. Each case is printing a value, but not returning anything.

Pattern matching can optionally have a guard clause on the left-hand side of a case, as shown here:

```
scala> num match {
    | case x if x % 2 == 0 => println("Even number.")
    | case _  => println("Odd number.")
    | }
```

In the preceding code example, we are using the _ placeholder to match everything and avoid `MatchError`:

```
scala> num match {
    | case x if x % 2 != 0 => println("Odd number.")
    | }
scala.MatchError: 10 (of class java.lang.Integer)
```

As this match expression is missing the *Checking of Even numbers or Default clause*, it throws a `MatchError`. In real-time projects, it is always recommended you use one of the default cases to avoid this kind of error.

It is always recommended you use pattern matching expressions, instead of `isInstanceOf/asInstanceOf` methods. We will discuss how to pattern match on case classes in the coming sections.

Scala's pattern matching follows the *Visitor Design* pattern.

Scala combinators

In Scala, a combinator is a Higher-Order Function and also a pure function.

As they are pure functions, we can easily compose them together very well as flexible, fine-grained building blocks for constructing larger, more complex programs.

Some of the frequently used Scala combinators are as follows:

- `map`
- `flatMap`
- `reduce`
- `fold`
- `recover`
- `filter`
- `fallbackTo`
- `zip`

Like the `try...catch` block in sequential programming, `Future` has the `Future.recover` block for asynchronous programming. If you are new to Scala Futures, please refer to `Chapter 3`, *Asynchronous Programming with Scala*:

```
def recover(pf: PartialFunction[Throwable, T])    (implicit e:
ExecutionContext): Future[T]
```

It is also a Scala combinator. We will discuss some Scala combinators, such as map and flatMap, in the coming sections.

For-comprehensions

Scala supports a very rich `For` loop construct known as **For-comprehension**. We can use it like Java's extended `For` loop, as shown here:

```
scala> val numList = List(1,2,3,4,5)
numList: List[Int] = List(1, 2, 3, 4, 5)

scala> for(num <- numList) yield num+1
res7: List[Int] = List(2, 3, 4, 5, 6)
```

When we observe the preceding example, we realize that For-comprehension results in the same container or object with a new set of elements.

For-comprehension = filter + map

We can use For-comprehension to replace the operation that uses both filter and map, as shown here:

```
scala> val numList = List(1,2,3,4,5)
numList: List[Int] = List(1, 2, 3, 4, 5)

scala> numList.filter(a => a %2 == 0).map(b => b*b)
res8: List[Int] = List(4, 16)

scala> for(num <- numList if num % 2 == 0) yield num*num
res10: List[Int] = List(4, 16)
```

Here, For-comprehension is picking one element at a time from `numList`, checking the condition `num % 2 == 0` (even number) and performing the *square root* operation, that is, `num*num`.

A combination of these two Higher-Order Functions, that is, `filter` and `map`, also does the same.

Scala implicits

Scala supports a powerful tool called **implicits** to ease the development of complex things in a concise and easy way. It reduces the verbosity of Scala applications.

We can use implicits to develop applications, DSLs, APIs, libraries, tools, and more, easily.

The main goal of Scala Implicits is to ease the process of extending the existing Scala Type system. We use the `implicit` keyword to define implicits in Scala.

Scala supports two kinds of implicits:

- Implicit parameters
- Implicit conversions

Implicit parameters

An implicit parameter is an actual parameter, which is a value passed to a function (or method) in a function (or method) call. When a method (or function) has an implicit parameter, it's up to the developer to pass it explicitly, or make it available in the current scope to pass it automatically to the Scala compiler.

Consider the following example:

```
scala> def add(x: Int, implicit y: Int) = x + y
<console>:1: error: identifier expected but 'implicit' found.
       def add(x: Int, implicit y: Int) = x + y
                       ^

scala> def add(x: Int)(implicit y: Int) = x + y
add: (x: Int)(implicit y: Int)Int

scala> add(11)
<console>:15: error: could not find implicit value for parameter y: Int
       add(11)
          ^

scala> implicit a:Int = 12
<console>:1: error: expected start of definition
       implicit a:Int = 12
                ^

scala> implicit val a:Int = 12
a: Int = 12

scala> add(11)
res1: Int = 23
```

Implicit conversions

Implicit conversions are used to convert an element from a type *A* to another type *B*, when the element is used in a place where *B* is expected. Let's check it with the following example:

```
scala> val num = 10
num: Int = 10

scala> val numInString = "20"
numInString: String = 20

scala> val result = num * numInString
<console>:14: error: overloaded method value * with alternatives:
  (x: Double)Double <and>
  (x: Float)Float <and>
  (x: Long)Long <and>
  (x: Int)Int <and>
  (x: Char)Int <and>
  (x: Short)Int <and>
  (x: Byte)Int
```

```
cannot be applied to (String)
        val result = num * numInString
                         ^

scala> implicit def str2Int(str:String) = str.toInt
str2Int: (str: String)Int

scala> val result = num * numInString
result: Int = 200
```

Explore our previously defined add() function, using Scala REPL here:

```
scala> def add (a: Int, b: Int)  = a + b
add: (a: Int, b: Int)Int

scala> add(100,10)
res1: Int = 110

scala> add(100,10)
res2: Int = 110

scala> add(100,20)
res3: Int = 120
```

If you observe the preceding code results, you will see that we are getting the same result for the same inputs. If we change the inputs, then we will get a different result.

Here, as the add function is dependent on its inputs only, we can say that this add function is a pure function.

> The major benefit or the main goal of pure functions is that there are *no side effects*.

There is an easy-to-understand and easy-to-remember rule of thumb about functions.

If a function does *not* return a result, that function has some side effects. It's not recommended you write this kind of function unless there is a specific requirement in our project:

```
scala> def display() = println("Hello Scala World!")
display: ()Unit

scala> display
Hello Scala World!
```

```
scala> display()
Hello Scala World!
```

Here, the `display()` function does *not* return anything, so the Scala compiler will infer its result type as `Unit`. If a function does NOT take parameters, then we can make a call to it, either using parenthesis or not. Both work fine.

However, if we define our `display()` function as shown in the following example, then we should make a call to it without parenthesis only:

```
scala> def display = println("Hello Scala World!")
display: Unit

scala> display
Hello Scala World!

scala> display()
<console>:12: error: Unit does not take parameters
       display()
              ^
```

 If we define a function with parenthesis, then we can make a call to it, either using parenthesis or not.

If we define a function without parenthesis, then we should make a call to it without using parenthesis only.

Scala anonymous functions

In previous sections, we defined a couple of Scala functions and came to know that each function has a meaningful name. Is it possible to define a function without a name? Yes, in Scala, we can define a function without a name.

An anonymous function is a function without a name. It is also known as a function literal. It works just like a normal function. Let's explore it with some examples now:

```
def add (a: Int, b: Int) = a + b
```

The following diagram shows the syntax of a Scala anonymous function:

```
( Inputs )  ⟹  Output

Scala Anonymous Function Syntax
```

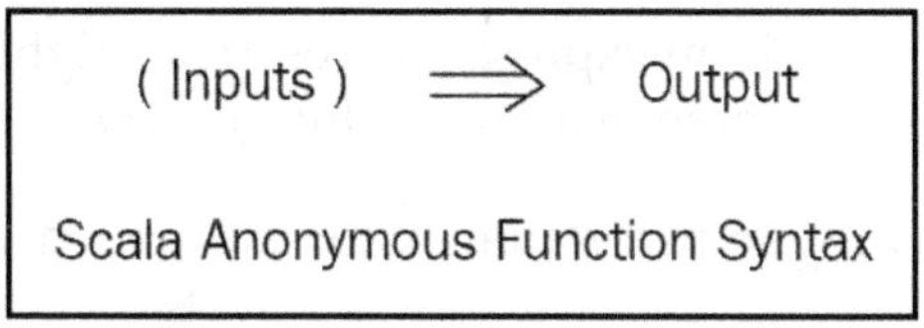

As we discussed with the add() function in the previous section, it is a normal Scala function.

We can write the same function as an anonymous function, as shown here:

```
scala> (a: Int, b: Int) => a + b
res0: (Int, Int) => Int = <function2>
```

Here, we have created an anonymous function of type Int, Int) => Int. It clearly explains what the inputs are and what the output of this function is:

Anonymous Function: Inputs ⟹ Output

Function Inputs	Function Output	Anonymous Function	Anonymous Function Type
(Int)	(Int)	(Int) ⟹ Int	funtion1
(Int, Int)	(Int)	(Int, Int) ⟹ Int	function2
(Int, Int, Int)	(Int)	(Int, Int, Int) ⟹ Int	function3
. . .			
(Int, Int, ... Int) 22 Parameters	(Int)	(Int, Int, ... Int) ⟹ Int	function22

Scala Anonymous function

Everything is an expression

Unlike Java, in Scala, everything is an expression. Yes, that's right. Then how about if...else expressions, For-comprehension (for loop), case statements, and more?

In Scala, we can use an if...else as a statement or expression, as shown here:

```
scala> val x = 10
x: Int = 10

scala> if (x % 2 == 0) "Even" else "Odd"
res4: String = Even

scala> val result = if (x % 2 == 0) "Even" else "Odd"
result: String = Even

scala> result
res5: String = Even
```

In the same way, we can assign anything to a variable, as everything is an expression.

Referential transparency

In Scala, **referential transparency** (**RT**) means that an expression or a function call may be replaced by its value, without changing the behavior of the application.

A value may be replaced by an expression or a function call without changing the behavior of the application.

We will explore these two points with some simple examples now.

Let's assume that we are using the y = x + 1 expression in our application:

```
scala> val x = 10
x: Int = 10

scala> val y = x + 1
y: Int = 11

scala> val y = 11
y: Int = 11
```

Here, when we replace an expression x+1 with its value 11, it does not change any behavior of the y in our application:

```
scala> val y = 11
y: Int = 11

scala> def addOne(a: Int) = a + 1
addOne: (a: Int)Int

scala> val y = addOne(x)
y: Int = 11
```

Here, the value of y is replaced by a function called addOne(). In this case too, there is no change in the behavior of our application.

RT means an expression can be replaced with its value without changing its behavior.

Functions are first-class citizens

In Scala, functions are first-class citizens because we can do the following things with them:

- We can use functions as values or like normal variables; we can replace a variable or value with a function
- We can assign a function literal to a variable
- We can pass one or more functions as another function's parameters
- We can return a function from another function

We will discuss the last two points in the Scala *Higher-Order Functions* section. Let's discuss the first two points here.

We can use a function like a normal value or variable, as shown here:

```
scala> def doubleIt(x: Int) = x * x
doubleIt: (x: Int)Int

scala> def addOne(x: Int) = x + 1
addOne: (x: Int)Int

scala> val result = 10 + doubleIt(20) + addOne(49)
result: Int = 460
```

We can assign an anonymous function to a variable, as shown in the following code snippet and use that variable where we have that function literal requirement:

```
val addFunction = (a: Int, b: Int) => a + b
```

Let us experiment this with Scala REPL:

```
scala> val addFunction = (a: Int, b: Int) => a + b
addFunction: (Int, Int) => Int = <function2>

scala> addFunction(10,20)
res10: Int = 30

scala> def display(x: Int) = println("x value = " + x)
display: (x: Int)Unit

scala> display(addFunction(10,20))
x value = 30
```

As shown in the preceding example, we can use a functional literal or anonymous function as a function parameter.

Partial functions

A partial function is a function that does not provide a result for every possible input value it can be given. It supports only a subset of possible inputs.

In Scala, we can use `scala.PartialFunction` to define partial functions.

In Scala source code, `PartialFunction` is defined as follows:

```
trait PartialFunction[-A, +B] extends (A) ⇒ B
```

Consider the following example:

```
scala> val numRange = 1 to 5
numRange: scala.collection.immutable.Range.Inclusive = Range(1, 2, 3, 4, 5)

scala> val isEven: PartialFunction[Int, String] = {
     |     case num if num % 2 == 0 => num +" is even"
     | }
isEven: PartialFunction[Int,String] = <function1>

scala> val evenNumbers = numRange collect isEven
evenNumbers: scala.collection.immutable.IndexedSeq[String] = Vector(2 is
even, 4 is even)
```

Function currying

Function currying means converting a function's single parameters list into a multiple parameters list. Take a look at the following code example:

```
scala> def add(a:Int,b:Int,c:Int) = a + b + c
add: (a: Int, b: Int, c: Int)Int

scala> add(1,2,3)
res2: Int = 6

scala> def add(a:Int)(b:Int)(c:Int) = a + b + c
add: (a: Int)(b: Int)(c: Int)Int

scala> add(1,2,3)
<console>:16: error: too many arguments (3) for method add: (a: Int)(b:
Int)(c: Int)Int
        add(1,2,3)
            ^

scala> add(1)(2)(3)
res4: Int = 6
```

One of the important use cases of currying is to support `implicit` parameters.

The following examples demonstrate how currying supports `implicit` parameters:

```
scala> def add(x: Int, implicit y: Int) = x + y
<console>:1: error: identifier expected but 'implicit' found.
        def add(x: Int, implicit y: Int) = x + y
                        ^

scala> def add(x: Int)(implicit y: Int) = x + y
add: (x: Int)(implicit y: Int)Int

scala> implicit val a:Int = 12
a: Int = 12

scala> add(11)
res1: Int = 23
```

Higher-Order Functions

In Scala, **Higher-Order Functions** (**HOF**) are functions that should have one or more of the following things:

- It should have one or more function(s) as its parameters
- It should return a function as its result

Let us explore a HOF which takes a function as a parameter, using Scala REPL function as a function parameter:

```
scala> val addOne = (x: Int) => x + 1
addOne: Int => Int = <function1>

scala> def hof(f: Int => Int) = f
hof: (f: Int => Int)Int => Int

scala> val result = hof(addOne)
result: Int => Int = <function1>

scala> result(10)
res14: Int = 11
```

Here, we are passing the `addOne()` function to the `hof()` function as a parameter.

We can observe these kind of functions a lot in Scala, Akka Toolkit, and Play Framework source code, for instance, the `map()` and `flatMap()` functions.

Let us explore a HOF which has a function as its result type, using Scala REPL:

```
scala> def fun(a:Int, b:Int): Int => Int = a => b
fun: (a: Int, b: Int)Int => Int

scala> fun(10,20)
res15: Int => Int = <function1>

scala> res15(30)
res17: Int = 20

scala> res15(1)
res18: Int = 20
```

Here, we are returning a function of type `Int => Int` from another function. So, that is also an example of a HOF.

Scala tail-recursion

Recursion is a technique defined as using a function or method that calls itself again and again, until it solves the problem.

The recursion technique helps us solve simple problems very easily and even makes it possible to solve complex problems. It is easy to reason about and needs a lot less code, as compared to the iterative approach.

What kind of problems can we solve using the recursion technique? Any problem that is defined in terms of itself.

Types of recursions

We can implement recursion in different ways. However, we are considering only the following two types:

- Linear recursion
- Tail-recursion

Tail-recursion is one form of recursion technique. We can say a recursive call is tail-recursive, when a recursive call is the last thing executed by that function and it does nothing after that, just returns its value.

Benefits of linear recursion

Unlike non-recursive approaches like loops, which use mutable variables, it supports immutability:

- We can write more readable code
- It avoids mutability
- It requires less code to solve complex problems

A linear-recursion example

Here, we will write a Scala Application to demonstrate a linear recursion technique:

```
package com.packt.publishing.recursion

object LinearRecursionApp extends App {

  val list = List(1,2,3,4,5,6,7,8,9)

  val list2 = linearRecursion(list)

  println("Original List = " + list)
  println("After Tail Recursion of List = " + list2)

  def linearRecursion[A](l: List[A]): List[A] = l match {
    case h :: tail => linearRecursion(tail) ::: List(h)
    case Nil => Nil
  }

}
```

When we run the preceding application, we can observe the following output:

```
Original List = List(1, 2, 3, 4, 5, 6, 7, 8, 9)
After Linear Recursion of List = List(9, 8, 7, 6, 5, 4, 3, 2, 1)
```

Both Scala and Java support this kind of recursion. However, it has the following drawbacks:

- It uses more stack-frames for recursive calls (it needs one stack-frame for each recursive call)
- It consumes or requires more memory
- There may be a chance of getting `StackOverflowError`

Benefits of tail-recursion

Apart from the preceding *linear recursion* benefits we discussed previously, it gives us the following benefits too:

- Uses very few stack-frames for tail-recursive calls
- Consumes less memory
- No more `StackOverflowException` issues

Chapter 2

 Unlike Java, which supports only the standard recursive approach, Scala supports both recursion and tail-recursion approaches.

A tail-recursion example

Here, we will write a Scala Application to demonstrate the tail-recursion technique.

Scala's @tailrec annotation ensures that tail recursive functions are optimized by the Scala compiler, to avoid StackOverflowErrors:

```
package com.packt.publishing.recursion

object TailRecursionApp extends App {

  val list = List(1,2,3,4,5,6,7,8,9)
  val list2 = tailRecursion(list)

  println("Original List = " + list)
  println("After Tail Recursion of List = " + list2)

  @tailrec
  def tailRecursion[A](listOfElements: List[A]): List[A] = {
    def reverse(updatedList: List[A], originalList: List[A]):
    List[A] = originalList match {
      case Nil => updatedList
      case head :: tail => reverse(head :: updatedList, tail)
    }

    reverse(Nil, listOfElements)
  }

}
```

When we run the preceding application, we can observe the following output:

```
Original List = List(1, 2, 3, 4, 5, 6, 7, 8, 9)
After Tail Recursion of List = List(9, 8, 7, 6, 5, 4, 3, 2, 1)
```

Scala Type class

In Scala, a Type class defines some behavior in terms of some operations. If a new class (or Type) wants to join as a member of that Type class, it must provide implementation to all operations, which are defined in that Type class.

So in simple words, a Type class is a group of classes which provides implementation to a contract (or an interface).

The main goal of Type classes is to define a contract or interface to its types.

Unlike sub-type polymorphism, which uses OOP inheritance, Type classes follow ad hoc polymorphism, using composition and support **DRY** (**Do NOT Repeat Yourself**) and **SRP** (**Single Responsibility Principle**).

Like generics or Type parameters, Type classes are resolved at compile time. The following diagram shows the main goal of Scala Type class:

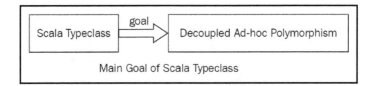

Types of polymorphism in brief:

- Parametric polymorphism—using generics:

  ```
  trait Json[T]
  ```

- Sub-type polymorphism:

  ```
  trait Json
    object StringJson extends Json
  ```

- Ad-hoc polymorphism—it is overloading:

  ```
  trait Json[T]
    object StringJson extends Json[String]
  ```

The preceding two examples just demonstrate how to use implicits. However, in our real-time projects we should never use these kinds of common types as implicits.

Benefits of Type classes

Scala Type classes provide us with the following benefits:

- It avoids lots of boilerplate code
- It avoids code redundancy
- It supports the DRY design principle very well
- We can write very flexible and more reusable code
- We can write extensible code
- We can write generic code easily
- It supports separation of concerns (Loosely Coupling) very well
- It encourages composition over inheritance
- It supports more type-safety

The following diagram shows the four main benefits of Scala Type classes:

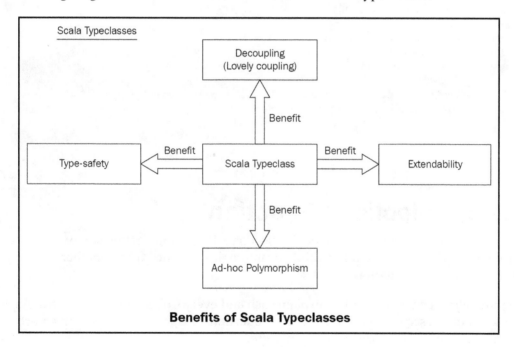

Benefits of Scala Typeclasses

Apart from Scala-based applications, Scala, Akka Toolkit, and Play Framework, source code uses Type classes extensively. For instance, the Cats library uses Type classes extensively. Please refer to this repository: `https://github.com/typelevel/cats`.

For instance, a Type class, `Json[T]` has the following operations:

```
trait Json[T] {
  def toJson(t: T) : Json
  def fromJson(json: Json): T
}
```

It is a Type class which defines a contract of two functions. We can use this contract and define any number of types by using type parameters as shown here:

```
object JSON {
    implicit object StringJson extends Json[Double] {
        def toJson(t: String) : Json
        def fromJson(json: Json): String
    }
    implicit object IntJson extends Json[Int] {
        def toJson(t: Int) : Json
        def fromJson(json: Json): Int
    }
    implicit object BooleanJson extends Json[Boolean] {
        def toJson(t: Boolean) : Json
        def fromJson(json: Json): Boolean
    }
}
```

Scala Collections in action

The Scala language supports a very rich Collection API. It supports two sets of Collections—one to support immutability (immutable Collections) and another to support mutability (mutable Collections).

It requires almost an entire book to explain each and every Collection API in depth. As we have only one subsection in this chapter for Collections, we will discuss only the most important and frequently used Collections here.

Scala List

In the Scala Collection API, List is a **LIFO**-based immutable Collection which represents an ordered linked list (where LIFO stands for **Last In First Out**). It is available as `scala.collection.immutable.List`.

It has two implementation case classes, `scala.Nil` and `scala.::` as shown here:

```
sealed abstract class List[+A]
object List
final case class :: extends List[B]
case object Nil extends List[Nothing]
```

Let's explore it with some examples:

```
scala> val numberList = List(1,2,3,4)
numberList: List[Int] = List(1, 2, 3, 4)

scala> number
numberList    numbersList

scala> number
numberList    numbersList

scala> numberList.map(x=> x.toString)
res0: List[String] = List(1, 2, 3, 4)

scala> val strList = "One" :: "Two" :: Nil
strList: List[String] = List(One, Two)
```

Here we are using List's Cons operator to construct the List object. Let's explore this in detail in the next section. Nil represents end of the List:

```
scala> val emptyList = Nil
emptyList: scala.collection.immutable.Nil.type = List()

scala> val emptyList = List()
emptyList: List[Nothing] = List()
```

Scala List Cons operator

In Scala, List has an operator : :, which is known as the Cons operator. It is useful to add new elements at the beginning of the List. Here, Cons is short for construct the new List object.

Let us explore the Cons operator with some simple examples (here : : is a double colon):

```
scala> var numbersList = List (1,2,3)
numbersList: List[Int] = List(1, 2, 3)

scala> numbersList = numbersList :: 4
<console>:11: error: value :: is not a member of Int
       numbersList = numbersList :: 4
                                  ^
```

We cannot use the Cons operator to add a new element at the end of the List. It accepts it only to add it at the beginning of the List:

```
scala> numbersList = 4 :: numbersList
numbersList: List[Int] = List(4, 1, 2, 3)

scala> numbersList = 6 :: 5 :: numbersList
numbersList: List[Int] = List(6, 5, 4, 1, 2, 3)
```

 In Scala, we don't have any operators except the = (equal to) assignment operator. All operators are functions only. Here, Cons is also a function, but we call it as an operator.

Right associative rule

In Scala, any operator ending with : (a colon) is right associative. Let's explore this in more detail with some examples.

In simple words, right associative means evaluate expressions from right to left, and left associative means evaluate expressions from left to right.

Take our previous example again:

```
scala> numbersList = numbersList :: 4
<console>:11: error: value :: is not a member of Int
       numbersList = numbersList :: 4
```

Here, we are getting a value :: is not a member of Int error owing to the right associative rule.

When we execute the numbersList :: 4 expression, it will interpret it in this way:

```
Expression = numbersList :: 4
```

As per the right associative rule, the Scala compiler starts evaluation of this expression from the right, as follows:

```
4.::(numbersList)
```

Here, the Scala compiler is trying to call the Cons `::` function on 4 (which is `Int`). If you go through the `Int` class in Scala API, we don't find the Cons function for this class. That's why we are getting the `value :: is not a member of Int` error.

Now, you will see a similar kind of thing for the left associative rule:

```
scala> val x = 10
x: Int = 10

scala> val y = x + 25
y: Int = 35
```

Here, `x + 25` is evaluated as `x.+(25)`.

As `x` is of type `Int` and has the + function, there is no error message for this expression evaluation.

 In Scala, all operators that end with : are right associative.

Scala Map

Scala Map is a map of key-value pairs. Like other Collections, Scala has the following two sets of maps:

```
scala.collection.mutable.Map
scala.collection.immutable.Map
```

If a package is not imported or not mentioned in the source code, the Scala compiler uses the default immutable Map:

```
scala> val numMap = Map("one" -> 1, "two" -> 2, "three" -> 3)
numMap: scala.collection.immutable.Map[String,Int] = Map(one -> 1, two ->
2, three -> 3)

scala> val phoneBook = "Ram" -> 1234567890
phoneBook: (String, Int) = (Ram,1234567890)
```

Scala Range

Range is an immutable Collection available at `scala.collection.immutable`. We can create a Range using the `to` and `upto` functions, as shown here:

```
scala> 1 to 5
res9: scala.collection.immutable.Range.Inclusive = Range 1 to 5

scala> 1 until 5
res11: scala.collection.immutable.Range = Range 1 until 5

scala> for(num <- 1 to 5) println(num)
1
2
3
4
5
```

Scala Functional Design Patterns

As a Java or Scala-experienced developer, I guess you are already familiar with some of the OOP design patterns. You may be not aware of Scala Functional Design Patterns.

Scala source code or applications use the following Functional Design Patterns extensively:

- Monoid
- Functor
- Monad

All these three terminologies come from **Mathematics Category Theory** (**MAT**). Let's delve into each of these, one by one in the following sections:

- **Monoid**: In Scala, Monoid is a type class or data structure with the following two rules:
    - **Associative rule**:

    ```
    (A1 Op A2) Op A3 == A1 Op (A2 Op A3)
    ```

- **Identity rule**: This rule states that, suppose we make a call to a function with two elements. This Identity rule states if that function returns a second element as is, without any change, then that first element is known as an Identity element:

    Left Identity rule:

    ```
    IndentityElement Operation Element  == Element
    ```

    Right Identity rule:

    ```
    Element Operation IndentityElement == Element
    ```

For instance, when we call a function with `Nil` and `List`, that function tries to add `Nil` to `List`. Finally, that function just returns the same `List` without any changes. In that case, `Nil` acts as the `Identity` element for Scala List:

```
scala> var numList = List(1,2,3,4)
numList: List[Int] = List(1, 2, 3, 4)

scala> numList = numList ++ Nil
numList: List[Int] = List(1, 2, 3, 4)

scala> numList = numList ++ Nil
numList: List[Int] = List(1, 2, 3, 4)
```

Irrespective of how many times we perform the `++` operation between a `List` and `Nil`, we will get the same `List` element.

- **Functors**: In Scala, Functor is a Type class or data structure which contains a `map()` function with the following signature:

```
trait MyFunctor {

  def map[A, B](f: A => B): C[A] => C[B]

}
```

Here, `MyFunctor` is a user-defined Functor trait with the `map()` function. `C` is any Scala container type such as `List`, `Option`, and more.

The `map()` function takes a function `f` of type `A => B` and returns a mapped function of type `C[A] => C[B]`.

For instance, we can translate this `map()` into a Scala option type as shown here:

```
def map[A, B](f: A => B): Option[A] => Option[B]
```

In other words, we can say that a Functor is a HOF that takes the function `f1` of type `A=>B` as input and transforms it into another function `f2` of type `C[A] => C[B]`.

In Scala, we don't have any specific trait or class type such as `trait Functor` or `class Functor`. We should use the existing Functor types such as `Option` or define your own Functor types, as per your requirement.

If we understand the Functor type very well, then it's easy to understand Monad. We will discuss it in the next section:

- **Monad**: In Scala, Monad is a Functional Design Pattern. It is a data structure that contains the following functions:
    - `apply()` (In FP terminology, it is also known as the `unit()` function)
    - `map()`
    - `flatMap()` (In FP terminology, it is also known as the `bind()` function) with the following signatures:

```
trait MyMonad[T] {
  def map[S](f: T => S): MyMonad[S]
  def flatMap[S](f: T => MyMonad[S]): MyMonad[S]
}
object MyMonad[T]{
  def apply[T](t: T): MyMonad[T]
}
```

Here, the `apply()` function is used to create that Monad (something like a constructor).

In Scala, Monad is a container type, which contains two or more elements. It is a Type class.

In Scala, we don't have any Monad type, such as `class Monad`, `trait Monad`, `case class Monad`, and so on. We need to define our own Monad types.

 Not only Scala source code, but also Play Framework and Akka Toolkit have used this Monad Design pattern.

Scala map() function

It is now a good time to understand how the `map()` function works in Scala. It's the same for all Scala containers such as Collections, Monads, and more. It is defined as shown in the following example in all Scala container classes:

```
final def map[B](f: (A) ⇒ B): C[B]
```

Here, `C` is a Scala container class such as `List`, `Option`, `Try`, `Future`, and so on.

The `map()` function takes a function `f` as an argument. The function `f` is defined as `f: A => B` that means it takes the element `A` as input, processes it and outputs element `B`.

Here, `A` and `B` are of the same type or may be different types.

When we apply this `map()` function on Container `C`, the `map()` function performs the following steps:

1. Picks up the first element from Container `C` of type `A` (if available).
2. Processes that element by the given logic.
3. Generates a new element of type `B`.
4. Generates a new container of the same type `C` and inserts that newly generated element into it.

It applies these same steps for all elements available in that container, one by one. If Container C is empty or contains nothing, the map() function does nothing. The following diagram shows how Scala's map() function works internally:

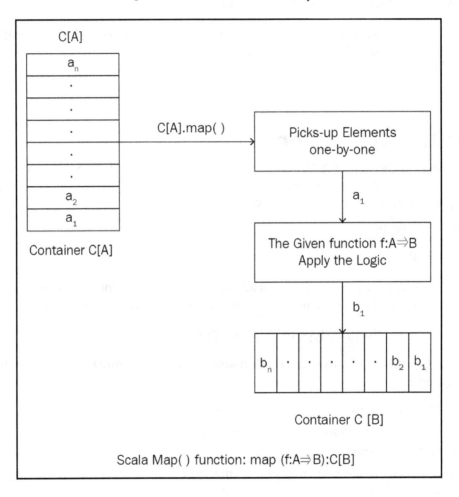

Let us explore Scala's `map()` function with some simple examples here:

```scala
scala> val numList = List(1,2,3,4,5)
numList: List[Int] = List(1, 2, 3, 4, 5)

scala> numList.map{ x => x+1 }
res0: List[Int] = List(2, 3, 4, 5, 6)
```

Scala flatMap() function

Unlike `Map`, which is just used to map one type element to another, `flatMap` is used to do the following two tasks in one call:

- Mapping
- Flattening

Advantages of flatMap

We can get the following benefits from the Scala `flatMap()` function:

- It avoids `if...else` blocks
- No nested `for` loops
- No callback hell
- We can write simple, elegant, readable, and neat code

The `flatMap()` function is defined, as shown here in all Scala Container classes:

```scala
final def flatMap[B](f: (A) => C[B]): C[B]
```

Here, `C` is a Scala container class like `List`, `Option`, `Try`, `Future`, and so on.

The `flatMap()` function takes a function `f` as an argument. The function `f` is defined as `f: A => C[B]`, meaning it takes element `A` as input, processes it, and outputs it as `C[B]`.

Here, A and B are of the same type or may be different types. The following diagram shows how the Scala `flatMap()` function works internally:

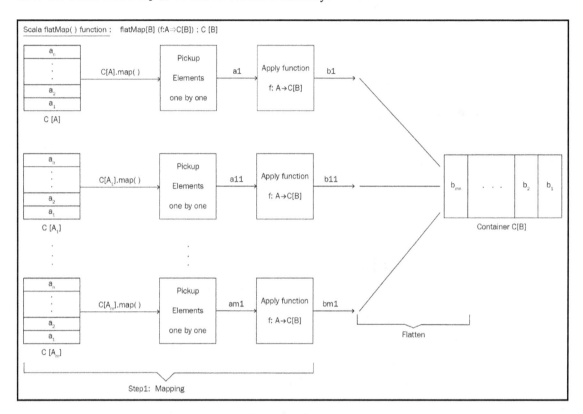

Let us explore the main difference between `map` and `flatMap` functions, using some simple examples here:

```scala
scala> val numList = List(List(1,2,3),List(4,5),List(6))
numList: List[List[Int]] = List(List(1, 2, 3), List(4, 5), List(6))
```

```scala
scala> numList.map{ x => x }
res2: List[List[Int]] = List(List(1, 2, 3), List(4, 5), List(6))
```

Here, we are still getting a `List` of `List` only. However, we are expecting only a `List`, so `flatMap` works well for this kind of scenarios, as shown here:

```scala
scala> numList.flatMap{ x => x }
res3: List[Int] = List(1, 2, 3, 4, 5, 6)
```

Scala Monads in action

In this section, we will discuss some of the import Monads available in Scala source code. Some example Monads from Scala source code are `Option`, `Try`, `Either`, `Future`, `Promise`.

Let's explore these Scala Monads, one by one, in the following sections.

Scala Option

In Scala, `Option` is used to represent whether a value is present or absent. It is a Type class like `scala.Option`. It is one of the frequently used Monad types in Scala-based applications.

The main advantages or goal of the `Option` type are as follows:

- To avoid lots of null checks for complex objects
- To avoid lots of boilerplate code to do null checks
- To avoid `NullPointerException`
- To write clean, neat, simple, and readable code

In the Scala source code, these three components are defined, as shown here:

```
sealed abstract class Option[+A]
case object None extends Option[Nothing]
final case class Some[+A] extends Option[A]
```

Let's take a value `T` into the `Option` type such as `Option[T]`. If a value is present in the `Option` type, then that type is known as `Some` type:

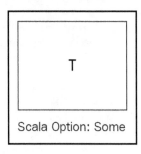

Scala Option: Some

Similarly, if a value is NOT present or absent in the `Option` type, then that type is known as `None` type:

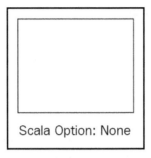

So, for a type parameter `T`, `Option[T]` has two types, `Some[T]` and `None`, as shown in the following diagram:

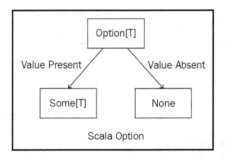

Like Option, Scala source code has another Monad —`Try`. It works similarly to `Option`. It is defined in the `scala.util` package. The `Try` type represents a computation that may either result in an exception or return a successfully computed value. It's similar to, but semantically different from, the `scala.util.Either` type.

Like `Option`, `Try[T]` represents two kinds of data:

- `Success[T]`
- `Failure[T]`

The following diagram represents Scala `Try` Monad and its subtypes:

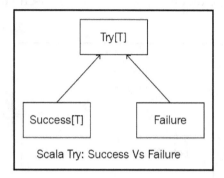

The following example demonstrates how to use `Try` Monad, using Scala Pattern matching:

```
import scala.util.{Try, Success, Failure}

result match {
    case Success(value) =>
      println("Success : $value")
    case Failure(error) =>
      println("Failure: $error")
  }
```

Scala Either

Like `Option`, Scala source code has another Monad—Either. It works similarly to `Option`. It is defined in the `scala.util` package.

Like `Option`, `Either[T]` represents two kinds of data:

- `Left[T]`
- `Right[T]`

Unlike `Option`, which cannot represent why data is missing, `Either` represents success cases as `Right`, and failure cases as `Left`.

Unlike `Try`, which can represent why data is missing in terms of exception only, `Either` can define a failure scenario, either as a plain text or any useful object. It is a kind of sum type:

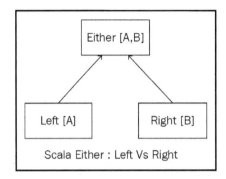

Scala Either : Left Vs Right

Here is an example:

```
import scala.util.{Either, Right, Left}
```

We can define a method signature using `Either`, as shown here:

```
val result: Either[String,Int] = ...
```

We can do pattern matching on `Either`, as shown here:

```
result match {
    case Right(value) =>
      println("Success : $value")
    case Left(error) =>
      println("Failure: $error")
}
```

 To understand Scala Future and Promise Monads, refer to Chapter 3, *Asynchronous Programming in Scala*.

Scala Case class and object

Case class is a special kind of class in Scala. In Scala-based applications, we define all our Models or Data Models using Case classes, only because it gives us many benefits for free.

In Scala, we can define a Case class or Case object, using the `case` keyword:

```
scala> case class Weather(day:String, temperature:String)
defined class Weather
```

By default, Case class constructors have `val` parameters, meaning that, we cannot change the values of `day` and `temperature`, once they are created.

A Case object is also an object that is defined using the `case` modifier. When we use a Case object, we will get some benefits for free to avoid boilerplate code.

Here is an example:

```
scala> case object WeatherAlert
defined object WeatherAlert
```

Benefits of Scala Case class

By default, the Scala compiler adds the following benefits to a Case class for free:

- The `toString`, `hashCode`, and `equals` methods. When we use the `case` keyword, the Scala compiler adds these methods for free to avoid boilerplate code.
- A companion object with `apply` and `unapply` methods, that's why there is no need to use new keywords to create instances of a Case classes copy method.
- Easy to use in pattern matching. It is immutable because, by default, its constructor parameters are `val`.

 In Scala, by default, `case` class and `case` objects are serializable.

Scala Traits in action

Scala Traits are somewhat similar to Java 8's interface, but they do more. We can use a Scala Trait as an interface (contract), abstract class, class, Mixin, and more.

In Scala, a Trait can contain abstract code, concrete code, or both. We can create a trait using the `trait` keyword, as shown here:

```
Trait Syntax:

trait <Trait-Name> {

  // Abstract members (Data and Functions)

  // Non-Abstract (Concrete) members (Data and Functions)

}
```

Let's explore them, one by one, now.

Trait as an interface

We can define a Trait only with abstract members, as shown here:

```
rambabuposa@ram$ scala -cp joda-time-2.9.6.jar
Welcome to Scala 2.12.3 (Java HotSpot(TM) 64-Bit Server VM, Java
1.8.0_121).

Type in expressions for evaluation. Or try :help.

scala> case class Weather(day: String, temparature: String)
defined class Weather

scala> :paste
// Entering paste mode (ctrl-D to finish)

import org.joda.time.LocalDate
trait IWeatherForecasting {
    def getWeatherForecasting(date:LocalDate) : Weather

}

// Exiting paste mode, now interpreting.

import org.joda.time.LocalDate
defined trait IWeatherForecasting
```

Here, `joda-time-2.9.6.jar` should be available in the current working directory.

Now, we can extend this Trait using a class, as follows:

```scala
scala> class WeatherForecasting extends IWeatherForecasting {
     |    def getWeatherForecasting(date:LocalDate) : Weather = {
     |         println("Getting weather ...")
     |         Weather(date.toString, "23")
     |    }
     | }
defined class WeatherForecasting
```

In the same way, we can define abstract data and concrete members.

Traits linearization

Unlike Java's interface, Scala's Traits are stackable. When we stack a set of Traits, they follow the **Traits linearization** rules to resolve them.

In Scala, there is no more **deadly diamond problem**, it is resolved automatically with this linearization technique.

Linearization rules

Scala Traits follow the following linearization rules in resolving the conflicts:

1. Take classes/traits available after the `extends` keyword.
2. Pick up the first one in that list from left to right.
3. Then, write down its complete hierarchy from left to right.
4. Pick up another trait from this list and perform the preceding step.
5. Repeat this step for all available traits.
6. Finally, the actual type of the instance.
7. Remove duplicates from top to bottom then left to right.
8. Write down the final list from bottom to top then left to right.

We can mix Scala Traits into classes using the `extends` keyword as the first entry, or `with` for the rest of the traits. We will explore it with one simple example here:

```scala
package com.packt.publishing.traits

trait BaseStep {
  def name: String = "BaseStep"
}
```

```
trait Step1 extends BaseStep {
  override def name: String = "Step1 >> " + super.name
}
trait Step2 extends BaseStep {
  override def name: String = "Step2 >> " + super.name
}
trait Step3 extends Step1 {
  override def name: String = "Step3 >> " + super.name
}

class FinalStep1 extends Step1 with Step2 {
  override def name = "FinalStep1 >> " + super.name
}
class FinalStep2 extends Step2 with Step1{
  override def name = "FinalStep2 >> " + super.name
}
class FinalStep3 extends Step3 with Step2 with Step1{
  override def name = "FinalStep3 >> " + super.name
}
class FinalStep4 extends Step2 with Step3  with Step1{
  override def name = "FinalStep4 >> " + super.name
}

object TraitsLinearizationApp extends App {
  println(new FinalStep1().name)
  println(new FinalStep2().name)
  println(new FinalStep3().name)
  println(new FinalStep4().name)
}
```

The output looks like this:

```
FinalStep1 >> Step2 >> Step1 >> BaseStep
FinalStep2 >> Step1 >> Step2 >> BaseStep
FinalStep3 >> Step2 >> Step3 >> Step1 >> BaseStep
FinalStep4 >> Step3 >> Step1 >> Step2 >> BaseStep
```

Analyze our rules here:

```
println(new FinalStep1().name)

class FinalStep1 extends Step1 with Step2
```

Take everything available after the extends keyword, as shown here:

```
extends Step1 with Step2
```

Pick up one class/trait at a time and write down complete hierarchy, as shown here:

```
Step1 >> BaseStep >> ScalaObject >> AnyRef >> Any
Step2 >> BaseStep >> ScalaObject >> AnyRef >> Any
FinalStep1
```

Start from bottom to top and from left to right, that is from `FinalStep1`, right down each entry in a row, as shown here, and if you find any duplicates, just leave them:

```
FinalStep1 >> Step2 >> Step1 >> BaseStep >> ScalaObject >> AnyRef >> Any
```

This is the order in which the Scala compiler applies the changes.

Summary

In this chapter, we discussed some Scala Basics and how to use the Scala app to execute standalone applications. We also discussed what is Scala REPL and how to access it.

We discussed a couple of Scala Functional Programming concepts with some simple examples, and gave an introduction to the Scala Collection API.

We discussed Scala FP Design Patterns such as Monoid, Functor, and Monad, and finally discussed a couple of Scala Source Code Monads.

Finally, we explored one of the greatest features of Scala—Traits. Java does not have a similar programming construct. We also explored linearization rules with one simple example.

In the next chapter, we will discuss the Scala asynchronous programming API.

3
Asynchronous Programming with Scala

In this chapter, we will discuss how Scala supports the asynchronous programming API, using the following two APIs—Scala Future API and Scala Async API.

The Scala **asynchronous programming (AP)** API supports both Concurrency and true Parallelism very well, in an asynchronous way.

We will also discuss how to use the Scala Future API in the Play Framework and the Akka Toolkit on a high level, so that we can write Reactive applications using the Scala Future API in the coming chapters, using Play, Scala, Akka, and Akka Streams.

In this chapter, you will learn the following concepts:

- Scala Futures API
- The benefits of Scala Futures
- A Scala Future and its API
- Scala Future examples
- Differences between Scala Future and threads
- A Scala Promise and its API
- Scala Promises examples

- The Scala Async API and examples
- Differences between a Scala Future and Scala Sync APIs
- How to utilize the Scala Future API in the Play Framework
- How to utilize the Scala Future API in the Akka Toolkit
- Differences between a Scala Future and a Promise
- Differences between a Scala Future and a Java Future

Introduction to Scala AP

Before starting with Scala AP, it is good to understand what asynchronous means and its benefits.

In this section, we will discuss what asynchronous is and how it differs from synchronous. We will also discuss how Scala supports asynchronous programming.

What is asynchronous?

We will define it in simple words in terms of computer programs. Let's assume we have two functions or methods or operations—function a() and function b(). Function b() uses function a() to fulfill its job.

The function a() is said to be asynchronous if function b() makes a call to function a() and does not wait for function a() response. Function b() continues doing it's next available tasks without waiting or blocking. Function b() utilizes function a() result once function a() finishes its computation and send response back to function b(). Here function a() is known as *called function* and function b() is known as *calling function*.

So, the calling function just make a call to called function, then continue doing its own computation and should not wait for the called function's response. It will process result once that called function finishes computation and send the result to it.

Here the called function's response or the result could be either a failure or success. The call flow is shown here:

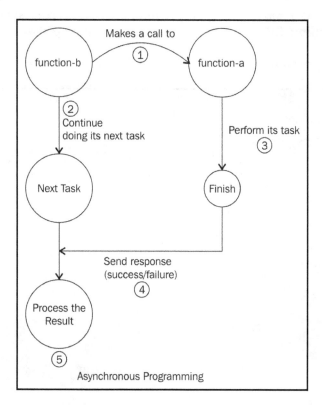

Asynchronous Programming

Differences between asynchronous and synchronous

We can observe the following differences between asynchronous and synchronous:

- Asynchronous means no waiting time. The caller function does not wait for a response from the called function; it continues doing its next task.
- Synchronous means waiting time. The caller function should wait for a response from the called function and it cannot continue doing its next task. The caller function should wait until the called function finishes its job and returns results (success or failure).

- An asynchronous function does not block or wait for it's called function's response. It will receive response asynchronously.
- AP supports a non-blocking programming style; whereas, **synchronous programming (SP)** supports a blocking programming style.

The following diagram shows how the synchronous process works internally:

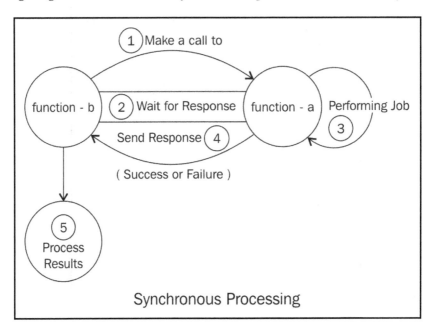

- An asynchronous function does not block or wait for it's called function's response. It will receive response asynchronously.
Synchronous Processing

Benefits of asynchronous programming

We will get the following benefits or advantages when we use AP constructs in our applications:

- No waiting time
- Supports the non-blocking programming model
- Efficient and effective use of valuable resources
- Better throughput
- Better performance

- We can simultaneously execute multiple tasks at a time
- Instant response to client requests
- Easy to write and understand the correct code
- Avoids lots of boilerplate code

Differences between Concurrency and Parallelism

Concurrency means executing multiple tasks at a time, by utilizing the underlying multi-core CPUs effectively. However, at any given point of time, only one task uses the CPU cores and the rest wait for their turn. They get timeslots to use the CPU and fulfill their job. This interleaving of timeslots and utilizing the CPU is known as context switching.

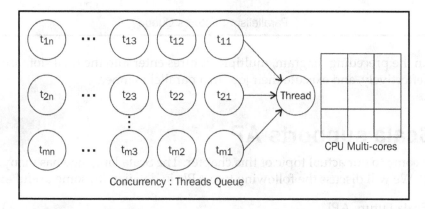

As shown in the preceding diagram, even though there are n number of queues for threads to use CPU cores and perform their job, only one thread will enter the final slot and use the CPU. The rest of the threads will wait in the CPU. The user may think that all the threads get executed simultaneously, but actually, only one thread is executed at a time.

Parallelism means executing multiple tasks simultaneously, by utilizing the underlying multi-core CPUs effectively. They use multi-core CPUs at a time and execute in a parallel manner.

The following diagram shows how Scala Futures' Parallelism works in gaining CPU cycles:

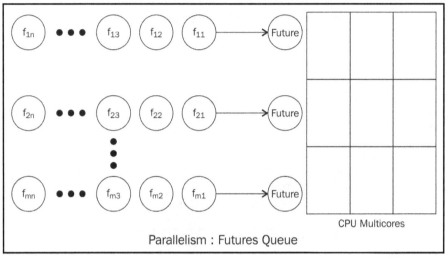

As shown in the preceding diagram, multiple Futures enter into the final slot, use multi-core CPUs effectively, and execute their jobs in a parallel manner.

How Scala supports AP

We've now come to our actual topic of this chapter. The Scala language has many APIs to support AP. We will discuss the following two APIs in detail, with some useful examples:

- Scala Future API
- Scala Async API

Both asynchronous APIs support Concurrency and true Parallelism, very well. We will first discuss the Scala Future API in the next section.

What is true Parallelism really?

True Parallelism means supporting Parallelism very well by efficiently utilizing the underlying multi-core processors at a time.

The Scala Future API

The Scala Future and Promise API is defined in the `scala.concurrent` package. This API is used to develop concurrent and parallel applications in the Scala language.

The Future represents a computation unit; this unit is executed by Promise and put into the Future.

In simple words, Future is an object to read that result and Promise is an object to execute that computation unit. Let's explore these concepts in depth, with some useful examples in the coming sections.

Building blocks of the Scala Future API

The Scala Future API has the following building blocks:

- Scala Future
- Scala Promise
- Scala ExecutionContext

The following diagram shows the main building blocks of the Scala Future API:

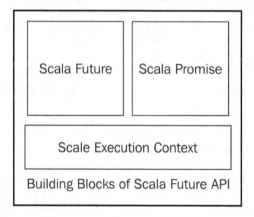

These are also known as the main components of the Scala Future API or the three Pillars of the Scala Future API. We will discuss these three Scala Future API components in depth, with some suitable examples in the coming sections.

Benefits of the Scala Future API

The Scala Future API has the following benefits:

- High-level concurrency programming
- No boilerplate code
- Easy-to-write, highly Scalable code
- Supports distributed applications very well
- More Type-safe
- No race conditions or deadlock issues
- Easy to avoid starvation and Livelocks
- No shared state
- Less resources utilization
- Unit testing is very easy
- Easy to write and understand the correct code
- No locks and no synchronization code
- Supports high performance
- Supports both Concurrency and true Parallelism very well
- Supports non-blocking functionality
- No context switching overhead

The Scala Future

In this section, we will discuss the Scala Future. Let's start by defining this component.

What is a Future in Scala?

In Scala, a Future is an object that represents a computation unit. It has some value at some point in the future. In other words, it is a programming construct in Scala used to write concurrency programs very easily. When a Future finishes its computation, we say that the Future is completed. However, it may be completed either successfully, or unsuccessfully.

If a Future is completed successfully, it has some computed value. If it has failed or completed unsuccessfully, it has some error.

The Scala Future API

Future[T] contains a computation unit of type T. This computation is done sometime in the future, either successfully or not.

What is a computation unit?

A computation unit is a block of code (which is used to perform a task or calculate some value and so on). Generally, this computation unit runs synchronously. If we place this computation unit in the Future, it runs asynchronously.

If this computation is completed successfully, the Future contains a value of type T. If this computation is completed with a failure, the Future contains an exception of type, Throwable.

The following diagram shows the Scala Future and its subtypes:

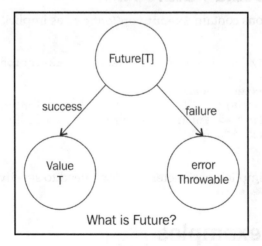

Like Scala constructs, such as Option, Either, Try, and so on, a Scala Future is also a container type. It may contain a value or an exception in the future.

It is a write-only-once container. Once it's completed, we cannot change its value, meaning that it becomes immutable. Do you know who writes that value into the Future? Promise (we will discuss this in the next section).

Future Trait definition

The following code is used for the Future Trait definition:

```
trait Future[+T] extends Awaitable[T]{
  def map[S](f: T => S) :Future[S]
  def flatMap[S](f: T => Future[S]) :Future[S]
}
```

Future Companion object

The following code is used for the Future Companion object:

```
object Future{
  def apply[T](body: => T): Future[T]
}
```

Here, the computation unit is the `body`. As it's computed asynchronously, it is defined as the by-name parameter.

The complete Scala Future API

Almost all Future functions contain `ExecutionContext` as implicit parameters:

```
object Future{
  def apply[T](body: => T)(implicit executor: ExecutionContext): Future[T]
}
trait Future[+T] extends Awaitable[T]{
  def map[S](f: T => S)(implicit executor: ExecutionContext) :Future[S]
  def flatMap[S](f: T => Future[S])(implicit executor:
   ExecutionContext) :Future[S]
}
```

Here, the executor is an implicit parameter; we don't need to specify it.

Scala Future examples

We have discussed lots of theory so far. It's good to start developing some examples to understand the Scala Future API. Let's start now with the Scala Hello World Future App:

1. Create a Scala SBT project in your favorite IDE (mine is IntelliJ IDEA):

```
Project Name: scala-future-app
```

build.sbt:

```
name := "scala-future-app"
version := "1.0"
scalaVersion := "2.12.3"
```

2. Create a Scala App:

```
object ScalaFutureHelloWorldApp extends App{
}
```

3. Create a HelloWorld Future Object:

ScalaFutureHelloWorldApp.scala:

```
import scala.concurrent.Future
object ScalaFutureHelloWorldApp extends App{
  val helloWordlFuture = Future("Hello World")
}
```

4. When we run this program, we can observe the following error:

```
[error] .../scala-future-
app/src/main/scala/com/packt/publishing/concurrent/future/ScalaFutureHelloW
olrdApp.scala:8: Cannot find an implicit ExecutionContext. You might pass
[error] an (implicit ec: ExecutionContext) parameter to your method
[error] or import scala.concurrent.ExecutionContext.Implicits.global.
[error] val helloWordlFuture = Future("Hello World")
```

5. When we make a call to `Future(someObject)`, internally it makes a call to the `Future.apply()` method and it has the following signature:

```
def apply[T](b: =>T)(implicit e: ExecutionContext): Future[T]
```

This method takes a by-name parameter of the type `T`. It also takes an implicit `ExecutionContext` parameter.

When we make a call to this `Future.apply` method, we can specify this `ExecutionContext` parameter like a normal parameter, or we can skip it. When we skip it, the Scala compiler looks for this implicit variable in the current scope.

If the Scala compiler does not find it, it throws the preceding error. If it finds that implicit parameter, it passes that parameter as the function method call, automatically.

As Future objects run in `ExecutionContext`, they need that object, which is why the `Future.apply()` function has an implicit object of type `ExecutionContext`. `Scala` that provides a default implicit `ExecutionContext` object so we can use it by using the following import:

```
import scala.concurrent.ExecutionContext.Implicits.global
```

We then import the global execution context from the `Implicits` object. This makes sure that Future computations execute on global, the default `ExecutionContext`.

6. Finally, our Scala Future app looks as follows:

ScalaFutureHelloWorldApp.scala:

```
package com.packt.publishing.concurrent.future

import scala.concurrent.ExecutionContext.Implicits.global
import scala.concurrent.Future
object ScalaFutureHelloWorldApp extends App{
  val helloWordlFuture1 = Future("Hello World")
  val helloWordlFuture2 = Future {
    "Hello World"
  }
  println(helloWordlFuture1)
  println(helloWordlFuture2)
}
```

7. We can create a Future object using parentheses, as shown here:

```
val helloWordlFuture = Future("Hello World")
```

Alternatively, we can use curly braces too, as shown here:

```
val helloWordlFuture = Future {
  "Hello World"
}
```

Both work in a similar way.

8. When we run the preceding application in your favorite IDE, we will see an output similar to the following:

```
Future(Success(Hello World))
Future(Success(Hello World))
```

As we know, a Future completes either successfully with a value, or failure with an error message. This program demonstrates how a Future completes with a value.

Let's develop another Scala App with a Future, which completes with an error. It does not do much complex real-time logic, just for demonstration purposes only:

1. Create another Scala Future app to demonstrate a Future with an error message like this:

ScalaFutureHelloWorldWithErrorApp.scala:

```
package com.packt.publishing.concurrent.future
import scala.concurrent.ExecutionContext.Implicits.global
import scala.concurrent.Future
object ScalaFutureHelloWorldWithErrorApp extends App{
  val helloWordlFuture1 = Future {
    "Hello World"
  }
  val helloWordlFuture2 = Future {
    throw new Throwable("Hello World")
  }
  println(helloWordlFuture1)
  println(helloWordlFuture2)
}
```

2. When we run the preceding application in your favorite IDE, we will see an output similar to the following:

```
Future(Success(Hello World))
Future(Failure(java.lang.Throwable: Hello World))
```

In the next section, we will discuss some more useful and simple Scala Future examples, by using Scala REPL:

```
scala> import scala.concurrent.Future
import scala.concurrent.Future

scala> import scala.concurrent.ExecutionContext.Implicits.global
import scala.concurrent.ExecutionContext.Implicits.global

scala> val intFuture = Future(10)
intFuture: scala.concurrent.Future[Int] =
scala.concurrent.impl.Promise$DefaultPromise@6b9ce1bf
```

Or we can use the following approach:

```
scala> val intFuture = Future{10}
intFuture: scala.concurrent.Future[Int] =
scala.concurrent.impl.Promise$DefaultPromise@6b9ce1bf
```

We can use either parentheses or curly braces:

```
scala> val nameFuture = Future("Rams")
nameFuture: scala.concurrent.Future[String] =
scala.concurrent.impl.Promise$DefaultPromise@19fe4644

scala> nameFuture.value
res5: Option[scala.util.Try[String]] = Some(Success(Rams))

scala> nameFuture.value.get
res6: scala.util.Try[String] = Success(Rams)

scala> nameFuture.value.get.get
res7: String = Rams
```

The Scala Promise

In this section, we will discuss the second component of the Scala Future API—**Promise**.

A Scala Promise is something similar to a Scala Future. Like a Scala Future, a Scala Promise may have a value or an exception. They have some minor differences in the actual functionality. Let's discuss them in the following sub-sections.

What is a Scala Promise?

Like a Scala Future, a Scala Promise is an object used to write AP. It is used to execute asynchronous code.

Like a Scala Future, a Scala Promise may have a value if it finishes successfully, or an exception or error if it finishes with some failure. We can say a Promise is completed if it finishes with a value or an exception. The following diagram defines what a Scala Promise is:

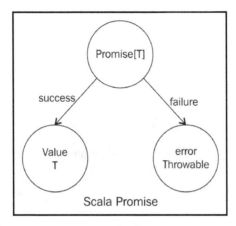

Scala Promise

As we discussed, a Future is a placeholder to hold a computation unit (which returns a value or exception and does not yet exist). It is used to read that result, whereas a Promise is used to finish that computation and write a value into the Future.

So, a Future is used to read that value, whereas a Promise is used to write that value.

In simple words, we can say that a Future is used to query or read the result, and a Promise is used to write or put the result:

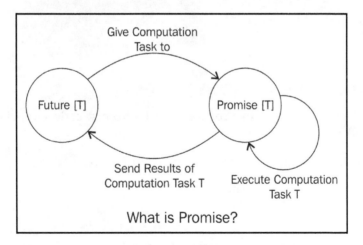

What is Promise?

As we discussed, we can write the result into a Future only once. Once it is done, we cannot change that value. So a Promise can write a value into a Future only once.

A Promise instance is always linked to exactly one, and only one instance of a Future.

The Scala Promise API

Let's understand the Scala API for a Promise. Scala has a trait for a Promise in the `scala.concurrent` package, which is as follows:

```
trait Promise[T] extends AnyRef
```

Scala Promise trait has the following important and frequently used functions:

```
trait Promise[T]{
  def success(value: T) : this.type
  def failure(cause: Throwabale): this.type
  def future: Future[T]
}
```

Its companion object is defined as shown here:

```
object Promise[T] {
  def apply[T](): Promise[T]
}
```

Scala Promise examples

In this section, let's experiment with a couple of Scala Promise code snippets, using Scala REPL (Scala Shell).

Let's explore how to create an empty Promise to a Future here:

```
scala> import scala.concurrent.Promise
import scala.concurrent.Promise

scala> val cityPromise = Promise[String]()
cityPromise: scala.concurrent.Promise[String] =
scala.concurrent.impl.Promise$DefaultPromise@7f36b021
scala> val cityFuture = cityPromise.future
cityFuture: scala.concurrent.Future[String] =
scala.concurrent.impl.Promise$DefaultPromise@7f36b021
scala> cityFuture.value
res11: Option[scala.util.Try[String]] = None
```

Once a Promise or a Future is completed (either successfully with a result, or unsuccessfully with an exception), we cannot rerun them. Doing so will throw an error, as shown in the following example:

```
scala> cityPromise.success("Hyderabad")
java.lang.IllegalStateException: Promise already completed.
```

To create a Promise to write a value to a Future, consider the following example:

```
scala>  val cityPromise = Promise[String]()
<console>:10: error: not found: value Promise
val cityPromise = Promise[String]()
                  ^
scala> import scala.concurrent.Promise
import scala.concurrent.Promise

scala> val cityPromise = Promise[String]()
cityPromise: scala.concurrent.Promise[String] =
scala.concurrent.impl.Promise$DefaultPromise@7d07e6aa
```

When we create a Promise object, it contains nothing. We should assign a value in the following way:

```
scala> cityPromise.success("Hyderabad")
res13: cityPromise.type =
scala.concurrent.impl.Promise$DefaultPromise@7d07e6aa

scala> cityPromise.future.value.get
res1: scala.util.Try[String] = Success(Hyderabad)

scala> cityPromise.future.value.get.get
res15: String = Hyderabad
```

We can use a Promise object's Future function to get its associated Future object, as follows:

```
scala> cityPromise.future
res7: scala.concurrent.Future[String] =
scala.concurrent.impl.Promise$DefaultPromise@707f7052
```

Scala ExecutionContext

In this section, we will discuss the third and important component of Scala Future API–ExecutionContext.

In simple words, ExecutionContext is something similar to a thread pool.

What is ExecutionContext?

ExecutionContext is a place where our Future's computation unit is executed. The Scala language gives us a ready-made static global ExecutionContext in scala.concurrent.ExecutionContext.global.

In simple words, ExecutionContext is home for both a Scala Future and a Promise to execute their tasks.

The relationship between Scala Future components

As we know, the Scala Future API is used to write asynchronous programs. It has three main components—Future, Promise, and ExecutionContext.

Let's discuss the relationship and differences between these components. The following diagram shows how the Scala Future API components work together:

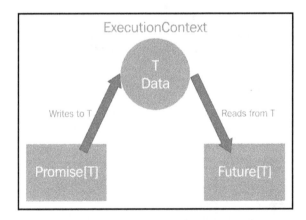

As shown in the preceding diagram, Future[T] contains a computation task of type T. Promise[T] executes that computation task T in ExecutionContext and writes the results back into the Future[T].

Differences between a Future and a Promise

In Scala, a Future and a Promise have the following differences:

- A Promise is used to compute a value, whereas a Future is used to read that value
- A Promise is used write the value, whereas a Future is a read-only object
- Once a Promise is completed, we cannot change its value, it becomes immutable
- Once a Future is completed, we cannot change its value, it becomes immutable
- A Future is for querying data and a Promise is for writing data
- In simple words, a Future is the getter and a Promise is the setter

Scala Future API callbacks

So far, we have demonstrated some of the useful ways to create a Scala Future and a Promise and displayed the results, using plain `println` statements. It's for understanding purposes only. In real-time projects, we don't use this approach.

We use the Scala Future API callback methods to check the following things from a Future object or a Promise object:

- Whether it is completed with a success result
- Whether it is completed with a failure
- Whether it is completed successfully or not completed

We use the following functions to check the preceding things, respectively:

- `onSuccess` (deprecated from Scala 2.12.0 onwards)
- `onFailure` (deprecated from Scala 2.12.0 onwards)
- `onComplete`

This example is about how to use a Scala Future's `onComplete` callback function. It refers to the `scala.util.Try` construct to check the Future value or exception. If you are new to this construct, refer to *Chapter 2, Functional Scala*, for more information. Let's explore Scala Future's `onComplete()` callback function with one simple application here:

```
package com.packt.publishing.concurrent.future
import scala.concurrent.ExecutionContext.Implicits.global
import scala.concurrent.Future
```

```
import scala.util.{Success,Failure}
object ScalaFutureWithOnCompleteCallbackApp extends App{

  val arthemeticFuture = Future {
    100/0
  }
  arthemeticFuture onComplete {
    case Success(_) => println("Future completed successfully.")
    case Failure(error) => println(s"Future completed with error:
${error}.")
  }
  Thread.sleep(1000)
}
```

The output is as follows:

Future completed with error: java.lang.ArithmeticException: / by zero.

 In Scala Future callbacks, `onComplete` = `onSuccess` + `onFailure`.

Let's now explore the `onSuccess` and `onFailure` callback functions. If you are using Scala 2.11.x version in your project, you can use these callback functions.

Because these callbacks are deprecated from Scala 2.12.0 version onward, it's not recommended you use them if you plan to upgrade Scala to the latest version. Let's explore Scala Future's callback functions with one simple application here:

```
package com.packt.publishing.concurrent.future
import scala.concurrent.ExecutionContext.Implicits.global
import scala.concurrent.Future
import scala.util.{Failure, Success}
object ScalaFutureWithOnSuccessFailureCallbacksApp extends App{
  val arthemeticFuture = Future {
  100/0
}
arthemeticFuture onSuccess {
  case value => println(s"Arthimetic Future completed successfully with
$value.")
}
arthemeticFuture onFailure {
  case error => println(s"Arthimetic Future completed with error:
${error}.")
}
```

```
val helloWorldFuture = Future {
  "Hello World"
}
helloWorldFuture onSuccess {
  case value => println(s"HelloWorld Future completed successfully with
$value.")
}
helloWorldFuture onFailure {
  case error => println(s"HelloWorld Future completed with error:
${error}.")
  }
  Thread.sleep(1000)
}
```

The output would be as follows:

HelloWorld Future completed successfully with Hello World.Arthimetic Future completed with error: java.lang.ArithmeticException: / by zero.

 In the next section, we will discuss some of the important and useful combinators of the Scala Future API. If you are new to Scala combinators, refer to Chapter 2, *Functional Scala*, to get some basic idea.

Scala Future API combinators

The Scala Future API supports a couple of Scala combinators to ease the way of extracting values from a Future or a Promise object.

Let's explore some of the useful and important Scala Future API combinators in this section:

- map
- flatMap
- recover
- filter

Let's explore Scala Future API combinators with some simple examples here:

```
scala> import scala.concurrent.Promise
import scala.concurrent.Promise
scala> import scala.concurrent.ExecutionContext.Implicits.global
import scala.conct.ExecutionContext.Implicits.global

scala> val cityPromise = Promise[String]()
```

```
cityPromise: scala.concurrent.Promise[String] =
scala.concurrent.impl.Promise$DefaultPromise@7d07e6aa
scala> cityPromise.success("Hyderabad")
res13: cityPromise.type =
scala.concurrent.impl.Promise$DefaultPromise@7d07e6aa
scala> cityPromise.future.map { value => println(value) }
scala> cityPromise.future.map { value => println(value) }
res16: scala.concurrent.Future[Unit] =
scala.concurrent.impl.Promise$DefaultPromise@770d65c2Hyderabad
```

Like Scala's `Try` API and a few more APIs, the Scala Future API also has a `recover` combinator to recover from a Future failure:

```
package com.packt.publishing.concurrent.future

import scala.concurrent.ExecutionContext.Implicits.global
import scala.concurrent.Futureobject ScalaFutureHelloWorldWithRecoverApp
extends App{
  val helloWordlFuture = Future {
    throw new Throwable("Hello World")
  }
  helloWordlFuture.map{
    value=>println(value)
  }
}
```

When we run the preceding program, we don't see any output on the console, because the Future object's `map()` function executes its body, only when that Future object completes successfully, meaning that it should contain a value, not an error or exception.

The Future completes with error examples:

```
package com.packt.publishing.concurrent.future
import scala.concurrent.ExecutionContext.Implicits.global
import scala.concurrent.Future
object ScalaFutureHelloWorldWithRecoverApp extends App{
  val arthemeticFuture = Future {
    100/0
  }
  arthemeticFuture.failed foreach {
    case t => println(s"Arthemetic Future failed with: $t")
  }
  arthemeticFuture.failed map {
    case t => println(s"Arthemetic Future failed with: $t")
  }
  Thread.sleep(1000)
}
```

The output is as follows:

```
Arthemetic Future failed with: java.lang.ArithmeticException: / by zero
Arthemetic Future failed with: java.lang.ArithmeticException: / by zero
```

Observe the following Scala application with `recover()` callback:

```
package com.packt.publishing.concurrent.future
import scala.concurrent.ExecutionContext.Implicits.global
import scala.concurrent.Future
import scala.util.{Success,Failure}
object ScalaFutureWithRecoverCallbackApp extends App{
  val arthemeticFuture = Future {
    100/0
  } recover {
      case t => 0
  }
  arthemeticFuture onComplete {
    case Success(value) => println(s"Future completed successfully with
${value}.")
    case Failure(error) => println(s"Future completed with error:
${error}.")
  }
  Thread.sleep(1000)
}
```

The output is as follows:

```
Future completed successfully with 0.
```

Scala Future.sequence()

When we have a sequence of Futures, or a list of Futures, or a collection of Futures, we should use one of the Future combinator APIs, `Future.sequence()`, to deal with this scenario.

This `Future.sequence()` function converts a list of Futures into a single Future that means collections of Futures into a single Future.

In simple words, `List[Future[T]]` ======> `Future[List[T]]`.

It is also known as composing Futures. The following diagram demonstrates how Scala Future's `sequence()` function converts `List[Future[T]]` into `Future[List[T]]`:

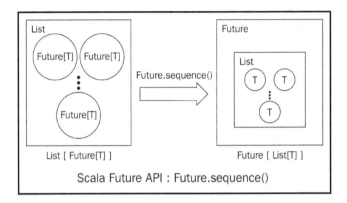

Consider the following example:

```
scala> val pricesList:List[Future[Int]] =
List(Future(1001),Future(999),Future(-2000),Future(1000))
pricesList: List[scala.concurrent.Future[Int]] =
List(scala.concurrent.impl.Promise$DefaultPromise@680a66dd,
scala.concurrent.impl.Promise$DefaultPromise@2dd8239,
scala.concurrent.impl.Promise$DefaultPromise@472698d,
scala.concurrent.impl.Promise$DefaultPromise@7b7683d4)

scala> val maxPrice:Future[Int] = Future.sequence(pricesList).map(_.max)
maxPrice: scala.concurrent.Future[Int] =
scala.concurrent.impl.Promise$DefaultPromise@14fded9d

scala> maxPrice.map { price => println("Max price = " + price) }
res0: scala.concurrent.Future[Unit] =
scala.concurrent.impl.Promise$DefaultPromise@ebda593
Max price = 1001
```

The Scala Async Library

So far, we have discussed one of the Scala's important Asynchronous Programming API, that is, the Scala Future API.

Scala has another API to support AP easily and very well, and that is the Scala Async API. Let's explore it in this section.

The Scala Async API does not add any extra features to the Scala Asynchronous Programming API. It is similar to the Scala Future API. However, it allows you to compose a set of Asynchronous computations in a simple and concise way.

The Scala Async library introduces two new methods—`async` and `await`.

It is available as a separate library in the Scala language. So we should add the following line to the SBT build file:

```
libraryDependencies += "org.scala-lang.modules" %% "scala-async" % "0.9.6"
```

The main aim of this library is to simplify Scala asynchronous and non-blocking concurrency programming.

The main difference between the Scala Future API (Future and Promise) and the Scala Async API is:

- The Scala Future API supports the composition of asynchronous computations (also known as control flow) up to some extent, using map and flatMap combinators
- Scala Async API supports the composition of asynchronous computations (or control flow) very well

Scala Async API

The Scala Async object is defined in the `scala.async` package. It has the following two functions:

```
object Async {
  def async[T](body: => T)(implicit execContext: ExecutionContext):
Future[T]
  def await[T](awaitable: Future[T]): T
}
```

The `async` function is similar to the `apply` function of the Future object. It takes an asynchronous computation as input and returns a Future object.

The `await` function takes a future object as input and returns that Future's value. It does not block the underlying thread that executes that computation logic.

An example of the Scala Async API:

1. Create a Scala SBT Project, `scala-async-app`.
2. Add the Scala Async library to the `build.sbt` file:

```
name := "scala-async-app"
version := "1.0.0"
scalaVersion := "2.12.3"
libraryDependencies += "org.scala-lang.modules" %% "scala-async"
 % "0.9.6"
```

3. Develop a Scala app to demonstrate the Async API:

```
package com.packt.publishing.scala.async
import scala.async.Async
import scala.concurrent.Future
import scala.concurrent.ExecutionContext.Implicits.global
object ScalaAsyncBasicApp extends App{
  val num1 = Future (10)
  val num2 = Future (20)
  // Scala for-comprehension example
  val forOutput = for{
    no1 <- num1
    no2 <- num2
  } yield no1 + no2
  Thread.sleep(1000)
  println(s"For comprehension addition output:
   ${forOutput.value}")
  // Scala Future API example
  val futureOuput = num1.map{ no1 =>
    num2.map { no2 =>
      no1 + no2
    }
  }
  Thread.sleep(1000)
  println(s"Scala Future API addition output:
   ${forOutput.value}")
  // Scala Async API example
  val asyncOuput = Async.async {
    Async.await(num1) +  Async.await(num2)
  }
  Thread.sleep(1000)
  println(s"Scala Async API addition output:
   ${asyncOuput.value}")
}
```

4. The output is as follows:

```
For comprehension addition output: Some(Success(30))
Scala Future API addition output: Some(Success(30))
Scala Async API addition output: Some(Success(30))
```

To know more about the Scala Async API, go through its source code at https://github.com/scala/scala-async.

Not only do Scala, Akka, and Play-based applications use the Scala Future API, the source code of Scala, Akka, and the Play Framework uses the Scala Future API, extensively.

The Scala Future API in Play Framework

As a Play Framework application developer, I think you have already come to know that the Scala Future API is very important to developing any Play Framework application.

We use the Scala Future API extensively in Play Framework applications to support asynchronous communication between components.

Let's take a Service class from a Play Framework web application. The following Service's getWeatherByCity() functions demonstrate how to return a value which is available in the future by using the Scala Future API:

```
class WeatherForecastingService extends CommonService {
  override def getWeatherByCity(city:String):
  Future[List[WeatherForecasting]] =
    Future{
      // Here, prepare WeatherForecasting object
    }
}
```

Here we are using the Future object to prepare a list of WeatherForecasting objects. As this component takes more time interacting with other components (for instance, external system or database and so on), this function call may take more time to prepare the data. In this case, it is good to use a Future to run that computation asynchronously.

Now, let's observe how we are using the Future object's combinator function such as map(), to get those details:

```
class WeatherForecastingController extends Controller {
  def weather(city:String) = Action.async {
```

```
        val weather = wfService.getWeatherByCity(city)
        weather.map { listOfWFObjects =>
         Ok(views.html.weather(listOfWFObjects))
        }
     }
  }
```

Here, weather view takes that list of `WeatherForecasting` objects and renders them to the user.

 Refer to `Chapter 6`, *Extending Application with Play* or `Chapter 8`, *Integrating Akka Streams to Play Application,* to understand this code very well.

The Play Framework source code also uses the Scala Future API extensively. Let's look at a couple of functions which use it:

```
/**
 * Components to create a Server instance.
 */
trait ServerComponents {
  def serverStopHook: () => Future[Unit] = () => Future.successful(())
}
```

And one more:

```
/**
 * Provides generic server behaviour for Play applications.
 */
trait Server extends ReloadableServer {
  def getHandlerFor(request: RequestHeader): Either[Future[Result],
    (RequestHeader, Handler, Application)] = {}

}
```

The Scala Future API in the Akka Toolkit

Both the Akka Toolkit and the Play Framework source code use Scala Futures extensively. The Akka Streams API also uses the Scala Future in all places.

Let's look at some Akka Streams source code examples here which are using the Scala Future API:

In the Akka Toolkit, the `ask` pattern returns a `Future[Any]`, shown as follows:

```
def ask (actorRef: ActorRef, message: Any)(implicit timeout: Timeout):
Future[Any]
```

Observe the following Akka Streams API:

```
val futureResult: Future[Seq[String]] = Source(in).runWith(Sink.seq)
```

Here, the `Souce.runWith[T]()` function returns its results as `Future[T]`. Not only this function, but most of the Akka Streams API uses Scala Futures extensively. We use the Scala Future API to write some unit tests, too.

Now you get what is the importance of this Scala Future API. Please experiment with some more examples to get more familiar with it.

We will also use Scala Futures extensively in our applications in the coming chapters. Refer to them, understand them well, and learn how to use them in your real-time projects.

A Scala Future versus a Java Future

We will discuss one of the important topics such as the differences between a Scala Future and a Java Future in this section:

- A Java Future works in a synchronous blocking way. It does not work in an asynchronous non-blocking way, whereas a Scala Future works in an asynchronous non-blocking way.
- If we want an asynchronous non-blocking feature, we should use Java 8's **CompletableFuture**. However, if we observe the CompletableFuture code, it is a bit clumsy, not elegant, and not concise, unlike that of Scala's Future. It is a bit tough to reason with.
- Scala Futures support very elegant and concise ways of writing concurrency code and support Concurrency and true Parallelism, very well. Java Futures/CompletableFutures support Concurrency, but do not support true Parallelism.

What is true Parallelism really?

True Parallelism means supporting Parallelism very well by utilizing the underlying multi-core processors very well.

- Scala Futures improve application performance and support Scalability very well, whereas, Java Futures/CompletableFutures support them up to some extent only.
- Both Scala Futures and Java's CompletableFutures use callbacks to support asynchronous non-blocking execution.

Summary

In this chapter, we discussed how Scala supports asynchronous programming using two different APIs—the Scala Futures API and the Scala Async API. We explored both of these APIs with examples.

We also discussed how to use the Scala Future API in the Play Framework and the Akka Toolkit. We will explore these two concepts in detail in the coming chapters.

As we discussed, both of Scala's APIs, Future and Async, support Concurrency well. Unlike Java threads, the Scala Future and Async API support true Parallelism and use the current multi-core processor architecture very well.

Not only the Scala, Akka-based and Play-based applications use the Scala Future API; the source code of Scala, Akka, and Play Framework uses the Scala Future API extensively.

Let's dive into developing Reactive Applications using the Akka Toolkit in `Chapter 4`, *Building Reactive Applications with Akka*.

4

Building Reactive Applications with Akka

In this chapter, we will discuss how to develop Reactive Applications using the **Akka** Toolkit. Unlike the **Shared-State Concurrency** model, which does not support true Parallelism, Akka's Actor-based Concurrency model supports true Parallelism. Akka is an open source library available on Apache License Version 2.0.

We can develop applications using Akka to utilize today's multicore CPUs efficiently to improve application performance. In the old versions, Scala had the Actors library; Lightbend has removed it from Scala and moved it to the Akka Toolkit. Now the `scala.actors` library is no longer useful, and it is deprecated.

Akka is an Event-Driven middleware framework for building high-performance, highly Scalable, highly available, and Reliable distributed applications in Java and Scala.

In this book, we will use the latest version of Akka Toolkit—2.5.9.

 The official Akka Toolkit website is here, `http://akka.io`, and its latest version documentation website is here, `http://doc.akka.io/docs/akka/current/scala/guide/introducti on.html`.

In this chapter, we will learn the following concepts:

- What is Akka and its features and benefits
- The Akka system and its components
- The Actor system and its properties and benefits
- What is an Actor and its components

- Akka supervision and supervision strategies
- Akka Actor's basic operations
- Akka examples

Introduction to Akka

In this section, we will introduce some basics of the Akka Toolkit to understand it well. If you are already familiar with it and have had good exposure with Akka, skip this section and move on to the next sections.

What is Akka?

Akka is an open source library or a toolkit and runtime from Lightbend Inc. (formerly known as Typesafe), written in the Scala language to develop these attributes:

- Concurrent
- Distributed
- Fault-Tolerant
- Message-Driven
- Responsive
- Highly Scalable
- Asynchronous
- Non-blocking
- Highly performant
- Highly available
- Ease of maintenance

Applications on the JVM (Java Virtual Machine)

We can develop Reactive Applications using the Akka Toolkit very easily.

The Akka Toolkit follows the Actor Model to support the Concurrency feature. It is one of the components used in the Lightbend Reactive Platform.

Akka is an open source toolkit and runtime which simplifies the construction of concurrent and distributed applications on the JVM. Akka is a library for building Reactive Applications, based on the Actor Model.

Akka was written in Scala and supports the following platforms:

- Java
- Scala
- Dot Net

The Akka Toolkit supports the development of concurrent, asynchronous, non-blocking, Resilient, Elastic, Event-Driven, and Responsive systems very easily.

Akka Toolkit supports Message-Driven programming using the Actor Model and without using any message brokers (such as RabbitMQ, Apache ActiveMQ, Apache Kafka, and more).

In this book, we will use the Scala language to develop Akka Reactive Applications.

Features of Akka

The Akka Toolkit supports the following features:

- Actor Model
- Distributed
- Concurrency and Parallelism
- Message-Driven
- Fault-Tolerant
- Highly Scalable
- Akka uses the Typesafe Config Library to support configuration
- Reactive
- Location Transparency
- Remote Actors
- Automatic load balancing
- Self-healing
- Clustering

- Developing WebServers using Akka HTTP
- Cluster sharding
- Remoting

Benefits of Akka (or why do we need Akka?)

As the Akka Toolkit has the following benefits, it's good to use Akka to develop your Reaction Applications/Systems:

- It is open source
- By design, it is distributed, and it's very easy to use distributed applications
- It supports clustering
- It supports Reactive Streams using the Akka Streams module
- It is easy to develop highly performant, highly scalable, highly maintainable, and highly available applications using Akka
- It supports concurrency using the Actor Model. Unlike Java's Shared-State Model (which is low-level API), the Actor-based Concurrency Model is a high-level API to write Concurrency and Parallelism programming without threads, locking, and other issues.
- It supports scalability in both directions:
    - Scale up (vertically)
    - Scale out (horizontally)
- It is easy to test Akka application's components
- By design, it supports Reactive Streams specifications—Message-Driven, Resilient (Fault-Tolerant), Elastic (Scalable), and Responsive
- It supports self-healing
- It supports Location Transparency, which means looking-up or identifying the Actors is the same for both local Actors (which are located in the same JVM) or remote Actors (which are located in the remote JVM)

Building blocks of the Akka Toolkit

The main building blocks of Akka Toolkit are as listed:

- ActorSystem
- Actor
- ActorContext
- ExecutionContext

We can depict these components in a diagram, as shown here:

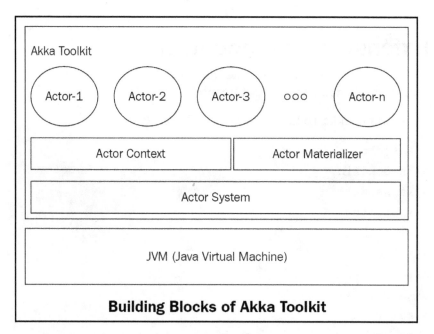

Building Blocks of Akka Toolkit

As shown in the preceding diagram, the **Actor System** is the base for the entire **Akka Toolkit**. It provides a runtime environment for Akka Actors and supports many features (refer to the *Akka ActorSystem* section for more details). On top of the **Actor System**, Akka uses a couple of components, such as **Actor Context**, **Actor Materializer**, and more, and finally, user-defined and system Actors.

The **Actor Context** is useful to expose contextual information for the Actor and the current message. It is not thread safe, so do not expose it to the outside world.

An Actor is the fundamental computation unit, which contains both state and behavior.

In the Akka Toolkit, if we want to execute Futures, we need `ExecutionContext`. By default, Akka's **Actor System** uses its default dispatcher as `ExecutionContext`, or we can create our required `ExecutionContext`.

We will discuss these components in detail in the coming sections with some useful examples.

Akka Extensions (or modules)

Akka is not just an Actor Model implementation; it has many other features. Each kind of feature in Akka is implemented as a separate module.

Some of the important Akka Toolkit modules are these:

- `akka-actor`
- `akka-contrib`
- `akka-stream`
- `akka-remote`
- `akka-cluster`
- `akka-persistence`
- `akka-osgi`
- `akka-camel`
- `akka-typed`
- `akka-agent`
- `akka-testkit`
- `akka-slf4j`

The Akka Toolkit comprises many modules. The following diagram shows the most important Akka Toolkit modules:

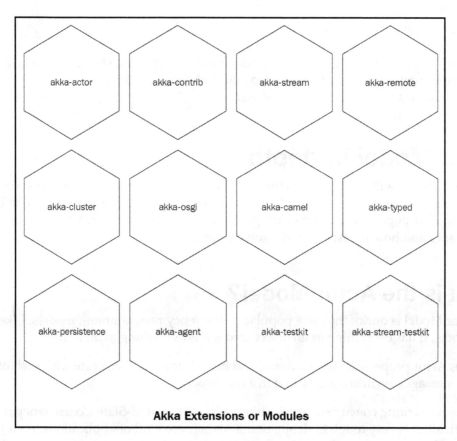

Akka Extensions or Modules

The Akka Toolkit is easily extendable using Akka Extensions or Akka Modules. We can easily enable and disable these modules in our application, using the Akka configuration.

Akka Clients

Popular clients who have been using the Akka Toolkit in their live systems for a long time, are as follows:

- Flipkart.com, Amazon.com, Walmart
- Twitter, LinkedIn, Paypal
- Cisco, HP, Samsung, Intel

- VMWare, CSC, Answers.com
- **HMRC (HM Revenue and Customs)**, **DWP (Department for Works and Pensions)**, BBC
- UBS, Barclays, HSBC

These are just a few clients. If you are interested to know the case studies about how these clients implemented their solutions, refer to this link from Lightbend:
`https://www.lightbend.com/case-studies.`

Actor Model in-depth

In this section, we will discuss the Actor Model conceptually, and how the Akka Toolkit implements this programming model to support concurrency programming. We will also discuss another popular concurrency programming model—the Shared-State Concurrency model issues and how the Actor Model solves them.

What is the Actor Model?

The Actor Model is one of the most popular concurrency programming models. Like the OOP Model, it has everything as an object, and it has everything as an Actor.

It defines Actor properties, Actor axioms, and how Actors communicate with each other by sending messages asynchronously and in a non-blocking way.

As we know, writing concurrent applications using the Shared-State Concurrency model is very difficult. It is very tough to debug or maintain these kind of applications. As a Java developer, I know you guys have already written many concurrent applications and faced many issues.

 To solve all these model problems, Carl Hewitt has introduced another Concurrency Model—the **Actor Model**.

The inventor of this Actor Model is Carl Hewitt, so he is also known as the **Father of the Actor Model**. As with Carl Hewitt, the Actor Model is inspired by physics (not like most of the other models, which are inspired by mathematics).

Principles of the Actor Model (or properties of Actor in the Actor Model)

The Actor Model has the following principles:

- Everything is an Actor
- In the Actor Model, an Actor is a first-class citizen
- An Actor has a mailbox to store data
- Actors should communicate with each other asynchronously
- Actors should communicate with each other in a non-blocking way
- Actors communicate with each other by sending messages
- All computations should be performed within an Actor
- An Actor can send or receive message to or from another Actor
- There is no direct communication between Actors
- Each Actor is identified using a unique name or address
- An Actor can send messages to other Actors whose addresses it has
- An Actor can have state or behavior or both
- An Actor can have state, but it's accessible by itself only, which means that only an Actor can modify its state; no other Actor or non-Actor can access or modify it—that's the beauty of the Actor Model
- An Actor should process only one message at a time
- An Actor should receive only one message at a time
- Messages are delivered arbitrarily, that is, messages are delivered to Actors in any order
- Messages are immutable objects, which means we cannot modify them once they are created
- An Actor can process any kind of messages
- Each message is delivered at most once only, which means a message is delivered from the sender Actor to the receiver Actor either zero times or once; so there is no chance of delivering duplicate messages in the Actor Model
- When an Actor receives a message, based on the context, it does one or more of the following things:
  - It can change its state
  - It can change its behavior
  - It can change both its state and behavior

- It can create some more Actors
- It can send messages to other Actors
- It can forward messages to other Actors
- It can acknowledge a message to a sender Actor
- It can decide what to do with the next message, that is, how to handle them

These are also known as Actor Principles in the Actor Model. If you are planning to implement a Toolkit like Akka or a framework to support the Akka Model, you should follow all these principles. Based on your requirements, you can provide some more features in your tool or framework.

Issues with the Shared-State Concurrency model

The Shared State Concurrency model has the following issues with low-level concurrency API (threading API):

- Lots of boilerplate code for locks and synchronized blocks
- Very hard and tedious to manage multi-threaded applications
- Low-level threading API
- Lots of concurrency issues—deadlock, race conditions
- Tight coupling between actual business logic and concurrency logic
- Less performance because of lots of blocking and synchronizations
- It uses the blocking communication approach
- It uses mutable data for communication between threads
- It does **not** utilize underlying multi-core CPUs effectively
- There are lots of context switches between threads to allocate CPU
- It does not support true Parallelism

Benefits of the Actor Model

When we compare the Actor Model with the Shared State Concurrency model, the Actor-based Concurrency Model has the following benefits:

- No boilerplate code, and no need for locks and synchronized blocks
- Easy to manage concurrency applications

- Higher level of abstraction over low-level threading API
- No more concurrency issues; we can solve them easily
- Loose coupling between actual business logic and concurrency logic
- Clear separation between two concerns: business logic and concurrency logic
- Better performance because it follows non-blocking and asynchronous
- It uses the non-blocking communication approach
- It uses **immutable messages** for communication between Actors
- It utilizes underlying multi-core CPUs very effectively
- There are no more context switches required to use the CPU
- It supports true Parallelism

Components of the Actor Model (or building blocks of the Actor Model)

The Actor Model has the following basic building blocks to support the high-level concurrency API:

- Actors
- Messages

These are also known as the two pillars of the Actor Model or the two essential components of the Actor Model.

In the OOP paradigm, an object is a fundamental unit of computation.

In the FP paradigm, a Function is a fundamental unit of computation.

In the Actor Model paradigm, an Actor is a fundamental unit of computation.

What are the benefits of immutable messages in the Actor Model?

The Actor Model recommends the use of immutable messages to communicate with Actors, because immutable data has the following benefits:

- The immutable state is easier to reason about
- It is easier to compose immutable behaviors
- It introduces much less boilerplate code for writing/reading behaviors
- It does NOT require the use of synchronization and locks, as no one can update it once it's created
- It is thread safe and fully shareable

How Akka implements the Actor Model

The Akka Toolkit implements the Actor Model to support the high-level concurrency API. It follows all the principles discussed in the previous section with some additional features.

In the Akka Toolkit, messages coming from one Actor are guaranteed to be received by another Actor in the same order. However, there is no guarantee that the messages are coming from more than one Actor.

The Akka Toolkit supports other major features, such as remoting, clustering, streams, and more.

In the Akka Toolkit, a recipient Actor can reply directly to the sender Actor, as shown here:

```
sender ! message
```

Refer to the *Akka Actors communicate example* section to understand it well.

The Akka Toolkit supports different kinds of dispatcher, mailboxes, and more, to support different scenarios. Based on our system or application requirements, we can pick up one of them to suit it well.

Other Actor Model implementations

Apart from the Akka Toolkit, we can find the following languages/frameworks/tools that implement the Actor Model:

- Erlang
- Akka.NET
- Haskell
- Groovy
- Python
- Clojure

Akka ActorSystem

In this section, we will discuss one of the important components or building blocks of the Akka Toolkit—the **ActorSystem**.

The ActorSystem is the key component of the Akka Toolkit and plays a very important role in any Akka Actor-based application/system.

What is the ActorSystem?

In the Akka Toolkit, the ActorSystem is the root of the Actors Hierarchy. It acts as a runtime environment for the Akka Actors and provides many features to help them perform their job.

In the Akka Toolkit, the ActorSystem is the entry point and manages all Actors that are created using it. The ActorSystem is placed at the root of the Actor Hierarchy. It acts as a root Actor for all Actors created, using that ActorSystem instance (object).

In the Akka Toolkit, each Actor needs some extra capabilities to do its computation, such as the following:

- Remoting
- Persistence
- Journal for durability
- Streaming

- Scheduling
- Clustering
- Logging
- Dispatching and more

Who is responsible for providing all these capabilities to an Actor? The Akka ActorSystem will take care of them under the hood.

Roles and responsibilities of ActorSystem

The Akka ActorSystem has the following roles and responsibilities:

- It acts as runtime for all Actors
- It creates Actors
- It can stop Actors
- It supervises related Actors
- It creates threads and assigns them to the Actor's dispatcher to process the messages
- It manages the lifecycle of Actors
- It can shut down the whole Akka Actor environment
- It creates the following three base Actors to help other Actors:
    - Root Actor (/)
    - User Guardian Actor(/user)
    - System Guardian Actor(/system)
- It supervises or monitors those top-level Actors
- When we run `ActorSystem.terminate()`, it is responsible for terminating all the available Actors automatically

When we create an Actor using `ActorSystem.actorOf()`, as shown in the following diagram, it creates an Actor object, but it does not return it. It returns `ActorRef`, which acts as a Proxy object to that Actor object:

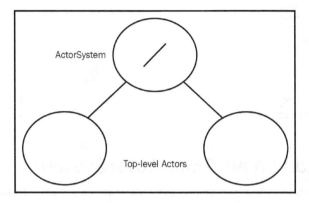

We have to shut down the **ActorSystem**; otherwise, the JVM keeps running forever.

How to create an Akka ActorSystem?

`ActorSystem` has one class and one object, as shown here:

```
object ActorSystem{ }
abstract class ActorSystem{ }
```

We can create an `ActorSystem` using one of its overload `create()` functions, as shown here:

```
val actorSystem1 = ActorSystem.create("FirstActorSystem")
println(actorSystem1)
```

When we call the `ActorSystem.create()` method, it internally calls its available `apply()` methods, so we can simply use the following code to create an `ActorSystem`:

```
val actorSystem2 = ActorSystem("SecondActorSystem")
println(actorSystem2)
```

In both of these examples, we are giving a name to the `ActorSystem`. If we don't provide a name, Akka will assign a default name. Consider the following example:

```
import akka.actor.ActorSystem
object ActorSystemTestApp extends App{
  val actorSystem = ActorSystem()
  println(actorSystem)
  val actorSystem1 = ActorSystem.create("FirstActorSystem")
  println(actorSystem1)
  val actorSystem2 = ActorSystem("SecondActorSystem")
```

```
    println(actorSystem2)
  }
```

This is the output:

```
akka://default
akka://FirstActorSystem
akka://SecondActorSystem
```

How to shut down an Akka ActorSystem?

Creating an ActorSystem is too expensive, because it takes a lot of resources and memory to initialize and work properly, so it's better to avoid creating a new one each time we need it.

After finishing our job and if we don't need the ActorSystem, we should shut it down using the following function:

```
actorSystem.terminate
actorSystem1.terminate
actorSystem2.terminate
```

When we execute `ActorSystem.terminate()`, before shutting down the system, it will stop all its child Actors (which are created using this ActorSystem), otherwise, JVM will run forever and never stop it.

Components of Akka's ActorSystem

In the Akka Toolkit, an ActorSystem is a hierarchical group of actors that share common configurations, for example, dispatchers, executors, schedulers, logging, threads, remote capabilities, and addresses. It is also the entry point for creating or looking up Actors.

To fulfill all its roles and responsibilities, it uses the following components:

- User Guardian Actor
- System Guardian Actor
- DeadLetter
- Scheduler
- Configuration
- EventStream
- Mailboxes
- Dispatchers

When we go through the Akka Actors module (`akka-actor`) API, we can observe the following things:

```
abstract class ActorSystem extends ActorRefFactory {
  // Components of ActorSystem
  def eventStream: EventStream
  def deadLetters: ActorRef
  def scheduler: Scheduler
  def dispatchers: Dispatchers
  def mailboxes: Mailboxes
}
```

Let us understand the components of Akka's `ActorSystem` one by one now:

- **User Guardian Actor** is responsible for taking care of all user-defined Actors, whereas System Guardian Actor is responsible for taking care of all system internal Actors.
- **DeadLetter** is used to store all undelivered messages. For instance, when an Actor sends a message to another Actor, if that Actor is already terminated or that is not an Actor or it's not able to receive the message, that message is delivered to DeadLetter.
- **Scheduler** is used to develop some kind of scheduling jobs to run them periodically. We can configure all **Akka configurations** such as scheduling, dispatcher, threads, executors, and more in the `application.conf` file in a Play Framework-based application (refer to the upcoming chapters for more information on this).
- **EventStream** is the main event bus of the Akka ActorSystem; it is useful to store all its events for instance-logging events.

What is materialization and Akka's implementation?

The Akka Toolkit has an `ActorMaterializer` component that is mainly useful in the Akka Streams module.

In the Akka Streams module, we design our flow execution in high level using Stream API components. That's it. Then who is responsible for creating the required Actors internally and executing that flow? It is `ActorMaterializer`.

Materialization means providing an implementation for the given data flow design.

`ActorMaterializer` is responsible for providing materialization to the Akka Toolkit. It will create all the required Actors under the hood and take care of executing the data streams with defined functionality. It needs the ActorSystem to create and manage those Actors.

 If you don't understand much of this, don't worry. We have not yet introduced Akka Streams. Refer to `Chapter 7`, *Working with Reactive Streams*, for more details.

Akka Actors

In this section, we will discuss what an Actor is, its components, and the Actor lifecycle in detail. We will also discuss the differences between `ActorPath` and `ActorRef`.

What is an Actor?

An Actor is the fundamental computation unit. As per Carl Hewitt's Actor Model, an Actor should perform one, and only one, responsibility. Actors are lightweight event-driven processes.

The Actor is the fundamental building block in the Actor Model as well as Akka-based applications. In simple words, we can say that an Actor is a computational unit of an entity. Like an OOP instance (object), it also has state and behavior.

 Like OOP's Object, *Actor = State + Behavior.*

Like an OOP's object, an Actor's state is maintained in instance variables. An Actor's behavior is a function, operation, or method to perform its job or task.

As a computational unit, it should embody the following three axioms:

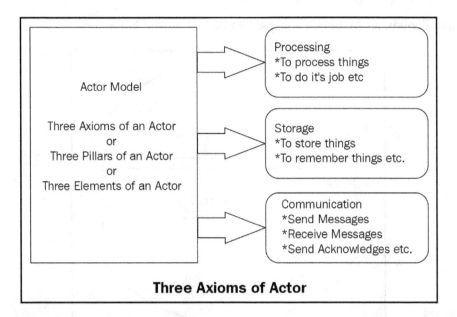

Three Axioms of Actor

Actors are completely abstract things or entities, which means they cannot share their state and behavior with other Actors or non-Actors.

Consider the following essential elements of computation:

- **Processing**: Each Actor should embody some kind of mechanism to process things (for instance, messages), which means to do some computation.
- **Storage**: Each Actor should embody some kind of storage to store things (for instance, messages) to remember and process them when required.
- **Communication**: Each Actor should embody some kind of communication mechanism, which means it should know how to communicate with other Actors.

So, an Actor is the fundamental computation unit, and it should embody all these three essential elements of computation.

In the Akka Toolkit, an Actor can encapsulate both state and behavior:

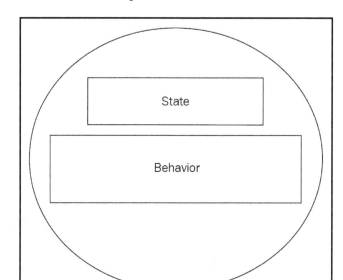

As shown in the preceding diagram, an *Actor = State + Behavior*. However, this state is accessible or modifiable by itself only. No other can access or modify it.

Like in the Shared-State Concurrency model, a thread is a basic unit of execution; in the Actor Model, an Actor is a basic unit of execution.

An Actor is also an object; however, it is not like a normal OOP's object. It has many components internally (which we will discuss in the next section) and does many more things.

Components of Akka Actor

In Akka Toolkit, an Actor is an object (instance). Unlike an **OOP (Object-Oriented Programming)** object, it is not a simple or plain object. Internally, an Akka's Actor contains many components to perform its job or computation easily.

An Akka's Actor contains the following main components under-the-hood:

- **ActorRef**
- **Dispatcher**
- **MailBox**
- **Actor**

The following diagram shows the internal components of an Actor and how they work with one another:

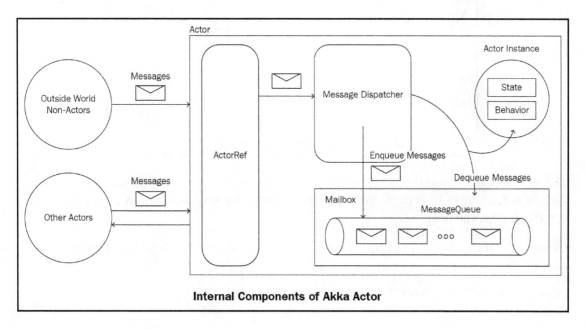

Internal Components of Akka Actor

In the Akka Toolkit, an Actor is not just a normal OOP's object. It contains many components under-the-hood to perform its job. Unlike an OOP's object, an Actor does many things using these components.

Each Actor component performs one specific kind of responsibility to ease its computation. We will understand each component role and responsibility in detail now.

Akka Actor – ActorRef

ActorRef acts as a proxy to the actual **Actor** instance or object. An **Actor** can interact with other Actors through this proxy only; they cannot communicate with them directly. It follows the Proxy Design Pattern:

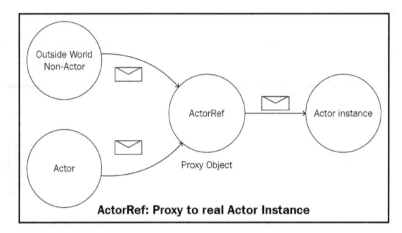

ActorRef: Proxy to real Actor Instance

The `ActorSystem.actorOf()` function is used to create Actors. It returns Actor's `ActorRef` only. It does not return the original Actor object. It is an immutable and serializable handle to an Actor.

Observe the following code snippet from `https://github.com/akka/akka/blob/v2.5.9/akka-actor/src/main/scala/akka/actor/ActorRef.scala`:

```
abstract class ActorRef extends Comparable[ActorRef] with Serializable {
}
```

Akka Actor – Dispatcher

In the Akka Toolkit, the Dispatcher component plays a very important role and acts as an engine. In simple words, it is responsible for coordination; it takes the incoming message and hands it over to its Actor. In the Akka Toolkit, the Dispatcher component is useful for working on messages, so we call it `MessageDispatcher`.

The Akka's dispatcher performs the following tasks:

- It picks up the incoming message from senders (Actor or non-Actor)
- It publishes that message to its Actor's mailbox message queue
- It checks whether its Actor is available or not to process that message

- If its Actor is available, it picks up the message from the message queue and hands it over to its Actor to take the necessary action
- It decouples the outside world from its Actor. In the Akka framework, the Dispatcher component follows the dispatcher design pattern
- If the required Actor is not available, it sends those messages to the DeadLetter Actor

Benefits of the dispatcher pattern

- It reduces dependencies between components, which means less coupling between components
- It increases application maintainability and testability
- It reduces boilerplate or duplicate code because we provide a common delegating logic at one place, that is, in the dispatcher

Akka Actor – Mailbox(MessageQueue)

It is a message queue for an Actor. It stores incoming messages and acts as a queue without any message broker.

In Akka Toolkit, each Actor typically has its own mailbox.

Actor picks up messages from the mailbox one by one and processes them, which means that it takes the necessary action.

The Akka Toolkit supports different kinds of mailboxes for different use case scenarios. Mainly, it supports the following types of mailboxes:

- Bounded mailbox
- Unbounded mailbox
- Priority mailbox

These are again divided into the following two categories:

- Blocking mailbox
- Non-blocking mailbox

The bounded mailbox supports storing incoming messages up to some limit. If it's blocking the bounded mailbox and reaches its capacity, it will block that sender.

The unbounded mailbox supports unlimited capacity to store incoming messages; it's up to the available memory in that server machine.

The priority mailbox delivers messages for Actors to process, based on that message's priority.

If required, we can create our own mailbox implementations. The Akka Toolkit has the following useful in-built mailboxes:

- `UnboundedMailbox`
- `SingleConsumerOnlyUnboundedMailbox`
- `NonBlockingBoundedMailbox`
- `UnboundedControlAwareMailbox`
- `UnboundedPriorityMailbox`
- `UnboundedStablePriorityMailbox`
- `BoundedMailbox`
- `BoundedPriorityMailbox`
- `BoundedStablePriorityMailbox`
- `BoundedControlAwareMailbox`

Refer to the following Akka Doc URL for more information on Akka's mailboxes:

`https://doc.akka.io/docs/akka/current/mailboxes.html`.

By default, messages from the Mailbox(MessageQueue) are evaluated (picked up, read, and processed) in the order they arrived in the queue.

In the Akka Toolkit, the default mailbox (if we don't specify any specific one) is an unbounded and non-blocking mailbox, which is backed by a `java.util.concurrent.ConcurrentLinkedQueue` implementation.

By default, the MailBox(MessageQueue) follows the **FIFO (First In First Out)** order to pick up and process messages from the queue.

Akka Actor – Actor

It is an actual Actor instance, which encapsulates state and behavior to perform its computation. It does NOT receive messages directly from the outside world (from Actors or non-Actors). It receives messages from `ActorRef` to dispatcher to itself only.

Both request and response messages between the sender Actor and the recipient Actor cannot be modified; they are immutable objects.

The `MessageDispatcher` component of an Actor manages the mailbox and routes the messages to the destination (receiver) Actor's mailbox. There is no direct communication between Actors.

When we execute the `ActorSystem.actorOf()` function, ActorSystem not only creates `ActorRef`, but also creates the actual Actor instance, MessageDispatcher, and Mailbox(MessageQueue). However, the ActorSystem returns only `ActorRef` to the clients.

Akka Actor – ActorPath

Apart from the preceding four components, an Actor has some more components such as the following:

- ActorPath
- Actor Selection

In the Akka Toolkit, every Actor has a name or address to look it up from the ActorSystem. This name must be unique per level in the Akka Actor hierarchy. This name is also known as ActorPath.

If we take one level from the Akka Actor Hierarchy, each Actor should have a unique name. No two Actors at the same level have the same name. Two actors at different levels in the Actors Hierarchy may have the same name. There is no restriction or conflict with this because they are at different levels and they form different Actor Paths to identify them uniquely.

An ActorPath is used to look up an Actor from the ActorSystem Hierarchy. We can use either an absolute or relative ActorPath for this purpose.

We will explore ActorPath in depth with some examples in the coming section.

Actor versus thread

When we compare our old Java friend, thread, with our new friend, Actor, we can see the following major differences:

- **Decoupling**: The multi-threaded programming model couples most of the concurrency logic into actual application business logic, so its very difficult to reason about and maintain it. Here, a developer has to concentrate on both, carefully.
  The Actor-based programming model decouples the concurrency logic from the application business logic, so it's very easy to reason about and maintain it. Here, a developer leaves concurrency issues to the programming model and concentrates on business logic only.
- **API**: Java threading API is a low-level concurrency API. The Akka Actor API is a high-level concurrency API.
- **Scaling**: Threads are good for scale-up, but not for scale-out. Actors are good for both scale-up and scale-out.
- **Concurrency versus parallelism**: Threads are good for only concurrency, but not for parallelism. We cannot execute threads in parallel.
  Actors are good for both concurrency and parallelism. We can execute Actors in parallel very well.
- **Lightweight**: Threads are not lightweight; they need more space from the RAM. We can only create around 4 K threads in 1 GB RAM.
  Actors are very lightweight, and we can create around 3 million Actors in 1 GB RAM.
- **Communication**: Threads communicate with each other in a synchronous and blocking way, whereas Actors communicate with each other in an asynchronous and non-blocking way.
- **Issues**: The threading API raises many issues such as synchronization, locking, deadlock, race condition, live locks, context switching, performance issues, inefficient code, and more.
  Actors do not raise these kind of issues.
- **Portable**: Threads are not portable, whereas Actors are portable.

The lifecycle of an Akka Actor

As we discussed, an Akka Actor is also an object or instance. Like any other object, an Akka Actor also has lifecycle methods. We will discuss them theoretically in this section and will provide some examples to understand them well in the coming sections.

Who manages the lifecycle of an Actor? The Actor's Supervisor, which may be either its parent Actor or the ActorSystem.

Akka Toolkit provides the following Actor lifecycle methods to manage it very well:

- `ActorSystem.actorOf()` or `ActorContext.actorOf()`
- `Actor.receive()`
- `Actor.preStart()`
- `Actor.postStop()`
- `Actor.preRestart()`
- `Actor.postRestart()`
- `ActorContext.stop()` or `ActorSystem.stop()`
- `ActorSystem.terminate()`

Consider the following diagram of the Akka Actor's lifecycle:

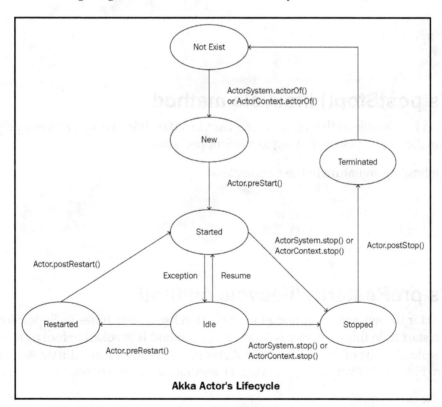

Akka Actor's Lifecycle

Actor's preStart() lifecycle method

This method is available in the `akka.actor.Actor` class. It is invoked immediately after creating a new Actor for the first time, and before moving to the Started state.

If required, we can override this method to perform any initialization activities (such as allocating resources, database connection, socket connection, and more) before the Actor moves to Started state and performs its computation.

It is invoked in two cases:

- Right after creating a new Actor for the first time and before moving to the Started state
- If an Actor is going to be restarted by its parent Actor (Supervisor Actor), its `postRestart()` method calls this method

It has the following signature in the `Actor` class:

```
trait Actor{
  def preStart(): Unit = ()
}
```

Actor's postStop() lifecycle method

This method is available in the `akka.actor.Actor` class. It is invoked immediately after stopping an Actor and before moving to the Stopped state.

It has the following signature in the `Actor` class:

```
trait Actor{
  def preStart(): Unit = ()
  def postStop(): Unit = ()
}
```

Actor's preRestart() lifecycle method

When an Actor throws any exception in its execution logic, sometimes its Supervior may decide to restart it. In this case, its `preRestart()` method is invoked before moving to the Restarted state. As part of this method, the Actor picks up all its subordinate Actors and stops them. Finally, it invokes its `postStop()` method, as shown here:

```
trait Actor{
  def preStart(): Unit = ()
```

```
def postStop(): Unit = ()
def preRestart(reason: Throwable, message: Option[Any]): Unit = {
  context.children foreach { child ⇒
    context.unwatch(child)
    context.stop(child)
  }
  postStop()
}
}
```

Actor's postRestart() lifecycle method

As discussed in the previous lifecycle method, the Actor's Supervisor decides to restart this Actor when it throws any exception. Its Supervisor makes a call to the Actor's postRestart() method immediately so that the Actor enters into the Restarted state.

This postRestart() method, in turn, makes a call to that Actor's preStart() method:

```
trait Actor{
  def preStart(): Unit = ()
  def postStop(): Unit = ()
  def preRestart(reason: Throwable, message: Option[Any]): Unit = {
    context.children foreach { child ⇒
      context.unwatch(child)
      context.stop(child)
    }
    postStop()
  }
  def postRestart(reason: Throwable): Unit = {
    preStart()
  }
}
```

Refer to the *Akka Actor's lifecycle example* section for the full example to understand it well.

Why Actors are lightweight?

In the Akka Toolkit, Actors are lightweight. They have only business logic. Other logic like such as supervision, dispatching messages, mailboxing, and more, are taken care of by other Akka components.

For instance, supervisions will be taken care of by parent Actors. Dispatching messages by the Akka Dispatcher component, mailboxing by the Akka mailbox component, and more.

In the Akka Toolkit, business logic concerns and other concerns are loosely coupled. That's why Akka Actors are very lightweight; they need space to do their job.

Actor basic operations

In this section, we will discuss some of the useful and frequently used Akka Actor operations. In the Akka Toolkit, an Actor can perform the following operations:

- Create an Actor
- Send messages
- Receive messages
- Stop an Actor
- Become/unbecoming an Actor
- Supervise an Actor

Let's define a simple Actor to explore all these operations, one by one, in the following sections.

Defining an Actor

Before creating an Actor and performing its operations, we need to define it.

In the Akka Toolkit, we can define an Actor class by extending the `Actor` Trait and providing implementation for the `receive` method, as follows:

```
class SampleActor extends Actor {
  def receive: Receive = {
    //Implmentation
  }
}
```

Here's the description:

- Here, `Actor` is a trait available in the `akka.actor` package
- The `Actor` trait has an abstract method—`receive`
- The `receive ()` function is a Scala Partial Function

- It takes a type of `Any` and returns `Unit`
- Its complete signature is this:

```
def receive: PartialFunction[Any,Unit] = ???
```

Alternatively, we can use the following simple syntax:

```
def receive: Receive= ???
```

- Here, `Receive` is a type, as shown here:

```
type Receive = PartialFunction[Any, Unit]
```

- We need to write this Actor logic in the `receive` function.

Creating an Actor

To create an Actor in Akka, we should first create its runtime environment, that is, the ActorSystem. We use this ActorSystem to create top-level Actors using the `actorOf()` function, as shown:

```
val actorSystem = ActorSystem("SimpleActorSystem")
val actorRef = actorSystem.actorOf(Props[SimpleActor])
// or use the following overloaded actorOf() function
val actorRef = actorSystem.actorOf(Props[SimpleActor], "Simple")
```

Here, `ActorSystem.actorOf()` takes `Props`, and we should provide the Actor name as the type annotation.

Like `ActorSystem.actorOf()` is useful to create top-level Actors; we can also use `ActorContext.actorOf()` with the same parameters to create subordinate or child Actors. However, we should use this function with an Actor, only as shown here:

```
class SampleActor extends Actor{
  def receive ={
    case _ =>
      // other computaion logic
      context.actorOf(Props[SimpleActor]
      // or use the following overloaded actorOf() function
      context.actorOf(Props[SimpleActor], "Simple")
  }
}
```

The following diagram explains how ActorSystem's `actorOf()` works in creating a new Actor with its components:

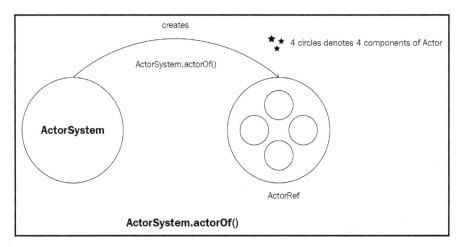

Props is a configuration object available in the `akka.actor` package. It is used to create an Actor. It is an immutable object, so it is thread safe and fully shareable.

Sending messages to an Actor

How do Actors communicate with each other? They communicate with each other by sending and/or receiving messages. The Akka Toolkit has provided a couple of functions to do this.

We can use one of the following functions to send messages to an Actor:

- The tell (!) function
- The ask (?) function

The tell (!) function

It follows the Fire and Forget model, which means send a message asynchronously and return immediately:

```
actor ! message
```

The ask (?) function

It follows the Send and Receive model, which means send a message asynchronously and return `Future` to retrieve results sometime in the future. It is known as the Ask pattern:

```
val result: Future[Result] = (actor ? message).mapTo[String]
```

In the Akka Framework API, this `ask` pattern is defined at the `akka.pattern` package:

```
import akka.pattern.ask

ask(actor, message) // use it directly
actor ask message   // use it by implicit conversion
actor ? message       // use it by implicit conversion
```

Replaying messages from an Actor

In this section, we will discuss how an Actor replies to a message (which is received from another Actor from `ActorWorld`) or processes a message (which is received from a non-Actor from the outside world).

Actor to Actor communication

Consider that an `Actor-1` sends a message to `Actor-2` using the `ask` function to know the response from that Actor; it is as shown here:

```
actor1 ? HelloMessage
```

In `Actor-2`, when it receives it, it should process it and reply to that `Actor-2`, as shown here:

```
def receive = {
   case HelloMessage =>
           println("Actor-2: Process the message")
           sender ! HowDoYouDo
}
```

Here, `Actor-2` uses the `sender` object to reply with a message back to that message sender directly.

Here, `sender` is a function defined in an Actor trait to access the current processing message's sender Actor reference directly, as follows:

```
final def sender(): ActorRef = context.sender()
```

Actor to non-Actor communication

If the sender of that message is a non-Actor coming from the outside world, then this sender cannot reply to that sender. If we try to do so, that message is delivered to the DeadLetter component of the Akka ActorSystem.

Stopping an Actor

Stopping an Actor means shutting it down gracefully, once its job is finished. We can use the following options to shut down an Actor.

Within an Actor, we can use the `context` object to stop it:

```
context.stop(self)
```

Here, `self` means referring itself, the Actor from which we are making this call to stop itself.

 When we stop an ActorSystem, it stops all its child Actors automatically.

As shown in the following example, we can also use ActorSystem's `terminate()` function to stop or shut down the whole ActorSystem so that all of its Actors are stopped automatically:

```
actorSystem.terminate()
```

Killing an Actor

If required, we can kill an Actor immediately, using one of these predefined messages:

- `akka.actor.Kill`
- `akka.actor.PoisonPill`

As shown in the following example, if we send either a `Kill` or `PoisonPill` message to an Actor, that Actor's `ActorSystem` will kill that immediately:

```
actor ! Kill
```

Or:

```
actor ! PoisonPill
```

Become/unbecoming an Actor

The Akka Toolkit ActorContext has two methods to change the state of an Actor from one to another: become() and unbecome(). These are useful to define **FSM (Finite State Machines)**.

Case object Switch

The following code snippet shows how to use ActorContext's become() and unbecome() functions:

```
class MyFSMActor extends Actor {
  def receive = {
    case Switch =>
      become({
        case Switch =>
          unbecome()
      })
  }
}
```

Here, when SwapActor receives a switch message for first time, it changes its state to become. Then, if it receives the same message the next time, it moves to the unbecoming state.

Akka has a decent FSM **DSL (Domain Specific Language)** API to ease the development of FST Machines.

Supervise an Actor

In the Akka Toolkit, an Actor supervises its child Actors automatically. When a child Actor crashes or fails to do its computation, it informs its status to its supervisor or parent Actor. Then, the parent Actor will take a decision and perform one of the following actions on that Actor only, or on all of its Actors:

- **Resume**: It resumes only the affected Actor or all of its subordinate Actors
- **Restart**: It restarts only the affected Actor or all of its subordinate Actors

- **Stop**: It stops only the affected Actor or all of its subordinate Actors permanently
- **Escalate**: If it cannot decide what to do, it escalates to its supervisor Actor about the failure and fails itself

The supervisor Actor decides what to do on only the affected Actor or all of its subordinate Actors, based on the configured supervision strategy. We will discuss what is supervision and its strategies in detail, in the coming sections.

Akka Supervision

In this section, we will discuss one of the important concepts of Akka Toolkit—**Supervision**.

First, we will discuss the supervision role in Akka and move to its strategies. We will explore Akka Supervision strategies with some examples in the practical section.

What is supervision?

Supervision is a technique to organize the Akka Actors into a hierarchy, which means creating a parent-child relationship between Actors.

In Akka terminology, the parent Actor is known as supervisor and the child Actor as subordinate:

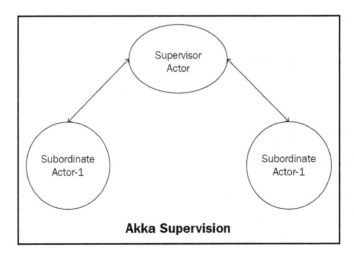

Akka Supervision

As shown in the preceding diagram, all Akka Actors are organized into a tree-like hierarchy. The supervisor Actor is responsible for supervising the subordinate Actors. These subordinate Actors again may have child Actors, which may also have subordinates. Final or leaf Actors are responsible for doing the actual work (Business logic).

 The Akka supervision concept is different than Akka's monitoring concept.

What is the main goal of Akka's supervision?

The main goal of this Akka's supervision is to implement fault-tolerance in the Akka Toolkit very easily. It makes it easy to isolate failures from the system.

Every system (or application) has two main concerns: one is its actual business logic and another is the non-business logic. For instance, non-business logic means taking care of system failures, child Actor failures, logging, monitoring, and more.

The Akka Supervision technique separates our system's actual business logic from the system's failure handling to make fault-tolerance very easy.

All supervisor (parent) Actors are responsible for taking care of the system's fault handling and its subordinate Actor's failures.

All subordinate Actors are responsible for doing actual application business logic, that is, its computation logic:

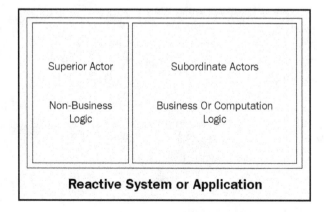

In simple words, the main goals of this Akka's supervision are these:

- Supporting fault-tolerance easily
- Supporting the **Single Responsible Principle** (**SRP**)

Benefits of supervision

The main benefits of the Akka supervision technique are as listed:

- Ease of supporting fault tolerance
- Ease of supporting the SRP
- Loose coupling between concerns—actual Business logic and non-Business logic
- Easy to test
- Easy to maintain
- Easy to develop reliable, robust, highly available, and Reactive systems
- Easy to support one of the principles of the Reactive Manifesto—react to failures

Why don't we write exceptions or failures handling in Actor itself?

- It increases the tight coupling between the Actor's computation logic and failure handling
- It makes Actors large or heavyweight components
- It decreases scalability and maintainability
- It violates the SRP

To avoid all these problems, the Akka Toolkit uses the Actors hierarchy model to implement failure handling.

So, an Akka Actor is as small as possible with Single Responsibility and lightweight features. There is a clear separation between an Actor's computation logic and failure handling.

Rules of Akka Supervision

The Akka Toolkit follows a set of rules in supporting its supervision technique:

- Every Actor must have one, and only one, supervisor's Actor
- This means no two supervisor Actors have the same subordinate Actor
- Akka supports a default supervision strategy concept
- If required, we should define and configure our required supervision strategies
- If we don't define it, Akka Toolkit uses the default supervision strategies
- Akka Toolkit's default supervision strategy is the one-for-one strategy

Akka Supervision strategies

The Akka Toolkit supports the following two supervision strategies:

- The one-for-one strategy
- The all-for-one strategy

They have provided two different classes to take care of them:

- `OneForOneStrategy`
- `AllForOneStrategy`

In the Akka Toolkit, the `OneForOneStrategy` is the default supervision strategy if we don't mention anything.

The one-for-one strategy means when one of the Actors fails to do its computation (for instance, it throws an exception), then its supervisor Actor will take an Action only to that Actor, and it does not affect other subordinates Actors, as shown:

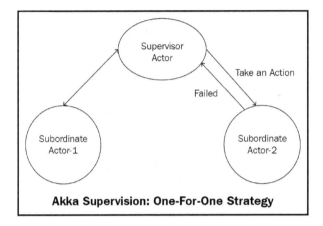

Akka Supervision: One-For-One Strategy

The all-for-one strategy means when one of the Actors fails to do its computation (for instance, it throws an exception), its supervisor Actor will take an Action to all of its Actors, as illustrated:

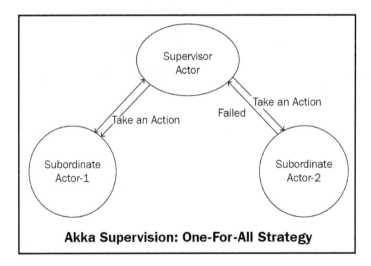

Akka Supervision: One-For-All Strategy

Akka's supervision hierarchy

In the Akka Toolkit, all Actors are organized into the following tree-like hierarchy:

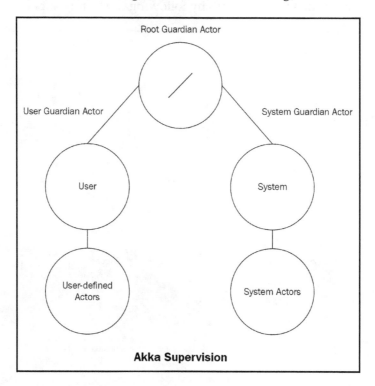

Akka Supervision

In the Akka Supervison hierarchy, there is one topmost supervisors Actor—"/" (**Root Guardian Actor**). It is responsible for taking care of the rest of the system.

It has two subordinates:

- /user (**User Guardian Actor**)
- /system (**System Guardian Actor**)

The User Guardian Actor is responsible for taking care of all user-defined Actors, whereas the System Guardian Actor is responsible for taking care of all the system's Actors.

Actor's Path

As we discussed in the previous section, ActorPath is the address of an Actor in the ActorSystem. We can form an Actor's Path by following the Actors supervision hierarchy:

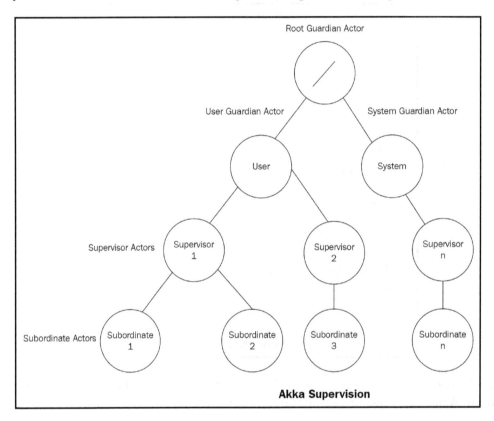

Akka Supervision

Supervisor1 forms its ActorPath as /user/Supervisor1, which means it starts first with Rootr Actor "/", then its child Actor user, and then itself, **Supervisor1**.

In the same way, **Subordinate3** forms its ActorPath as /user/Supervisor2/Subordinate3.

If you are familiar with trees, graphs, and more, it is not a big job to understand it well.

What is Akka's Let It Crash model?

The Akka Toolkit follows the **Let it Crash** model to take care of fault handling. When a subordinate Actor crashes, let it crash and do that fault handling with the help of another Actor. This means the subordinate does not need to worry how to handle that situation. The supervisor of that Actor will take care of that fault handling based on the configured supervision strategy.

This Akka's approach clearly defines who is responsible for taking care of fault handling (supervisor Actors) and who is responsible for actual business logic (Subordinate Actors). This loose coupling and the **SRP (Single Responsibility Principle)** approach gives us the ease of fault handling and lightweight Actors. Refer to the *Supervisor strategies* section for more information on this.

 The Akka Team was using `http://letitcrash.com` for updates. Now they have moved the blog to `http://blog.akka.io`.

Akka HelloWorld Actor example

As a developer, you guys know that it's good to start learning any new language, tool, or framework with a simple HelloWorld example to understand its basics and execution flow.

In this section, we will develop an Akka-based HelloWorld example to understand *how to write Actors, how to run them*, and more:

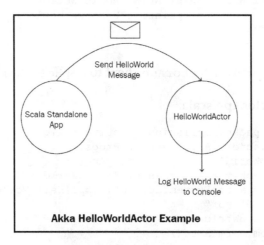

Follow these steps to develop and test this `helloworld-app` application:

1. Create a SBT project in IntelliJ IDEA IDE. (Here, I'll use `helloworld-app` as my SBT project name).

2. Add the `akka-actor` module configuration to the `build.sbt` file:

   build.sbt:

   ```
   name := "helloworld-app"
   version := "1.0"
   scalaVersion := "2.12.2"
   libraryDependencies ++= Seq("com.typesafe.akka" %% "akka-actor" %
    "2.5.9")
   ```

3. Create the `HelloWorld` message as the `case` class:

   ```
   HelloWorld.scala
   package com.packt.publishing.reactive.hello
   case class HelloWorld()
   ```

4. Create the `HelloWorldActor` Actor with the `HelloWorld` message processing logic:

   HelloWorldActor.scala:

   ```
   package com.packt.publishing.reactive.hello
   import akka.actor.Actor
   class HelloWorldActor extends Actor{
     override def receive: PartialFunction[Any, Unit] = {
       case HelloWorld => println("Hello World")
       case _          => println("Unknown World")
     }
   }
   ```

5. Create the `HelloWorldActorApp` client to test `HelloWorldActor`:

   HelloWorldActorApp.scala:

   ```
   package com.packt.publishing.reactive.hello
   import akka.actor.{ActorSystem, Props}
   object HelloWorldActorApp extends App{
     val actorSystem = ActorSystem("helloworld")
     val actor = actorSystem.actorOf(Props[HelloWorldActor],
      "HelloWorldActor")
     actor ! HelloWorld
     actorSystem.terminate()
   ```

}

6. Execute the Scala App and observe the output.

   When we run the `HelloWorldActorApp` client in IDE, we will see the following expected output:

   Hello World

Congratulations! You have successfully developed and tested it using a simple Scala standalone App. That's good news to start this chapter. Go ahead and learn some more Akka Toolkit concepts in the coming sections.

Akka Actors communicate example

In this example, we will discuss how Actors communicate with each other, which means how one Actor sends a message to second Actor, and how it receives and processes the messages from the second Actor:

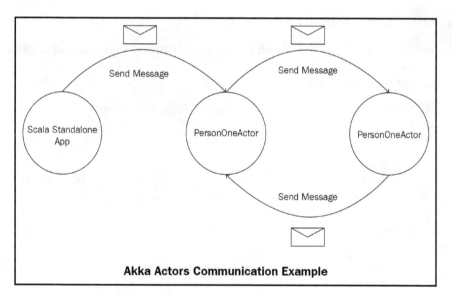

Akka Actors Communication Example

Follow these steps to develop and test this `akkacommunicate-app` application:

1. Create an SBT Project in IDE. Here, I'll use `helloworld-app` as my SBT project name.
2. Add the `akka-actor` module configuration to the `build.sbt` file:

    build.sbt:

    ```
    name := "akkacommunicate-app"
    version := "1.0"
    scalaVersion := "2.12.2"
    libraryDependencies ++= Seq("com.typesafe.akka" %% "akka-actor" %
      "2.5.9")
    ```

3. Create greeting messages as Case classes and Case object(s), as shown:

    GreetingMessages.scala:

    ```
    package com.packt.publishing.reactive.communicate
    case class GoodMorning(name: String)
    case object HowDoYouDo
    case class GoodBye(name: String)
    ```

4. Create `PersonOneActor` with its messages processing logic, as illustrated:

    PersonOneActor.scala:

    ```
    package com.packt.publishing.reactive.communicate
    import akka.actor.Actor
    class PersonOneActor extends Actor {
      override def receive = {
        case GoodMorning(name:String) =>
          println(s"PersonOneActor Received: Good Morning ${name}.")
          sender ! GoodMorning(sender.path.name)
        case HowDoYouDo =>
          println(s"PersonOneActor Received: How do you do?.")
          sender ! GoodBye
        case GoodBye =>
          println(s"PersonOneActor Received: GoodBye.")
      }
    }
    ```

5. Create `PersonTwoActor` with its messages processing logic, as follows:

PersonTwoActor.scala:

```scala
package com.packt.publishing.reactive.communicate
import akka.actor.Actor
class PersonTwoActor extends Actor {
  override def receive = {
    case GoodMorning(name:String) =>
      println(s"PersonTwoActor Received: Good Morning ${name}.")
      sender ! HowDoYouDo
    case HowDoYouDo =>
      println(s"PersonTwoActor Received: How do you do?.")
      sender ! GoodBye
    case GoodBye =>
      println(s"PersonTwoActor Received: GoodBye.")
      sender ! GoodBye
  }
}
```

6. Create a client Scala application to create `ActorSystem`, Actors, and initiate the communication between two actors, as demonstrated here:

ActorCommunicateApp.scala:

```scala
package com.packt.publishing.reactive.communicate
import akka.actor.{ActorSystem, Props}
object ActorCommunicateApp extends App{
  val actorSystem = ActorSystem("ActorCommunicate")
  val personOneActor = actorSystem.actorOf(Props[PersonOneActor],
   "PersonOne")
  val personTwoActor = actorSystem.actorOf(Props[PersonTwoActor],
   "PersonTwo")
  personOneActor.tell(GoodMorning(personOneActor.path.name),
   personTwoActor)
  actorSystem.terminate()
}
```

7. Execute the client application and observe the following output:

```
PersonOneActor Received: Good Morning PersonOne.
PersonTwoActor Received: Good Morning PersonTwo.
PersonOneActor Received: How do you do?.
PersonTwoActor Received: GoodBye.
PersonOneActor Received: GoodBye.
```

Akka Actor's lifecycle example

In this section, we will develop a couple of Actors to explore Akka Actor's lifecycle methods in detail. Perform the following steps to explore Akka Actor's lifecycle:

1. Create a Scala/Akka SBT project in your favorite IDE (I am using IntelliJ IDEA IDE):

```
Project name: akka-actor-lifecycle-app
```

2. Add the following configuration to the sbt file:

build.sbt:

```
name := "akka-actor-lifecycle-app"
version := "1.0"
scalaVersion := "2.12.2"
libraryDependencies ++= Seq("com.typesafe.akka" %% "akka-actor" %
  "2.5.9")
```

3. Create the ActorLifecycleApp file, as shown:

ActorLifecycleApp.scala:

```scala
package com.packt.publishing.actor.lifecycle

import akka.actor.{Actor,ActorSystem,Props}

class LifecycleActor extends Actor{
  override def preStart(): Unit = {
    println("LifecycleActor::preStart() invoked.")
  }
  override def receive: PartialFunction[Any, Unit] = {
    case _ =>
      println("LifecycleActor::receive() invoked.")
      //throw new Exception
  }
  override def postStop(): Unit = {
    println("LifecycleActor::postStop() invoked.")
  }
  override def preRestart(reason: Throwable,
  message: Option[Any]): Unit = {
    println("LifecycleActor::preRestart() invoked.")
  }
  override def postRestart(reason: Throwable): Unit = {
    println("LifecycleActor::postRestart() invoked.")
```

```
    }
  }
  object ActorLifecycleApp extends App {
    val actorSystem = ActorSystem("LifecycleSystem")
    val actor = actorSystem.actorOf(Props[LifecycleActor],
     "LifecycleActor")
    actor ! 2017
    actorSystem.terminate()
  }
```

Here's the output:

```
LifecycleActor::preStart() invoked.
LifecycleActor::receive() invoked.
LifecycleActor::postStop() invoked.
```

4. In the `ActorLifecycleApp` file, comment one line and uncomment another line to see the different Actor lifecycle (or refer to the `ActorLifecycleApp2.scala` file):

   ActorLifecycleApp2.scala:

```
//actorSystem.terminate() from ActorLifecycleApp
throw new Exception  // From LifecycleActor
```

5. Now, again execute the application; you'll see the following output from the console:

```
LifecycleActor::preStart() invoked.
LifecycleActor::receive() invoked.
LifecycleActor::preRestart() invoked.
LifecycleActor::postRestart() invoked.
[ERROR] [07/05/2017 14:57:19.979]
[LifecycleSystem-akka.actor.default-dispatcher-4]
[akka://LifecycleSystem/user/LifecycleActor] null
java.lang.Exception
at
com.packt.publishing.actor.lifecycle
.LifecycleActor2$$anonfun$receive$1.applyOrElse(
 ActorLifecycleApp2.scala:14)
```

Explore a similar way for another Akka Actor lifecycle method.

Akka parent-child Actors example

As we discussed in the previous sections, Akka's ActorSystem creates all top-level actors, which may act as parent or supervisor Actors. So, how do we create subordinate Actors?

When we execute the `ActorSystem.actorOf()` function, it creates all top-level Actors. However, Akka Toolkit has provided an implicit variable, context of the `ActorContext` type in the `Actor` class, as follows:

```
trait Actor {
   implicit val context: ActorContext = {
     // Code goes here
   }
}
```

Like `ActorSystem.actorOf()`, the ActorSystem also has `actorOf()` with the same set of parameters to create child or subordinate Actors from a supervisor or parent Actor:

```
package com.packt.publishing.supervision
import akka.actor.{Actor,Props,ActorSystem}

sealed trait Work
case object DevWork extends Work
case object TestingWork extends Work
class LeadDeveloperActor extends Actor{
  def receive = {
    case DevWork =>
      val devActor = context.actorOf(Props[DevActor],"Dev")
      devActor ! DevWork
    case TestingWork =>
      val qaActor = context.actorOf(Props[QAActor],"QA")
      qaActor ! TestingWork
  }
}
class DevActor extends Actor{
  def receive = {
    case DevWork =>
      println("Should Develop the application.")
    case _ =>
      println("No work.")
  }
}
class QAActor extends Actor{
  def receive = {
    case TestingWork =>
      println("Should test the application.")
```

```
      case _ =>
         println("No work.")
    }
}
object ParentChildApp extends App{
  val projectLeadSystem = ActorSystem("ProjectSystem")
  val leadDevActor =
    projectLeadSystem.actorOf(Props[LeadDeveloperActor],"LeadDev")
  leadDevActor ! DevWork
  leadDevActor ! TestingWork
  projectLeadSystem.terminate
}
```

This is the output:

```
Should Develop the application.
Should test the application.
```

Actor's Path versus Reference

In this section, we will compare the two important components of an Akka Actor:

- ActorRef: ActorRef is a reference of an Actor object. When we create an Actor using ActorSystem, it returns ActorRef but not an Actor object:

```
val actorRef:ActorRef =
  actorSystem.actorOf(Props[SimpleActor],"SimpleActor")
```

As the outside world cannot interact with an Actor object directly, an outside Actor or a non-Actor can interact with another Actor indirectly using this ActorRef. When we create another Actor, ActorSystem returns a different ActorRef to that newly created Actor.

ActorRef is the same for a single Actor. It does not change during an Actor lifecycle. Two different Actor objects cannot have the same ActorRef.

- `ActorPath`: `ActorPath` is the address of an Actor in the `ActorSystem`. In Akka, Actors are created in the hierarchy fashion, so each Actor in that hierarchy has a different address to reference that Actor uniquely.

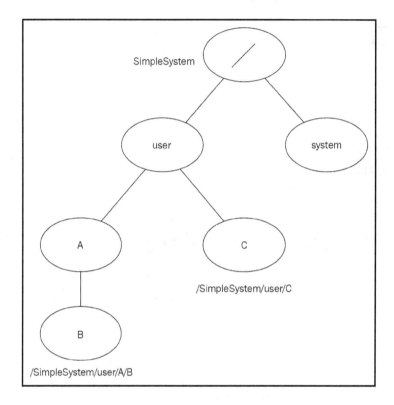

As shown in the preceding diagram, Actor **B** has **/SimpleSystem/user/A/B** as its address (`ActorPath`) and Actor **C** has **/SimpleSystem/user/C**.

Differences between ActorRef and ActorPath

- `ActorRef` is different for two different Actors; no two Actors can have the same `ActorRef`.
- `ActorPath` may be the same or different for two different Actors. We can create two different Actors having the same `ActorPath`. However, we cannot create them at a time. When Actor one dies or shuts down, we can create Actor two with the same `ActorPath`. However, Actor two has a different `ActorRef`.

An ActorPath is used to look up an Actor in `ActorSystem`.

Two actor references are compared equal when they have the same path and point to the same actor incarnation.

Let's explore these differences with a simple example:

```
import akka.actor.{Actor, ActorPath, ActorRef, ActorSystem, PoisonPill,
Props}
case object Shutdown
class SimpleActor extends Actor {
  def receive = {
    case Shutdown => context.stop(self)
  }
}
object ActorRefActorPathApp extends App {
  val actorSystem = ActorSystem("SimpleSystem")
  val actorRef1:ActorRef =
actorSystem.actorOf(Props[SimpleActor],"SimpleActor")
  println(s"Actor Reference1 = ${actorRef1}")
  println(s"Actor Path1 = ${actorRef1.path}")
  val actorPath:ActorPath = actorSystem / "SimpleActor"
  println(s"Actor Path = ${actorPath}")
  actorRef1 ! Shutdown
  Thread.sleep(1000)
  val actorRef2:ActorRef =
   actorSystem.actorOf(Props[SimpleActor],"SimpleActor")
  println(s"Actor Reference2 = ${actorRef2}")
  println(s"Actor Path2 = ${actorRef2.path}")
  actorSystem.terminate
}
```

Here's the output:

```
Actor Reference1 = Actor[akka://SimpleSystem/user/SimpleActor#1117950189]
Actor Path1 = akka://SimpleSystem/user/SimpleActor
Actor Path = akka://SimpleSystem/user/SimpleActor
Actor Reference2 = Actor[akka://SimpleSystem/user/SimpleActor#1063378319]
Actor Path2 = akka://SimpleSystem/user/SimpleActor
```

As shown in the preceding example, we can create an `ActorPath` using the following notation too:

```
val actorPath:ActorPath = actorSystem / "SimpleActor"
```

Here, we are using the "/" (forward slash) notation to walk the ActorSystem tree hierarchy.

If we don't use unique names for Actors in the same ActorSystem, we will get the `InvalidActorNameException` error, as in the following example:

```
val actorSystem = ActorSystem("SimpleSystem")
val actorRef1:ActorRef = actorSystem.actorOf(Props[SimpleActor],
 "SimpleActor")
val actorRef2:ActorRef = actorSystem.actorOf(Props[SimpleActor],
 "SimpleActor")
akka.actor.InvalidActorNameException: actor name [SimpleActor] is not
unique!
```

Example-1:

It explores some basics of both the `ActorRef` and `ActorPath` concepts:

```
import akka.actor.{Actor, ActorSystem, Props}
case object HelloWorld
class HelloWorldActor extends Actor{
  override def receive: Receive = {case HelloWorld =>
  println("Hello World")
  case _ =>
  "Unknown Message"
  }
}
object HelloWorldApp extends App{
  val actorSystem = ActorSystem("HelloWorld")
  var actorRef1 = actorSystem.actorOf(Props[HelloWorldActor],
  "FirstActor")
  val actorRef2 = actorSystem.actorOf(Props[HelloWorldActor],
  "SecondActor")
  val actorRef3 = actorRef1
  println("Actor 'actorRef1' Reference= " + actorRef1)
  println("Actor 'actorRef2' Reference = " + actorRef2)
  println("actorRef1 == actorRef1 = " + (actorRef1 == actorRef1))
  println("actorRef1 == actorRef2 = " + (actorRef1 == actorRef2))
  println("actorRef1 == actorRef3 = " + (actorRef1 == actorRef3))
  println("Actor 'actorRef1' path = " + actorRef1.path)
  println("Actor 'actorRef2' path = " + actorRef2.path)
  println("Actor 'actorRef3' path = " + actorRef3.path)
  actorRef1 ! HelloWorld
  actorSystem.terminate}
```

This is the output:

```
Actor 'actorRef1''' Reference=
Actor[akka://HelloWorld/user/FirstActor#-276253961]
Actor 'actorRef2''' Reference =
Actor[akka://HelloWorld/user/SecondActor#1861673652]
```

```
actorRef1 == actorRef1 = true
actorRef1 == actorRef2 = false
actorRef1 == actorRef3 = true
Actor 'actorRef1''' path = akka://HelloWorld/user/FirstActor
Actor 'actorRef2''' path = akka://HelloWorld/user/SecondActor
Actor 'actorRef3''' path = akka://HelloWorld/user/FirstActor
Hello World
```

Example-2:

We create non-top-level Actors within another Actor using the `context.actorOf()` function, as demonstrated:

```
import akka.actor.{Actor, ActorSystem, Props}
case object HelloWorld
class HelloWorldActor extends Actor{
  val dummyActorRef = context.actorOf(Props.empty, "DummyActor")
  override def receive: Receive = {
    case HelloWorld =>
     println("Actor 'dummyActorRef' Reference = " + dummyActorRef)
     println("Hello World")
    case _ =>
     "Unknown Message"
  }
}
object HelloWorldApp extends App{
  val actorSystem = ActorSystem("HelloWorld")
  var actorRef = actorSystem.actorOf(Props[HelloWorldActor],
   "FirstActor")
  actorRef ! HelloWorld
  actorSystem.terminate
}
```

The following is the output:

```
Actor 'dummyActorRef' Reference =
Actor[akka://HelloWorld/user/FirstActor/DummyActor#436541392]
Hello World
```

When we execute actorRef.tell (message), what happens internally?

This section explains what happens under the hood to understand the things well. If you are not interested in knowing this, skip this section and move on to the next parts of this chapter.

On a high level, Actor Toolkit components perform the following steps:

1. `ActorRef` makes a call to its `!()` function.
2. `ActorRef` hands over the message to the dispatcher.
3. Dispatcher enqueues the message into the mailbox.
4. Dispatcher creates an `executorService` (Executor).
5. Dispatcher creates a mailbox thread—`mbox`.
6. Dispatcher makes a call to the `execute()` function of `executorService`:

   ```
   executorService.execute(mbox)
   ```

7. The `executorService.execute()` method invokes the mailbox's `run()` function:

   ```
   mbox.run()
   ```

8. Mailbox's `run()` function dequeues the message.
9. Mailbox's `run()` function hands over that message to the actual Actor instance or object.
10. Now, finally, the real Actor instance processes that message and does the necessary job.

MessageDispatcher

The `MessageDispatcher` performs the following functionality:

1. It picks up the incoming message from `ActorRef` (coming from non-Actor client or other Actors).
2. It enqueues that message into MailBox(MessageQueue).

3. MailBox(MessageQueue) is a thread.

   Look at this from `https://github.com/akka/akka/blob/v2.5.9/akka-actor/src/main/scala/akka/dispatch/Mailbox.scala`.

   Look at the following code snippet from Actor's `Mailbox` component to understand how it deals with messages:

```
private[akka] abstract class Mailbox(val messageQueue: MessageQueue)
  extends ForkJoinTask[Unit] with SystemMessageQueue with Runnable {
  override final def run(): Unit = {
    processAllSystemMessages() //First, deal with any system messages
    processMailbox() //Then deal with messages
  }
}
```

   It is part of Akka's INTERNAL API.

4. It creates an executor to process Actor's mailbox.

   Look at this from `https://github.com/akka/akka/blob/v2.5.9/akka-actor/src/main/scala/akka/dispatch/Dispatcher.scala`.

   Look at the following class definition for Actor's Dispatcher component and how it uses `ExecutorService` to execute that Actor's mailbox:

```
class Dispatcher(.....) extends MessageDispatcher(_configurator) {
  protected[akka] def systemDispatch(receiver: ActorCell,
    invocation: SystemMessage): Unit = {
    val mbox = receiver.mailbox
    mbox.systemEnqueue(receiver.self, invocation)
    registerForExecution(mbox, false, true)
  }
  protected[akka] override def registerForExecution(mbox:
   Mailbox,......): Boolean = {
    executorService execute mbox
  }
}
```

It is part of Akka's INTERNAL API.

 Most of the `ActorRef`, mailbox, and dispatcher functions are part of Akka's INTERNAL API (Private API).

How to configure a dispatcher?

In the Akka framework, each AkkaSystem has a default `MessageDispatcher`. An Actor uses that default dispatcher, if no dispatcher is configured to it. If required, we can configure our application required `MessageDispatcher`.

In the Akka framework, the Dispatcher component internally uses Java's Executor framework to execute tasks asynchronously. The Akka framework has provided the following implementations of Java's Executor framework:

- `default-executor`: It is the default Executor implementation used by the Akka framework if we don't provide this configuration. It uses `java.util.concurrent.ExecutorService` to execute asynchronous tasks.
- `fork-join-executor`: It uses Java's Fork/Join Executor framework to execute asynchronous tasks.
- `thread-pool-executor`: It uses a predefined thread pool to execute asynchronous tasks.

The Akka dispatcher works based on the configured underlying threading model.

We can configure a dispatcher to work with only one Actor, a group of Actors, only one dispatcher per ActorSytem, or one dispatcher per Akka application.

To improve our application performance, throughput, availability, and scalability, we should pick up the right dispatcher and mailbox and should configure them.

Akka Configuration

We can develop Akka applications without using any configuration because the Akka framework provides sensible default configuration values for each and every Akka component. If required, we can change configuration values to improve application performance, scalability, and more.

In this section, we will discuss some of the following important Akka framework configuration details:

- Dispatcher
- Executor
- Logging

Akka framework uses the Typesafe Configuration library for this purpose. In the Akka framework, this configuration is read and used by the ActorSystem. By default, the ActorSystem uses all configuration details available in the `application.conf` file. If required, we can customize it.

Akka Configuration starts with `akka`, as depicted in the `application.conf` file:

```
akka{
}
```

We can set a log level and default dispatcher for Actors, as shown:

```
akka{
  loglevel = "DEBUG"
  actor {
    default-dispatcher {
      type = "Dispatcher"
      executor = "default-executor"
      default-executor {
        fallback = "fork-join-executor"
      }
    }
  }
}
```

Here, `executor` specifies which kind of `ExecutorService` to use for this dispatcher. The default value is `default-executor`.

The `default-executor` requires a `default-executor` section.

Akka SBT Templates

Lightbend will decommission **activator** by the end of 2017. So, it's better to use **Giter8** templates to start initial Play, Scala, Akka, and more, based projects.

> For more information, read https://www.lightbend.com/community/core-tools/activator-and-sbt.

To use this new approach, install sbt 0.13.13 (or higher), and use the `sbt new` command. To see all available Giter8 templates, go through the GitHub URL `https://github.com/foundweekends/giter8/wiki/giter8-templates`.

Here's an example:

To create a basic simple Scala project:

```
$ sbt new <path-to-your-new-project>/scala-app scala/scala-seed.g8
```

To create a basic simple Scala and Akka project:

```
$ sbt new <path-to-your-new-project>/scala-app akka/akka-scala-seed.g8
```

To create a basic simple Scala, Akka, and Play project:

```
$ sbt new <path-to-your-new-project>/scala-app playframework/play-scala-
seed.g8
```

Alternatively, you can use the `git` command to clone those repositories, as shown:

```
$ git clone https://github.com/playframework/play-scala-seed.g8.git
```

Akka Logging

Akka Toolkit has provided a `akka.actor.ActorLogging` component to support the logging feature. It is a trait useful with an Actor only and has a `log` function, as follows:

```
trait ActorLogging { this: Actor ⇒
  def log: LoggingAdapter = {
    // only used in Actor, i.e. thread safe
  }
}
```

We can use `ActorLogging`, as shown here:

```
class SimpleActor extends Actor with ActorLogger {
  def receive = {
    case _ =>  log.info("SimpleActor: receive inovoked.")
  }
}
```

Business problem

In this section, we will discuss our real business problem in detail. Understand this section well, as we will use our **Reactive Ecosystem**—Scala, Akka, Akka Streams, and Play Framework to solve this problem, step by step.

Problem discussion

We will develop a **WeatherForecasting (WF)** Reactive System using the Lightbend Reactive Ecosystem. This system contains three main subsystems:

- **WF Admin System**: It acts as a **Satellite Interface System**. In real-time applications, satellites send weather forecasting data frequently to one of our systems, which is responsible for processing them in different stages and storing them in a data store in a required format, as illustrated:

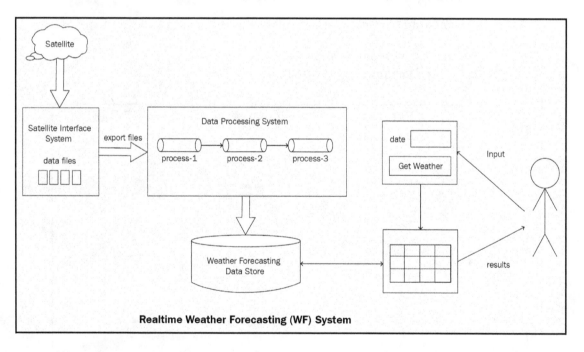

As we cannot implement this kind of complex system to understand our Lightbend Reactive Ecosystem, we will simplify this system with a Fileupload functionality in the WF Admin System.

The WF Admin System provides a nice UI to upload files in a specific format, as depicted in the following diagram:

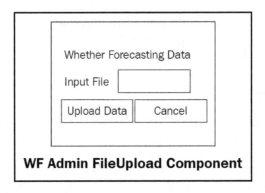

WF Admin FileUpload Component

Then, our system will process that file data into a useful format and store it into our data store (Mongo or Apache Cassandra data store).

So, our WF Admin System mainly contains the following two components:

- Fileupload component
- Data processing component

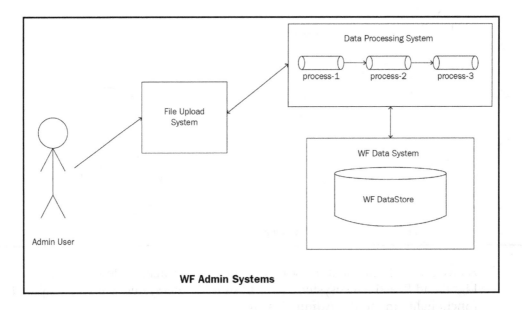

- **WF User System**: It is a real user of our application. The user can access our application and see the WeatherForcasting by giving one of the following inputs to our system:
  - Date
  - City
  - Postcode

Once the user enters one of these values, they will see the hourly-based WeatherForecasting in a nicely designed UI:

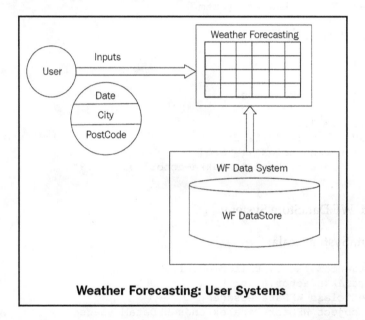

Weather Forecasting: User Systems

- **WF DataStore System**: It is a database system to store our **WF (WeatherForecasting)** data. We can implement this system using one of the popular NoSQL data stores, such as MongoDB or Apache Cassandra.

In the coming chapters, we will develop this WF Reactive System step by step as separate programs, which may miss some components. However, this is intentional. After reading this whole book, try to implement this Reactive completely as your homework.

Akka Actor's implementation

In this section, we will try to implement some of the components using the Akka Toolkit to understand it well. Anyhow, it is not a real WF System, just a simple and dummy solution. We will improve this system, step by step in the coming chapters.

Perform the followings steps one by one:

1. Create an SBT Project in your favorite IDE (I am using IntelliJ IDEA):

   ```
   Project Name: akka-wf-system
   ```

2. Update the `build.sbt` file:

   build.sbt:

   ```
   name := "akka-wf-system"

   version := "1.0"
   scalaVersion := "2.12.2"
   libraryDependencies ++= Seq(
    "com.typesafe.akka" %% "akka-actor" % "2.5.9"
    )
   ```

3. Create WF DataStore System:

   WFDataSystem.scala:

   ```
   package com.packt.publishing.wfsystem
   import akka.actor.Actor
   sealed class WFDataMessage
   case object WFStoreData extends WFDataMessage
   case object WFRetrieveData extends WFDataMessage
   class WFDataSystem extends Actor {
     override def receive: Receive = {
       case WFStoreData    => println("WF DataStore: Storing Data")
       case WFRetrieveData => println("WF DataStore: Retrieving Data")
     }
   }
   ```

4. Create the WF Admin System:

   WFAdminSystem.scala:

   ```
   package com.packt.publishing.wfsystem
   import akka.actor.{Actor, Props}
   ```

```scala
sealed trait WFMessage
case object   WFAdminLogin          extends WFMessage
case object   WFAdminFileUpload  extends WFMessage
case object   WFAdminWFUI             extends WFMessage
case object   WFAdminWFResults  extends WFMessage
case object   WFAdminSignout          extends WFMessage
class WFAdminSystem extends Actor{
  override def receive: Receive = {
    case WFAdminLogin       => println("WF Admin: Login")
    case WFAdminFileUpload =>
      println("WF Admin: FileUpload")
      val wfDataStoreSystem1 =
       context.actorOf(Props[WFDataSystem], "WFAdminData1")
      wfDataStoreSystem1 ! WFStoreData
      context.stop(wfDataStoreSystem1)
    case WFAdminWFUI        =>
      println("WF Admin: WFUI")
      val wfDataStoreSystem2 =
       context.actorOf(Props[WFDataSystem], "WFAdminData2")
      wfDataStoreSystem2 ! WFRetrieveData
      context.stop(wfDataStoreSystem2)
    case WFAdminWFResults  => println("WF Admin: WFUI Results")
    case WFAdminSignout     => println("WF Admin: Singout")
  }
}
```

5. Create the WF User System:

WFUserSystem.scala:

```scala
package com.packt.publishing.wfsystem
import akka.actor.{Actor, Props}
sealed class WFUserMessage
case object   WFUserLogin     extends WFUserMessage
case object   WFUSerInputs    extends WFUserMessage
case object   WFUserResults  extends WFUserMessage
case object   WFUserSignout  extends WFUserMessage
class WFUserSystem extends Actor {
  override def receive: Receive = {
    case WFUserLogin    => println("WF User: Login")
    case WFUSerInputs   =>
      println("WF User: Inputs Date or City or Postcode")
      val wfDataStoreSystem =
       context.actorOf(Props[WFDataSystem], "WFUserData")
      wfDataStoreSystem ! WFRetrieveData
      context.stop(wfDataStoreSystem)
    case WFUserResults => println("WF User: Results")
```

```
            case WFUserSignout => println("WF User: Singout")
      }
    }
```

6. Create the WF Admin System app to test the WF Admin System flow:

   WFAdminSystemApp.scala:

   ```
   package com.packt.publishing.wfsystem
   import akka.actor.{ActorSystem, Props}
   object WFAdminSystemApp extends App {
      val wfSystem = ActorSystem("WFSystem")
      val wfAdmin = wfSystem.actorOf(Props[WFAdminSystem],"WFAdmin")
      wfAdmin ! WFAdminLogin
      wfAdmin ! WFAdminFileUpload
      Thread.sleep(1000)
      wfAdmin ! WFAdminWFUI
      Thread.sleep(1000)
      wfAdmin ! WFAdminWFResults
      wfAdmin ! WFAdminSignout
      wfSystem.terminate
   }
   ```

7. When we execute this app, we will observe the following output:

   ```
   WF Admin: Login
   WF Admin: FileUpload
   WF DataStore: Storing Data
   WF Admin: WFUI
   WF DataStore: Retrieving Data
   WF Admin: WFUI Results
   WF Admin: Singout
   ```

   By observing this output, we can understand the WF Admin System flow and how it interacts with the WF Data Store System to store or retrieve data.

8. Create the WF User System app to test the WF User System flow:

   WFUserSystemApp.scala:

   ```
   package com.packt.publishing.wfsystem
   import akka.actor.{ActorSystem, Props}
   object WFUserSystemApp extends App {
      val wfSystem = ActorSystem("WFSystem")
      val wfUser = wfSystem.actorOf(Props[WFUserSystem],"WFUser")
      wfUser ! WFUserLogin
      wfUser ! WFUSerInputs
   ```

```
    Thread.sleep(1000)
    wfUser ! WFUserResults
    wfUser ! WFUserSignout
    wfSystem.terminate
}
```

9. When we execute this app, we will observe the following output:

```
WF User: Login
WF User: Inputs Date or City or Postcode
WF DataStore: Retrieving Data
WF User: Results
WF User: Singout
```

By observing this output, we can understand the WF User System flow and how it interacts with WF Data Store System to retrieve data.

Summary

In this chapter, we discussed what the Akka Toolkit is and its features and benefits. We developed a couple of simple examples.

We also discussed how the Akka Toolkit eases the development of Reactive systems. Akka is an open source runtime and middleware framework designed to develop distributed and Reactive System, easily.

Akka is a toolkit, not a framework. By design, it supports distributed and Reactive features. It is not just an implementation of the Actor Model. It supports many other features, in terms of Akka Modules or Akka Extensions.

Let's continue our journey into building a WF Reactive System using the Lightbend Reactive Ecosystem in the coming chapters.

5
Adding Reactiveness with RxScala

In this chapter, we will discuss **Reactive Extensions** (**RX**) and one of the RX implementations—RxScala.

RxScala stands for **Reactive Extensions for Scala**. RxScala is an adapter on top of **RxJava** (**Reactive Extensions for Java**).

In this chapter, we will discuss the following topics:

- What are Reactive Extensions and RxScala?
- What are the building blocks of RxScala?
- How the RxScala components are connected
- How to develop Reactive applications using RxScala
- How to use Subscriber to utilize the back-pressure feature
- RxScala Marble diagrams
- Limitations of RxScala

To understand these Rx frameworks well, it's good to go through their source code at the following URLs:

- RxScala GitHub repository:
  `https://github.com/ReactiveX/RxScala`
- RxJava GitHub repository:
  `https://github.com/ReactiveX/RxJava`

We can find more information on RxScala from its official website at `http://reactivex.io/rxscala/`.

Introduction to RxScala

Nowadays, developing an application is not that much easier by following old design principles, design patterns, architectures, and technologies. We should develop our new systems to do the following things:

- Our system should support today's multicore processor architecture
- Our system should support Multicluster, Distributed, and Cloud environments
- Our system should support today's big data environments
- Our system should support **very quick response** to customer requests
- Our system should support high traffic or a huge amount of users; that is, it should support heavy loads
- Our system should be available all the time
- Our system should utilize resources effectively

A Reactive system supports all these features easily. In this book, a Reactive system means developing our system or application by following the **Reactive Manifesto** principles.

A Reactive system may be a Reactive web application, Reactive microservice, and more.

To support all the preceding features, our programming paradigm should be able to do the following things:

- Write code to support low latency, high scalability (both scale-up and scale-out), and 24/7 availability (100% up-time)
- Write code to support concurrency and parallelism easily and utilize today's multicore processor architecture effectively

- Write code to support asynchronous and non-blocking approaches easily
- Develop Responsive applications
- Develop Resilient applications; they should be able to recover from failures (self-healing)
- Write Message-Driven code easily
- Write Event-Driven code easily

In this chapter, we will pick up on only one kind of RP implementation, that is, Reactive Extensions. We will discuss this with RxScala.

Reactive Extensions

RX (also known as ReactiveX), or Reactive Extensions is an API or library from Microsoft for asynchronous and event-based stream programming.

Initially, Erik Meijer from Microsoft implemented this RX library for C# to resolve the Observer pattern issues. Later, the Netflix team developed a new library by implementing that RX concept for RxJava. As of today, Netflix is using RxJava for its backend system development.

Reactive Extensions takes the best things or positive points from the Observer pattern and Iterator pattern and supports the **FP** (**Functional Programming**) paradigm:

ReactiveX = Observer Pattern + Iterator Pattern + FP

Initially, Microsoft Corporation implemented this RX library for .NET as Rx.NET. Later, Netflix developed a Java library by implementing Microsoft's RX library as RxJava.

 Here, **Rx.NET** stands for **Reactive Extensions for .NET** and **RxJava** stands for **Reactive Extensions for Java**.

The following are the main goals of Microsoft's RX library:

- To support composability with listeners
- To support **RP** (**Reactive Programming**)

In the Observer pattern, it is not possible to compose listeners. When we compose listeners, we can solve some complex problems easily:

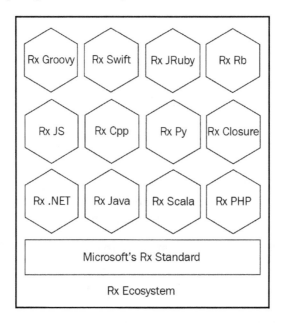

RP is a kind of declarative programming *that reacts to changes in a timely manner*. It gives us the following benefits:

- The ability to express data flows easily
- The ability to propagate changes automatically

Refer to `Chapter 1`, *Getting Started With Reactive and Functional Programming*, for more information on this.

Understanding Rx implementations

After Microsoft successfully implemented Rx for the .NET platform, Netflix implemented Rx implementation for Java, that is, RxJava. Then, following this RxJava, everybody started implementing Rx implementations for all JVM and non-JVM languages.

Currently, there are plenty of RX implementations in the market. Take a look at the following diagram:

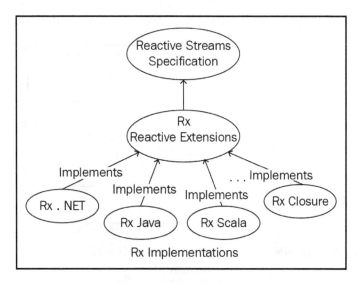

The following are some important RX implementations:

- **RxJava**: Reactive Extensions (RX) implementation for the Java language
- **RxScala**: Reactive Extensions (RX) implementation for the Scala language
- **RxPHP**: Reactive Extensions (RX) implementation for the PHP language
- **RxCPP**: Reactive Extensions (RX) implementation for the CPP language
- **Rx.NET**: Reactive Extensions (RX) implementation for the .NET platform
- **RxJS**: Reactive Extensions (RX) implementation for JavaScript

The following are some other important implementations:

- **RxAndroid**: Reactive Extensions (RX) for Android (`https://github.com/ReactiveX/RxAndroid`)
- **RxJava-JDBC**: Reactive Extensions (RX) for Java JDBC (`https://github.com/davidmoten/rxjava-jdbc`)
- **RxNetty**: Reactive Extensions (RX) for Netty (`https://github.com/ReactiveX/RxNetty`)
- **RxJavaFX**: Reactive Extensions (RX) for JavaFX (`https://github.com/ReactiveX/RxJavaFX`)

RxScala

RxScala stands for Reactive Extensions for Scala. Rx Scala is an adapter on top of RxJava. The following diagram shows the relationship between RxJava and RxScala:

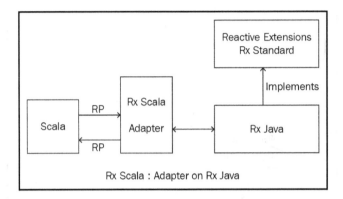

Rx Scala : Adapter on Rx Java

In this chapter, we will use the latest stable version of RxScala—0.26.5, so we will need to use the following SBT configuration in our examples:

```
libraryDependencies += "io.reactivex" %% "rxscala" % "0.26.5"
```

We can find the latest RxScala library information at its bintray at https://bintray.com/reactivex/RxJava/RxScala.

In other words, RxScala is just a wrapper on top of Netflix's RxJava, as shown in the following diagram, and this wrapper was created by Samuel Gruetter:

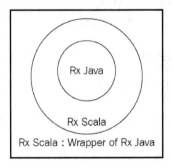

Rx Scala : Wrapper of Rx Java

Samuel Gruetter has a BSc degree at EPFL. As a student assistant and member of the Scala team at EPFL, he developed RxScala. He was also a teaching assistant in *Principles of Reactive Programming* at Coursera.

We can observe the following code snippet from the RxScala `Subscription` trait. It has a wrapper of RxJava's `Subscription` function calls:

```
trait Subscription {

  // Other code
  def unsubscribe() = {
    asJavaSubscription.unsubscribe()
  }

  def isUnsubscribed = {
    asJavaSubscription.isUnsubscribed
  }

}
```

RxScala's `Subscription.unsubscribe()` is just a wrapper of RxJava's `Subscription.unsubscribe()`. RxScala is not doing anything new; it just wraps the RxJava and provides the Scala syntax features to Scala-based applications.

Reactive Extensions quickly emerged as a cross-language specification to bring RP into the market. RxJava has become a base specification for all JVM languages, as shown here:

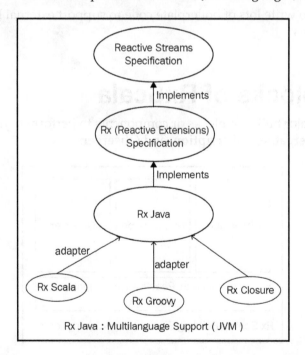

Benefits of Reactive Extensions

Rx implementations provide the following benefits with RP:

- We can write simple, elegant, and more expressive asynchronous and event stream programming
- It provides an easy way to design asynchronous data flows
- It provides easy-to-write Event-Driven applications
- It is easy to work with
- It supports backpressure

Limitations of Reactive Extensions

Apart from its benefits, an RX framework has the following limitations or drawbacks:

- It does not support Message-Driven architecture
- We will lose all the benefits we get from Message-Driven architecture, such as loose coupling between components, Location Transparency, and immutability by design
- We need to write lots of boilerplate code to support external Message-Driven components

Building blocks of RxScala

RXScala has three major building blocks or components to perform asynchronous stream programming—**Observable**, **Subscription**, and **Observer**:

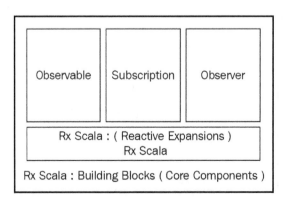

Here, we can observe the following things:

- **Observable** works as a producer; that means it emits the data
- **Observer** works as a consumer; that means it consumes the data
- **Subscription** works as a channel between **Observable** and **Observer** to emit and consume data through this channel

The following diagram shows the relationship between RxScala components and how they work with each other:

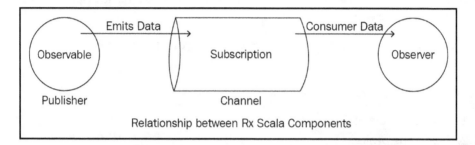

Relationship between Rx Scala Components

There are two more components to perform the asynchronous data stream processing:

- Subscriber
- Scheduler

Understanding the Observable

It is the `Observable` interface that implements the Reactive pattern. It has the `subscribe()` method to subscribe the `Observer` or `Subscriber` to send items and notifications to them:

```
observable.subscribe(observer)   // To subscribe an Observer
observable.subscribe(subscriber) // To subscribe an Subscriber
```

An `Observable[T]` instance is responsible for accepting all subscriptions and notifying all observers and subscribers for that item. The `subscribe()` method does the following:

- It stores a reference to the `Observer` in a Collection object, such as a `List[T]` object.

- This will return a reference to the Subscription interface. This will enable the Observers to unsubscribe that is, to stop receiving items and notifications before the Observable stops sending them, which also invokes the Observer.onCompleted() method.

Developing RxScala HelloWorld with an Observable

As with our other chapters, we will start RxScala with a simple and standard *HelloWorld* example. In this section, we will develop a basic application and extend it further in the coming sections.

In this example, we will concentrate on only two components out of the three: Observable and Subscription.

Perform the following steps to develop and explore it:

1. Create a Scala SBT project in the IDE.
2. Name the project rxscala-helloworld-app.
3. Add the RxScala library to build a .sbt file, as shown in the following code snippet:

   build.sbt:

   ```
   name := "rxscala-helloworld-app"
   version := "0.1"
   scalaVersion := "2.12.3"
   libraryDependencies += "io.reactivex" %% "rxscala" % "0.26.5"
   ```

4. Develop HelloWorldApp, as shown here:

   RxScalaHelloWorld_With_Observable_Subscription.scala:

   ```
   package com.packt.publishing.rxscala.hello

   import rx.lang.scala.Observable

   object RxScalaHelloWorld_With_Observable_Subscription extends App {
     val helloWorld: String = "Hello RxScala World!"
     val observable = Observable.from(helloWorld)

     observable.subscribe { msg =>
       print(s"$msg")
     }
   ```

```
}
```

Here, we have imported the RxScala `Observable`, available from
the `rx.lang.scala` package:

```
def from[T](iterable: Iterable[T]): Observable[T]
```

This preceding method converts an Iterable into an Observable. In our example, a
simple Java `String` is an Iterable, and the preceding method will convert this into
a RxScala `Observable`:

```
def subscribe(onNext: T => Unit): Subscription
```

The preceding method creates a subscription and executes an `onNext` function on
the emitted data by `Observable`.

5. When we run this Scala app, we will get the following output:

```
Hello RxScala World!
```

The `subscribe()` function picks up one letter at a time from `Hello RxScala World!` and
prints it to the console.

As we are using `print(s"$msg")`, it prints letter by letter in the same line. If we
use `println(s"$msg")` instead, we will see each letter in a new line. Just verify it for your
clarification.

Observer

`Observer` provides a technique for receiving push-based notifications. It will subscribe
with an `Observable` using its `subscribe()` method.

Once an `Observer` makes a call to an `Observable.subscribe()` method and the
subscription is done, the `Observable` calls the `Observer.onNext()` method to provide
notifications to that `Observer`.

Asynchronous data stream processing may finish either successfully or with some errors. If it's done successfully, `Observable` will make a call to the `Observer.onCompleted()` method. If it's done with errors, `Observable` will make a call to the `Observer.onError()` method.

> A well-behaved `Observable` will call an Observer's `onCompleted` or `onError` methods exactly once.

Extending RxScala HelloWorld with Observer

In the preceding example, we explored only two RxScala components—`Observable` and `Subscription`. Now, it's time to explore all three components with the same example. We will use the same project and create a new Scala app for this purpose.

Perform the following steps to develop and explore it:

1. Develop `HelloWorldApp` as shown here:

   RxScalaHelloWorld_With_Observable_Subscription_Observer.scala:

   ```scala
   package com.packt.publishing.rxscala.hello

   import rx.lang.scala.Observable
   import rx.lang.scala.Observer
   import scala.language.{implicitConversions, postfixOps}

   object RxScalaHelloWorld_With_Observable_Subscription_Observer
     extends App {

     val helloWorld: String = "Hello RxScala World!"

     val observable = Observable.from(helloWorld)

     val observer = new Observer[Char] {
       override def onNext(char: Char): Unit = {
         print(char)
         if(char == '!') println("")
       }

       override def onError(error: Throwable): Unit = {
         println("Executing onError...")
   ```

```
      error.printStackTrace()
    }

    override def onCompleted(): Unit = {
      println("Executing onCompleted...")
    }
  }

  observable.subscribe(observer)

}
```

2. Execute the Scala App and observe the results, as follows:

```
Hello RxScala World!
Observer: Executing onCompleted...
```

In the following code snippet, we have implemented `Observer`:

```
val observer = new Observer[Char] {
  override def onNext(char: Char): Unit = ...

  override def onError(error: Throwable): Unit = ...

  override def onCompleted(): Unit = ...
}
```

Just as `Observable` sends `Char` one by one into `Subscription`, `Observer` should also do the same; for instance, `Observer[Char]`.

A `Subscription` is created between `Observable` and `Observer`, as follows:

```
observable.subscribe(observer)
```

Subscriber

This is an extension of the `Observer` trait, which adds the following two new features:

- **Subscription handling**: This has the implementation of the `unsubscribe()`, `isUnsubscribed()`, and `add()` methods to take care of the handling subscription process.
- **Back-pressure handling**: This has the implementation of the `onStart()` and `request()` methods to take care of the handling back-pressure process.

Once a `Subscriber` makes a call to an `Observable.subscribe()` method and the subscription is done, the `Observable` calls the `Subscriber.onNext()` method to provide notifications to that `Subscriber`. The asynchronous data stream processing may either finish it successfully or have some errors. If it's done successfully, `Observable` will make a call to the `Subscriber.onCompleted()` method. If it's done with errors, `Observable` will make a call to the `Subscriber.onError()` method.

> A well-behaved `Observable` will call an Observer's `onCompleted` or `onError` methods only once.

Extending RxScala HelloWorld with Subscriber

In the preceding example, we have explored all three RxScala components—`Observable`, `Subscription`, and `Observer`—very well. I hope that you now have a clear idea about how these three components interact with each other to perform asynchronous data stream processing.

One point to note about `Observer` is that it does not support `Subscription` and back-pressure handling methods. We should use `Subscriber` for this purpose.

`Subscriber` extends the `Observer` with the following two new features:

- Subscription handling
- Back-pressure handling

Now it's time to explore **backpressure** with the same example. We will use the same project and create a new Scala app for this purpose.

Perform the following steps to develop and explore it:

1. Develop `HelloWorldApp`, as follows:

   RxScalaHelloWorld_With_Observable_Subscription_Subscriber.scala:

   ```
   package com.packt.publishing.rxscala.hello

   import rx.lang.scala.Observable
   import rx.lang.scala.Observer
   import scala.language.{implicitConversions, postfixOps}

   object RxScalaHelloWorld_With_Observable_Subscription_ Subscriber
   ```

```
    extends App {

  val helloWorld: String = "Hello RxScala World!"

  val observable = Observable.from(helloWorld)

  val subscriber = new Observer[Char] {
    override def onNext(char: Char): Unit = {
      print(char)
      if(char == '!') println("")
    }

    override def onError(error: Throwable): Unit = {
      println("Subscriber : Executing onError...")
      error.printStackTrace()
    }

    override def onCompleted(): Unit = {
      println("Subscriber : Executing onCompleted...")
    }
  }

  observable.subscribe(subscriber)

}
```

2. Execute the Scala app and observe the following results:

Hello RxScala World!
Subscriber: Executing onCompleted...

Here, we have implemented Observer, as shown here:

```
val subscriber = new Subscriber[Char] {
  override def onNext(char: Char): Unit = ...

  override def onError(error: Throwable): Unit = ...

  override def onCompleted(): Unit = ...
}
```

Just as Observable sends Char one by one into Subscription, Subscriber should also do the same; for instance, Subscriber[Char].

A Subscription is created between Observable and Subscriber, as follows:

```
observable.subscribe(subscriber)
```

Subscription

A subscription is returned from all `Observable.subscribe()` methods to allow unsubscribing. It supports `unsubscribe()` to stop receiving notifications on the `Observer` that was registered when the subscription was received.

Scheduler

The main goal of the Scheduler component is to take care of scheduling threads. It has the following methods to support this scheduling:

- `schedule()`: This schedules a unit of task for execution
- `scheduleRec()`: This schedules a unit of task for recursively repeated execution
- `schedulePeriodically()`: This schedules a cancelable unit of task to be executed periodically

It manages a set of worker threads to take care of the scheduling threads for both the `Observable` and `Observer` components.

RxScala Marble diagrams

This section is a continuation of the *Marble diagrams* section of Chapter 1, *Getting Started with Reactive and Functional Programming*. Refer to that section to understand what a Marble diagram is and its rules and benefits.

In this section, we will discuss the following things:

- How to represent Marble diagrams for RxScala components
- How to represent Marble diagrams for RxScala basic operations

The following diagram shows what our RxScala application's input Observable looks like:

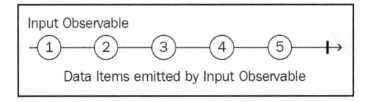

An input `Observable` (that is, a data stream) is represented, as shown in the following diagram; when the `Observable` (the input data stream) emits the data elements, its associated Observer's `onNext ()` function is executed to take data elements one by one to apply the data transformation:

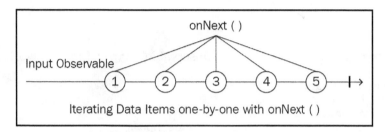

An `Observer` that is completed successfully is represented as follows. In the following diagram, the `onNext ()` function represents iterating elements one by one from the input `Observable`. When it successfully completes iterating all input data elements, it calls the `onCompleted()` function, as shown in the following diagram:

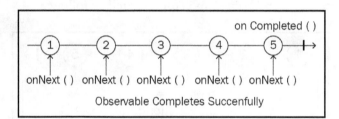

We can represent an `Observer` that is completed in the middle of an iteration with failures; this means that it throws some errors, as follows. In the following diagram, the `onNext ()` function represents iterating elements one by one from the input `Observable`. When it completes with some errors at a given input data element, it calls its `onError ()` function, as shown in the following diagram:

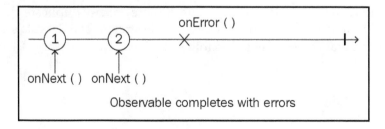

RxScala's map() function

Like the Scala language, RxScala also has a `map()` function. In RxScala, Observable's `map()` function returns an `Observable` that applies the given function to each item emitted by an `Observable` and emits the result. It is defined as follows:

```
def map[R](func: T => R): Observable[R]
```

The following example demonstrates how Observable's `map()` function works:

RxScalaMapFunctionExample.scala:

```
import rx.lang.scala.Observable
object RxScalaMapFunctionExample extends App {

  val observable = Observable.just(1)

  observable.map(x => x)
}
```

RxScala's `map()` function Marble diagram is represented as follows:

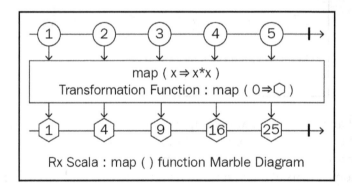

RxScala's `distinct()` function picks up each element from the given input Observable (data stream) and returns only distinct elements. If there are any duplicate elements, they will be removed from the resulting output Observable stream. The RxScala's `distinct` function Marble diagram is represented as follows:

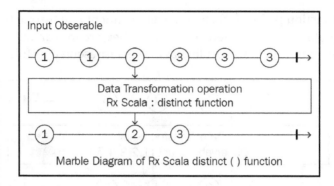

Marble Diagram of Rx Scala distinct ( ) function

RxScala's `first()` function picks up the first available element from the given input Observable (data stream) and returns it to output an Observable stream. RxScala's `first()` function Marble diagram is represented as follows:

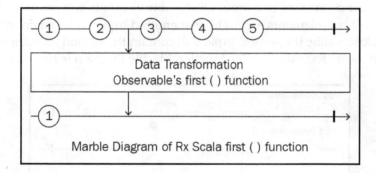

Marble Diagram of Rx Scala first ( ) function

RxScala's `last()` function picks up each and every element one by one from the given input Observable (data stream) and returns only the last element to output an Observable stream. RxScala's `last()` function Marble diagram is represented as follows:

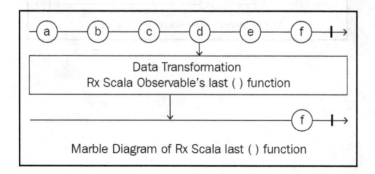

Marble Diagram of Rx Scala last ( ) function

RxScala's `just()` function picks up each and every element one by one from the given input Observable (data stream) and returns them as they are into an output Observable stream. RxScala's `just()` function Marble diagram is represented as follows:

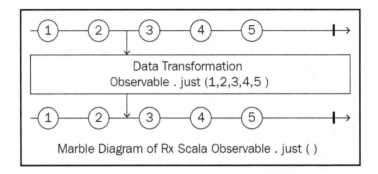

RxScala's `zip()` function takes two input Observable elements and returns an Observable that emits tuples of two elements each. The first emitted tuple will contain the first element of each source Observable, the second tuple will contain the second element of each source Observable, and so on. RxScala's `zip()` function Marble diagram is represented as follows:

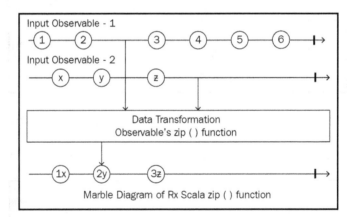

Summary

In this chapter, we discussed RxScala basics, its building blocks, and features. It is just a wrapper on top of Netflix's RxJava. RxScala has three main building blocks or core components, that is, `Observable`, `Subscription`, and `Observer`, and two more components, that is, `Subscriber` and `Scheduler`.

We have developed a simple *HelloWorld* example to explore the building blocks of RxScala. As it has lots of limitations, we cannot use it to implement our Reactive system. Let's move on to the next chapter to understand how to solve these limitations using Akka Streams.

6
Extending Applications with Play

In this chapter, we will discuss what Play Framework is and how to develop Reactive Web Applications using Scala, Akka, and Play Framework.

In this book, we will use the latest version of Play Framework, 2.6.11, which was released in July 2017. It requires a minimum of JDK 1.8, SBT 0.13.15, and Scala 2.11.x or 2.12.x.

Play is a very flexible framework such that it does not force developers to use a predefined flow/components/approach. We can use the best suitable approach to develop our applications.

Its official website is https://www.playframework.com/ and you can find its source code on GitHub at https://github.com/playframework/playframework.

In this chapter, we will learn the following concepts:

- What is Play Framework and what are its features, benefits, and building blocks?
- Play Architecture and its Project structure
- Play Framework simple examples
- How to use Twirl's Scala Templates in Play Framework
- How to integrate Play Framework with Akka Toolkit
- Extend our WeatherForecasting Application using Play Framework

Introduction to Play Framework

In this section, we will introduce you to some of the important and basic theoretical concepts of Play Framework.

It is an open source framework licensed under the Apache License 2.0.

What is Play Framework?

Play Framework is a full stack modern open source and Reactive Web Framework for Java and Scala languages from Lightbend (formerly known as Typesafe).

It is based on modular, asynchronous, and non-blocking architecture. Play 1.x was written in Java. Play 2.x was rewritten from scratch in Scala language. It has native support for Scala language.

It supports the **MVC** (**Model-View-Controller**) architecture. It supports **Dependency Injection** (**DI**) using the Guice framework and uses Twirl to support View Templates. Play Framework's View Templates need some Scala code.

Play Framework makes it easy to build web applications with Java and Scala. Play is based on a lightweight, stateless, web-friendly architecture.

Built on Akka Toolkit, Play Framework provides predictable and minimal resource consumption (CPU, memory, and threads) for highly Scalable, distributed, highly available, low latency, and Reactive Web Applications or Reactive Systems or Reactive microservices.

Features of Play Framework

Play Framework has the following best features to develop Reactive Web Applications easily:

- Open source.
- Supports DI.
- Uses Twirl (Scala) as a View Template engine.
- By default, Play Framework uses Google Guice to support the DI feature. However, we can replace it with our required framework.
- Supports the stateless HTTP REST API.
- Supports JSON extensively.

- JSON is a first-class citizen.
- Supports hot reloading to ease development and improve productivity.
- Built on Akka Toolkit.
- Supports I18N, WebSocket, **Server-Side Events** (**SSE**), HTTP Streaming, non-blocking IO, and so on.
- Supports the JBoss Netty Server.
- Built-in support for the SBT tool.
- Uses Ivy to manage a local Maven repository.
- Supports modules (or extensions).
- Uses the Akka Streams API for asynchronous data streaming.
- Multi-environment configurations.

Benefits of Play Framework

When we compare it with other web frameworks, Play Framework has the following benefits:

- Open source modern web framework.
- Developer-friendly Full Stack Web Framework.
- Displays errors on the browser itself with friendly, useful, and meaningful error messages.
- No restart of the server or application.
- More productivity with hot-reloading.
- Follows asynchronous and non-blocking architecture.
- Supports hot-reloading so there is no need to restart the server or application.
- Easy to extend with modules.
- Strong Typesafe framework. All components are type safe—Scala or Java code, View Templates, and Routes.
- It follows a stateless HTTP nature and does not support sharing states.
- Lightweight, a stateless and user-friendly web framework.
- Highly scalable, concurrent, parallel, and available framework.
- Highly productive web framework.
- Easy to test the components.
- By design, Play supports responsiveness. Easy to develop responsive web applications.

- *Responsive = asynchronous + non-blocking.*
- By design, Play is Reactive because it is built on Akka under the hood. Easy to develop Reactive Web Applications.
- It follows modular architecture. Easy to extend with new modules.
- *Reactive = responsive + resilient (fault tolerant) + elastic + message-driven.*
- Play uses the Actor model to support concurrency using Akka Toolkit.
- Play supports the Java NIO.2 based JBoss Netty server under the hood. It doesn't use the one thread per client request model.
- Event-driven framework with Akka and Netty.
- Java EE application or web servers are not required. It supports embedding a HTTP server (JBoss Netty server).
- Auto-compilation support for JS Frameworks—CoffeeScript, LESS, and many more.
- It has built-in unit testing support.
- Supports multi-environment configurations.

Why Play Framework is so fast?

When we compare Play Framework with other modern web frameworks, Play Framework is so much faster for the following reasons:

- It is built on Akka Toolkit
- It uses the Java NIO.2 API
- Play Framework 2.5.x uses the Java NIO.2 based JBoss Netty Server as the default backend server
- Play Framework 2.6.x uses the Akka HTTP Server as the default backend server
- By default, the Java NIO2 API or the JBoss Netty Server support non-blocking functionality
- By design, it is a responsive web framework (*responsive = asynchronous + non-blocking*)
- By design, it is a reactive web framework (*Reactive = Responsive + Resilient + Elastic + Message-Driven*)
- It does not use a HTTP Request-Response Based Service 3.x API to support asynchronous

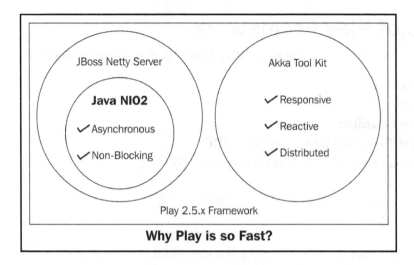

The preceding diagram shows us why Play 2.5.x Framework is so fast. There are mainly two reasons:

- JBoss Netty Server
- Akka Toolkit:

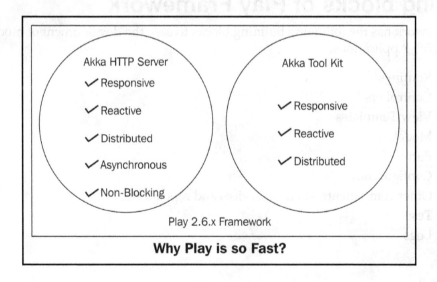

Clients of Play Framework

Popular real-time clients who are using Play Framework extensively include:

- Walmart
- LinkedIn
- The Guardian
- **HM Revenue and Customs (HMRC)**
- **Department for Work and Pensions (DWP)**
- Verison
- Coursera
- Atlassian

 Here we have listed only a few clients for our reference. You can find more at the following link:

`https://www.lightbend.com/case-studies`

Building blocks of Play Framework

Play Framework has the following building blocks to ease the development of modern and Reactive Web Applications:

- Routings
- Controllers
- View Templates
- Model
- Forms
- Configuration
- Other components, such as services and repositories
- Tests
- Logs

Play Routings

The routings file defines all your application Routes. Then, what is a Route? A Route is a link between a client request and a Controller's Action, as shown here:

```
Route = <Client Request>  <Controller Action>

Client Request = <HTTP Request Method>  <Client Request URI>

Controller Action = <Fully Qualified ControllerName>.<FunctionName>

          Play Framework: Route
```

Client Request

Client Request is the combination of both HTTP Request Method and Client Request URI. Take a look at the following table to understand it very well:

Client request parts	Meaning
HTTP request method	We can use any HTTP request methods, such as GET, POST, PUT, and DELETE
Client request URI	This is the URI to identify an application resource uniquely

For instance, GET /helloWorld.

Here GET is the HTTP Request method and /helloWorld is the Client Request URI.

Controller Action

Controller Action contains mainly two parts—one is Play Controller name and another is that Controller's function name. We can represent this as <Fully Qualified Controller Name>.<That Controller's Function Name>. Take a look at the following table and example to understand it very well:

Controller Action parts	Meaning
Fully Qualified Controller Name	Fully qualified means including package name (if any)
Function Name	Any required controller's function or method name

For instance, controllers.HelloWorldDIController.helloWorld

Here `controllers` is a package name, `HelloWorldDIController` is a Play Controller name, `controllers.HelloWorldDIController` is fully qualified controller name. `helloWorld` is that Controller's function name.

Let's observe some Play Framework Routes examples here:

GET	/helloWorld	controllers.HelloWorldController.helloWorld
POST	/books	controllers.BooksController.saveBooks

We can define all application routings in this `Routings` file. We can use a single `Routings` file or multiple `Routings` files.

By default, Play Framework uses the routes filename as the `Routing` filename and it should be available under the `/project-name/conf` folder.

Let's take the following Route to understand the Routing Role in Play Framework.

Routes

In Play Framework, Route is the combination of Client Request and Controller Action, that means each Route contains mainly three parts—first one is HTTP Request method (that is GET), second is Client Request URI (that is `/helloWorld`) and last one or third one is the Controller Action. Consider the following table to understand it completely:

GET	/helloWorld	controllers.HelloWorldController.helloWorld

In Play Framework, each Route from the Routings file does the following activities:

1. When the user (Customer or Client) sends a request to the application, first Play Routing receives that Request.

   Here, the Client HTTP Request is GET `/helloWorld`.

2. Play Routing checks whether the Request is available in the application Routes file(s) or not.

- If found:
    - Try to hand over that request to the matched controller (in this example, `HelloWorldController`)
    - If the matched controller has the defined function, the Routing component hands over that client request to the Controller and leaves it
    - If the matched controller does not have that defined function, it shows the following compilation error on the client browser:

      ```
      Compilation error value helloWorld2 is not a member
      of controllers.HelloWorldNoDIController.
      ```

- If not found:
    - Let's assume that the client sent this Request: `GET /helloWorld2`
    - As this routing is not found in our routes file, it throws the following error on the browser (if required, we should handle it properly to avoid these kinds of error messages shown to the end user):

      ```
      Action Not Found
      For request GET /helloWorld3
      ```

Here, it displays all the available routings that are the content of the routes file:

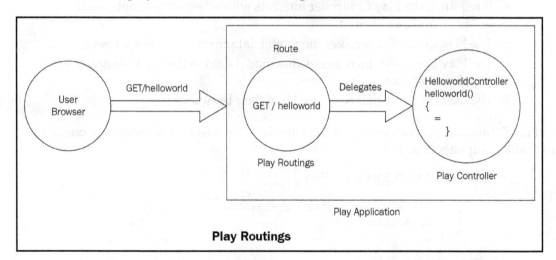

Play Routings

Note that all routes are case-sensitive.

For instance, our routes file has the following entry:

GET	/helloWorld	controllers.HelloWorldController.helloWorld

3. If the user sends a request to `/helloworld`, then the user sees the following error message in their browser:

```
Action Not Found
For request 'GET /helloworld'
```

Play Controllers

Play Controller is a class with a set of related actions. Here Action means a function or method defined in that Controller.

In Play Framework, each Controller does the following activities:

1. When the user (customer or client) sends a request to the application, first Play Routing receives that Request.
2. Play Routing then hands over that request to the matched Controller. It makes a call to that matched Controller's method.
3. Then, Play Controller executes that method.
4. If required, the Play Controller interacts with other components, such as `Utils` and `Service`.
5. The Play Controller receives the model data from other components.
6. The Play Controller then passes that model data to the View Template to populate that data.
7. The users then see that response UI in their browser.

In Play Framework, we can define a Controller by implementing or extending one of the available components, as follows:

- Play 2.3.x/2.4.x/2.5.x Controller:

```
class HomeController extends Controller {
  // Actions
}
```

In Play 2.6.x Framework, a controller is deprecated. We should extend `AbstractController`, `BaseController`, or `InjectedController` instead.

- Play 2.6.x Controller:

```
class HomeController @Inject()
(cc:MessagesControllerComponents)(implicit executionContext:
ExecutionContext)
extends MessagesAbstractController(cc) {
// Actions
}
```

Or:

```
class HelloWorldDIAndScalaFutureController
@Inject()(helloWorldService: THelloWorldService)(cc:
ControllerComponents) extends AbstractController(cc) {
  // Actions
}
MessagesActionBuilder = I18nSupport + MessagesRequestHeader
MessagesControllerComponents = MessagesActionBuilder +
ControllerComponents
```

Use `MessagesControllerComponents` at the controller side and `MessagesRequestHeader` at the View Template side.

View Templates

Play Framework uses the Twirl template engine for its View Components. As Twirl template is a Scala-based typesafe template, Scala developers can write them very easily.

Benefits of Twirl Templates

The various benefits of Twirl Templates are as follows:

- Typesafe
- As it's based on the Scala language, there is no need to learn new technology
- The templates are compiled and evaluated, so if there are any errors, we can see these errors in the browser

We will discuss this more in the *Play Framework View Templates Constructs* section with some simple examples.

Model and Forms

In Play Framework, we use Scala sealed classes, case classes, and case objects to define model objects. Scala case classes are immutable and serializable.

Consider the following code, for example:

```
sealed class Message
case object SuccessMessage extends Message
case object FailureMessage extends Message
```

We also define some Forms using the Play Form API. Refer to the *Play Framework Form-based web application* section of this chapter for more information.

Other components – services and repositories

We use some other user-defined components, such as services, repositories, and `Utils`, to decouple the code from controllers.

We define our business logic in Services and Data Access logic (such as DAO components) in repositories. Services use repositories and controllers use service components.

We will explore these things in detail in the coming examples.

Configuration

We will use the following components to define Play Framework Scala-based SBT projects:

- Routes to define Play routings
- `application.conf` to define Play application configuration
- `plugins.sbt` to define SBT plugins, such as the Play Framework plugin
- The sample `plugins.sbt` file:

```
addSbtPlugin ("com.typesafe.play" % "sbt-plugin" % "2.6.3")
```

- The logging configuration in the `logback.xml` file

- `build.sbt` configuration to define any Play modules, such as the Play WS module and Google Guice module, project name, Scala version and so on, as shown as follows:

  Sample build.sbt file:

  ```
  name := "play-scala-fileupload-app"
  version := "1.0.0"
  lazy val root = (project in file(".")).enablePlugins(PlayScala)
  scalaVersion := "2.12.2"
  libraryDependencies += guice
  libraryDependencies += ws
  Sbt version in build.properties file
  Sample build.properties
  sbt.version=0.13.16
  ```

  You will observe the following while developing our examples in the upcoming sections:

  - `build.properties` and `plugins.sbt` files under the `${PROJECT_HOME}/project` folder
  - `application.conf` and routes files under the `${PROJECT_HOME}/conf` folder

Play Framework View Template constructs

Play Framework uses the Twirl Template engine for its View Components. We will discuss some of the important, useful, and frequently used Twirl Template engine constructs so that we don't get confused while developing Play Framework examples in the upcoming sections.

Twirl View Templates

Play Framework supports different View Templates using the Twirl Template engine. We can even create our own View Template types.

Some of the important Play View Template types are as follows:

- **Scala Template**: `main.scala.html`

  Here we use `main` as the template name and `scala` to identify this as a Scala-based HTML template type.

- **Text Template**: `main.scala.txt`

  Here we use `main` as the template name and `txt` to identify this as a Scala-based Text template type.

- **XML Template**: `main.scala.xml`

  Here we use `main` as the template name and `scala` to identify this as a Scala-based XML template type.

For instance, we have a project with `play-scala-app` as the base directory. Let's assume `PROJECT_HOME = play-scala-app`.

For each template, Play generates a class at `${PROJECT_HOME}/target/scala-2-12/twirl/main/<FQPN>/index.template.scala` using Scala Compiler.

We have a view template, `index.scala.html` at `${PROJECT_HOME}appviewsindex.scala.html`. Here, `index` is a View template name and it is a Scala Template.

Then, Scala compiler generates a class `index` under the `views.html` package name, because we have placed our `index.scala.html` template under the `views` folder and its `html` template.

Similarly, if we use a text template, such as `index.scala.txt`, Scala compiler generates the `index` class under the `views.txt` package name.

Some people may use different project structures instead of just `views`. For instance, let's assume we have placed our `index.scala.html` at `${PROJECT_HOME}appcompacktpublishingviewsindex.scala.html`.

Then, Scala Compiler generates the `index` class under
the `com.packt.publishing.views.html` package name.

If we observe our generated `index.template.scala` class, we can see the following code
snippet:

```
package views.html
class definition extends BaseScalaTemplate ... {
  apply():play.twirl.api.HtmlFormat.Appendable = {
  }
}
package views.txt
class definition extends BaseScalaTemplate ... {
  apply():play.twirl.api.TxtFormat.Appendable = {
  }
}
```

We will use the following:

- `play.twirl.api.TxtFormat.Appendable` for Text View Template
- `play.twirl.api.HtmlFormat.Appendable` for Text HTML Template
- `play.twirl.api.XmlFormat.Appendable` for Text XML Template

In the Twirl Scala View Template, the @ sign plays a very key role. We use it to write both
Twirl Constructs and Scala code in Play's View Templates.

Twirl Template Constructs

Let's explore some of the Twirl Template Engine constructs now:

- **Twirl Imports**: We use this at sign @ to import any external classes or objects into
  the Play View template.

  For instance, we can import our `UserData` into our View template, as shown here:

  ```
  @import model.UserData
  ```

  Here, `UserData` is a case class or object that is available under the `model`
  directory directly under our `${PROJECT_HOME}` app.

- **Twirl comments**: We can write comments in Play View Templates using `@*` and `*@` constructs, as follows:

```
@* End of HTML Form block *@
```

Here, `@*` denotes the beginning of the comment and `*@` denotes the end of the comment.

- **Twirl If condition**: We can use the `@if` construct to write a Twirl `If` condition, as follows:

```
@if(result) {
  <h3>Some HTML Code snippnet</h3>
} else {
  <h2>Other HTML Code snippnet</h2>
}
```

The Twirl template does not support Scala/Java, such as the `else...if` block. We should use the nested `if` block to solve this issue.

- **Twirl for comprehension**: We can use the `@for` construct to write Twirl for comprehension, which is shown as follows:

```
@for(user <- usersList){
  <tr>
  <td>@user.name</td>
  <td>@user.age</td>
  </tr>
}
```

We will discuss some more Twirl constructs as and when we use them in the upcoming sections.

Architecture of Play Framework

In this section, we will discuss the typical architecture of a Play Framework web application. Here, some components are mandatory for all applications, such as the routes file, Controller, View Templates, and so on; some are optional:

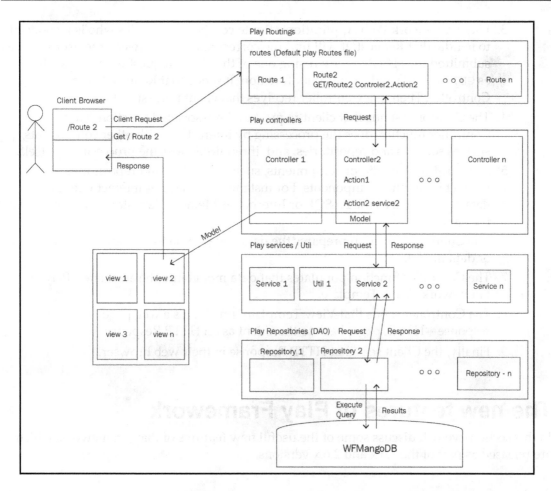

We can observe the following steps in any Play Framework Web Application:

1. The users access a Play Web Application, using the application URL and a web browser.
2. When the user sends a HTTP request to a Play Web Application, such as /route2 in our example, first that request reaches the Play Framework's Routing component (the default route filename is routes). However, we can use any name. Some applications may have more than one route file; finally, they have one top-level routes file.

3. Play Framework Web Application's Route component decides who is responsible to handle that Request. It will find the correct mapping between the user who has submitted the HTTP request (using one of the HTTP request methods, such as GET or POST) and a Controller function. It sends that Request to that Controller. Then that Controller receives that client request.

4. The Controller sends that client request to the associated function. That Controller function does the processing by interacting with other components, such as services and repositories, and, if required, does the processing by itself.

5. Some utility or mediator components, such as services and repositories, may interact with other components. For instance, repositories interact with external data stores, such as the NoSQL or Internal In-Memory data store, to get or update the data.

6. The Controller function prepares the data and populates it to an associated model or data model.

7. The Controller function populates that data model into the associated Play Frameworks View Template.

8. The Controller sends that View Template (finally, it's a web page response—HTML page) back to the Client as an HTTP Response.

9. Finally, the Client sees that HTTP Response in their web browser.

The new features of Play Framework

In this section, we will discuss some of the useful new features of Play Framework, which are released as part of the 2.5.x and 2.6.x versions.

Play Framework 2.5.x features

Play Framework 2.5.x has the following new or updated features:

- It supports new streaming APIs based on Akka Streams
- There is full support for Java 8
- This supports other logging frameworks
- This supports Play performance improvements
- This supports Play WS API improvements

For more details, go to the following Lightbend page: https://www.playframework.com/documentation/2.5.x/Highlights25.

Play Framework 2.6.x features

Play Framework 2.6.x has the following new or updated features:

- Support for both Scala 2.12.2 and Scala 2.11.11.
- Play new default backend server: Akka HTTP server.

  Prior to Play 2.6.x, it had the JBoss Netty server as the default backend server. From 2.6.x onwards, it has a new default backend server, Akka HTTP server, which is built on the `akka-http` module. It still supports the JBoss Netter server with some configuration changes.

- If required, we can still use old Netty Server by changing the default configurations, as follows:

```
lazy val root = (project in file("."))
  .enablePlugins(PlayScala, PlayNettyServer)
  .disablePlugins(PlayAkkaHttpServer)
```

- Play Framework API improvements.
- Improvements for Play WSClient, JSON, Testing, FileUpload, and so on.
- Play Global Application instance (`Play.current`) is deprecated to support `Global State Free` applications.
- Play has support for HTTP/2 on the Akka HTTP server.
- Supports Injectable Twirl Templates:

```
@this(wfc: WFComponent)
@(wf: WeatherForecasting)
@{wfc.render(wf)}
```

 Further details can be found at the following Lightbend URL:
https://www.playframework.com/documentation/2.6.x/Highlights26

Play Application project structure

Before starting Play Framework Web Applications, I feel it's good to understand the Play Application/Project structure. If you are new to this framework, this section is mandatory to understand this chapter's examples.

Like any other applications, we can create Play Projects in many ways. We will use two of them in this book:

- Using an IDE such as IntelliJ IDE or Eclipse IDE
- Using Lightbend (typesafe) Activator Templates (old approach now)
- Using Giter8 Templates
- Using Play Framework GitHub repositories

When we generate our Play Framework skeleton project using one of the available techniques, we will observe the following main folders:

- Top-level project name
- Under the project, we will have the following main folders:
    - app: Here, we will place all our Project source code
    - conf: Here, we will place all our Project configuration
    - project: Here, we will place all our Project related SBT configuration
    - test: Here, we will place all our Project unit tests
    - it: Here, we will place all our Project integration tests
- Under the app folder, we can find the following things.

We can use one of the following methods in our projects. Both are recommended, but it's up to you which one you choose:

First way:

- `controllers`: Play Framework application controller components
- `services`: Play Framework application service components
- `repositories`: Play Framework application repository or DAO components
- `models`: Play Framework application Data Model or Model components
- `views`: Play Framework application View Template components

Second way:

- `com.packt.publishing.wfsystem.controllers`: Controller components
- `com.packt.publishing.wfsystem.services`: Service components
- `com.packt.publishing.wfsystem.repositories`: Repository or DAO components
- `com.packt.publishing.wfsystem.models`: Data Model or Model components
- `com.packt.publishing.wfsystem.views`: View Template components

 We can find Play Framework sample projects at:
`https://github.com/playframework?utf8=%E2%9C%93&q=&type=&languag e=scala`

The following diagram shows the complete Play Scala SBT-based project structure:

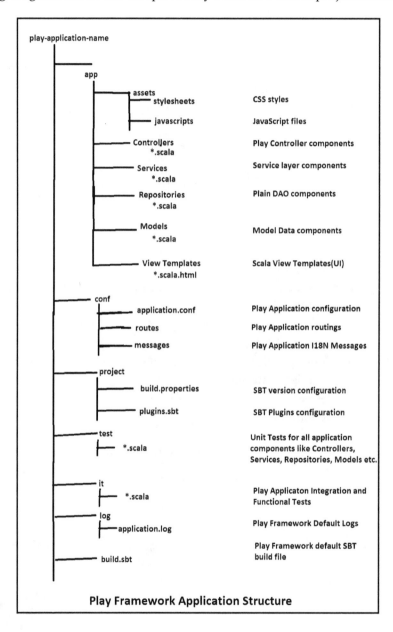

Play Framework Application Structure

Play/Scala HelloWorld example

In this section, we will start learning Play Framework with our simple old-style HelloWorld Web Application example.

This `HelloWorld` example is using Play 2.6.11 without Play DI with Scala 2.12.4 and SBT 0.13.15. Perform the following steps to experiment this example:

1. Create a Play Framework SBT Project from your favorite IDE (I am using my favorite IDE: IntelliJ IDEA):

   ```
   Project Name: play-scala-helloworld-app
   ```

2. Create a `HelloWorld` Play Controller without using DI, as follows:

   HelloWorldNoDIController.scala:

   ```
   package controllers

   import play.api.mvc.{Action, Controller}

   class HelloWorldNoDIController extends Controller {
     def helloWorld = Action {
       Ok(views.html.helloWorld("Hello World Without DI."))
     }
   }
   ```

3. Create a `HelloWorld` View Template, as follows:

   ```
   helloWorld.scala.html
   @(message: String)
    @message
   ```

4. Configure a Routing for `HelloWorldNoDIController` in the routes file available at `/play-scala-helloworld-app/conf`:

   routes:

   ```
   # Routes
   # This file defines all application routes (Higher priority
   routes first)
    # ~~~~# HelloWorldController without using Play DI
    GET      /helloworld
   controllers.HelloWorldNoDIController.helloWorld
    # Map static resources from the /public folder to the /assets
   URL path
   ```

```
GET      /assets/*file
controllers.Assets.versioned(path="/public", file: Asset)
```

5. Start the application using the `sbt` command:

```
$sbt run
play-scala-helloworld-app$ sbt run
 [info] Loading global plugins from
/home/rambabu/.sbt/0.13/plugins
[info] Loading project definition from
/home/rambabu/Applications/RamsApps/PlayFrameworkExamples/play-
scala-starter-example/project
[info] Set current project to play-scala-starter-example (in
build
file:/home/rambabu/Applications/RamsApps/PlayFrameworkExamples/
play-scala-starter-example/)
--- (Running the application, auto-reloading is enabled) ---
[info] p.c.s.AkkaHttpServer - Listening for HTTP on
/0:0:0:0:0:0:0:0:9000
(Server started, use Enter to stop and go back to the
console...)
```

Here, we can observe that the Play Netty Server is started at the default port number 9000 successfully.

6. Access the application from the browser:

```
http://localhost:9000/helloworld
```

The following is the output:

Hello World Without DI.

7. If required, we can start our application on a different port number using the following `sbt` command:

```
play-scala-helloworld-app$ sbt   "run 9999"
```

8. Now we should use the new port number to access our application:

```
http://localhost:9999/helloworld
```

The following is the output:

Hello World Without DI.

Congratulations! We have successfully developed our first Play Reactive Web Application and tested it using our web browser. Let's explore some more Play Framework features in the coming sections:

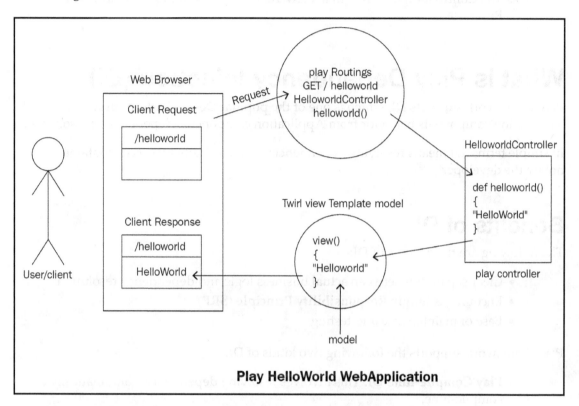

Play HelloWorld WebApplication

When we look at the preceding diagram, we can understand how a Play Application works:

1. When the user or client or customer sends an HTTP request to a Play Web Application, first that request reaches the Play Framework's Routing component (routes).
2. The Play Framework Web Application's Route decides who is responsible to handle that request. It will find the correct mapping between the user's HTTP request and a Controller function, and send that request to that Controller.
3. Then, the Controller or Controller function receives that client request.
4. Then, the Controller function does the processing by interacting with other components, such as services and repositories.

5. The Controller function prepares the data (data model).
6. The Controller function populates that data into the associated View Template.
7. The Controller then sends that View Template back to the Client as HTTP Response.

What is Play Dependency Injection (DI)

Play Framework supports DI, which is one of the popular Design Patterns used to decouple Application components behavior from Application components dependencies resolution.

In simple terms, DI means resolving dependencies automatically by server/container, but not by the developer.

Benefits of DI

The following are the benefits of DI:

- Clear separation between actual business logic and dependency resolution
- Encourages **Single Responsibility Principle (SRP)**
- Ease of maintenance and testing

Play Framework supports the following two kinds of DI:

- **Play Compile-time DI:** This involves resolving dependencies automatically at compile-time.
- **Play Run-time DI:** This involves resolving dependencies automatically at runtime. Play Framework supports the Run-time DI based on JSR-330 (https://jcp.org/en/jsr/detail?id=330).

By default, Play Framework supports the Compile-time DI out of the box using Guice.

Let's explore the Play Compile-time DI in the next section using a simple Play `HelloWorld` Web Application.

Extend HelloWorld Example With DI

In the previous example, we have developed our first Play Framework HelloWorld Web Application.

For a clear separation between the Play Web Application with DI and without DI, I'll create a new project with the same content without changing the previous project:

1. Create a Play Framework SBT Project from your favorite IDE (I am using IntelliJ IDEA):

   ```
   Project Name: play-scala-helloworld-di-app
   ```

2. Copy the complete content of `play-scala-helloworld-app` into this project.

3. Create a HelloWorld Play Controller with DI:

   HelloWorldDIController.scala:

   ```
   package controllers
   import javax.inject._
   import play.api.mvc._
   @Singleton
   class HelloWorldDIController @Inject() extends Controller {
     def helloWorld = Action {
       Ok(views.html.helloWorld("Hello World With DI."))
     }
   }
   ```

 We will use the same Play View Template for both `HelloWorld` Controllers.

The following table describes the most important and frequently used Play Web Application annotations:

Annotation	Description
`@Inject`	To inject dependencies at runtime. It is available in the `javax.inject` package.
`@Singleton`	To have only one instance of the component per application.

- @Inject annotation: We can use this annotation when our application components, such as Controller, have a dependency on the other components. We can use this annotation at two different places:
  - At the Field Level
  - At the Constructor Level

We always recommend using this annotation at the Constructor level. If we use it at the constructor level, we should follow this rule—the @Inject annotation must come after the class name, but before the constructor parameters, and must have parentheses.

Explore this rule with our HelloWorld example:

```
class HelloWorldDIController @Inject() extends Controller
```

In this example, @Inject comes after the Controller class name, that is, HelloWorldDIController and before the HelloWorldDIController constructor's parameters. It has empty parentheses like this: Inject().

In Play Framework, we can use any DI Framework. In our example, we have used Java CDI (Context and Dependency Injection). However, if you are crazy enough to use other DI Frameworks, such as Google Guice, we can use them as shown here:

```
import com.google.inject.Inject
```

- @Singleton annotation:

```
class HelloWorldDIController @Inject() extends Controller {
}
```

If we observe this controller, we have just replaced the @Inject annotation by the Google Guice API: import com.google.inject.Inject. There is no difference; it works similar to the Java CDI API.

4. Configure a Routing for HelloWorldDIController in the routes file available at /play-scala-helloworld-app/conf:

Routes:

```
# Routes
# This file defines all application routes (Higher priority
  routes first)
# ~~~~
```

```
# HelloWorldController without using Play DI
GET /helloWorld controllers.HelloWorldNoDIController.helloWorld
# HelloWorldController with Play DI
GET /helloWorldDI controllers.HelloWorldDIController.helloWorld
# Map static resources from the /public folder to the /assets
  URL path
GET /assets/*file controllers.Assets.versioned(path="/public",
  file: Asset)
```

5. Start the application with the default port number and access the application from the browser:

    ```
    http://localhost:9000/helloWorldDI
    ```

    The following is the output:

    Hello World With DI.

Extending HelloWorld example with Scala Futures

As we discussed in Chapter 3, *Asynchronous Programming with Scala,* Scala Futures are very useful APIs to write asynchronous programming with non-blocking.

Not only do Scala, Akka, and Play-based applications use the Scala Future API, the source code of Scala, Akka, and Play Framework also use the Scala Future API extensively.

In the previous example, we have developed our Play Framework HelloWorld Web Application using DI. We will extend that Application with Scala Futures in this example. Let's start now.

To have a clear separation between the Play Web Application with DI and with Scala Futures, I'm going to create a new project with the same content and not touch the previous project:

1. Create a Play Framework SBT Project from your favorite IDE (I'm using IntelliJ IDEA):

    ```
    Project Name: play-scala-helloworld-future-app
    ```

    Copy the complete content of play-scala-helloworld-di-app into this project.

2. Create the `HelloWorld` Message Model object:

HelloWorld.scala:

```
package models
case class HelloWorld(message:String)
```

3. Create the `HelloWorldService` service class:

HelloWorldService.scala:

```
package services
import com.google.inject.ImplementedBy
import models.HelloWorld
import scala.concurrent.Future
import scala.concurrent.ExecutionContext.Implicits.global
@ImplementedBy(classOf[HelloWorldService])
trait THelloWorldService {
  def hello: Future[HelloWorld]
}
class HelloWorldService extends THelloWorldService {
  override def hello = Future{
    HelloWorld("Hello Future!")
  }
}
```

Here, `THelloWorldService` is a trait, which defines the `hello` function. `HelloWorldService` is a class, which implements the `hello` function for the `THelloWorldService` trait.

We can use the `@ImplementedBy` Google Guice annotation to specify the actual implementation class of a trait. Here, `HelloWorldService` is an implementation class of the `THelloWorldService` trait.

4. Create the `HelloWorld` Play Controller with the Scala Future API:

HelloWorldDIAndScalaFutureController.scala:

```
package controllers
import javax.inject._
import models.HelloWorld
import play.api.mvc._
import services.THelloWorldService
import scala.concurrent.ExecutionContext.Implicits.global
import scala.concurrent.Future
@Singleton
```

```
class HelloWorldDIAndScalaFutureController @Inject()
(helloWorldService: THelloWorldService)(cc: ControllerComponents)
 extends AbstractController(cc) {
  def helloWorld = Action.async {
    val helloMsg: Future[HelloWorld] = helloWorldService.hello
     helloMsg.map{ msg =>
      Ok(views.html.helloWorldExtended(msg))
    }
  }
}
```

Here we are declaring our controller as singleton using `@Singleton` annotation and injecting the required Service using `@Inject` annotation.

5. Develop the main View Template:

main.scala.html

```
@(title: String)(content: Html)
<!DOCTYPE html>
<html>
  <head>
   <title>@title</title>
  </head>
  <body>
    @content
  </body>
</html>
```

This is a Play View Template, which defines just a skeleton or design or structure or blueprint of a Play Template. If any other view is following a similar kind of structure, we can reuse it. There is no need to write each and everything again and again.

If we feel lots of redundant or boilerplate code is present in our View Templates, we can extract them into a View like this and reuse them:

6. Develop the actual `helloWorld` view template by reusing our main View Template:

helloWorldExtended.scala.html:

```
@import models.HelloWorld
@(hello: HelloWorld)
@main(hello.message) {
   <h1>@hello.message</h1>
```

```
}
```

Here, we are not rewriting the HTML tags redundantly. We are just reusing the main template and passing the values.

We use the `@import` Twirl View Template construct to import any components into the views, as follows:

```
@import models.HelloWorld
```

7. Add new routing to the routes file, as follows:

```
# HelloWorldController with Play DI and Scala Futures
GET /helloWorldDIFuture
  controllers.HelloWorldDIAndScalaFutureController.helloWorld
```

To observe the output, please start the Play server using SBT's `run` command as shown here:

```
play-scala-helloworld-future-app$ sbt run
```

When we access the following URL from browser:

```
http://localhost:9000/helloWorldDIFuture
```

we will see our expected response:

```
Hello Future!
Play Framework Form Basics
```

Before diving into developing a Play Framework Form-based application, we will first discuss the following:

- How does Play Framework support Forms?
- How do we design Data Models in Play Framework?
- How does Play Framework map data between a Form and Data Model?
- How do we write Form Data Validations, and so on?

Let's start discussing these things one by one in this section. Then, we will develop one simple Form-based Web Application in the next section.

Play Form – Data Model

The first and foremost point we need to understand is how we design our Model or Data Model in Play Framework Scala-based applications. This may be a bit different for Play Framework Java-based applications.

In Play Framework Scala-based applications, we use a concept called Scala Case classes to design our Data Models, because they are very handy and provide a lot of free benefits. For instance, we don't need to write getters at all. Scala provides them for free automatically.

You can refer to the *Scala Case Classes* section in `Chapter 2`, *Functional Scala*, , for more information on the benefits of Scala Case Classes.

Play Framework Form API

Play Framework has a rich Form API to support Forms in a handy and easy way. It supports simple Forms very easily, and complex Forms are also possible.

We should understand the following two Play Form APIs to develop Play Form-based Web applications:

```
Form case class
Forms object
```

Both Play APIs are available in the same package, `play.api.data`.

In the Play Framework `play.api.data`, the Form case class is responsible for handling forms. It binds the user-submitted Form data (Request Data filled and submitted by the HTTP `POST` method) to the Model class (user-defined case class).

Play Framework's Form is a case class and object with some utility functions, which are useful to handle forms and form submissions.

Play Framework's Form API also has another important API, Forms object. `play.api.data.Forms` contains the following set of Form helper functions:

- Form Data Mapping functions
- Form Data Validation functions
- Form Data manipulation functions

Forms object contains the following useful functions:

```
object Forms {
  // Overloaded mapping function
  def mapping(..............)
  // Data Validation functions
  def text
  def nonEmptyText
  def number
  // And more
}
```

Consider the following example:

```
val form = Form(
  mapping(
    "username" -> nonEmptyText,
    "password" -> nonEmptyText(minLength = 6,maxLength = 8)
  )(UserData.apply)(UserData.unapply)
)
```

Here, we have defined a Form object using the Forms object utility functions:

- `mapping()`—It is used to map data from Form to case class object and vice versa
- Plain `nonEmptyText` function means that text should not be empty, it must contain some text
- `nonEmptyText` function with two validations—`minLength` and `maxLength` that means this must not be empty should contain some text within the specified limitations only

We will explore all this Form object's functions in the next example in detail.

Play Form – Binding Data

Play Framework follows a concept called Binding Data to handle Forms and their submissions.

Here, Binding Data means mapping or binding data between Play Form Data (user filled and submitted data using the HTTP `POST` request) and user-defined (or application) case class object, as shown in the next diagram.

When the user fills the Form data and submits it, Play Framework's Form object receives that data from the user (user interface - UI).

Play Framework's Form object binds that data to user-defined data (in Scala terminology, it is also known as applying data).

This means, here we use the user-defined case class's `apply()` function to bind data from the Form to the case class object.

Next, when the users or applications want to retrieve that data, Play Framework's Form object unbinds that data from the user-defined data (here the user submits a HTTP GET request).

Play Framework's Form object unbinds that data to show it to the user (in Scala terminology, it is known as unapplying data). This means, here we use the user-defined case class's `unapply()` function to unbind data from the case class object to the Form.

Let's understand this process or concept of Binding Data by going through the following diagram:

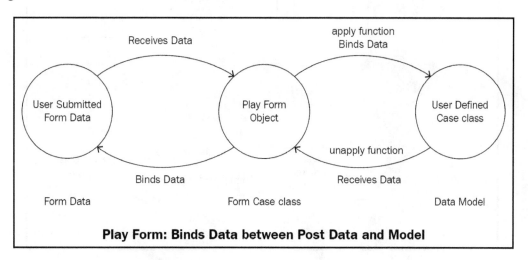

Play Form: Binds Data between Post Data and Model

Consider the following example:

```
val form = Form(
  mapping(
    "username" -> nonEmptyText,
    "password" -> nonEmptyText(minLength = 6,maxLength = 8)
  )(UserData.apply)(UserData.unapply)
)
```

`UserData` is a user-defined case class.

Form is Play Framework's Form API case class.

`UserData.apply` is an `apply()` function of the user-defined case class `UserData` to bind data from the user-submitted HTTP `POST` request to this case class object.

`UserData.unapply` is an `unapply()` function of the user-defined case class, `UserData`, to unbind data from this case class object to the user Form (HTTP `GET` request).

Let's understand this complete Play Framework's Form handling and binding data process using the following simple diagram:

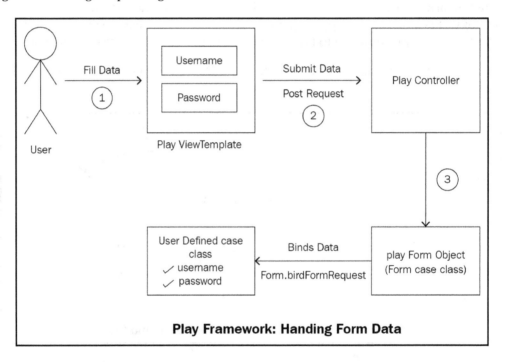

Play Framework: Handing Form Data

We will explore this Play Framework's Form handling process with a simple web application in the upcoming example.

Play Form functions

The Play Framework Form case class has many functions to handle the Form submissions, such as binding data, validating data, and unbinding data.

Now, we will discuss the following two important Form API functions:

- `Form.bindFromRequest()`: This binds request data (user-submitted HTTP POST request data) to the Form, that is, it handles the Form submission. It returns a copy of this Form filled with the new data:

```
def bindFromRequest()(implicit request:
play.api.mvc.Request[_]): Form[T] = {
}
```

- `Form.fold()`: This takes care of handling form results and takes two parameters:
    - **First parameter:** This is a function to handle the form errors
    - **Second parameter:** This is a function to handle form submission success

If the form has errors, it executes the first parameter function.

If form submission is done successfully without any errors, it executes the second parameter function, which is done as follows:

```
def fold[R](hasErrors: Form[T] => R, success: T => R): R = value match {
  case Some(v) if errors.isEmpty => success(v)
  case _ => hasErrors(this)
}
```

Consider the following example:

```
UserData.form.bindFromRequest().fold(
  formWithErrors => {
  },
  user => {
  }
)
```

 If you want more information about Play Framework Scala Forms, you can visit: https://www.playframework.com/documentation/2.6.x/ScalaForms

Play Framework Form-based web application

In this section, we will develop a Play Framework Web Application, which handles Form-based submissions. Like any other web application framework, Play also supports very rich and easy-to-use tools to develop Form-based applications.

Let's start developing a Form-based login web application. We will use this application in future chapters to support Login components for our WF Reactive System.

Perform the following steps to develop this application:

1. Create a Play Scala-based SBT Project from your IDE Project Name: `play-scala-login-from-app`

2. Update the `build.sbt` file:

   build.sbt:

   ```
   name := "play-scala-login-form-app"
   organization := "com.packt.publishing"
   version := "1.0.0"
   lazy val root = (project in file(".")).enablePlugins(PlayScala)
   scalaVersion := "2.12.2"
   libraryDependencies += guice
   ```

   Here, we have configured the Google Guice module, as we are going to use the Guice DI in our controllers.

3. Configure the SBT version in the `build.properties` file:

   ```
   build.properties
   sbt.version=0.13.16
   ```

4. Create a user data model and its associated Form:

   UserData.scala:

   ```
   package forms

   import play.api.data.Forms._
   import play.api.data._
   case class UserData(username: String, password: String)
   object UserData {
     val form = Form(
       mapping(
         "username" -> nonEmptyText,
         "password" -> nonEmptyText(minLength = 6,maxLength = 8)
   ```

```
    )(UserData.apply)(UserData.unapply)
  )
}
```

Here, we can observe two things:

- **Case class UserData**: This is the Data Model to represent user data
- **Case class UserData**: `UserData` object with a Play Form to map data between case class and form

The following code snippet defines a Play Form object with `apply` and `unapply` functions:

```
val form = Form(
  mapping(
    "username" -> nonEmptyText,
    "password" -> nonEmptyText(minLength = 6,maxLength = 8)
  )(UserData.apply)(UserData.unapply)
)
```

Let us understand this form object definition with the following table:

Case class field name	Form field name	Description
username	username	This represents the User login name. Here, we mapped it to Play Framework Form object's `nonEmptyText` validation. This means that the field is mandatory.
password	password	This represents the User login password. Here, we mapped it to Play Framework Form object's `nonEmptyText` validation. This means that the field is mandatory. We have also added two more restrictions on this field: `minLength = 6`: This password should have minimum six characters (alpahnumberic) `maxLength = 8`: This password should have a maximum of eight characters (alpahnumberic)

You can refer to the *Play Framework Form Basics* section to learn more about it.

5. Create a User Repository to check logins:

UserRepository.scala:

```scala
package repositories
import forms.UserData
class UserRepository {
  var userDataList = List[UserData] (
    UserData("adminone","adminone"),
    UserData("userone","userone"),
    UserData("usertwo","usertwo")
  )
  def isValidUser(user:UserData):Boolean = {
    val index = userDataList.indexOf(user)
    if(index >= 0) true
    else false
  }
}
```

Here we have mocked our data directly into the repository. In our real application in the next chapter, we will contact the data store, get the data, and validate the login credentials.

As of now, we are simply using In-Memory Data Store and not using much logic to interact with external data stores, such as RDBMS, NoSQL, and more. We will work on this topic in the upcoming chapters.

6. Create a Service component to interact with the Repository component:

LoginService.scala:

```scala
package services
import com.google.inject.Inject
import forms.UserData
import repositories.UserRepository
class LoginService @Inject()(userRepository: UserRepository){
  def checkLogin(user:UserData): Boolean =
    userRepository.isValidUser(user)
}
```

Here, we are using the Google Guice DI API, that is, @Inject, to automatically resolve dependencies.

7. Develop the login controller to take care of serving user requests to this Login web application:

LoginController.scala:

```scala
package controllers
import javax.inject.Singleton
import com.google.inject.Inject
import forms.UserData
import play.api._
import play.api.mvc._
import play.api.i18n.Messages.Implicits._
import play.api.Play.current
import services.LoginService
import scala.concurrent.ExecutionContext
@Singleton
class LoginController @Inject()(loginService:LoginService)
 (cc:MessagesControllerComponents)(implicit executionContext:
 ExecutionContext) extends MessagesAbstractController(cc) {
  def showLoginPage: Action[AnyContent] = Action {
    implicit  request =>
     Ok(views.html.loginPage(UserData.form))
  }
  def submitLogin = Action {
    implicit request =>
     UserData.form.bindFromRequest().fold(
       formWithErrors => {
         BadRequest(views.html.loginPage(formWithErrors))
       },
       user => {
         val isValidUser = loginService.checkLogin(user)
         if(isValidUser)
           Redirect(routes.LoginController.homePage).flashing(
           "loginStatus" ->"User logged-in successfully.")
          else
            Ok(views.html.loginPage(UserData.form))
       }
     )
  }
  def homePage = Action{
    implicit request =>
     Ok(views.html.homePage())
  }
}
```

Here, we have implemented the following three different functions to take care of the Login process:

- `showLoginPage()`: This is used to display the login form to the user. It uses the `loginPage()` View template, as shown here:

```
Ok(views.html.loginPage(UserData.form))
```

- `submitLogin()`: This is used to submit the user Login data to the Play Form object, and then that Form data is validated.

  Based on the validation result, the Form does one of the following two steps:

  - If validation fails, it sends a BadRequest to the same login form so that the user can submit another request
  - If validation passes, it does the login authentication

- `homePage()`: This is used to display our application home page to the valid login user. It uses the `homePage()` View template.

8. Develop the following two Play View Templates to refer them from `LoginController`:

- **loginPage.scala.html**: This Scala template is used to display our WF Reactive System Login page:

```
@(userForm:Form[forms.UserData])(implicit flash: Flash,
  request: MessagesRequestHeader)
@if(userForm.hasGlobalErrors) {
  <ul>
  @for(error <- userForm.globalErrors) {
    <li>@error.message</li>
  }
  </ul>
}
<h1>WF Reactive System Login</h1>
@helper.form(action = routes.LoginController.submitLogin) {
  @helper.inputText(userForm("username"))
  @helper.inputPassword(userForm("password"))
  @helper.CSRF.formField
  <input type="submit" value="Submit"/>
}
```

- **homePage.scala.html**: This Scala template is used to display user login status:

```
@()(implicit flash: Flash)
@flash.get("loginStatus").map { message =>
  <h2>@message</h2>
```

```
      }
```

9. Add the following routings for the Play `routes` file:

    routes:

    ```
    # Routes
    # This file defines all application routes (Higher priority
      routes first)
    # https://www.playframework.com/documentation/latest/ScalaRouting
    # ~~~~
    # Managing a User
    GET        /login
     controllers.LoginController.showLoginPage
    POST       /submitLogin
     controllers.LoginController.submitLogin
    GET        /homePage
     controllers.LoginController.homePage
    # Map static resources from the /public folder to
      the /assets URL path
    GET       /assets/*file
     controllers.Assets.versioned(path="/public", file: Asset)
    ```

We have finished developing our Play Framework Form-based web application. Let's test it now.

For the output, we will test our Play Framework Form-based web application using one of the web browsers:

1. Start the Akka HTTP server from our project root folder:

    ```
    play-scala-login-form-app$ sbt run
    ```

2. Here we can see that our Akka HTTP server starts at port number `9000`.

3. Access our login from the URL of the web browser:

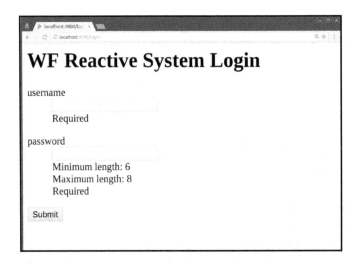

4. Access this page using this URL: `http://localhost:9000/login`.

5. Click on the **Submit** button without providing any data or provide wrong data. You will see errors in the same page, as shown here:

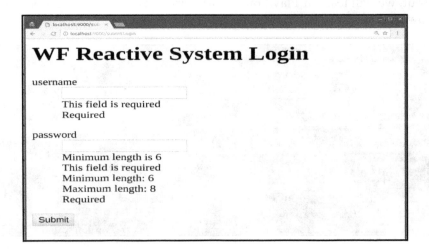

Here, we can see a new message for each field—**This field is required**.

6. Provide the correct login details and click on the **Submit** button to see the home page of the WF Reactive System:

- username: `adminone`
- password: `adminone`

Use `adminone` as username and password to login to our system:

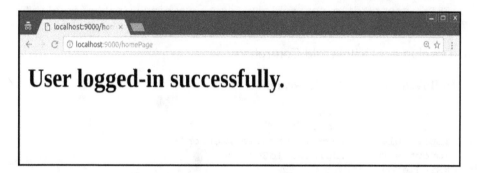

We have successfully developed and tested the Play Framework Form-based web application.

Extending Play/Scala HelloWorld example with Akka Toolkit

In this section, we will use the same previous Play Framework/Scala based HelloWorld example and extend it with Akka Toolkit. I'll use the content from the previous example to demonstrate this.

Perform the following steps:

1. Import the previously developed Play/Scala HelloWorld example into your favorite IDE.
2. I just renamed this Project Name as `play-scala-akka-helloworld-app`.
3. Define the configurations `routes` file:

routes:

```
# Routes
# This file defines all application routes (Higher priority
```

```
   routes first)
# ~~~~
# HelloWorldController without using Play DI
GET /helloWorldNoDI
 controllers.HelloWorldNoDIController.helloWorldNoDI
# HelloWorldController with Play DI
GET /helloWorldDI controllers.HelloWorldDIController.helloWorld
# Map static resources from the /public folder to the /assets
 URL path
GET /assets/*file controllers.Assets.versioned(path="/public",
 file: Asset)
```

4. Develop our HelloWorld Controllers:

HelloWorldDIController.scala:

```
package controllers
import javax.inject._
import play.api.mvc.{Controller,Action}
import services.HelloWorldService
@Singleton
class HelloWorldDIController @Inject()  extends Controller {
  val helloWorldService:HelloWorldService = HelloWorldService
  def helloWorld = Action {
    helloWorldService.helloWorldWithDI
    Ok(views.html.helloWorld("Hello World With DI."))
  }
}
```

HelloWorldNoDIController.scala:

```
package controllers
import play.api.mvc.{Action, Controller}
import services.HelloWorldService
class HelloWorldNoDIController extends Controller {
  val helloWorldService:HelloWorldService = HelloWorldService
  def helloWorldNoDI = Action {
    helloWorldService.helloWorldWithoutDI
    Ok(views.html.helloWorld("Hello World Without DI."))
  }
}
```

5. Define the Service component:

HelloWorldService.scala:

```
package services
import actors.HelloWorldActorController
```

```
trait HelloWorldService {
  def helloWorldController: HelloWorldActorController
  def helloWorldWithDI = helloWorldController.helloWorldWithDI
  def helloWorldWithoutDI = helloWorldController.helloWorldWithoutDI
}
object HelloWorldService extends HelloWorldService {
  val helloWorldController: HelloWorldActorController =
   HelloWorldActorController
}
```

6. Define the ActorController component:

HelloWorldActorController.scala:

```
package actors
import akka.actor.{ActorRef, ActorSystem, Props}
trait HelloWorldActorController {
  protected def system: ActorSystem
  protected def helloWorldActor: ActorRef
  def helloWorldWithDI = {
    implicit val dispatcher = system.dispatcher
    helloWorldActor ! HelloWorldWithDI
  }
  def helloWorldWithoutDI = {
    implicit val dispatcher = system.dispatcher
    helloWorldActor ! HelloWorldWithoutDI
  }
}
object HelloWorldActorController extends
 HelloWorldActorController {
  val system = ActorSystem("HelloWorldSystem")
  val helloWorldActor =
    system.actorOf(Props[HelloWorldActor],"HelloWorldActor")
}
```

7. Define the Actor component:

HelloWorldActor.scala:

```
package actors
import akka.actor.Actor
case object HelloWorldWithDI
case object HelloWorldWithoutDI
class HelloWorldActor extends Actor{
  override def receive: Receive = {
    case HelloWorldWithDI =>
     println("Hello World With DI")
```

```
      case HelloWorldWithoutDI =>
       println("Hello World Without DI")
      case _ =>
       println("Unknown Message")
    }
  }
```

The following is the output:

```
Start the server
http://localhost:9000/helloWorldNoDI
Hello World Without DI
```

We can see this message on both the client browser and SBT console:
```
http://localhost:9000/helloWorldDI
Hello World With DI
```

Play Fileupload web application

In this section, we will develop a Play Framework Scala and SBT-based Fileupload web application, which is useful to develop our final WF Reactive Systems in the coming chapters.

One of the new features of Play 2.6.x Framework is Fileupload functionality improvements.

We will follow these steps to develop and experiment with this example:

1. Create a Play/Scala SBT project with the following name:

   ```
   Project name: play-scala-fileupload-app
   ```

2. Update `build.sbt` file:

   build.sbt:

   ```
   name := "play-scala-fileupload-example"
   version := "1.0.0"
   lazy val root = (project in file(".")).enablePlugins(PlayScala)
   scalaVersion := "2.12.2"
   libraryDependencies += guice
   ```

```
libraryDependencies += ws
```

3. Configure the SBTversion in the `build.properties` file, as follows:

build.properties:

```
sbt.version=0.13.16
```

4. Configure SBT plugins like Play Framework library:

plugins.sbt:

```
resolvers += Resolver.typesafeRepo("snapshots")
resolvers += Resolver.jcenterRepo
addSbtPlugin("com.typesafe.play" % "sbt-plugin" % "2.6.11")
```

5. Define the case class as a Data model and its associated form:

FileData.scala:

```
case class FileData(filename: String)
object FileData {
  val form = Form(
    mapping(
      "filename" -> text
    )(FileData.apply)(FileData.unapply)
  )
}
```

6. Define some file-related utilities, as follows:

FileUtils.scala:

```
object FileUtils {
  private val logger = Logger(this.getClass)

  type FilePartHandler[A] = FileInfo => Accumulator[ByteString,
   FilePart[A]]

  def handleFilePartAsFile: FilePartHandler[File] = {
    case FileInfo(partName, filename, contentType) =>
     val path: Path = Files.createTempFile("multipartBody",
      "tempFile")
     val fileSink: Sink[ByteString, Future[IOResult]] =
      FileIO.toPath(path)
     val accumulator: Accumulator[ByteString, IOResult] =
      Accumulator(fileSink)
```

```
      accumulator.map {
        case IOResult(count, status) =>
         logger.info(s"count = $count, status = $status")
        FilePart(partName, filename, contentType, path.toFile)
      }
    }

  def operateOnTempFile(file: File) = {
    val size = Files.size(file.toPath)
    logger.info(s"size = ${size}")
    Files.deleteIfExists(file.toPath)
    size
  }
}
```

7. Define the Controller to handle the Fileupload functionality, as follows:

HomeController.scala:

```
@Singleton
class HomeController @Inject() (cc:MessagesControllerComponents)
  (implicit executionContext: ExecutionContext)
  extends MessagesAbstractController(cc) {
    private val logger = Logger(this.getClass)
    def uploadForm = Action {
      implicit request =>
      Ok(views.html.fileupload(FileData.form))
  }
  def upload =
   Action(parse.multipartFormData(handleFilePartAsFile)) {
     implicit request =>
     val filePart = request.body.file("filename")
     val fileOption = filePart.map {
       case FilePart(key, filename, contentType, file) =>
       val data = operateOnTempFile(file)
       data
     }
     Ok(s"WF Reactive System: Uploaded file
      '${filePart.get.filename}' and it's size =
      ${fileOption.getOrElse("no file")}")
   }
}
```

8. Define `routes`, as follows:

routes:

```
# Routes
# This file defines all application routes (Higher priority
  routes first)
# ~~~~
GET     /uploadForm
 controllers.HomeController.uploadForm
POST    /upload
 controllers.HomeController.upload
# Map static resources from the /public folder to the /assets URL
  path
GET     /assets/*file
 controllers.Assets.versioned(path="/public", file: Asset)
```

9. Define Play View Templates, as follows:

main.scala.html:

```
@(title: String)(content: Html)
<!DOCTYPE html>
<html lang="en">
<head>
  <title>@title</title>
  <link rel="stylesheet" media="screen"
   href="@routes.Assets.versioned("stylesheets/main.css")">
  <link rel="shortcut icon" type="image/png"
   href="@routes.Assets.versioned("images/favicon.png")">
  <script src="@routes.Assets.versioned("javascripts/hello.js")"
   type="text/javascript"></script>
</head>
<body>
  @content
</body>
</html>
```

fileupload.scala.html:

```
@(form: Form[forms.FileData])(implicit request:
   MessagesRequestHeader)
 <h1>WF Reactive System: Upload Data</h1>
 @main("Welcome to WF App") {
   @helper.form(action = routes.HomeController.upload,
     'enctype ->"multipart/form-data") {
       @helper.inputFile(field = form("filename"),
```

```
      '_label ->"File Name",'class ->"form-control input-lg")
      @helper.CSRF.formField
    <input type="submit" value="Upload Weather Data"/>
  }
}
```

As of Play 2.6.x Framework, we need CSRFFilter to validate the authorization of accessing the Play Forms. To add this to the functionality of Play Framework automatically, we need to include `@helper.CSRF.formField` when submitting the form, preferably as a hidden field. This allows the CSRF token to be generated and validated with the server automatically.

The following is the output:

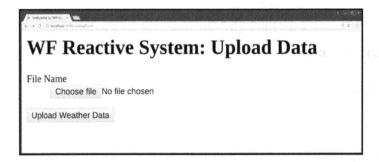

10. Start the Akka HTTP server, as follows:

    play-scala-fileupload-app$ sbt run

11. Access the fileupload form, using `http://localhost:9000/fileuploadForm`.

12. Select the file from your local system to upload:

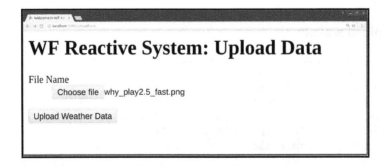

11. Click on the **Upload Weather Data** button:

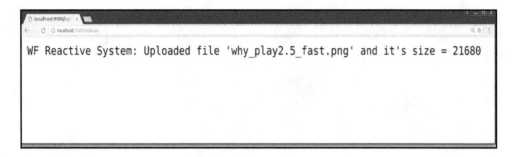

Now, observe the results.

Summary

In this chapter, we have discussed the Play Framework basics, looking at its benefits and features. We have discussed the Play MVC components, such as Views, Controllers, Models, Routes, and more.

We started with the basic Play HelloWorld web application and extended it to different Play features, such as DI, Forms, file upload, and more.

As we discussed in Chapter 3, *Asynchronous Programming with Scala*, Play Framework applications use Scala Futures extensively. We have converted our simple example to use Futures.

We have discussed Play Framework and its component architecture in detail with some simple diagrams, and we have also explained the Play Framework SBT project structure.

So far, in this book, we have discussed many concepts, such as Scala Functional Programming, Asynchronous Programming, Akka Toolkit, and Play Framework. It's good to start building our **Weather Forecasting** (**WF**) system using all of these concepts.

Before developing this WF System in Chapter 8, *Integrating Akka Streams to Play Application*, let's first discuss Akka Streams in the next chapter.

7
Working with Reactive Streams

In this chapter, we will discuss the use of the Akka Streams API to easily perform asynchronous data stream processing with non-blocking backpressure. We will also discuss what the CQRS/ES pattern is and how the Akka Persistence module uses this pattern to support the development of Event-Driven systems or applications.

Its shares the same Akka Toolkit office website (`http://akka.io/`) and GitHub source code location is available at `https://github.com/akka/akka`.

In this chapter, you will learn the following concepts:

- Streams and the benefits of streaming data
- Akka Streams and their features and benefits
- How Akka Streams support data streaming
- Backpressure and its importance
- How Akka Streams implements backpressure, and why we need it in data streaming
- Akka Streams API examples
- How to use the Akka Streams `GraphDSL` API
- Akka Persistence and its features and benefits
- How the EQRS/ES pattern works and its benefits
- How Akka Persistence supports the EQRS/ES Model

Introduction to Akka Streams

In this section, we will introduce you to data streaming, the Akka Streams API, its features and benefits and more concepts.

What is a stream?

A **stream** is a sequence of things that is flowing continuously from a source to a destination. Stream elements are processed sequentially. It is also known as a data stream, data streaming, or streaming data.

Here, things can refer to anything, for instance, data elements, components, entities, objects, bytes, elements, files, and so on. Take a look at the following diagram:

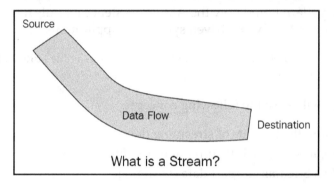

In the real world, a stream will form only when at least one source and at least one destination are connected and have data flowing between them. Remember these three terminologies as discussed in this section—source, destination, and flowing. These three are the key concepts that we should understand well in order to learn the Akka Stream's API.

In the Akka Streams API, this source is designed as a Source component, the destination is designed as a Sink component, and flowing is designed as a Flow component.

Goals of data streaming

Data streaming has the following goals:

- Streaming huge amounts of data
- Streaming data at very fast
- Streaming data in real time or near real time

- Streaming a variety of data
- Streaming data at different rates

These points also answer the question *why do we need streaming data.*

What is Akka Streams?

Akka Streams is one of Akka Toolkit's APIs or modules, and is useful for data streaming in an asynchronous and non-blocking way using backpressure. It follows the Reactive Manifesto standard or specification (`http://www.reactivemanifesto.org/`). It is one of the implementations of Reactive Streams (`http://www.reactive-streams.org`):

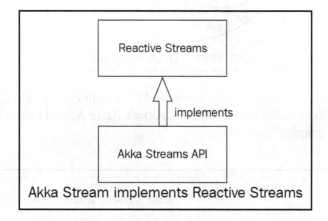

- Streaming a variety of data

Goals of the Akka Streams API

Akka Streams API has designed and developed with the following main goals in mind to ease the Streaming data easier and faster:

- To support asynchronous streaming data with non-blocking backpressure
- To support better performance
- To support reactiveness by implementing Reactive Streams specification
- To support distributed feature using Akka Toolkit and its Actor Model

Some APIs, tools, or frameworks support backpressure. However, they support using synchronous blocking backpressure. It solves some of the streaming data problems; however, it is not the right solution.

Internally, the Akka Streams API uses some of the Akka Toolkit components and also Akka Actor Model to ease and fulfill its job:

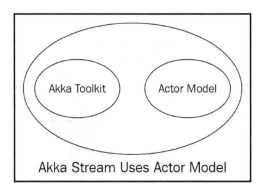

Akka Stream Uses Actor Model

Apart from Reactive Streams, the Akka Streams API is built on top of Akka Toolkit to utilize all the benefits of Akka for free. It uses Akka's Actor Model under the hood to take care of running the graphs:

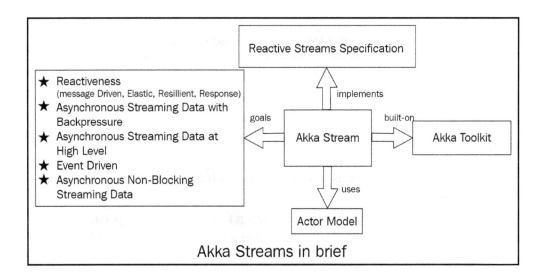

Akka Streams in brief

The main goal of the Akka Streams API is *asynchronous streaming data with non-blocking backpressure.*

Features of the Akka Streams API

Akka Streams API has the following best features to support real-time or near real-time Streaming data in asynchronous and non-blocking way using backpressure:

- It is open source
- It supports Graph DSL
- It supports streaming data
- It supports the streaming IO API to handle file IO and TCP connection
- It supports unit testing and integration testing of its core components easily, using its own Testing kit
- It supports pipelining and parallel processing

Benefits of the Akka Streams API

The Akka Streams API has the following benefits:

- It avoids lots of boilerplate code to implement Actors. Akka Stream's Materializer creates the required Actors under the hood to execute the Graphs.
- It offers reusability. Once we design **Data Flow Graph** (**DFG**), we can reuse it any number of times.
- It offers composability. We can compose Akka Streams components easily to solve complex data-processing problems.
- It is built on Akka Toolkit. We will get all Akka Toolkit benefits, such as Reactiveness, Distributed, Location Transparency, Clustering, Remoting, and more, for free.
- It is very useful for fast streaming data.
- It is best suited for big data-based applications.
- It is best suited for Cloud-based applications.

Why do we need Akka Streams and why not just Akka?

It's really important to know the answer to this question.

Why can't we use just plain Akka Actors to support data streaming process? Why do we need another separate API or Library or Module—Akka Streams?

In this context, Akka Actors have two things going against them:

- Akka Actors do not support type safety very well. We know that Actor's `receive()` function supports any kind of message type that is Any (Scala type name). Even though the Akka Team is working on Typed Actors, as of now, we are all using Untyped Actors only.
- Plain Akka Actors do not support dynamic push/pull backpressure.

Because of these two reasons, the Akka Team has introduced a new module called Akka Streams, which solves both problems very well.

Other Reactive Streams implementations

Apart from Akka Streams, there are a number of Frameworks, Languages, Tools, and so on, that were implemented by the following Reactive Manifesto. Here is a list for reference:

- Spring 5 Reactor Module
- Reactive MongoDB
- Slick
- Reactive Rabbit
- Play Framework (integrated Akka Streams API), and more

There are many other APIs, frameworks, tools, and more that are implemented in the Reactive Streams.

Components of Akka Streams

The Akka Streams module has the following components to ease data stream processing:

- Source
- Sink
- Flow
- RunnableGraph or Graph
- Fan-in function
- Fan-out function

These components are also known as the building blocks or pillars of the Akka Streams API.

The Akka Streams API

In the Akka Streams API, there are mainly the following three main APIs. They are also known as Components of the Akka Streams API. We can also treat them as different processing stages in Akka Streams:

- Source
- Sink
- Flow

The Akka Streams API has two sets of DSL APIs. One set for Java-defined at `akka.stream.javadsl`, and another for Scala-defined at `akka.stream.scaladsl`.

All the preceding three Akka Streams API components are defined in the `akka.stream.scaladsl` package.

Apart from the preceding three major components, the Akka Streams API has one imported API, ActorMaterializer.

It also uses the Akka Actor module's ActorSystem. In this section, we will first discuss the three APIs—Source, Sink, and Flow, and will then discuss the rest of the APIs in the coming sections.

What is streaming data?

Streaming data means generating huge amounts of data and analyzing, processing, and transforming it between the Source and Destination components in different stages. In Akka Streams terminology, we can say that in these stages, Source is Source only, Destination is Sink, and there is another component to perform operations (such as analyze, process, and transforming, and more) known as Flow.

Streaming data is also known as data streaming. As we discussed, we use the Akka Streams API for streaming data.

We will discuss these components one by one in depth in the coming sections.

The Akka Streams Source component

In the Akka Streams API, Source is a Producer of streaming data and has only one output and no input.

The main responsibility of a Source is producing data elements (or emitting data elements) to Sink or Flow when it's ready to receive them. Here, we can call Source the **upstream processing stage** and Sink the **downstream processing stage**.

A Source can have either only one step or a set of stream-processing steps, depending on our requirements. A Source can be anything like a File, String, Collection, Map, Database, and so on.

In the Akka Streams API, a Source is defined as a `final` class in the `akka.stream.scaladsl` package, as shown here:

```
final class Source[+Out, +Mat] {
   // Only Out (Output)
}
```

Akka Materialization (or simply Materialization) turns a Source into a Reactive stream Publisher. The Reactive Streams API defines a Subscriber as `org.reactivestreams.Publisher`. Refer to `Chapter 1`, *Getting Started with Reactive and Functional Programming*, to learn more about the Reactive Streams API (Specification).

It is a mandatory Akka Streams component to form a RunnableGraph or Graph. The following diagram shows the Akka Stream's Source component structure:

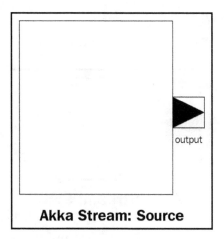

Akka Stream: Source

It is used to produce data elements in a Graph or RunnableGraph. It is a mandatory element. For outside world, it looks like a single step or stage. However, internally, it can have only one stage or a set of stages to fulfill its job. Please refer to the *Akka Streams API* section for more information. In Akka Streams API, Sink is a **Consumer** of Streaming data and has only one Input and no Output as shown in the next section.

The Akka Streams Sink component

In the Akka Streams API, Sink is a Consumer of streaming data and has only one input and no output.

The main responsibility of a Sink is to consume data elements from Source or Flow only when they are available. Here, we can say Source as **Upstream Processing Stage** and Sink as **Downstream Processing Stage**.

Like the Source component, a Sink can also have either only one step or a set of stream-processing steps, depending on our requirements.

In the Akka Streams API, Sink is defined as the final class in the `akka.stream.scaladsl` package, as shown here:

```
final class Sink[-In, +Mat] {
  // Only In (Input)
}
```

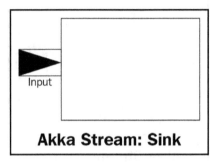

Akka Stream: Sink

For outside world, it looks like a single step or stage. Please refer *Akka Streams API* section for more information

Like the Source component, forming a RunnableGraph or Graph is also a mandatory Akka Streams component. Akka Materialization (or simply Materialization) turns a Sink into a Reactive Streams Consumer. The Reactive Streams API defines Subscriber as `org.reactivestreams.Subscriber`. Refer to `Chapter 1`, *Getting Started with Reactive and Functional Programming*, to learn more about the Reactive Streams API (Specification).

The Akka Streams Flow component

In the Akka Streams API, Flow is a connector or mediator between Source and Sink for streaming data and has one input and one output.

Akka Streams' Flow is used to connect a Source to a Sink and is responsible for doing one or more of the following operations:

- Analyzing data elements
- Updating/reading/deleting data elements
- Transforming data elements into a required format
- Grouping/mapping/filtering data elements and more

In the Akka Streams API, Flow is defined as a final class in the `akka.stream.scaladsl` package, as shown here:

```
final class Flow[-In, +Out, +Mat] {
  // Both In (Input) and Out (Output)
}
```

We can understand this Flow component by going through the following diagram:

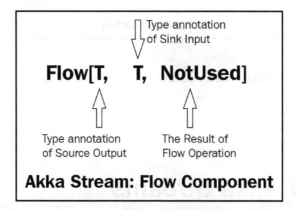

Unlike the Source and Sink components, forming a RunnableGraph or Graph is not a mandatory Akka Streams component (it is optional). In real-time applications, we should use it to perform our data-processing activities. However, we can omit it, if not required:

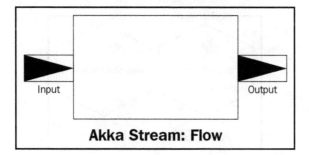

RunnableGraph or Graph

In the Akka Streams API, when we connect two mandatory components or all components, it will form a Graph or RunnableGraph, as shown in the following diagram.

Here, the Source and Sink components are mandatory and Flow is an optional component:

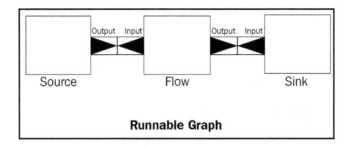

Runnable Graph

 Graph is also known as RunnableGraph or Data Flow Graph.

Modules of Akka Streams

In Akka Toolkit, Akka Streams have the following modules or extensions:

- Akka Stream (`akka-stream`)
- Akka Stream Testkit (`akka-stream-testkit`)

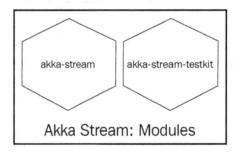

Akka Stream: Modules

The Akka Stream (`akka-stream`) module is an API in Akka Toolkit for providing streaming data solutions with DSLs (Scala DSL and Java DSL).

Akka Stream Testkit (`akka-stream-testkit`) is a Testing API in Akka Toolkit for performing Unit testing and Integration (Functional) testing of Akka Streams components easily.

Akka Materialization

In this section, we will talk about one of the important key concepts of Akka Streams—Materialization. If you are not that keen to know *what happens when we run a Graph or RunnableGraph under the hood*, you can skip this section and move on to the next section.

What is materialization?

In general, materialization means *generating a value (or a set of values) by performing an operation (or some set of operations) on a data element (or a set of data elements)*.

In simple Akka Streams API terminology:

> Materialize = Execute or Run

Then *why do we need to know this in Akka Streams*? *What is the relationship between this concept and Akka Streams*? Good questions.

Let's explore this Akka Toolkit's component in more detail in the coming sections.

Akka's Materializer

Akka Toolkit has a Materializer **SPI (Service Provider Interface)** to support the Materialization component for Akka Stream-based Graphs:

```
package akka.stream
abstract class Materializer {
  // SPI
}
```

If we want our own customized Materializer, we should provide the implementation to this abstract class. However, the Akka Streams API has provided a default implementation for running Akka Stream's Graph—ActorMaterializer:

- If required, we can create our own Materializer
- We can use any Materializer implementation to execute our Data Flow Graphs (Graphs or RunnableGraphs)

- The Akka Streams API uses ActorMaterializer as the default Materializer

Akka's ActorMaterializer

In Akka Streams, we (as developers) are responsible for designing Graphs (or RunnableGraphs) to fulfill our requirements. So, who is responsible for running or executing those Graphs? The answer is **Akka ActorMaterializer**.

ActorMaterializer is useful for running or executing our Graphs or RunnableGraphs and gives us a value. This value is also known as **materialized value**.

The Akka Streams API has `akka.stream.ActorMaterializer` to support this feature.

In simple words, ActorMaterializer is a Akka Streams running tool or Akka Stream's Data Flow Graphs running tool:

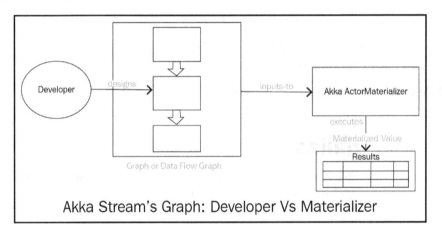

Akka Stream's Graph: Developer Vs Materializer

As shown in the preceding diagram, developers are responsible for designing Graphs based on their application requirements, and ActorMaterializer is responsible for executing those Graphs and providing the results (materialized values).

Roles and responsibilities of Akka's ActorMaterializer

Akka Stream's ActorMaterializer is responsible for doing the following:

- Creating required Actors under the hood to execute Graphs
- Allocating the required resources to execute Graphs

- Executing Graphs
- Executing different stages of Graphs step by step
- Taking inputs of one stage and using them to provide output for the next stage (Source, Sink, Flow, and so on)

Akka's Actor versus Akka Stream's ActorMaterializer

It is very important to understand why we need a separate component—ActorMaterializer in Akka Toolkit. Why can't we use Akka's Actor to fulfill the Streaming Data purpose?

```
Akka Actors => Design + Execute        Akka Streams => Design
    ✸ We should create Actors              ✸ No need to create Actors
    ✸ Lots of Boilerplate                  ✸ No Boilerplate code
    ✸ We should write logic                ✸ Actor Materializer will take care of
      to process different stages            executing different stages, passing
    ✸ We should pass one stage              them to next stage
      results to next

       Akka Data Streaming: Actor Vs ActorMaterializer
```

If we use Akka Actors to implement Graphs for streaming data, we need to write lots of boilerplate code to process the data and send it to the next stage. I'm not saying it's impossible; we can implement it. However, we need to write lots of boilerplate code and it is a very tedious approach.

If we use Akka Streams to implement Graphs for streaming data, we are just responsible for designing Graphs, and that's it. Akka Streams' component, Materializer, will take care of creating the required Actors under the hood, executing them, sending one stage's results to the next stage, and finally giving us the expected results.

Backpressure

In this section, we will discuss backpressure, one of the most important key concepts of Akka Streams supported features, with some simple and useful diagrams.

The main goal of the Akka Streams API is to support asynchronous streaming data with non-blocking backpressure, so as to support better performance and ease of maintainability for fast data-processing applications. It's therefore very important to understand what backpressure is, how it works, and why we need it in Akka Streams.

In Akka Streams, backpressure is a technique for flow-control between a Producer and a Consumer. It gives a way for the Consumer to inform the Producer about the number of data elements or messages it can accept so that the Producer sends only that number of data elements to the Consumer to avoid failures such as OutOfMemory issues.

Before moving to Akka-style backpressure, we will first discuss how to solve these kinds of problems in a traditional way.

The traditional backpressure approach

There are many traditional backpressure approaches to solving these kinds of problems. However, we will take buffer-based backpressure approach and understand it well to find out the problems.

This approach may have the following two scenarios:

- Push-based backpressure approach
- Pull-based backpressure approach

Let's consider the following two kinds of scenarios for both push-based and pull-based backpressure applications:

- Fast Producer / Slow Consumer
- Slow Producer / Fast Consumer

Push – Fast Producer / Slow Consumer

In this section, we will try to explore a pull-based backpressure application with the Fast Producer/Slow Consumer scenario. In this application, if we have a Fast Producer/Slow Consumer in the buffer-based backpressure approach, we will face OutOfMemory errors. Let's explore this in detail.

In this Producer/Consumer message communication application, we will observe the three major roles—Producer, Consumer, and Buffer. Let's assume they have the following capacities to fulfill their jobs:

- Producer components have a Publishing capacity (sending messages to Consumer) of 10 messages per second at a time

- Consumer components have a Consuming capacity (receiving messages from Publisher) of one message per second at a time
- Buffer components have a Buffering capacity (storing messages in memory) maximum of 10 messages

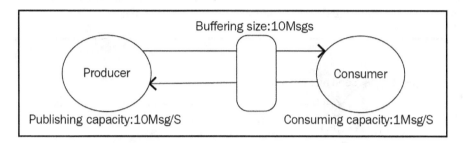

Producer sends the first 10 messages to Consumer, as shown here:

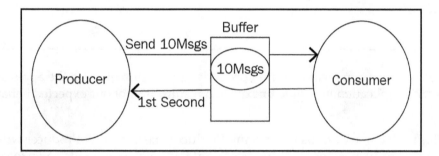

Then, Consumer reads the first message from the Buffer and does its job. Now, the Buffer has the remaining nine messages, as shown here:

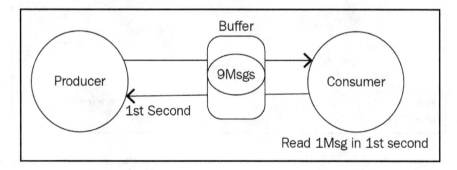

In the second Second, Producer sends another set of 10 messages to Consumer, and, at the same time, Consumer reads the second message from Buffer and does its job. Now, the Buffer component should have a total of 18 messages (the previous set of eight messages + the new set of 10 messages). However, it can store a maximum of 10 messages in its available memory. It may discard eight messages and store only 10 messages (eight old messages + two new messages) or throw an OutOfMemory error:

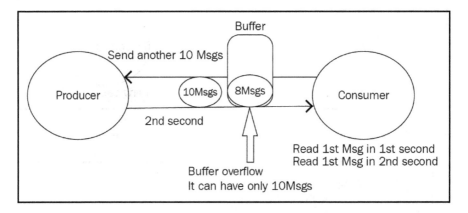

In this scenario, if we don't handle errors properly, it may stop or crash the application from working or the application may give unexpected results. It's not our expected behavior, is it?

To solve this problem, we can use a blocking Producer, meaning that Producer will wait to send another set of 10 messages to Consumer until that Consumer reads and processes all 10 messages:

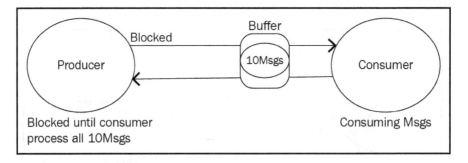

Here, the major problem is Blocking Producer. It may impact the application's performance and user responsiveness.

In simple words, a push-based backpressure application with Fast Producer/Slow Consumer has the following problems:

- OutOfMemory buffer issues
- Blocking Producer
- Less performance and responsiveness

So, the push-based backpressure approach is not safe for the Fast Producer/Slow Consumer scenario. It may be OK for Slow Producer/Fast Consumer. (It also faces fewer performance and responsiveness issues).

Pull – Slow Producer/Fast Consumer

Let's consider another scenario in this section. For instance, a pull-based backpressure application has a Slow Producer/Fast Consumer scenario.

In this case, Consumer should always try to pull more messages from Producer, and Producer is a bit slow in sending messages to Consumer. So, Consumer should wait to receive new messages. This is also not a good approach.

So finally, neither the pull-based approach nor the push-based approach is an ideal solution for solving streaming data problems. We should find a new approach that combines both of these two approaches. This new approach should work dynamically, meaning that it should pick up one of these approaches depending on the context and try to solve the problems.

We will explore this new approach in the next section.

The dynamic push/pull model

In Akka Toolkit, the Akka Streams API uses Dynamic pull/push backpressure model to solve the fast streaming data issues that we discussed in the previous section.

In dynamic pull/push mode, sometimes it uses a pull-based model, and sometimes it uses a push-based model.

If a System has a Fast Producer/Slow Consumer, this model uses a pull-based approach, which means Consumer always requests how many messages (data elements) it can process to Producer, then only that Producer sends that many messages to Consumer:

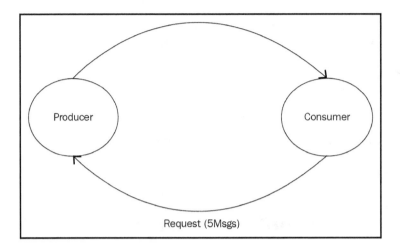

As shown in the preceding diagram, **Consumer** sends a **Request** of five messages to **Producer**. Then, **Producer** sends a **Response** of five messages to that **Consumer**:

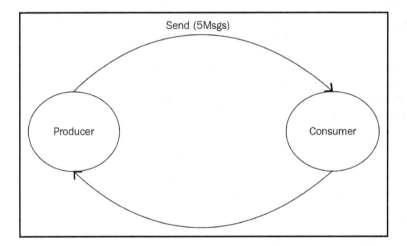

Here, if Consumer is able to process more elements, it sends a request for more elements. If it can process only fewer elements, it sends a request for fewer elements. It follows the pull-based model.

For instance, if a system has a Slow Producer/Fast Consumer scenario, this model uses the push-based approach to continue the communication between Producer and Consumer:

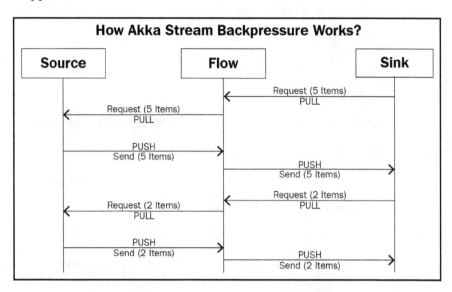

In this way, Akka Streams' backpressure follows the Dynamic Push/Pull model to support fast streaming data easily.

Akka Streams programming basics

Before we develop some Akka Streams applications in this chapter, we will first take some baby steps to understand the Streams API very well.

Creating a Source

To create an Akka Stream's Source, we need to use one of its functions, such as single, by providing some input elements. For instance, create a Source that contains the numbers 1 to 10 as shown here:

```
val numbersSource = Source.single(1 to 10)
```

If we add this code snippet to a Scala App and run it from your favorite IDE or using the `sbt` command, we don't see any output. This is because Akka Streams components are executed only when we run them manually:

```
package com.packt.publishing.akka.streams.hello
import akka.stream.scaladsl.Source
object AkkaStreamsBabyStepsApp extends App{
    val numbersSource = Source.single(1 to 10)
}
```

Similarly, we can create a Source from a String, Collection, Map, File, Database, and so on.

We can also create a Source using its apply method, as shown here:

```
val source = Source(1 to 10)
```

The following demonstrates a source with a type annotation:

```
val source: Source[Int, NotUsed] = Source(1 to 10)
```

It creates a Source with a number ranging from 1 to 10. If we want to run this Source independently, we can use its `runForeach` function, as shown here:

```
source.runForeach(num => println(num))
```

This will execute or run the Source component and supply each number to the `println` function. We will see the output of this statement soon:

```
val strSource = Source("Hello World")
```

This creates a String Source.

Creating a Sink

To create an Akka Stream's Sink, we need to use one of its functions, such as `foreach`, as shown here:

```
val sampleSink = Sink.foreach(println)
```

Here, the `Sink.foreach` function is attached to the `println` function, which means that anything it receives as input from other Akka Streams components is passed to the `println` function to display it on the console.

We will explore this more in the coming sections and also in HelloWorld examples.

Connect a Source to a Sink

As we discussed in the Akka Streams API section, only the Source and Sink components are mandatory to form a Graph or RunnableGraph. The rest of the API components are optional.

Even though we cannot do much with just the Source and Sink components, we can use and run the Graph:

```
val numbersSource = Source(1 to 10)
val numberSink = Sink.foreach(println)
```

Here, we have created both Source and Sink:

```
val numberRunnableGraph = numbersSource.to(numberSink)
```

Now we have connected our Source to our Sink using the to functions available in the Source component. It forms a simple RunnableGraph. When we run this code in a Scala App, it executes successfully without any output to the console.

Creating a Flow

We can create a Flow component easily using its map function, as shown here:

```
val numberFlow = Flow[Int].map(num => num + 1)
```

Here, Flow takes an Int and increments it by 1 by using this anonymous function:

```
num => num + 1
```

Connecting a Source to a Flow to a Sink

Now, we will try to connect all three major components of the Akka Streams API:

```
val numbersSource = Source(1 to 10)
val sampleSink = Sink.foreach(println)
val numberFlow = Flow[Int].map(num => num+1)
```

Create all three components to work on numbers. We can use Source's via function to connect a Source to Flow and Flow's to function to connect a Flow to Sink.

```
val numberRunnableGraph = numbersSource.via(numberFlow).to(sampleSink)
```

This is a fully connected RunnableGraph with all three components. When we run this code, it also does give any output.

Why do we need ActorSystem and ActorMaterializer?

Now, it's time to run our RunnableGraph here and find the results. We can run a RunnableGraph by calling its run function, as follows:

```
import akka.stream.scaladsl.{Flow, Sink, Source}
object AkkaStreamsNumbersApp extends App{
  val numbersSource = Source(1 to 10)
  val sampleSink = Sink.foreach(println)
  val numberFlow = Flow[Int].map(num => num+1)
  val numberRunnableGraph =
   numbersSource.via(numberFlow).to(sampleSink)
  numberRunnableGraph.run
}
```

When we run the preceding program, we will get the following error messages:

```
Error:(18, 23) could not find implicit value for parameter materializer:
akka.stream.Materializer
   numberRunnableGraph.run

Error:(18, 23) not enough arguments for method run: (implicit materializer:
akka.stream.Materializer)akka.NotUsed.
Unspecified value parameter materializer.
   numberRunnableGraph.run
```

The first one says that `numberRunnableGraph.run` needs a materializer parameter of the `akka.stream.Materializer` type. We can pass it manually or pass it as an implicit variable.

The second error says that the `run` function does not have enough arguments. It expects a parameter of the `akka.stream.Materializer` type, but it is missing.

So, how do we create Materializer as an `implicit` object?

```
implicit val materializer = ActorMaterializer()
```

Add the preceding statement to our program as shown here and run it again to check the output:

```
import akka.stream.scaladsl.{Flow, Sink, Source}
object AkkaStreamsNumbersApp extends App{
    implicit val materializer = ActorMaterializer()
  val numbersSource = Source(1 to 10)
  val sampleSink = Sink.foreach(println)
  val numberFlow = Flow[Int].map(num => num+1)
  val numberRunnableGraph =
   numbersSource.via(numberFlow).to(sampleSink)
  numberRunnableGraph.run
}
```

When we run the preceding program, we will get the following four errors:

```
Error:(9, 48) implicit ActorRefFactory required: if outside of an Actor you
need an implicit ActorSystem, inside of an actor this should be the
implicit ActorContext
    implicit val materializer = ActorMaterializer()
Error:(9, 48) not enough arguments for method apply: (implicit context:
akka.actor.ActorRefFactory)akka.stream.ActorMaterializer in object
ActorMaterializer.
Unspecified value parameter context.
    implicit val materializer = ActorMaterializer()
Error:(18, 23) could not find implicit value for parameter materializer:
akka.stream.Materializer
    numberRunnableGraph.run
Error:(18, 23) not enough arguments for method run: (implicit materializer:
akka.stream.Materializer)akka.NotUsed.
Unspecified value parameter materializer.
    numberRunnableGraph.run
```

If we observe the first error message, **implicit ActorRefFactory required: if outside of an Actor you need an implicit ActorSystem, inside of an actor this should be the implicit ActorContext**.

We can understand that we need ActorSystem because we are trying to run this code outside an Actor, that is, in a Scala App. If we run the same piece of code within an Actor, we can use ActorContext for the same purpose.

ActorMaterializer creates one or more Actors to run the Akka Stream's Graphs (refer to the ActorMaterializer section for more information) and runs them on ActorSystem, so even ActorMaterializer also needs ActorSystem to run the RunnableGraph using it's internal Actors.

So we should also create `ActorSystem` as an implicit object, as shown here:

```
implicit val actorSystem = ActorSystem("NumberSystem")
```

Now if we add this statement to our Scala App and run it, we will see the expected results:

```
import akka.stream.scaladsl.{Flow, Sink, Source}
object AkkaStreamsNumbersApp extends App{
   implicit val actorSystem = ActorSystem("NumberSystem")
   implicit val materializer = ActorMaterializer()
  val numbersSource = Source(1 to 10)
  val sampleSink = Sink.foreach(println)
  val numberFlow = Flow[Int].map(num => num+1)
  val numberRunnableGraph =
   numbersSource.via(numberFlow).to(sampleSink)
  numberRunnableGraph.run
  actorSystem.terminate
}
```

The output is as follows:

```
2
3
4
5
6
7
8
9
10
11
```

Great! Congratulations. We have successfully developed an Akka Stream's RunnableGraph and executed it very well.

Let's start developing some simple programs using the Akka Streams API in the coming sections.

Akka Streams HelloWorld example

In this section, we will develop our first Akka Streams simple and old-fashioned HelloWorld application. In this example, we will use or experiment with only two of the Akka Streams API components, as shown here:

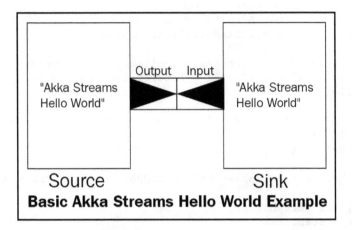

Basic Akka Streams Hello World Example

Perform the following steps to experiment with this example:

1. Create a Scala SBT project in your favorite IDE:

    ```
    Project Name: akka-streams-scala-helloworld-app
    ```

2. Add the `akka-streams` dependency in the `build.sbt` file:

    build.sbt:

    ```
    name := "akka-streams-scala-helloworld-app"
    version := "1.0.0"
    scalaVersion := "2.12.2"
    libraryDependencies ++= Seq(
      "com.typesafe.akka" %% "akka-stream" % "2.5.9"
    )
    ```

    Here, we are using `akka-stream` `"2.5.9"`, the latest stable version.

3. Create a AkkaStreams HelloWorld App with Source ~> Sink:

AkkaStreams_Source2Sink_HelloWorldApp.scala:

```scala
package com.packt.publishing.akka.streams.hello

import akka.actor.ActorSystem
import akka.stream.ActorMaterializer
import akka.stream.scaladsl.{Sink, Source}

object AkkaStreams_Source2Sink_HelloWorldApp extends App{
  implicit val actorSystem = ActorSystem("HelloWorldSystem")
  implicit val materializer = ActorMaterializer()

  val helloWorldSource = Source.single("Akka Streams Hello
   World")
  val helloWorldSink = Sink.foreach(print)

  val helloWorldGraph =  helloWorldSource.to(helloWorldSink)

  helloWorldGraph.run
  actorSystem.terminate
}
```

4. Run the application and observe the output:

```
AKKA STREAMS HELLO WORLD
```

Refer to the *HelloWorld example description* section to understand this example very well.

Extending the Akka Streams HelloWorld example with the Flow component

In this example, we will experiment with the full RunnableGraph, meaning that we will use Flow to connect both Source and Sink. Flow has one input to connect to Source and retrieve incoming data elements. It has one output to connect to Sink and send data elements to it.

We will use the previous HelloWorld example and add a couple of new applications to test different scenarios:

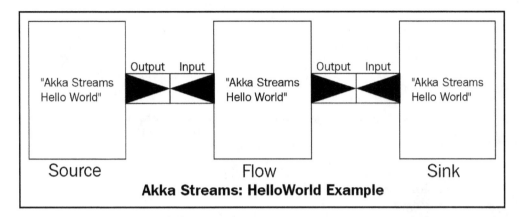

Akka Streams: HelloWorld Example

Perform the following steps to understand this example:

1. Create a Akka Streams HelloWorld App with Source | Flow | Sink:

```
package com.packt.publishing.akka.streams.hello
import akka.actor.ActorSystem
import akka.stream.ActorMaterializer
import akka.stream.scaladsl.{Flow, Sink, Source}

object AkkaStreams_Source2Flow2Sink_HelloWorldApp extends App{

  implicit val actorSystem = ActorSystem("HelloWorldSystem")
  implicit val materializer = ActorMaterializer()
  val helloWorldSource = Source.single("Akka Streams Hello World")
  val helloWorldSink = Sink.foreach(print)
  val helloWorldFlow = Flow[String].map(str => str.toUpperCase)
  val helloWorldGraph =
   helloWorldSource.via(helloWorldFlow).to(helloWorldSink)
  helloWorldGraph.run
  actorSystem.terminate
}
```

2. When we run this application, we will observe the same output:

   AKKA STREAMS HELLO WORLD

3. If you are eager to know the type annotations for each and every step, refer to this example:

```
package com.packt.publishing.akka.streams.hello
import akka.{Done, NotUsed}
import akka.actor.ActorSystem
import akka.stream.ActorMaterializer
import akka.stream.scaladsl.{Flow, RunnableGraph, Sink, Source}
import scala.concurrent.Future

object AkkaStreamsHelloWorldApp_WithTypeAnnotations extends App{
  implicit val actorSystem = ActorSystem("HelloWorldSystem")
  implicit val materializer = ActorMaterializer()
  val helloWorldSource:Source[String,NotUsed] =
   Source.single("Akka Streams Hello World")
  val helloWorldSink: Sink[String,Future[Done]] =
   Sink.foreach(print)
  val strToUpperCase: String => String = str => str.toUpperCase
  val helloWorldFlow:Flow[String,String,NotUsed] =
   Flow[String].map(strToUpperCase)
  val helloWorldGraph:RunnableGraph[NotUsed] =
   helloWorldSource.via(helloWorldFlow).to(helloWorldSink)
  helloWorldGraph.run
  actorSystem.terminate
}
```

HelloWorld example description

We will dissect each step one by one to understand the basics of Akka Streams components.

1. Create a Akka Streams Source as follows:

```
val helloWorldSource = Source.single("Akka Streams Hello World")
```

Here, we create the `Akka Streams Hello World` text message as a Source for this application. We can use the `Source.single` function to create a Source with one element.

The type annotation of the `Source.single` function is `Source[T,NotUsed]`, where `T` is the string in our example. So we can also write the preceding code snippet as follows:

```
val helloWorldSource:Source[String,NotUsed] =
  Source.single("Akka Streams Hello World")
```

`NotUsed` is a sealed abstract class and has one case object, as shown here:

```
sealed abstract class NotUsed
case object NotUsed extends NotUsed { }
```

`NotUsed` is a generic type used to represent the materialized value of an Akka Stream, where no result will be returned from materialization.

Akka Stream's *NotUsed = Scala's Unit + Java's Void*:

2. Create an Akka Streams `Sink`:

```
val helloWorldSink = Sink.foreach(print)
```

Here, we try to create an Akka Stream's Sink component by using the `foreach` function. This Sink does nothing, just takes the input and prints it to the console.

The type annotation of the `Source.single` function is `Sink[T,Future[Done]]`, where `T` is String in our example. So we can also write the preceding code snippet as follows:

```
val helloWorldSink: Sink[String,Future[Done]] =
  Sink.foreach(print)
```

3. Create an Akka Streams `Flow`:

```
val helloWorldFlow = Flow[String].map(str => str.toUpperCase)
```

Here, we try to create an Akka Stream's Flow component by using an anonymous function:

```
val strToUpperCase: String => String = str => str.toUpperCase
```

The return type annotation of the `Flow.map()` function is `Flow[T,T,NotUsed]`, where `T` is `String`. So we can also write the preceding code snippet as follows:

```
val helloWorldFlow:Flow[String,String,NotUsed] =
  Flow[String].map(str => str.toUpperCase)
```

4. Create an Akka Streams `RunnableGraph`:

```
val helloWorldGraph=
  helloWorldSource.via(helloWorldFlow).to(helloWorldSink)
```

Here, we try to create an Akka Streams `RunnableGraph` by linking the `Source` and `Sink` components with a `Flow` component:

```
RunnableGraph = Source → Flow → Sink
```

We can connect a Source with Flow using one of the following functions available in the Source class:

- via
- viaMat

We can also directly connect a Source to Sink (without the mediator—Flow component) by using one of the following functions:

- to
- toMat

We try to create Akka Stream's RunnableGraph by connecting Source to Sink directly as shown here:

```
RunnableGraph= Source → Sink
```

We can connect a Flow with Sink by using one of the following functions:

- toMat

Both `to` and `via` functions keep materialized value of the stream they are called on.

Consider the following example:

```
source.to(sink)
```

Here the `to()` function keeps materialized value of the source, but not its argument, which is sink, which can be explained as follows:

```
source.to(sink)(Keep.Left)
```

Whereas, `toMat` and `viaMat` functions keep materialized values for both streams:

- One Stream they are called on
- Another Stream of their arguments

For instance, `source.toMat(sink)` will prepare materialized values for both source and sink streams which means:

```
source.to(sink)(Keep.Both)
```

The return type annotation of Graph is `RunnableGraph[NotUsed]`. So we can also write the preceding code snippet as follows:

```
val helloWorldGraph:RunnableGraph[NotUsed] = helloWorldSource
.via(helloWorldFlow)
.to(helloWorldSink)
```

Akka Streams GraphDSL

The Akka Streams API supports two kinds of Graphs:

- **Linear graphs**: These graphs are simple graphs with only basic building blocks of Akka Streams (Source | Flow | Sink). They have no complexity:

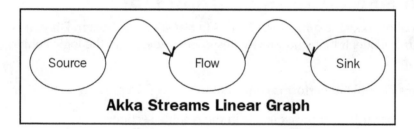

Akka Streams Linear Graph

- **Non-linear graphs**: These graphs are complex graphs with the basic building blocks of Akka Streams + Akka Streams junctions:

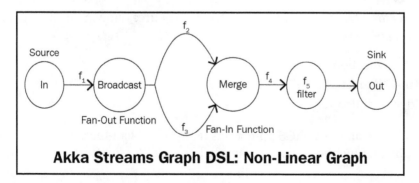

Akka Streams Graph DSL: Non-Linear Graph

To support these two kinds of Akka Streams Graphs, the Akka Streams API has the following two kinds of Graph **DSL (Domain-Specific Language)** APIs:

- **Akka Streams DSL**: This is a DSL API used for Akka Streams linear graphs, that is, only for simple graphs. It has two sets of APIs:
  - Akka Streams DSL for Java
  - Akka Streams DSL for Scala
- **Akka Streams Graph DSL**: This is a DSL API used for Akka Streams non-linear graphs, that is, only for complex graphs. Like Akka Streams DSL, this too has two sets of APIs:
  - Akka Streams Graph DSL for Java
  - Akka Streams Graph DSL for Scala

Akka Streams Graph DSL is useful for expressing data stream processing in nicer, simple, and easy-to-understand graphs.

Goal of Akka Streams Graph DSL

The main goal of Akka Streams GraphDSL is to translate our Design Diagrams into Akka Streams Source Code. It helps non-techy designers understand the logic behind the code using that Graph.

Akka Streams GraphDSL performs computations using Graphs.

Let's explore this with a simple example in the coming section.

Building blocks of Akka Streams Graph DSL

Like Akka Streams, DSL has basic building blocks—Source, Flow, Sink, and so on. Akka Streams Graph DSL has the following building blocks:

- Fan-In junctions
- Fan-Out junctions
- Edge operator

These two Akka Streams GraphDSL junctions (Fan-In and Fan-Out) are known as Akka Streams GraphDSL functions. They are simply known as Graph functions or Graph junctions.

Fan-In functions

In Akka Streams GraphDSL, a Fan-In function is a function with multiple inputs and single output.

In simple words, Fan-In means multiple inputs. A GraphDSL Fan-In function is also known as GraphDSL Fan-In junction:

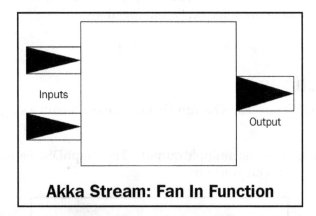

Akka Stream: Fan In Function

As shown in the preceding diagram, it takes two inputs from other components from the RunnableGraph and performs a given operation to result it to one output:

Fan-In Function = Multiple Inputs

Fan = Multiple

In = Input

Akka Streams GraphDSL has the following Fan-In junctions:

- `Merge[In]`: (*N* inputs, 1 output) This picks randomly from inputs pushing them one by one to the output
- `MergePreferred[In]`: This is like Merge, but if elements are available on the preferred port, it picks from it; otherwise, it picks randomly from others
- `ZipWith[A,B,...,Out]`: (*N* inputs, 1 output) This takes a function of *N* inputs that given a value for each input emits one output element

- `Zip[A,B]`: (2 inputs, 1 output) This is a `ZipWith` specialized to zipping input streams of *A* and *B* into an (A, B) tuple stream
- `Concat[A]`: (2 inputs, 1 output) This concatenates two streams (first consume one, then the second one)

Refer to the Akka Streams GraphDSL documentation at `http://doc.akka.io/docs/akka/2.5.3/scala/stream/stream-graphs.ht ml` for more information on Fan-In functions.

Fan-Out functions

In Akka Streams GraphDSL, a Fan-Out function is a function with a single input and multiple outputs.

In simple words, Fan-Out means multiple outputs. The GraphDSL Fan-Out function is also known as a GraphDSL Fan-Out junction:

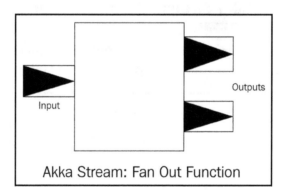

Akka Stream: Fan Out Function

As shown in the preceding diagram, it has exactly one input point and two output points. This means that it takes one input from the other component and splits it into two outputs based on the given requirements:

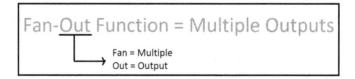

An Akka Streams GraphDSL has the following Fan-Out junctions:

- `Broadcast[T]`: (1 input, *N* outputs) given an input element emits to each output
- `Balance[T]`: (1 input, *N* outputs) given an input element emits to one of its output ports
- `UnzipWith[In,A,B,...]`: (1 input, N outputs) takes a function of one input that, given a value for each input, emits N output elements (where `N <= 20`)
- `UnZip[A,B]`: (1 input, 2 outputs) splits a stream of (`A`, `B`) tuples into two streams, one of type A and one of type B

> Refer to the Akka Streams GraphDSL documentation at `http://doc.akka.io/docs/akka/2.5.3/scala/stream/stream-graphs.html` for more information on Fan-Out functions.

We will explore some of the Fan-In and Fan-Out junctions in the coming section with one simple example.

Edge operator

In Akka Streams GraphDSL, we use an operator known as Edge operator to build graphs in an easy and concise way. It is depicted as ~>. We can also read it as connect, via, or to.

The main goal of this operator in Akka Streams GraphDSL is *to translate our Design Diagrams into Akka Streams Source Code*. It helps non-techy designers also understand the logic of the code using that Graph. We will explore it in the coming example with one image.

In our programs, we can get this operator implicitly by importing `GraphDSL.Implicits` as follows:

```
import GraphDSL.Implicits._
```

> Both Graph and RunnableGraph are immutable, thread safe, and freely shareable.

An Akka Streams GraphDSL example

In this section, let's develop one complex non-linear graph using Akka Streams Graph DSL.

Refer to the Akka Streams Graph DSL's *Non-Linear Graph* image in the *Akka Streams GraphDSL* section. We will develop the same example here.

Follow these steps to execute this example:

1. Create a Scala SBT project in your favorite IDE:

```
Project name: akka-streams-scala-graphdsl-example
```

2. Add the `akka-streams` module to `build.sbt`:

build.sbt:

```
name := "akka-streams-scala-graphdsl-app"
version := "1.0.0"
scalaVersion := "2.12.2"
libraryDependencies ++= Seq(
  "com.typesafe.akka" %% "akka-stream" % "2.5.9"
 )
```

 The Akka Streams module (`akka-stream`) contains Akka Streams API, Akka Streams DSL, and Graph DSL.

3. Create a Scala App with the Akka Streams Graph DSL code:

AkkaStreamsGraphApp.scala:

```
package com.packt.publishing.akka.streams.graphdsl
import akka.NotUsed
import akka.actor.ActorSystem
import akka.stream.scaladsl.{Broadcast, Flow, GraphDSL, Merge,
 RunnableGraph, Sink, Source}
import akka.stream.{ActorMaterializer, ClosedShape}
object AkkaStreamsGraphApp extends App{
  implicit val actorSystem = ActorSystem("NumberSystem")
  implicit val materializer = ActorMaterializer()
  val graph = RunnableGraph.fromGraph(GraphDSL.create() {
    implicit builder: GraphDSL.Builder[NotUsed] =>
    import GraphDSL.Implicits._
    val in = Source(1 to 10)
    val out = Sink.foreach(println)
    val bcast = builder.add(Broadcast[Int](2))
    val merge = builder.add(Merge[Int](2))
    val f1, f2, f3, f4 = Flow[Int].map(_ + 1)
```

```
val f5 = Flow[Int].filter(x => x % 2 ==0)
in ~> f1 ~> bcast ~> f2 ~> merge ~> f4  ~> f5 ~> out
                 bcast ~> f3 ~> merge
ClosedShape
})
graph.run
actorSystem.terminate
}
```

4. Execute the preceding Scala App and observe the following output:

```
4
4
6
6
8
8
10
10
12
12
```

We will go through our previous Akka Streams Graph DSL app step by step here to understand it well. Finally, we will compare our source code to our Graph diagram to check whether they look similar or not:

1. Create a RunnableGraph by making a call to fromGraph like
   `RunnableGraph.fromGraph()`.

2. Create a Closed Graph using `GraphDSL.create()`, as shown here:

   ```
   GraphDSL.create() {
       ...
     ClosedShape
   }
   ```

 A Closed Graph means all ports (all input and output points) are connected; no single point is open to connect to another. Refer to our non-linear graph diagram; all inputs and outputs are closed, meaning that they are connected to other points.

3. Create our Source and Sinks:

   ```
   val in = Source(1 to 10)
   val out = Sink.foreach(println)
   ```

A Source is an Akka Streams component that consumes elements (for instance, consuming a number from a Scala range like `1` to `10` from the preceding program).

4. Create Graph DSL Fan-In and Fan-Out junctions:

```
val bcast = builder.add(Broadcast[Int](2))
val merge = builder.add(Merge[Int](2))
```

Here, `bcast` is the Broadcast function, which is a Fan-Out function, and `merge` is Merge function, which is a Fan-In function.

5. Create user-defined functions, which are not GraphDSL functions:

```
val f1, f2, f3, f4 = Flow[Int].map(_ + 1)
```

These functions do the same thing. They take one number and add 1 to it.

6. Create our Closed Graph by using the Edge operator:

```
in ~> f1 ~> bcast ~> f2 ~> merge ~> f4  ~> f5 ~> out
            bcast ~> f3 ~> merge
```

7. Run the graph by using the run function like `graph.run`.

If we observe our source code and our Graph diagram, they look the same:

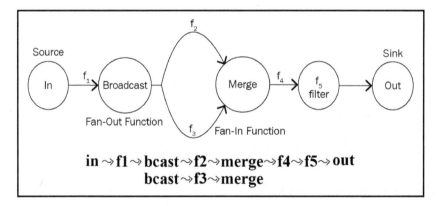

For simple, straight-line, and linear graphs, we should use Akka Streams DSL. Data streaming is processed using Akka Core building blocks (Source, Flow, and Sink)

For complex and non-linear graphs, we use both Akka Streams DSL and Akka Streams Graph DSL. Data streaming is done by using both Akka Core building blocks (Source, Flow, and Sink) and Akka Streams GraphDSL building blocks (Fan-In and Fan-Out functions).

Akka Persistence

Akka Toolkit has a module to support the persistence feature, Akka Persistence. Initially, Akka Toolkit has an eventsourced Scala library for the same purpose.

The Akka Persistence module was inspired and developed by following that eventsourced Scala library. However, that eventsourced library is now deprecated.

Akka Persistence has mainly the following two modules:

- akka-persistence
- akka-persistence-query

Consider the following Akka Persistence modules:

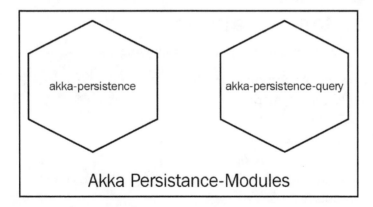

Eventsourced and Akka Persistence are both Akka Extensions or Modules.

In Akka Toolkit, the main goal of the Akka Persistence module is to provide a way to persist Stateful Actor's internal state to a Data Store, File System, In-Memory, and more. The Akka Persistence module stores only the changes to that Actor's internal state, not its current state.

When that Actor is crashed/started/restarted by its JVM or Supervisor, the Akka Persistence module uses those storages to recover that Actor to the previous state.

 In an Akka Persistence module, these data stores are known as **journals**.

Unlike other data store techniques, Akka Persistence stores a sequence of events generated in a system (application), not just the current state of the system. It follows the CQRS/ES pattern to ease this process.

So, before diving into the Akka Persistence module, let's first understand what the CQRS/ES pattern is and how it works.

 The Akka Persistence module follows this rule—*First persist the Event then update the State.*

Akka Persistence features

In Akka Toolkit, Akka Persistence supports the following features:

- The persisting Stateful Actor's State
- The Event Sourcing model
- The EQRS pattern
- The Persistence query
- The Plug-ins API to develop journals
- Different journals, such as MongoDB and Apache Cassandra
- The Snapshots feature
- We can answer both What and Why questions
- Easy to maintain event-based architectures/systems/applications with EQRS/ES
- Event adapters to decouple the Data Model from the Domain Model

The ES (Event Sourcing) model

ES model has two main components—Event and Event Stream. They are also known as the building blocks of event sourcing. ES is an architectural pattern.

What is an Event?

An Event is a significant change in the state of a thing. Here, a thing can be anything, such as a model, domain, entity, and more.

When a user performs any change action (that means an update operation such as CREATE, UPDATE, or DELETE operations), it updates the state of one or more entities in that system. Each change creates an Event. So, every system generates a sequence of events. Then how do we track them? What is the use of those events? The answer is Event Streams.

An Event Stream

An Event Stream is a streams or a data store for storing all those system events. It is a sequence of events generated by the system. It stores events sequentially:

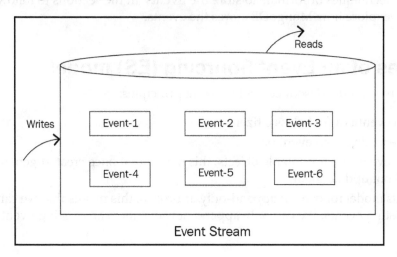

When a user queries the current state of an entity of the system, then the system queries the Event Stream to get a list of events generated to that entity. The system runs or executes all those events one by one to get the current state of the entity.

Let's explore it with a **WF** (**Weather Forecasting**) system. For a specific hour of the current day, the WF system has the following events:

- *Event-1(Day=Current Day, Hour=11, "Temperature set 20 Degrees")*
- *Event-2(Day=Current Day, Hour=11, "Temperature increased 3 Degrees")*
- *Event-3(Day=Current Day, Hour=11, "Temperature decreased 2 Degrees")*
- *Event-4(Day=Current Day, Hour=11, "Temperature increased 4 Degrees")*

When our system queries these events from the Event Stream and executes them sequentially, so Event-1, Event-2, Event-3, and Event-4, we will get the Temperature of the 11th hour of Current Day, which is 20 + 3 - 2 + 4 = 25 Degrees.

This kind of events execution is also known as events replier or replaying of events.

 Here, I have given the Event Data in a simple format to help you understand the concept well. Different data store vendors use different techniques or formats to store the Events. In the sections to follow, we will explore how MongoDB stores the events.

Principles of an Event Sourcing (ES) model

An event sourced model describes the following principles:

- An event is a first-class citizen.
- Everything is an event only.
- All events are immutable objects; this means that once created/generated, we cannot update them.
- This model follows an append-only approach; this means that we cannot update existing events. We can only append new events to an existing Event Stream.

Event sourcing

Event Sourcing is a technique to store, process, and analyze a sequence of events that happened in a system, not just the current state of the system. It is mainly useful in Event-Driven architecture or Event-Driven applications to get more benefits, such as the following:

- By replaying events, we can answer any kind of user queries.
- For instance, what is the temperature at a specific hour of a day and how does it come to this state? We can answer this by playing a sequence of events one by one. It is not possible to answer this question if we use a normal data store and store only the current temperature of that day.
- It is easy to know the state of the system at any given point of the time.
- It is easy to support the CQRS pattern.
- It is easy to maintain the system.
- It supports the Append A-only model, so there is no point in getting inconsistent data.
- No need to Audit the system's activities separately, as it stores each and every system change (event) clearly.

 You can learn more about Event Sourcing at
http://cqrs.nu/Faq/event-sourcing.

The CQRS pattern

CQRS stands for Command Query Responsibility Segregation. CQRS is an architectural pattern created by Greg Young, based on Bertrand Meyer's Command and Query Separation principle.

Greg Young, the father of CQRS, coined this term. The CQRS pattern was inspired by the **Command Query Separation (CQS)** technique.

Wikipedia defines this CQS as follows:

> *It states that every method should either be a command that performs an action, or a query that returns data to the caller, but not both. In other words, asking a question should not change the answer. More formally, methods should return a value only if they are referentially transparent and hence possess no side effects.*

We know that every system or application has two kinds of operation:

- Write operation (CREATE, UPDATE, and DELETE)
- Read operation (READ)

If we don't follow the CQRS pattern, I mean using old-style traditional CRUD style pattern, we use the same model or domain object to perform both Write and Read operations. There is no coupling between those two operations. So it is very hard to manage those operations and the system:

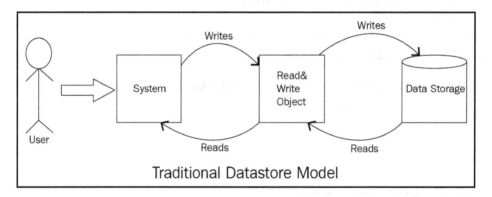

A single model or domain object is not sufficient to handle the things properly. However, in the CQRS pattern, we separate those two operations clearly. We use two different domain or model objects to manage those two operations.

As Write operations need some kind of locking to avoid data inconsistency issues, it may cause some performance issues if we don't use CQRS for Read operations. Read operations are blocked and should wait until a Write operation finishes its job.

It is not the case in the CQRS pattern. As we separate Write and Read operations clearly, we will get better performance for all Query operations.

In the CQRS pattern terminology, a Write operation is known as Command and a Read operation is known as Query.

Commands are write operations or functions that update the state of the model, entity, or Actor, which are side-effect functions and should not return any value:

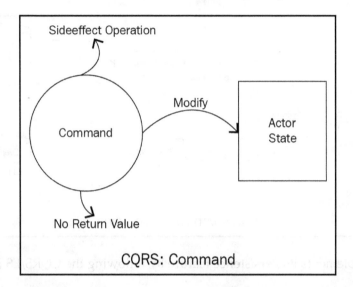

Queries are Read operations or functions that do not update the state of the model, entity, or Actor; they just query the results, which are NOT side-effect functions, and should return query results:

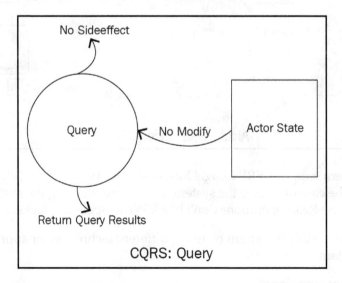

As it has clear separation (segregation) of two responsibilities, we call this technique **CQRS** (**Command Query Responsibility Segregation**):

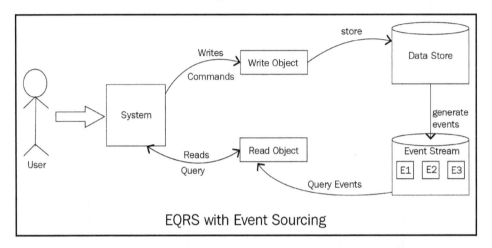

EQRS with Event Sourcing

Akka Toolkit implements its Persistence feature by following the CQRS/ES pattern as shown here:

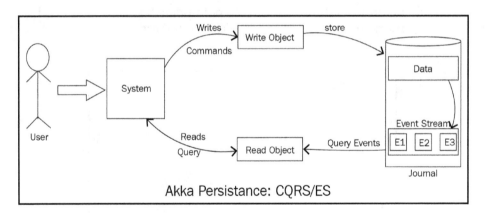

Akka Persistance: CQRS/ES

As the CQRS pattern supports SRP (Single Responsibility Principle) clearly, it gives many benefits, such as the ease of testing the system, ease of maintaining the system, better performance because Read operations don't block Write operation locks, and more.

We can implement the CQRS pattern by using different techniques or approaches. Here are a couple of important approaches:

- **ES (event sourcing)**
- **Command sourcing (CS)**

Both CQRS and ES are architectural patterns.

Benefits of CQRS

If we follow the CQRS pattern to implement our systems, we will get the following benefits:

- Easy to maintain our system for a long time
- Provides better performance
- Easy to test the system
- Easy to scale the system
- Gives better responsiveness to our system
- Better performance, scalability, and responsiveness

How Akka Persistence implements CQRS/ES

Akka Persistence supports the CQRS/ES pattern very well. The main goal of Akka Persistence is to support event stream processing.

As shown in the following diagram, we use two different objects—one for Read and another for Write operations. If our system is small, not complex, then we can use a single data store for both Read and Write operations. If our system is too big and needs to support complex architecture, then it is recommended that we use two separate data stores—one for Read and another for Write operations:

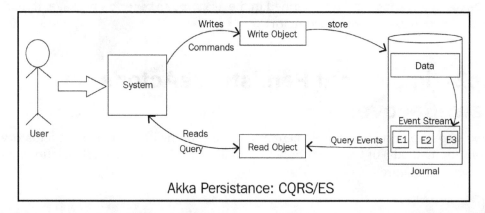

In Akka Persistence terminology, a data store is known as a journal. We can use any journal to store our Read and Write data.

In the next example, we will use MongoDB as a journal. We will also experiment with Apache Cassandra journal in the coming chapters.

 You can learn more about the CQRS pattern at
`http://cqrs.nu/Faq/command-query-responsibility-segregation`.

How to develop Akka Persistence Actors

Before diving into the development of Akka Persistence application, we will consider some steps on how to develop an Akka Persistence Actor, covering which components are important, which functions are required to provide implementation, how to interact with Journals, and so on.

Step1 – Use the PersistenceActor trait

If want to develop an Akka Persistence component or Actor, add the `PersistenceActor` trait to this Actor, as shown here:

```
class HelloWorldActor extends PersistentActor{
  // Actor State goes here
  // Actor Operations goes here
}
```

Here, `PersistentActor` is a trait defined in the `akka.persistence` package. It marks our `HelloWorldActor` as a Persistence Actor.

Step2 – Implement PersistenceActor's receiveRecover

The next step is to provide an implementation for one of the important and mandatory functions (or methods) of `PersistentActor` trait—`receiveRecover`. It is defined with the following signature:

```
def receiveRecover: Receive
```

This function is also known as the recovery handler. It is used to restore the state of our Persistence Actor from its journal (such as MongoDB, Apache Cassandra, and so on) when an Actor is crashed, started, or restarted by its JVM or its Supervisor. This `receiveRecover()` function works in one the following two kinds of behaviors:

- **Normal behavior (without the Snapshots feature)**: When this function is executed, it retrieves all available events related to that Persistence Actor from the journal and replay those events sequentially to get the current state of the Actor.
- **Snapshots behavior (with Snapshots feature)**: If we have implemented the Snapshots feature, this handler receives only the related events that are younger than the offered Snapshot from journal and replay those events sequentially to get the current state of the Actor.

 Other than updating the Actor's state, this function should not do any other side-effect activities.

Like plain Actor's `receive` function, it is also a `PartialFunction` and it has the following:

- Receive as a return type
- Receive is a type of `PartialFunction[Any, Unit]`
- `PartialFunction[Any, Unit]` means it can handle any type and return nothing

 Refer to `Chapter 4`, *Building Reactive Applications with Akka*, for more information on Actor's receive function description.

Step3 – Implement PersistenceActor's receiveCommand

The next step is that we need to provide implementation for another important and mandatory function (or method) of the `PersistentActor` trait—`receiveCommand`. It is defined with the following signature:

```
def receiveCommand: Receive
```

It is also known as command handler. It receives commands and validates them. If those commands are valid, then it generates one or more events and runs a persist function to persist those events to the journal or data store. Then it updates the state of the `PersistentActor`.

As we discussed in the previous section, the Akka Persistence module first persists the generated event to the journal, and only then updates.

If the persisting of the events steps fail, it won't update the state of the Actor. It leaves the current state of the Actor as it is.

Like the `receiveRecover` function, the `receiveCommand` function also has a type of Receive.

 Refer to `Chapter 4`, *Building Reactive Applications with Akka*, for more information on Actor's receive function description.

Step4 – Implement PersistenceActor's persistenceId

Our next step is to provide the implementation for another important and mandatory function of the `PersistentActor` trait—`persistenceId`. It is defined with the following signature:

```
def persistenceId: String
```

It should provide a unique ID for our persistent entity or Actor for which messages should be replayed. It is useful to provide our entity events in the journal uniquely.

Finally, our Persistence Actor looks like this:

```
class HelloWorldActor extends PersistentActor{
  // Actor State
  val entity: HelloWorldEntity = ....
  def receiveRecover: Receive = {
      // Implementation to recover the state of HelloWorldEntity
        from Journal
  }
  def receiveCommand: Receive = {
      // Implementation to Validate and Store HelloWorldEntity's
        Commands to Journal
```

```
    }
    def persistenceId: String = {
        // Implementation to provide Unique ID for HelloWorldEntity
    }
}
```

Step5 – Configure our journal details in application.conf

The last step is that we should provide our journal (or data store, for instance, MongoDB) with config details in the `application.conf` file.

Let's develop one of the scenarios of our Weather Forecasting Systems using Akka Persistence CQRS/ES with MongoDB journal in the next section.

Akka Persistence MongoDB Weather example

In this section, we will develop a simple Akka Persistence Weather Application to explore the CQRS/ES pattern. We will use MongoDB as our application Akka Persistence journal to store our events.

Use the following steps to experiment with Akka Persistence with MongoDB:

1. Create an SBT Scala project from your favorite IDE:

   ```
   Project name: akka-persistence-mongodb-weather-ap
   ```

2. Update `build.sbt` with the following content:

   build.sbt:

   ```
   name := "akka-persistence-mongodb-weather-app"
   version := "1.0.0"
   scalaVersion := "2.12.4"
   libraryDependencies ++= {
     Seq(
       "com.typesafe.akka" %% "akka-actor" % "2.5.9",
       "com.typesafe.akka" %% "akka-persistence" % "2.5.9",
       "com.typesafe.akka" %% "akka-slf4j" % "2.5.9"
   ```

```
    )
  }
  build.properties
  sbt.version = 0.13.16
```

3. Create the Model:

```
package com.packt.publishing.wf.persist.model
case class WeatherForcastPerHour(city:String, date:String,
  day:String, hour:String,  temparature:Int )
```

4. Create the events:

Events.scala:

```
sealed trait WeatherForecastEvent
case class TemparatureIncreased(
  temparature:WeatherForcastPerHour) extends WeatherForecastEvent
case class TemparatureDecreased(
  temparature:WeatherForcastPerHour) extends WeatherForecastEvent
```

5. Create the commands:

Commands.scala:

```
sealed trait WeatherForcastHour
case class IncreaseTemparature(temparature:
  WeatherForcastPerHour) extends WeatherForcastHour
case class DecreaseTemparature(temparature:
  WeatherForcastPerHour) extends WeatherForcastHour
case object PrintTemparature extends WeatherForcastHour
case object GetTemparature extends WeatherForcastHour
```

6. Create the service:

TemparatureService.scala:

```
object TemparatureService {
  def decreaseTemparature(prevTemparature:WeatherForcastPerHour,
    currTemparature:Int): WeatherForcastPerHour =
    prevTemparature.copy(temparature =
    (prevTemparature.temparature - currTemparature))
  def increaseTemparature(prevTemparature:WeatherForcastPerHour,
    currTemparature:Int): WeatherForcastPerHour =
    prevTemparature.copy(temparature =
    (prevTemparature.temparature + currTemparature))
}
```

7. Create the Persistent Actor:

WFPersistenceActor.scala:

```scala
class WFPersistenceActor(initialTemparature:
WeatherForcastPerHour) extends PersistentActor with ActorLogging {

  var temparature: WeatherForcastPerHour = initialTemparature
   override def receiveRecover: Receive = {
    case event:WeatherForecastEvent =>
      updateTemparature(event)
    case RecoveryCompleted => log.info("Recovering data
      completed.")
  }
   override def receiveCommand: Receive = {
    case DecreaseTemparature(temp) =>
      persist(TemparatureDecreased(temp))(updateTemparature)
      sender ! "Decreased the Temparature successfully."
    case IncreaseTemparature(temp) =>
      persist(TemparatureIncreased(temp))(updateTemparature)
      sender ! "Increased the Temparature successfully."
    case PrintTemparature => log.info(s"Current Temparature:
      $temparature")
    case GetTemparature => sender ! temparature
  }

  override def persistenceId: String = WFPersistenceActor.name
  val updateTemparature:WeatherForecastEvent => Unit = {
    case TemparatureDecreased(temp) => temparature =
      TemparatureService.decreaseTemparature(
      temparature,temp.temparature)
    case TemparatureIncreased(temp) => temparature =
      TemparatureService.increaseTemparature(
      temparature,temp.temparature)
  }
}
object WFPersistenceActor {
  val name = "WFPersistenceActor"
}
```

8. Configure the journal:

reference.conf:

```
akka {
  stdout-loglevel = off
  log-dead-letters-during-shutdown = off
```

```
      loglevel = info
      log-dead-letters = off
      log-config-on-start = off

      loggers = ["akka.event.slf4j.Slf4jLogger"]
      logging-filter = "akka.event.slf4j.Slf4jLoggingFilter"

      persistence {
        journal {
          plugin = "casbah-journal"
        }
      }
    }

    casbah-journal {
      mongo-url = "mongodb://localhost:27017/weatherforecast.events"
      woption = 1
      wtimeout = 10000
      load-attempts = 5
    }
```

The output should be as follows:

I will add the Robomongo tool screenshot at the time of final review.

Please refer to `Appendix B`, *Installing Robomongo*, for more information on How to install and use the Robomongo tool.

Summary

In this chapter, we discussed what Akka Streams are and why we need them, and also their features and benefits with some simple examples.

The Akka Streams API has two kinds of DSL for easy data streaming; Akka Streams DSL and Akka Streams GraphDSL. Both DSL have two sets of APIs—one for Java and one for Scala.

Akka Streams has three core and basic building blocks—Source, Flow, and Sink. We have discussed them thoroughly, with examples. It also has two GraphDSL building blocks, Fan-In and Fan-Out junctions, which support complex and non-linear Graphs.

In next chapter, we will develop our WF application completely using our Lightbend Reactive Stack-Play Framework, Akka, Scala, and Akka Streams.

8

Integrating Akka Streams to Play Application

In this chapter, we will discuss Akka Dynamic Streams components, MergeHub, BroadcastHub, and PartitionHub in detail with some simple examples. Dynamic Streams allow us to execute an Akka Stream's component multiple times, based on our requirements; this is not possible with Basic Akka Static Streams components (discussed in Chapter 7, *Working with Reactive Streams*).

Once we are comfortable with Akka Dynamic Streams components, we will design a Reactive Chat Application graph using both Akka Static and Dynamic Streams components. We will understand how to use Dynamic Streams components to implement our application.

We will develop a Reactive Chatting System using Scala, Play Framework, Web Socket, Akka Streams API, SBT, and so on.

Finally, we will discuss the Akka Persistence Query API with some simple examples. We will use a similar kind of Persistence Query in Chapter 9, *Reactive Microservices with Lagom*. I consider it good to understand some Akka Persistence Query basics here before we use them in our real WF Reactive System.

In this chapter, you will learn the following concepts:

- What are Akka Dynamic Streams components?
- Developing examples to understand Akka Dynamic Streams
- Integrating the Akka Streams API into Play Framework
- Learning the Akka Persistence Query API

Akka Streams

You have already learned many concepts and developed a couple of Akka Streams examples in `Chapter 7`, *Working with Reactive Streams*. As the current chapter is an extension of `Chapter 7`, *Working with Reactive Streams*, I recommend that you refer to that chapter and practice those examples before going through this chapter.

Akka Streams revisited

Before moving into the integration of Akka Streams to the Play Framework web application, we will recollect our knowledge about Akka Streams API basics here.

The Akka Streams API has predominantly the following three components:

- Source
- Flow
- Sink

Source is a **Producer** of a streaming data and has only one Output and no Input points. **Sink** is a Consumer of a streaming data and has only one Input and no Output.

Flow is a connector or mediator between Source and Sink for a streaming data and has a one Input and one Output.

Apart from these three components, the Akka Streams API has few more components:

- Fan-In function
- Fan-Out function
- RunnableGraph

Fan-In function has two Inputs and one Output. This means that it takes two inputs of other components from RunnableGraph, performs some given operation, and sends that result into one Output.

Fan-Out function has exactly one Input and two Output points. This means that it takes one Input of other components from RunnableGraph, performs some given operation, and splits the result into two Outputs based on the given requirements.

When we connect two or more Akka Stream components to perform a task and generate a result, it will form a RunnableGraph.

Types of Akka Stream components

Apart from components, Akka Stream also has many other data streaming components. Based on the functionality and nature of these components, we can categorize them into the following types:

- Static Data Stream components
- Dynamic Data Stream components

As we discussed in `Chapter 7`, *Working with Reactive Streams,* all these components are also known as **Stages** of the Graph.

Akka Dynamic Streams

When we know the complete flow from Producer to Consumer in advance, we can create that Graph using simple Source, Flow, and Sink components (if required, use Fan-In and Fan-Out functions too). We should use that Graph as it is to compute a task. This is why they are known as **Static Data Stream components**. This means that all the Graph component's connections must be known in advance and be connected upfront.

However, there are some scenarios where we don't know how the Graph components are connected and how many components are required to fulfill a computation. We don't know this kind of dynamic nature in advance. So, we should create those graphs dynamically using some of the Akka Streams components. This kind of Akka Stream components with dynamic nature are known as **Dynamic Data Stream components**.

The Akka Streams API has many Dynamic Data Stream components. These are also known as Hubs. We will discuss the following three components:

- MergeHub
- BroadcastHub
- PartitionHub

These are also known as Dynamic Fan-In/Fan-Out Streams.

How do Dynamic Data Stream components work? How do they connect dynamically?

Yes, these are good questions. In the Dynamic Fan-In and Fan-Out functions, we connect basic Stream components using Source, Sink, Flow, and so on. However, based on our system requirements, one of these components will be materialized or executed multiple times to generate the Dynamic Fan-In and Fan-Out functions.

MergeHub

In the Akka Streams API, MergeHub acts as a Source of elements. We can attach this Hub into only one Sink or single Consumer. This means that we can materialize this Hub value into a Sink, which inturn can be materialized any number of times.

MergeHub allows us to implement a Dynamic Fan-In junction point in a Graph, where elements coming from different Producers are emitted in a first-come-first-served fashion:

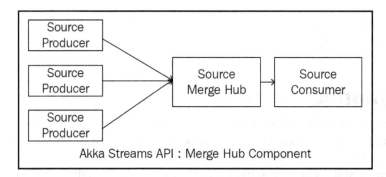

Akka Streams API : Merge Hub Component

As shown in the preceding diagram, we can attach any number of producers to a MergeHub component; however, we can connect this Hub to a single consumer only.

BroadcastHub

In the Akka Streams API, BroadcastHub acts as a Sink for incoming elements or values. We can attach this Hub into any number of dynamic consumers. This means that we can materialize this Hub value into any number of consumers and any number of times. This Hub allows us to implement a Dynamic Fan-Out Junction point in a Graph:

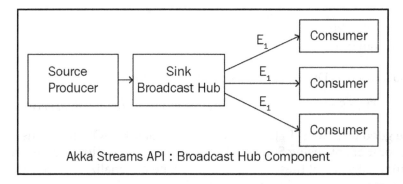

Akka Streams API : Broadcast Hub Component

As shown in the preceding diagram, we can attach only one producer to a BroadcastHub component; however, we can connect this Hub to any number of consumers.

PartitionHub

In the Akka Streams API, PartitionHub acts as a Sink from a common producer to a dynamic set of consumers. We can attach this Hub into any number of dynamic consumers. This Hub allows us to implement a Dynamic Fan-Out Junction point in a Graph.

As shown in the preceding diagram, we can attach only one Producer to a PartitionHub component; however, we can connect this Hub to any number of consumers.

The major difference between BroadcastHub and PartitionHub is this:

- In BroadcastHub, each element should be routed to all consumers
- In PartitionHub, each element can be routed to only one consumer

Developing Akka Dynamic Streams

Before integrating Akka Streams into our Play web application, in this section, we will develop and explore Akka Streams Dynamic components with one simple example.

Perform the following steps to explore Akka Streams Dynamic components:

1. Create a Scala SBT project in your favorite IDE:

   ```
   Project Name: akka-dynamic-streams-scala-app.
   ```

2. Add the `akka-streams` dependency in the `build.sbt` file as shown here:

   build.sbt

   ```
   name := "akka-dynamic-streams-scala-app"
   version := "1.0.0"
   scalaVersion := "2.12.4"
   libraryDependencies ++= Seq(
    "com.typesafe.akka" %% "akka-stream" % "2.5.9"
    )
   ```

3. Develop and test `AkkaStreamsMergeHubApp,` as shown here:

```
object AkkaStreamsMergeHubApp extends App{
    implicit val actorSystem = ActorSystem("MergeHubSystem")
    implicit val materializer = ActorMaterializer()
    val consumer = Sink.foreach(println)
    val mergeHub = MergeHub.source[String](perProducerBufferSize = 16)
    val runnableGraph: RunnableGraph[Sink[String, NotUsed]] =
     mergeHub.to(consumer)
    val toConsumer: Sink[String, NotUsed] = runnableGraph.run()
    Source.single("Hello!").runWith(toConsumer)
    Source.single("MergeHub!").runWith(toConsumer)
    Source.single("World!").runWith(toConsumer)
    Thread.sleep(500)
    actorSystem.terminate
}
```

Now let us understand the preceding Scala Application step by step:

1. We can create MergeHub using its utility function—`source().` It requires a parameter—`perProducerBufferSize,` as shown here:

```
val mergeHub = MergeHub.source[String](perProducerBufferSize = 16)
```

2. Once we create a RunnableGraph with MergeHub, we should run and materialize it before attaching this to multiple Sources:

```
val runnableGraph = mergeHub.to(consumer)
```

3. As discussed in the previous section, we have attached our Hub to multiple producers, but it is attached to a single consumer only.

4. When we run the preceding `AkkaStreamsMergeHubApp` in the IDE, we can observe the following output from the console:

If we observe the preceding output, we can understand that the order of the output is not guaranteed. If we run the same app again, we may see a different order output.

5. Develop and test `AkkaStreamsBroadcastHubApp`, as shown here:

```
object AkkaStreamsBroadcastHubApp extends App{
  implicit val actorSystem = ActorSystem("BroadcastHubSystem")
  implicit val materializer = ActorMaterializer()
  val producer = Source.tick(1.second, 1.second, "New message")
  val runnableGraph: RunnableGraph[Source[String, NotUsed]] =
   producer.toMat(BroadcastHub.sink(bufferSize = 256))(Keep.right)
  val fromProducer: Source[String, NotUsed] = runnableGraph.run()
  fromProducer.runForeach(msg ⇒ println("consumer1: " + msg))
  fromProducer.runForeach(msg ⇒ println("consumer2: " + msg))
  Thread.sleep(5000)
  actorSystem.terminate
}
```

Description:

1. We can create BroadcastHub using its utility function—`source()`. It requires a parameter, `bufferSize`, as shown here:

   ```
   BroadcastHub.sink(bufferSize = 256)
   ```

2. We create a producer to send one message per second:

   ```
   Source.tick(1.second, 1.second, "New message")
   ```

3. We connect our Hub to two consumers.

When we run the preceding `AkkaStreamsBroadcastHubApp` in the IDE, we can observe the following output from the console:

```
Run   AkkaStreamsBroadcastHubApp
  /usr/lib/jvm/java-8-oracle/bin/java ...
  consumer2: New message
  consumer1: New message
  consumer1: New message
  consumer2: New message
  consumer2: New message
  consumer1: New message
  consumer1: New message
  consumer2: New message

  Process finished with exit code 0
```

If we observe the preceding output, we can understand that the order of the output is not guaranteed. If we run the same app again, we may see a different order output.

4. Develop and test `AkkaStreamsPartitionHubApp`, as shown here:

```scala
object AkkaStreamsPartitionHubApp extends App{

  implicit val actorSystem = ActorSystem("PartitionHubSystem")
  implicit val materializer = ActorMaterializer()

  val producer = Source.tick(1.second, 1.second, "message")
    .zipWith(Source(1 to 10))((a, b) ⇒ s"$a-$b")

  val runnableGraph: RunnableGraph[Source[String, NotUsed]] =
   producer.toMat(PartitionHub.sink(
     (size, elem) ⇒ math.abs(elem.hashCode) % size,
      startAfterNrOfConsumers = 2, bufferSize = 256))(Keep.right)

  val fromProducer: Source[String, NotUsed] = runnableGraph.run()

  fromProducer.runForeach(msg ⇒ println("consumer1: " + msg))
  fromProducer.runForeach(msg ⇒ println("consumer2: " + msg))

  Thread.sleep(5000)
  actorSystem.terminate
}
```

Let's understand the preceding Scala Application step by step now:

1. We can create `PartitionHub` using its utility function—`source()`. It requires three parameters, as shown here:
   - `PartitionHub.sink((size, elem) ⇒`
     `math.abs(elem.hashCode) % size`
   - `startAfterNrOfConsumers = 2`
   - `bufferSize = 256)`

2. We connect our Hub to two consumers.

3. Each message is sent to a specific consumer only.

4. We create a producer to send one message per second:

   ```
   Source.tick(1.second, 1.second, "message")
   ```

5. When we run the preceding `AkkaStreamsPartitionHubApp` in the IDE, we can observe the following output from the console:

```
Run   AkkaStreamsPartitionHubApp
      /usr/lib/jvm/java-8-oracle/bin/java ...
      consumer2: message-1
      consumer1: message-2
      consumer2: message-3
      consumer1: message-4

      Process finished with exit code 0
```

Here we used `Thread.sleep(5000)` in ms. As this Producer can send only one message per second and it sends each message to a specific Consumer, we can observe only four or five messages in the output console because of that `Thread.sleep(5000)`.

As usual, the order of output is not guaranteed. If we run the same App again, we may see a different order output.

Integrating Akka Streams into Play

In this section, we will develop a Reactive Multi-User Chat application using the following technology stack:

- Play Framework
- Play Web Socket API
- Akka Streams API
- Scala

Designing a Reactive Chat System

In this section, we will design and discuss our Reactive Multi-User Chat System, so that its easy for us to understand how our chat system works and how to develop our application in the next section.

We can assume our **Reactive Chat System** to be on a high level, as shown here:

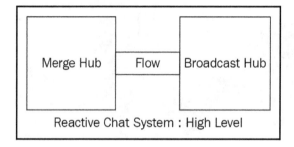

In our Reactive Chat System, MergeHub acts a Source and BroadcastHub acts as a Sink:

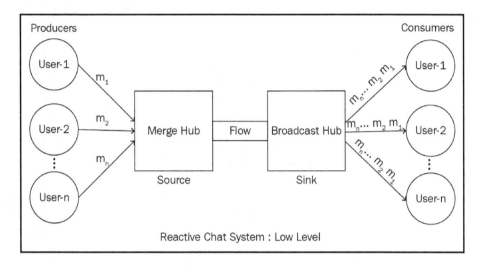

Reactive Chat System : Low Level

Here multiple users connect to our system and send messages to others through the MergeHub component. So those message senders will become Producers.

At the same time, other users connect to our system and receive messages from BroadcastHub, as shown in the preceding diagram. So those message receivers will become consumers.

Developing the Reactive Chat System

In this section, we will develop and discuss our **Reactive Chat System** using Play/AkkaStreams/Scala Technology Stack.

Perform the following steps to explore Akka Streams Dynamic components:

1. Create a Scala SBT project in your favorite IDE:

   ```
   Project Name : play-akka-streams-scala-chatroom-app
   ```

2. Add the akka-streams dependency in the build.sbt file, as shown here:

   build.sbt:

   ```
   name := "play-akka-streams-scala-chatroom-app"
   scalaVersion := "2.12.4"
   val akkaVersion = "2.5.9"
   lazy val root = (project in file(".")).enablePlugins(PlayScala)
   crossScalaVersions := Seq("2.11.12", "2.12.4")
   ```

```
libraryDependencies += guice
libraryDependencies += "org.webjars" %% "webjars-play" % "2.6.1"
libraryDependencies += "org.webjars" % "flot" % "0.8.3"
libraryDependencies += "org.webjars" % "bootstrap" % "3.3.6"
libraryDependencies += "net.logstash.logback" %
 "logstash-logback-encoder" % "4.11"
libraryDependencies += "com.typesafe.akka" %%
 "akka-slf4j" % akkaVersion
libraryDependencies += "ch.qos.logback" % "logback-classic" % "1.2.3"
```

3. Add the Play Framework plugins to the `plugins.sbt` file:

```
addSbtPlugin("com.typesafe.play" % "sbt-plugin" % "2.6.11")
```

4. Develop the `ContentSecurityPolicyFilter` filter:

```
class ContentSecurityPolicyFilter @Inject()(implicit ec:
 ExecutionContext) extends EssentialFilter {
  override def apply(next: EssentialAction): EssentialAction =
   EssentialAction { request: RequestHeader =>
    val webSocketUrl =
     routes.ChatController.chat().webSocketURL()(request)
    next(request).map { result =>
     result.withHeaders("Content-Security-Policy" ->
      s"connect-src 'self' $webSocketUrl")
    }
   }
 }
```

5. Configure the `ContentSecurityPolicyFilter` filter in the `application.conf` file, as shown here:

application.conf:

```
akka {
  loggers = ["akka.event.slf4j.Slf4jLogger"]
  loglevel = "DEBUG"
  logging-filter = "akka.event.slf4j.Slf4jLoggingFilter"
}
play.filters.headers.contentSecurityPolicy = null
play.filters.hosts.allowed = ["localhost:9000",
 "localhost:19001"]
play.filters.enabled += filters.ContentSecurityPolicyFilter
```

6. Develop `RequestMarkerContext,` as shown here:

```
trait RequestMarkerContext {
  implicit def requestHeaderToMarkerContext(implicit request:
  RequestHeader): MarkerContext = {
    import net.logstash.logback.marker.LogstashMarker
    import net.logstash.logback.marker.Markers._
    val requestMarkers: LogstashMarker = append("host",
      request.host).and(append("path", request.path))
    MarkerContext(requestMarkers)
  }
}
```

7. Develop our actual `ChatController`:

```
@Singleton
class ChatController @Inject()(cc: ControllerComponents)
 (implicit actorSystem: ActorSystem, mat: Materializer,
  executionContext: ExecutionContext,
  webJarsUtil: org.webjars.play.WebJarsUtil)
  extends AbstractController(cc) with RequestMarkerContext {
    private type WSMessage = String
    private val logger = Logger(getClass)
    private implicit val logging =
      Logging(actorSystem.eventStream,
      logger.underlyingLogger.getName)
    private val (chatSink, chatSource) = {
      val source = MergeHub.source[WSMessage].log("source")
        .recoverWithRetries(-1, { case _: Exception ⇒ Source.empty })
      val sink = BroadcastHub.sink[WSMessage]
        source.toMat(sink)(Keep.both).run()
    }
    private val userFlow: Flow[WSMessage, WSMessage, _] = {
      Flow.fromSinkAndSource(chatSink, chatSource)
    }
    def index: Action[AnyContent] = Action {
      implicit request: RequestHeader =>
       val webSocketUrl =
         routes.ChatController.chat().webSocketURL()
         logger.info(s"index: ")
         Ok(views.html.index(webSocketUrl))
    }
    def chat(): WebSocket = {
      WebSocket.acceptOrResult[WSMessage, WSMessage] {
        case rh if sameOriginCheck(rh) =>
         Future.successful(userFlow).map { flow =>
          Right(flow)
```

```scala
      }.recover {
        case e: Exception =>
         val msg = "Cannot create websocket"
          logger.error(msg, e)
          val result = InternalServerError(msg)
          Left(result)
      }
      case rejected =>
       logger.error(s"Request ${rejected} failed same origin
        check")
      Future.successful {
        Left(Forbidden("forbidden"))
      }
    }
  }
  private def sameOriginCheck(implicit rh: RequestHeader):
   Boolean = {
    logger.debug("Checking the ORIGIN ")
    rh.headers.get("Origin") match {
      case Some(originValue) if originMatches(originValue) =>
       logger.debug(s"originCheck: originValue = $originValue")
       true
      case Some(badOrigin) =>
       logger.error(s"originCheck: rejecting request because
        Origin header value ${badOrigin} is not in
        the same origin")
       false
      case None =>
       logger.error("originCheck: rejecting request
        because no Origin header found")
       false
    }
  }
  private def originMatches(origin: String): Boolean = {
    try {
      val url = new URI(origin)
      url.getHost == "localhost" &&
      (url.getPort match { case 9000 | 19001 => true;
       case _ => false })
    } catch {
        case e: Exception => false
    }
  }
}
```

Let us understand the preceding Scala application step by step now:

1. First, develop Source using `MergeHub` to send messages, as shown here:

```
val chatSource = MergeHub.source[WSMessage]
```

As discussed, `MergeHub` is a source to which multiple message senders send messages. This means that it receives messages from multiple users.

2. Develop Sink using `BroadcastHub` to receive messages, as shown here:

```
val chatSink = BroadcastHub.sink[WSMessage]
```

As discussed, `BroadcastHub` is a Sink from which multiple message receivers receive messages. This means that it broadcasts each message to all receivers.

3. Create our complete Reactive system user flow, as shown here:

```
val userFlow = Flow.fromSinkAndSource(chatSink, chatSource)
```

 The `Flow.fromSinkAndSource()` function creates a Flow from a Sink and a Source. Here the Flow's output will come from the Source and the Flow's input will be sent to the Sink.

4. Add routings in the routes file:

routes:

```
GET / controllers.ChatController.index
GET /chat controllers.ChatController.chat
# Map static resources from the /public folder to the /assets
  URL path
GET /assets/*file controllers.Assets.at(path="/public", file)
-> /webjars webjars.Routes
```

Test Reactive Chat Application

To test our chat application, start our application, as shown here:

```
$ cd play-akka-streams-scala-chatroom-app
$ sbt run
```

Access the application using the `http://localhost:9000/` URL as a Ram user:

When we access the `http://localhost:9000/` URL, we can find the following logs in the server console:

```
[info] c.ChatController - index:
[debug] c.ChatController - Checking the ORIGIN
[debug] c.ChatController - originCheck: originValue = http://localhost:9000
```

Access the application using the `http://localhost:9000/` URL as Posa user:

```
"Ram" user sent the following Messages:
Hello Posa
"Posa" user sent the following Messages:
Hello Ram
How are you doing
```

Observe this output in the following diagram:

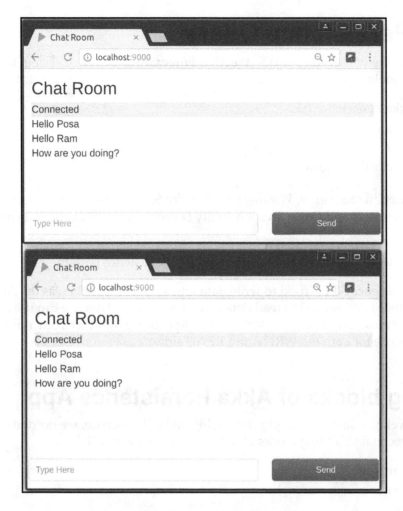

We can observe both user logs on the server console, as shown here:

```
[info]  play.api.Play - Application started (Dev)
[info]  c.ChatController - index:
[debug] c.ChatController - Checking the ORIGIN
[debug] c.ChatController - originCheck: originValue = http://localhost:9000
[info]  c.ChatController - index:
[debug] c.ChatController - Checking the ORIGIN
[debug] c.ChatController - originCheck: originValue = http://localhost:9000
[debug] c.ChatController - [source] Element: Hello Posa
[debug] c.ChatController - [source] Element: Hello Ram
[debug] c.ChatController - [source] Element: How are you doing?
```

Akka Persistence Query

In this section, we will develop a **WF** (**Weather Forecasting**) Reactive system using the following technology stack:

- Akka Persistence API
- Akka Persistence Query API
- Scala
- Apache Cassandra

As we discussed in `Chapter 7`, *Working with Reactive Streams*, Akka Persistence supports the CQRS/ES (Command and Query Responsibility Segregation with Event Sourcing) Design pattern.

CQRS/ES is a Reactive Statement Management and Persistence pattern.

The Akka Persistence API is used to write data into a data store, whereas the Akka Persistence Query API is used to read data from a data store. Here we can use any RDBMS or No SQL database as a data store. We will use Apache Cassandra as our WF Reactive System data store for both the WRITE and READ sides.

Building blocks of Akka Persistence App

When we develop a data store application using Akka Persistence, we need to consider the following three main building blocks of the Akka Persistence API:

- Command
- Event
- State

The following diagrams show the main building blocks or components of an Akka Persistence application:

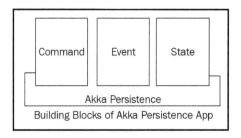

The following are present in an Akka Persistence application:

- **Commands**: These are user actions generated when user interacts with our application or system, our system generates a set of user actions They are known as commands in Akka Persistence terminology:

```
AddWeatherForecast
RemoveWeatherForecast
UpdateWeatherForecast
GetWeatherForecast
```

- **Events**: These are when a user performs any action (Command), which is stored into a data store as an Event. For instance, the following are the Events stored in a WF Reactive System data store when the user generates the aforementioned commands:

```
WeatherForecastAdded
WeatherForecastRemoved
WeatherForecastUpdated
```

- **State**: It means the state of a Persistence Actor.

Developing WF Reactive Akka Persistence App

In this section, we will develop our **WF (Weather Forecasting)** Reactive Akka Persistence application using Apache Cassandra as its data store.

Execute the following steps to develop this application:

1. Create a Scala SBT project in your favorite IDE:

   ```
   Project Name : play-akka-streams-scala-chatroom-app
   ```

2. Add all dependencies in the `build.sbt` file, as shown here:

   build.sbt:

   ```
   name := "wf-akka-persistence-query-cassandra-scala-app"
   version := "1.0.0"
   scalaVersion := "2.12.4"
   lazy val akkaVersion = "2.5.9"
   libraryDependencies ++= Seq(
     "com.typesafe.akka" %% "akka-actor" % akkaVersion,
     "com.typesafe.akka" %% "akka-testkit" % akkaVersion,
   ```

```
"com.typesafe.akka" %% "akka-persistence" % akkaVersion,
"com.typesafe.akka" %% "akka-persistence-query" % akkaVersion,
"com.typesafe.akka" %% "akka-persistence-cassandra" % "0.80-RC3",
"org.scalatest" %% "scalatest" % "3.0.1" % "test"
)
```

3. Develop our `WeatherForecasting` model:

```
case class WeatherForecasting(city: String, weather: String)
```

4. Develop the Akka Persistence App's three main building blocks. Develop Events, as shown here:

```
sealed trait WFEvent
case class WFAdded(wf: WeatherForecasting) extends WFEvent
case class WFRemoved(wf: WeatherForecasting) extends WFEvent
```

5. Develop Commands, as shown here:

```
case class AddWF(wf: WeatherForecasting)
case class RemoveWF(wf: WeatherForecasting)
case object PrintWF
case object SnapshotWF
```

6. Develop our `WeatherForecasting` state, as shown here:

```
case class WFState(wfs: Vector[WeatherForecasting] =
 Vector.empty[WeatherForecasting]) {
   def update(evt: WFEvent) = evt match {
     case WFAdded(wf) => copy(wfs :+ wf)
     case WFRemoved(wf) => copy(wfs.filterNot(_ == wf))
   }
   override def toString = wfs.mkString(",")
}
```

7. Develop one useful logger utility:

```
object WFLogger {
   def log(system: ActorSystem, eventid: String, event: Any) = {
     system.log.info(s"Id [$eventid] Event [$event]")
   }
}
```

8. Develop a Persistence Actor, as shown here:

```
object WFActor {
   def props(id: String, recovery: Recovery) =
```

```
        Props(new WFActor(id, recovery))
    }
    class WFActor(id: String, rec: Recovery) extends PersistentActor
     with ActorLogging {
      override val persistenceId = id
      override val recovery = rec
      var state = WFState()
      def updateState(event: WFEvent) = state = state.update(event)
      val receiveRecover: Receive = {
        case evt: WFEvent => log.info(s"Replaying event: $evt")
        updateState(evt)
        case SnapshotOffer(_, recoveredState : WFState) =>
         log.info(s"Snapshot offered: $recoveredState")
        state = recoveredState
        case RecoveryCompleted => log.info(s"Recovery completed.
         Current state: $state")
      }
      val receiveCommand: Receive = {
        case AddWF(wf) => persist(WFAdded(wf))(updateState)
        case RemoveWF(wf) => persist(WFRemoved(wf))(updateState)
        case SnapshotWF => saveSnapshot(state)
        case PrintWF => log.info(s"Current state: $state")
      }
    }
```

Testing WF Reactive Akka Persistence App

Here we will develop some Akka Persistence and Akka Persistence Query applications to test our WF Reactive Akka Persistence application:

1. Develop the Akka Persistence application, as shown here:

```
object WFApp extends App {
  val system = ActorSystem("WFSystem")
  val hyd = system.actorOf(WFActor.props("Hyd", Recovery()))
  val vja = system.actorOf(WFActor.props("Vja", Recovery()))
  hyd ! AddWF(WeatherForecasting("Hyd","12"))
  hyd ! AddWF(WeatherForecasting("Hyd", "19"))
  vja ! AddWF(WeatherForecasting("Vja", "21"))
  vja ! AddWF(WeatherForecasting("Vja", "18"))
  system.scheduler.scheduleOnce(5 second, vja,
   AddWF(WeatherForecasting("Vja","15")))
  system.scheduler.scheduleOnce(10 second, vja,
   RemoveWF(WeatherForecasting("Vja","21")))
  vja ! SnapshotWF
  hyd ! PrintWF
```

```
        Thread.sleep(25000)
        system.terminate()
    }
```

2. When we run our application, we can observe the following output on the IDE console:

Output for first run:
```
[WFSystem-akka.actor.default-dispatcher-4] [akka://WFSystem/user/$b]
```
Recovery completed. Current state:
```
[WFSystem-akka.actor.default-dispatcher-2] [akka://WFSystem/user/$a]
```
Recovery completed. Current state:
```
[WFSystem-cassandra-plugin-default-dispatcher-7]
[akka.serialization.Serialization(akka://WFSystem)] Using the default Java
serializer for class [com.packt.publishing.cassandra.events.WFAdded]
[WFSystem-akka.actor.default-dispatcher-4] [akka://WFSystem/user/$b]
```
Current state:WeatherForecasting(Vja,21),WeatherForecasting(Vja,18)
```
[WFSystem-akka.actor.default-dispatcher-5] [akka://WFSystem/user/$a]
```
Current state:WeatherForecasting(Hyd,12),WeatherForecasting(Hyd,19)
```
[WFSystem-cassandra-plugin-default-dispatcher-6]
[akka.serialization.Serialization(akka://WFSystem)] Using the default Java
serializer for class [com.packt.publishing.cassandra.state.WFState]
[WFSystem-cassandra-plugin-default-dispatcher-9]
[akka.serialization.Serialization(akka://WFSystem)] Using the default Java
serializer for class [com.packt.publishing.cassandra.events.WFRemoved]
```

3. If you run the same application the second time, you will see a different output. We will see the following `Snapshot` and `Recovery` output:

```
[WFSystem-akka.actor.default-dispatcher-9] [akka://WFSystem/user/$b]
Snapshot offered: WeatherForecasting(Vja,21),WeatherForecasting(Vja,18)
[WFSystem-akka.actor.default-dispatcher-11] [akka://WFSystem/user/$a]
Replaying event: WFAdded(WeatherForecasting(Hyd,12))
[WFSystem-akka.actor.default-dispatcher-11] [akka://WFSystem/user/$a]
Replaying event: WFAdded(WeatherForecasting(Hyd,19))
[WFSystem-akka.actor.default-dispatcher-11] [akka://WFSystem/user/$a]
Recovery completed. Current state:
WeatherForecasting(Hyd,12),WeatherForecasting(Hyd,19)
[WFSystem-akka.actor.default-dispatcher-9] [akka://WFSystem/user/$b]
Replaying event: WFAdded(WeatherForecasting(Vja,15))
[WFSystem-akka.actor.default-dispatcher-8] [akka://WFSystem/user/$b]
Replaying event: WFRemoved(WeatherForecasting(Vja,21))
[WFSystem-akka.actor.default-dispatcher-8] [akka://WFSystem/user/$b]
Recovery completed. Current state:
WeatherForecasting(Vja,18),WeatherForecasting(Vja,15)
```

4. Develop the Akka Persistence Query application, as shown here:

```
object WFJournalReaderApp extends App {
  implicit val system = ActorSystem("WFSystem")
  implicit val mat = ActorMaterializer()(system)
  val queries =
   PersistenceQuery(system).readJournalFor[CassandraReadJournal]
    (CassandraReadJournal.Identifier)
  queries.persistenceIds().map(id => system.log.info(s"Id
   received [$id]")).to(Sink.ignore).run()
  Thread.sleep(2000)
  system.terminate()
}
```

`queries.persistenceIds()` is used to get all Persistence Entity's IDs stored in the Apache Cassandra data store.

5. When we run the preceding Akka Persistence Query application, we can observe the following output:

```
[WFSystem-akka.actor.default-dispatcher-4]
[akka.actor.ActorSystemImpl(WFSystem)] Id received [Hyd]
[WFSystem-akka.actor.default-dispatcher-4]
[akka.actor.ActorSystemImpl(WFSystem)] Id received [Vja]
```

6. Develop another Akka Persistence Query application, as shown here:

```
object WFJournalReaderApp2 extends App {
  implicit val system = ActorSystem("WFSystem")
  implicit val mat = ActorMaterializer()(system)
  val queries =
   PersistenceQuery(system).readJournalFor[CassandraReadJournal]
    (CassandraReadJournal.Identifier)
  queries.eventsByPersistenceId("Hyd",1,2).map(e => log(system,
   e.persistenceId, e.event)).to(Sink.ignore).run()
  Thread.sleep(10000)
  system.terminate()
}
```

The `queries.eventsByPersistenceId()` function is useful to retrieve all events stored in a data store based on Persistence ID.

7. When we run the preceding Akka Persistence Query application, we can observe the following output:

```
[WFSystem-akka.actor.default-dispatcher-4]
```

```
[akka.actor.ActorSystemImpl(WFSystem)] Id [Vja] Event
[WFAdded(WeatherForecasting(Vja,21))]
[WFSystem-akka.actor.default-dispatcher-4]
[akka.actor.ActorSystemImpl(WFSystem)] Id [Vja] Event
[WFAdded(WeatherForecasting(Vja,18))]
[WFSystem-akka.actor.default-dispatcher-4]
[akka.actor.ActorSystemImpl(WFSystem)] Id [Vja] Event
[WFAdded(WeatherForecasting(Vja,15))]
[WFSystem-akka.actor.default-dispatcher-4]
[akka.actor.ActorSystemImpl(WFSystem)] Id [Vja] Event
[WFRemoved(WeatherForecasting(Vja,21))]
```

Here we assume that our Akka Persistence application, WFApp, ran only once. If you run it more than once, we will see more events here.

Summary

In this chapter, we started with learning about the Akka Streams API, which has mainly two kinds of components:

- Static Stream components
- Dynamic Stream components

Akka Dynamic Streams have mainly the following components to support the dynamic nature of Graphs:

- MergeHub
- BroadcastHub
- PartitionHub

Then we developed a Reactive Play Multi-User Chatting Web application using Play Framework, Akka Dynamic Streams components, Play Web Socket, and Scala technology stack.

In Chapter 7, *Working with Reactive Streams*, we discussed how to develop CQRS/ES Persistence applications using the Akka Persistence API. In this chapter, we developed and explored a couple of Akka Persistence Query APIs.

We need to understand these Persistence and Persistence Query APIs very well because we are going to develop a Lagom Framework-based WF Reactive System in the next chapter using a similar kind of Lagom APIs.

9

Reactive Microservices with Lagom

In this chapter, we will discuss Lightbend's Reactive Platform. It has a Reactive Microservice Framework, that is, the Lagom Framework. We will be developing our **WF (Weather Forecasting)** Reactive System, using this framework.

Nowadays, like Reactive, microservices or microservice architectures are becoming more popular. Everyone is moving to the microservices architecture. All greenfield projects are starting with this architecture, and old monolithic applications are also converting to microservices step by step to get their benefits.

The Lagom Framework home page can be found at `https://www.lightbend.com/lagom-framework`.

If you are interested in finding out about the source code of the Lagom Framework, go to the repository at `https://github.com/lagom/lagom`.

In this chapter, we will discuss the following concepts:

- What is Lagom Framework?
- Lagom Framework features and benefits
- Lagom Framework architecture
- Basics of microservice architecture
- Building blocks of Lagom Framework
- Internal components of Lagom Framework

- Developing Lagom Framework HelloWorld Service example
- Developing our WF Reactive System using Lagom Framework
- Testing the WF Reactive System

Introduction to Lagom Framework

In this section, we will introduce you to a new Reactive Framework, that is, the Lagom Framework. We will discuss Lagom Framework basics, its features, benefits, and architecture.

What is Lagom Framework?

Lagom Framework is an Opinionated Reactive microservices framework from the Lightbend team. Lagom is a Swedish word which means *just the right amount*. It also means adequate, sufficient, just right, and more.

We should pronounce it as *Laah-Gome*.

It implements the Reactive Manifesto.

It is built on top of the two popular frameworks from Lightbend, as shown in the following diagram:

- **Akka Toolkit**
- **Play Framework**

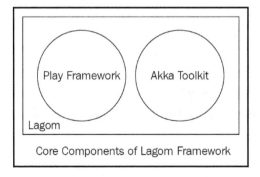

Core Components of Lagom Framework

Features of Lagom Framework

Lightbend's Lagom Framework supports the following features:

- Open source
- Microservice architecture
- Development environment
- Production environment with ConductR
- Persistence
- **CQRS (Command Query Responsibility Segregation)** with **ES (Event Sourcing)**
- Single command to start the service, for instance, `sbt runAll`
- Default embedded data store (Cassandra) and message broker (Kafka)

Benefits of Lagom Framework

Lightbend's Lagom Framework has the following benefits:

- Open source framework
- Supports developing Reactive microservices by design
- Supports reactiveness by design
- Supports distributed applications by design
- Develops distributed systems faster and more easily
- Easily develops highly Scalable, high-performance, Resilient, robust, and highly-available (100% up time) applications
- Supports concurrency and parallelism very well
- Supports Message-Driven (and Event-Driven) architecture by design
- Better productivity
- Supports hot-reloading with the help of Play Framework under-the-hood
- A modular framework has divided the whole Lagom Framework into different modules

Drawbacks of monolith architecture

Our old monolith applications were good a decade ago. Now, they are obsolete and not useful anymore with the current demand. This architecture has the following limitations or drawbacks:

- Tight coupling between components, as everything is in one application
- Less reusability
- Large code base; tough for developers and QA to understand the code and business knowledge
- Less Scalable
- Does not follow **SRP** (**Single Responsibility Principle**)
- More deployment and restart times

Benefits of microservice architecture

When we use the microservice architecture to develop our system, we will get the following benefits:

- More reusability
- Loose coupling between services
- We can deploy and scale them independently
- We can use different technology stacks to develop different microservices
- Easy for developers and QA to understand their services
- Clear separation of concerns
- Does only one thing very well
- Ease of testing and maintenance
- Fault isolation
- High Cohesion, Reliable, and more Resilient
- Very flexible
- Requires less deployment time

Principles of microservices

When we have to plan to design and develop microservices, we should remember the following principles:

- They should be small and autonomous services.
- They should work together.
- Each microservice should have its own data store to store its data.
- External microservices should not access the data store directly. They should get that data through the microservice only. This means they should hide their data and implementation details.
- They should follow SRP.
- They should support fault isolation.
- They should support automation and continuous deployment.
- They should support business domain-driven modeling.

Lagom Reactive Platform architecture

Lightbend's Reactive Platform is an application development solution powered by an open source core and the commercial enterprise suite for building, deploying, and managing Scalable Reactive Systems on the **JVM (Java Virtual Machine)**. The following diagram represents the Lagom Reactive Platform architecture:

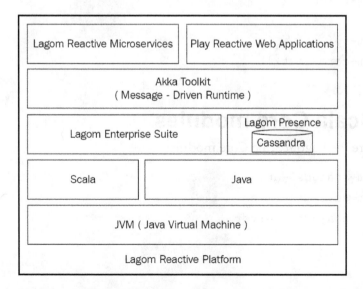

The Lagom Reactive Platform has the following benefits when developing Reactive Systems:

- More reliable infrastructure
- More profitable infrastructure
- Massive scalability and elasticity
- Higher developer productivity
- Rapid time to value
- Access to real-time insights
- Disrupted markets

Modules of Lagom Framework

Lagom Framework is a modular framework. It is divided into different modules, as we will see further.

Lagom Core modules

The following are the Lagom Core modules:

- `lagom-api`
- `lagom-client`
- `lagom-server`
- `lagom-spi`
- `lagom-core-testkit`

Lagom Scala Core modules

The following are the Lagom Scala Core modules:

- `lagom-scaladsl-api`
- `lagom-scaladsl-client`
- `lagom-scaladsl-server`

- `lagom-scaladsl-testkit`
- `lagom-scaladsl-dev-mode`
- `lagom-scaladsl-play-json`

Lagom Persistence modules

The following are the Lagom Persistence modules:

- `lagom-persistence-core`
- `lagom-persistence-cassandra-core`
- `lagom-scaladsl-persistence`
- `lagom-scaladsl-persistence-cassandra`

Lagom Clustering modules

The following are the Lagom Clustering modules:

- `lagom-cluster-core`
- `lagom-scala-cluster`

Lagom Kafka modules

The following are the Lagom Kafka modules:

- `lagom-kafka-broker`
- `lagom-kafka-client`
- `lagom-scaladsl-broker`
- `lagom-scaladsl-kafka-broker`
- `lagom-scalkafka-scaladsl-client`

Lagom logging module

The Lagom Logging module is `lagom-lagback`.

If you want to look at the Lagom Modules source code, you can go to the Lagom Github repository at `https://github.com/lagom/lagom/`.

For instance, we can find the Lagom Play JSON module at `https://github.com/lagom/lagom/tree/master/play-json`.

Similarly, you can find Lagom Framework modules for Java DSL.

Building blocks of Lagom Framework

In this section, we will explore Lagom Framework's building blocks at a high level and low level.

When we observe the Lagom Framework, it contains the following high-level components:

- Service API
- Persistence API
- Message Broker API
- Development environment
- Production environment

Consider the following diagram of the building blocks of Lagom Framework:

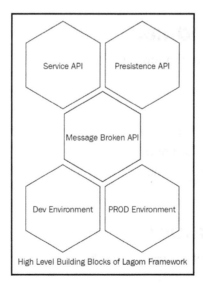

High Level Building Blocks of Lagom Framework

The Service API is used to define the Lagom Framework-based API and its implementation.

The Persistence API is used to store our Reactive System's persistent entities into a data store using the CQRS/ES technique.

The Message Broker API is used to support the Publish/Subscribe model using Topic.

It supports both development and production environments. We will explore the production environment, that is, Lagom ConductR, in detail in `Chapter 11`, *Managing Microservices in ConductR*.

If we observe Lagom services in detail, we can identify the following low-level components:

- Service Call
- Service Descriptor
- Service Locator
- Web Gateway
- JSON Serializer Registry
- Lagom Application Loader
- Persistent Entity

Lagom Service Locator

Lagom Framework has an embedded Service Locator in the development environment. It allows services to discover and communicate with each other. By default, this Service Locator runs on port `9008`, but it is possible to use a different port.

The major goal or benefit of the Lagom Service Locator is to support Location Transparency. This means that the client does need to know where those services are available. Even though they are available remotely somewhere in a clustered environment, the client feels that they are available locally.

We can find the implementation of this component in the `lagom-service-locator_2.11-1.3.10.jar` file. When we start our local application using `sbt runAll`, we can observe the following log on the console:

```
[info] Service Locator is running at http://localhost:9008.
```

Lagom Service Gateway

Lagom Framework has an embedded Service Gateway in the development environment. It allows us to expose our public endpoints to the clients who does not have access to our Service Locator.

Lagom Framework supports the following two flavors of Service Gateways:

- Akka HTTP-based Service Gateway (default)
- Netty-based Service Gateway (legacy)

The Service Gateway default port number is `9000` and, if required, we can change it. When we start our local instance, we can observe the following log on the server console:

```
[info] Service gateway is running at http://localhost:9000.
```

Lagom Service Descriptor

In Lagom Framework, we use the Service Descriptor to define the Lagom API interface. We define this Service Descriptor by overriding the `descriptor` function, which is defined in the service interface.

The service trait is defined with that `descriptor` function and some utilities, as shown here:

```
package com.lightbend.lagom.scaladsl.api
trait Service {
  def descriptor: Descriptor
}

object Service {
  def named(name: String): Descriptor = Descriptor(name)

  def call[Request, Response](method: ScalaMethodServiceCall[Request,
  Response]): Call[Request, Response]
  def namedCall[Request, Response](name: String, method:
  ScalaMethodServiceCall[Request, Response]): Call[Request, Response]
  def pathCall[Request, Response](pathPattern: String, method:
  ScalaMethodServiceCall[Request, Response]): Call[Request, Response]
  def restCall[Request, Response](method: Method, pathPattern: String,
  scalaMethod: ScalaMethodServiceCall[Request, Response]):
  Call[Request, Response]
  def topic[Message](topicId: String, method:
  ScalaMethodTopic[Message]):
```

```
        TopicCall[Message]
}
```

Consider the following example:

```
trait HellolagomService extends Service {

  def hello(id: String): ServiceCall[NotUsed, String]
  override final def descriptor = {
    named("hello-lagom")
      .withCalls(
        pathCall("/api/hello/:id", hello _)
      )
  }
}
```

Here, our `HellolagomService extends Service` interface implements the `descriptor` function for one hello endpoint: `"/api/hello/:id"`. Here, we use the `pathCall` identifier to define our endpoint.

This endpoint is pointed to the `hello()` function that should actually provide a logic on how to handle incoming requests and serve the response to the clients. We will explore `ServiceCall` in the coming sections.

 By observing this, we can say that Lagom Framework's Service Descriptor is similar to Play Framework's Routings (routes file).

Lagom Framework's identifiers

Lagom Framework supports the following kinds of identifiers to define our endpoints in a Lagom API service:

- **Call identifier**: Example: `call(sayHello)`

- **Named Call identifier**: Example: `namedCall("hello", sayHello)`

- **Path-based parameter identifier**: Example: `pathCall("/hello/:message", sayHello _)`

- **Query String parameter identifier**: Example:
  `pathCall("/hello/:message?name&greeting", sayHello _)`

- **REST identifier**: Example: `restCall(Method.GET, "/hello/message", sayHello _)`

We will explore these identifiers a bit more in the example section.

Lagom ServiceCall in detail

Before starting to develop our first example, one of the important concepts we should understand is `ServiceCall`.

`ServiceCall` is a trait defined as shown here:

```
package com.lightbend.lagom.scaladsl.api

trait ServiceCall[Request, Response] {

  def invoke(request: Request): Future[Response]

}
```

It is used to define or implement a service call for an entity in a Lagom API or implementation microservice:

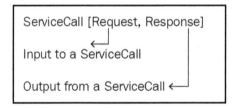

Description

Here, **Request** is an input to that service call. It can be any of the Scala built-in types or any user-defined types, as follows:

```
ServiceCall[String, Response]
```

This service call has an input of the `String` type.

The response is an output to that service call. Like input, it can be any of the Scala built-in types or any user-defined type, as shown here:

```
ServiceCall[String, String]
```

This service call has an input of the `String` type and an output of the `String` type.

If we don't want to specify a type of `ServiceCall` input, we define its input of type akka.`NotUsed`, as shown here:

```
ServiceCall[NotUsed, WeatherForcasting]
```

This service call does not have an input; however, it has an output of the `WeatherForecasting` type (user-defined type).

Like the input type, we can also use NotUsed for the output type:

```
ServiceCall[Id, NotUsed]
```

There are two kinds of Request/Response messages:

- Strict
- Streamed

Before processing, strict messages are fully loaded into memory. Sometimes, it may cause memory issues.

For example, `ServiceCall[Id, NotUsed]`.

Streamed Messages are of Source type (Akka Streams API). It allows processing of very big messages asynchronously. It is mainly used for Data Streaming purposes.

For example, `ServiceCall[Id, Source[String,_]]`.

We will explore this usage in more detail in the coming sections with some examples.

It's now time to start our simple HelloWorld example with Lagom Framework. It gives us a better idea of how to develop Lagom Framework-based microservices.

Internal components of Lagom Framework

Lagom Framework uses the following components under the hood to fulfill its job easily. We can say that these are default components used by Lagom Framework. We can change a few components to use our own external components:

- Scala
- Java
- Play Framework
- Kafka with Zookeeper
- Akka Toolkit, Akka Persistence, Akka Streams
- SBT
- Apache Cassandra
- Guice
- ConductR
- Architectural design patterns - Circuit Breaker, CQRS, and ES
- Logging

Lagom Framework has two separate APIs: one for Scala (Scala API) and the other for Java (Java API).

In Lagom Framework, both are first-class citizens.

Like Akka Streams namespaces convention, the Java API has a package name of `javadsl`:

```
com.lightbend.lagom.javadsl
```

The Scala API has a package name of `scaladsl`:

```
com.lightbend.lagom.scaladsl
```

Lagom Framework is built on top of Play Framework and Akka Toolkit. It uses Akka Toolkit extensively, such as Akka Persistence, to support the Persistence API and the Akka Streams API to support Data Streaming.

It uses SBT as default build tool. However, it also supports Maven.

By default, Lagom Framework uses Macwire as its **DI (Dependency Injection)** framework.

Kafka with ZooKeeper

By default, Lagom Framework supports an embedded Kafka server as a message broker in a development environment to exchange information or data between services.

This embedded Kafka server's default port number is 9092. Kafka uses ZooKeeper, which is a distributed coordination service. ZooKeeper server's default port number is 2181.

When we start our Lagom Reactive System or service using the sbt runAll command, it starts both the embedded server's Kafka and Zookeeper. We can find the Lagom's implementation of Kafka and Zookeeper in the lagom-kafka-server_2.11-1.3.10.jar file.

If required, we can configure Kafka externally by updating the build.sbt file. We will explore more about this in our examples:

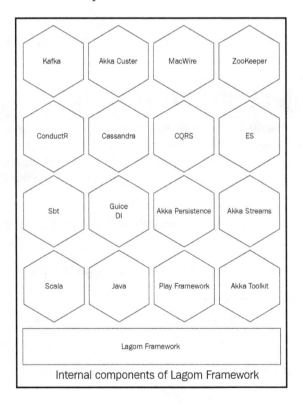

Internal components of Lagom Framework

Cassandra

By default in Lagom framework, microservices that need to persist data use Cassandra as a data store. For developer convenience, Lightbend supplies an embedded Cassandra server in the development environment so that we don't have to worry about installing it. We can use this in-built data store in a development environment. However, we need to use an external data store in production environments.

When we start our development environment using `sbt runAll`, by default it also starts that embedded Cassandra data store at the default port number. We will discuss how to configure an external data store and how to change the default port number in the coming sections.

If we observe the external Cassandra server, by default it starts at `9042`. However, Lagom's Cassandra server starts by default at port number `4000`.

Lagom framework uses Akka Persistence for Apache Cassandra for doing Persistence and its source code is available at `https://github.com/akka/akka-persistence-cassandra`.

Lagom project structure

In this section, we will discuss the high-level structure of a Lagom project or Lagom service or Lagom microservice. Lagom Framework follows a different approach to organize its project structure. As we are new to this framework, I bet we will definitely get confused about the project structure. If newbies look at a Lagom project for the first time, they won't be able to understand it well.

So it is very important to understand this section to develop our Lagom-based projects in the coming sections.

Lagom Framework has organized its project structure into two parts:

- API Microservice (or project)
- Implementation Microservice (or project)
- Frontend Microservice (or project)

We can create all their microservices as separate projects or combine them into one Reactive System.

There is a very strong reason why they have divided a Lagom project into two projects. The main reason is a clear separation between a Contract and its implementation. We should not expose our implementation to the outside world, that is, its clients. We should expose only our Contract (the interface or API) to clients. Even clients do not need to know the implementation. They only need to know about the interface:

```
Lagom - project - name
        ├ lagom - project - name - api
        ├ lagom - project - name - implementation

    High Level Lagom Project Structure
```

Lagom System API

In a Lagom Reactive System, the API (`servicename-api`) part contains the blueprint or interface or contract of that service. It defines the contract or skeleton or template of that API endpoint.

Each API may have one or more endpoints. We define each API endpoint's details in this service, such as the URI of that endpoint, any path parameters, any query parameters, and how to handle a request.

We define a function that actually does the handling of API endpoint requests coming from users, customers, or clients.

We can define this API service as a separate microservice. We will explore how to define API endpoints and how to map them to functions in the coming sections.

Lagom System – implementation

In a Lagom Reactive System, implementation (`servicename-impl`) contains the actual implementation of the previously defined API. It should provide implementations to all endpoints functions.

We share only that API with clients so that they understand how to consume that API and do not share this implementation with the outside world.

Lagom System – frontend

Not all services have a frontend. Some services may have only an API and implementation, as shown in the preceding diagram. In that case, that system provides only the API to its clients or consumers.

Some Reactive Systems may have a frontend service too. Clients can access this frontend and see the API results in the UI:

```
Lagom - reactive - system - name
        ├ lagom - servicename - api
        ├ lagom - servicename - impl
        ├ lagom - servicename - frontend

High Level Lagom Project Structure With Frontend
```

We will explore all these concepts in detail by developing some simple examples in the coming sections.

Lagom Hello Reactive System

In this section, we will develop and explore our first Lagom Framework microservice, that is, the `Hello` Reactive System. Even though it is a simple example, we will explore most of the required concepts in detail so that it is easy to develop our actual WF Reactive System in the coming section.

Getting Hello Service code

Fortunately, we don't need to create Lagom services from scratch. Like Play Framework, Lagom Framework also has some built-in examples. We can use them as the base to develop our services.

Perform the following steps to get the base project:

1. Access *Tech Hub Project Starter* using the following URL:

    ```
    https://developer.lightbend.com/start/?group=lagom&project=lagom-scala
    -sbt
    ```

    It looks like this:

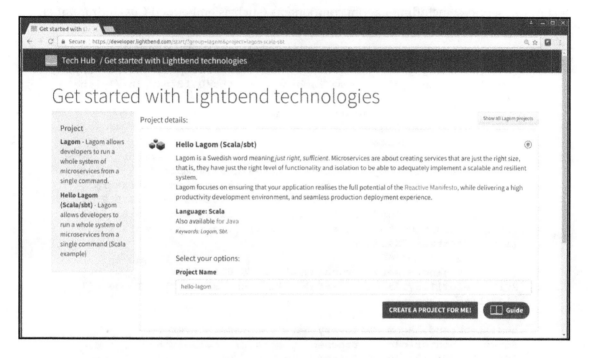

2. Click on the **CREATE A PROJECT FOR ME!** button; it will download the `lagom-scala-sbt.zip` file into your filesystem.
3. Alternatively, we can clone Giter8 repositories using the following SBT command:

    ```
    sbt -Dsbt.version=0.13.16 new https://github.com/lagom/lagom-scala.g8
    ```

4. Unzip it, and open it in the IntelliJ IDE (or your favorite IDE).

Testing the Hello Reactive System

Before going through and understanding the HelloWorld service code, we will simply run the services and see the output. One of the beautiful features of Lagom Framework is that we can start all services with just one simple SBT command, as shown here:

```
$ sbt runAll
```

It starts all services, including Lagom components (such as embedded Cassandra, Kafka, Zookeeper, and more), as shown here:

```
lagom-scala-sbt$ sbt runAll
    [info] Loading global plugins from /home/rambabuposa/.sbt/0.13/plugins
    [info] Updating {file:/home/rambabuposa/.sbt/0.13/plugins/}global-
plugins...
    [info] Resolving org.fusesource.jansi#jansi;1.4 ...
    [info] Done updating.
    [info] Starting Kafka
    [info] Updating {file:/home/rambabuposa/Documents/Personal/
           PaktPublishing/Chapter-9%20Notes/ch9-examples/
           lagom-scala-sbt/}lagom-internal-meta-project-cassandra...
    [info] Resolving org.codehaus.jackson#jackson-core-asl;1.9.2 ...
    SLF4J: Failed to load class "org.slf4j.impl.StaticLoggerBinder".
    SLF4J: Defaulting to no-operation (NOP) logger implementation
    [info] Starting Cassandra
    ...............
    [info] Cassandra server running at 127.0.0.1:4000
    2017-11-20T11:57:38.625Z [info] akka.event.slf4j.Slf4jLogger [] -
    Slf4jLogger started
    2017-11-20T11:57:40.686Z [info]
    com.lightbend.lagom.discovery.ServiceLocatorServer [] -
    Service locator can be reached at http://localhost:8000
    2017-11-20T11:57:40.687Z [info]
    com.lightbend.lagom.discovery.ServiceLocatorServer [] -
Service gateway can be reached at http://localhost:9000
    [info] Service locator is running at http://localhost:8000
    [info] Service gateway is running at http://localhost:9000
    11:57:44.456 [info] play.core.server.NettyServer [] -
    Listening for HTTP on /0:0:0:0:0:0:0:0:55115
    11:57:44.467 [info] play.core.server.NettyServer [] -
    Listening for HTTP on /0:0:0:0:0:0:0:0:49848
    11:57:57.480 [info] akka.event.slf4j.Slf4jLogger [] -
    Slf4jLogger started
    11:57:59.982 [info] play.api.Play [] - Application started (Dev)
    11:58:04.221 [info] akka.event.slf4j.Slf4jLogger [] -
    Slf4jLogger started
    11:58:06.464 [info] akka.cluster.singleton.ClusterSingletonProxy
```

```
[sourceThread=hello-lagom-impl-application-akka.actor.default-
 dispatcher-18, akkaSource=akka.tcp://hello-lagom-impl-
 application@127.0.0.1:40195/user/cassandraOffsetStorePrepare-
 singletonProxy, sourceActorSystem=hello-lagom-impl-application,
 akkaTimestamp=11:58:06.464UTC] - Singleton identified at
 [akka://hello-lagom-impl-application/user/
  cassandraOffsetStorePrepare-singleton/singleton]
11:58:07.314 [info] play.api.Play [] - Application started (Dev)
[info] Service hello-lagom-stream-impl listening for HTTP on
 0:0:0:0:0:0:0:0:55115
[info] Service hello-lagom-impl listening for HTTP on
 0:0:0:0:0:0:0:0:49848
[info] (Services started, press enter to stop and go back
 to the console...)
11:58:09.651 [info] com.lightbend.lagom.internal.persistence
 .cluster.ClusterStartupTaskActor
[sourceThread=hello-lagom-impl-application-akka.actor.default-
 dispatcher-17, akkaTimestamp=11:58:09.651UTC,
 akkaSource=akka.tcp://hello-lagom-impl-
 application@127.0.0.1:40195/user/cassandraOffsetStorePrepare-
 singleton/singleton/cassandraOffsetStorePrepare,
 sourceActorSystem=hello-lagom-impl-application] -
 Cluster start task cassandraOffsetStorePrepare done.
```

Here, just to save some space, we have removed some unwanted logs. It shows everything we need to understand. We can observe the following things:

- Starting Cassandra server
- Starting Kafka server
- Starting `hello api` and `hello impl`
- Starting Service Locator, Gateway, and others

Access the service using this URL:

```
http://localhost:9000/api/hello/World
```

Lagom Hello Reactive System microservices

Even though this basic Lagom HelloWorld System looks very simple, we can learn many Lagom concepts. Let's pick up each service and understand the code.

It mainly has two services (microservices):

- Hello Lagom service
- Hello Lagom Stream service

Again, each microservice has two parts: one is for the API and another for the implementation.

The Hello (hello) Microservice has the following two parts:

- Hello API service (hello-lagom-api)
- Hello implementation service (hello-lagom-impl)

In the same way, the Hello Stream (hello-lagom-stream) microservice has two parts:

- Hello Stream API service (hello-lagom-stream-api)
- Hello Stream implementation service (hello-lagom-stream-impl)

The whole HelloWorld System looks like the following in the IntelliJ IDE:

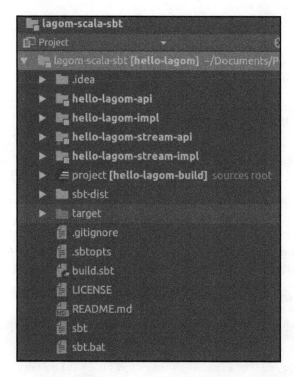

It's time to understand the code in both the API and the implementation projects.

Understanding the Hello Service API code

In this section, we will try to understand the HelloWorld API (`hello-lagom-api`) service code. This is an API microservice for the HelloWorld system.

It has the `GreetingMessage` data model, as shown here:

```scala
case class GreetingMessage(message: String)

object GreetingMessage {
  implicit val format: Format[GreetingMessage] =
    Json.format[GreetingMessage]
}
```

It has a `GreetingMessageChanged` event, as shown here:

```
case class GreetingMessageChanged(name: String, message: String)

object GreetingMessageChanged {
  implicit val format: Format[GreetingMessageChanged] =
    Json.format[GreetingMessageChanged]
}
```

It has a `greetings` Topic, as follows:

```
object HellolagomService  {
  val TOPIC_NAME = "greetings"
}
```

This topic is used by embedded Lagom's Kafka or explicitly configured Kafka server to exchange information between microservices available in that Lagom Reactive System.

In this example, both `hello-lagom` and `hello-lagom-stream` microservices use this Kafka's Topic to exchange data between each other.

It has a `HellolagomService` service, as depicted here:

```
trait HellolagomService extends Service {

  def hello(id: String): ServiceCall[NotUsed, String]
  def useGreeting(id: String): ServiceCall[GreetingMessage, Done]

  def greetingsTopic(): Topic[GreetingMessageChanged]

  override final def descriptor = {
    named("hello-lagom")
      .withCalls(
        pathCall("/api/hello/:id", hello _),
        pathCall("/api/hello/:id", useGreeting _)
      )
      .withTopics(
        topic(HellolagomService.TOPIC_NAME, greetingsTopic _)
          .addProperty(
            KafkaProperties.partitionKeyStrategy,
            PartitionKeyStrategy[GreetingMessageChanged](_.name)
          )
      )
      .withAutoAcl(true)
  }
}
```

This service defines two `Hello` service functions:

```
def hello(id: String): ServiceCall[NotUsed, String]

def useGreeting(id: String): ServiceCall[GreetingMessage, Done]
```

It defines one Topic function to handle `GreetingMessage` events:

```
def greetingsTopic(): Topic[GreetingMessageChanged]

Lagom Service Descriptor:
```

When our `HellolagomService` extends Lagom's service, it should override the `descriptor` function. This service overrides that function and defines the following two Hello Service endpoints:

Endpoint	Associated function call to handle the request	Function input (request)	Function output or result (response)
/api/hello/:id	hello	NotUsed	String
/api/hello/:id	useGreeting	GreetingMessage	Done

If we observe the preceding two endpoints' URIs, both have the same URI:`/api/hello/:id`. It's a little strange, right? Can you guess how Lagom Framework distinguishes those two endpoints?

If we observe the input and output of both endpoints' associated functions, they have different signatures:

The `hello()` function takes no input that is `NotUsed` and outputs a `String` value. If you are familiar with HTTP request methods, I think you will guess which HTTP `Request` method has this kind of behavior. It is an HTTP `GET` request method because it does not take any input in its body and has some result as an output.

The `useGreeting()` function takes `GreetingMessage` as an input and no output. If you are familiar with HTTP request methods, I think you will guess which HTTP `Request` method has this kind of behavior. It is an HTTP `POST` request because its body has some data (input) and no result (output).

By following the HTTP request method's standards, Lagom Framework distinguishes those two endpoints. If a user sends a POST request with the `/api/hello/:id` endpoint, then Lagom Framework makes a call to the `useGreeting()` function. In the same way, if the user sends a GET request with the same `/api/hello/:id` endpoint, then Lagom Framework makes a call to the `hello()` function.

Lagom Framework will take care of this under the hood.

 If you are new to the REST API, it's good to understand the difference between an API and endpoint.

Here, we have defined one API that is the Hello Service API with the following two endpoints:

```
GET        /api/hello/:id
POST       /api/hello/:id
```

These two endpoints are linked to `HellolagomService.TOPIC_NAME`. We will discuss how Lagom Framework uses this Topic in the coming WF Reactive System example.

We are done with the Hello Service API part. Now, let's move to its implementation microservice.

Understanding HelloService implementation code

In this section, we will try to understand the Hello Service implementation (`hello-lagom-impl`) code. This is an implementation microservice for the Hello Reactive System.

It has the `HellolagomState` state, as shown here:

```
case class HellolagomState(message: String, timestamp: String)

object HellolagomState {
  implicit val format: Format[HellolagomState] =
  Json.format[HellolagomState]
}
```

It has the `HellolagomEvent` event, as show here:

```
sealed trait HellolagomEvent extends AggregateEvent[HellolagomEvent] {
  def aggregateTag = HellolagomEvent.Tag
}

object HellolagomEvent {
  val Tag = AggregateEventTag[HellolagomEvent]
}
```

We have defined the following `GreetingMessageChanged` event to represent the change in the `GreetingMessage` state:

```
case class GreetingMessageChanged(message: String) extends HellolagomEvent

object GreetingMessageChanged {
  implicit val format: Format[GreetingMessageChanged] =
                                          Json.format[
GreetingMessageChanged
}
```

It has the `HellolagomCommand` command to represent our Hello Service commands:

```
sealed trait HellolagomCommand[R] extends ReplyType[R]
```

We have the following two command types:

→ **UseGreetingMessage Command**
```
case class UseGreetingMessage(message: String) extends
HellolagomCommand[Done]

object UseGreetingMessage {
  implicit val format: Format[UseGreetingMessage] =
Json.format[UseGreetingMessage]
}
```

→ **Hello Command**
```
case class Hello(name: String) extends HellolagomCommand[String]

object Hello {
  implicit val format: Format[Hello] = Json.format[Hello]
}
```

1. Create a serializer registry for our Hello Service implementation JSON objects. It is known as `JsonSerializerRegistry`. It is one of the internal components of Lagom Framework:

```
object HellolagomSerializerRegistry extends
 JsonSerializerRegistry {
  override def serializers: Seq[JsonSerializer[_]] = Seq(
   JsonSerializer[UseGreetingMessage],
   JsonSerializer[Hello],
   JsonSerializer[GreetingMessageChanged],
   JsonSerializer[HellolagomState]
  )
 }
```

Here, we have created a concrete subclass of `JsonSerializerRegistry` and initialized the Actor System manually by creating a serialization setup and passing it to the `ActorSystem` constructor.

The next step is persistence.

2. Develop the Hello persistence entity by extending `PersistentEntity` (it is one of the internal components of Lagom Framework), as shown here:

```
class HellolagomEntity extends PersistentEntity {

  override type Command = HellolagomCommand[_]
  override type Event = HellolagomEvent
  override type State = HellolagomState

  override def initialState: HellolagomState =
   HellolagomState("Hello", LocalDateTime.now.toString)

  override def behavior: Behavior = {
    case HellolagomState(message, _) =>
     Actions().onCommand[UseGreetingMessage, Done] {
       case (UseGreetingMessage(newMessage), ctx, state) =>
        ctx.thenPersist(GreetingMessageChanged(newMessage))
        { _ => ctx.reply(Done)
        }
     }.onReadOnlyCommand[Hello, String] {
       case (Hello(name), ctx, state) =>
        ctx.reply(s"$message, $name!")
     }.onEvent {
       case (GreetingMessageChanged(newMessage), state) =>
        HellolagomState(newMessage, LocalDateTime.now().toString)
     }
```

```
    }
  }
```

Here, we have defined the following three core components of the CQRS/ES design pattern:

- **Command**: `HellolagomCommand`
- **Event**: `HellolagomEvent`
- **State**: `HellolagomState`

 If you are new to the EQRS/ES design pattern, go through `Chapter 7`, *Working with Reactive Streams*, first.

3. Define the initial state of our Hello Service Reactive System:

```
override def initialState: HellolagomState =
  HellolagomState("Hello", LocalDateTime.now.toString)
```

4. Define our persistent entity behavior by overriding the `behavior` function, as demonstrated here:

```
override def behavior: Behavior = {
  case HellolagomState(message, _) =>
    Actions().onCommand[UseGreetingMessage, Done] {
      case (UseGreetingMessage(newMessage), ctx, state) =>
        ctx.thenPersist(
          GreetingMessageChanged(newMessage)
        ) { _ =>
          ctx.reply(Done)
        }
    }.onReadOnlyCommand[Hello, String] {
      case (Hello(name), ctx, state) =>
        ctx.reply(s"$message, $name!")
    }.onEvent {
      case (GreetingMessageChanged(newMessage), state) =>
        HellolagomState(newMessage, LocalDateTime.now().toString)
    }
  }
}
```

Let's understand this behavior function step by step now:

- `onCommand()`: This adds a command handler. For each command class, the handler is a `PartialFunction`. It is used to persist events into data store using the `ctx.thenPersist()` function.

- `onReadOnlyCommand()`: This is used to provide `READ-SIDE` commands. It adds a command handler that will not persist any events.

5. Provide implementation to our Hello Service API, as shown here:

```
class HellolagomServiceImpl(persistentEntityRegistry:
PersistentEntityRegistry) extends HellolagomService {

  override def hello(message: String) = ServiceCall { _ =>
   val ref = persistentEntityRegistry.refFor[HellolagomEntity]
    (message)
   ref.ask(Hello(message))
  }

  override def useGreeting(message: String) =
   ServiceCall { request =>
    val ref = persistentEntityRegistry.refFor[HellolagomEntity]
     (message)
    ref.ask(UseGreetingMessage(message))
  }

  override def greetingsTopic():
   Topic[api.GreetingMessageChanged] =
    TopicProducer.singleStreamWithOffset {
     fromOffset => persistentEntityRegistry.eventStream(
      HellolagomEvent.Tag, fromOffset)
      .map(ev => (convertEvent(ev), ev.offset))
  }

  private def convertEvent(helloEvent:
   EventStreamElement[HellolagomEvent]):
   api.GreetingMessageChanged = {
     helloEvent.event match {
       case GreetingMessageChanged(msg) =>
         api.GreetingMessageChanged(helloEvent.entityId, msg)
      }
    }
  }
```

Here our `HellolagomServiceImpl` class takes a constructor parameter that is `PersistentEntityRegistry`.

It provides implementation to all of our API functions:

```
hello()
useGreeting()
greetingsTopic()
```

`PersistentEntityRegistry` is a registry for all of our application-persistent entities. At our WF Reactive System startup, we must register all of our `PersistentEntity` classes with `PersistentEntityRegistry`, using its `register()` function.

6. Develop our `Hello` Service application, as follows:

```
abstract class HellolagomApplication(context:
 LagomApplicationContext) extends LagomApplication(context)
 with CassandraPersistenceComponents with LagomKafkaComponents
 with AhcWSComponents {
    override lazy val lagomServer = serverFor[HellolagomService]
    (wire[HellolagomServiceImpl])

    override lazy val jsonSerializerRegistry =
     HellolagomSerializerRegistry

    persistentEntityRegistry.register(wire[HellolagomEntity])
 }
```

Here, the most important thing we need to understand is how to bind our API and implementation classes.

7. We should override the `lagomServer` function to bind or map or link our API class with its implementation class, as follows:

```
override lazy val lagomServer = serverFor[HellolagomService]
  (wire[HellolagomServiceImpl])
```

- `serverFor()`: It binds our Lagom server for the `HellolagomService` service and it's factory service that is `HellolagomServiceImpl`.
- `wire()`: Here we are using Lagom's default DI framework that is Mocwire.

8. We should override `jsonSerializerRegistry()` using our `HellolagomSerializerRegistry`, as shown here:

```
override lazy val jsonSerializerRegistry =
  HellolagomSerializerRegistry
```

Last but not least, we should register our entity with our `PersistentEntityRegistry`, as shown here:

```
persistentEntityRegistry.register(wire[HellolagomEntity])
```

9. Develop Lagom Loader for our `HelloService` application, as illustrated here:

```
class HellolagomLoader extends LagomApplicationLoader {

  override def load(context: LagomApplicationContext):
  LagomApplication = new HellolagomApplication(context) {
    override def serviceLocator: ServiceLocator =
      NoServiceLocator
  }

  override def loadDevMode(context: LagomApplicationContext):
   LagomApplication = new HellolagomApplication(context)
   with LagomDevModeComponents

  override def describeService =
   Some(readDescriptor[HellolagomService])
}
```

10. Configure our Lagom application loader in the `application.conf` file, as shown here:

```
play.application.loader = com.example.hello.impl.HellolagomLoader
```

11. Configure our Cassandra Persistence details, such as the keyspace in the `application.conf` file, as demonstrated here:

```
hello-lagom.cassandra.keyspace = hello_lagom

cassandra-journal.keyspace = ${hello-lagom.cassandra.keyspace}
cassandra-snapshot-store.keyspace =
 ${hello-lagom.cassandra.keyspace}
lagom.persistence.read-side.cassandra.keyspace =
 ${hello-lagom.cassandra.keyspace}
```

That's it. Now it's time to start the implementing of our real WF Reactive System by following the same approach.

Developing Lagom WF Reactive System

In this section, we will start developing our WF Reactive System using Lagom Framework. Unlike our previous simple *Hello Reactive System*, we will develop some **UI** (**User Interface** or frontend) service for our WF system.

WF Reactive System architecture

Before developing our Reactive System, first we will understand its architecture. Our WF Reactive System has the following three main microservices:

- WF Frontend (UI)
- WF Producer (API and Implementation)
- WF Consumer (API and Implementation)

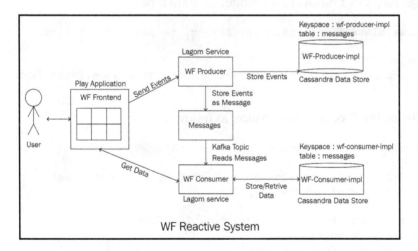

As shown in the preceding diagram, the **User** interacts with our System through the **WF Frontend** Service. When the **User** generates any events in our system, they will be sent to the Cassandra data store `wf-producer-impl` through our **WF Producer** Service. When the **User** sends any queries to our system, they will send them to the WF Consumer Service and serve those requests.

All these services are developed using the following microservices:

```
wf-frontend
wf-producer-api
wf-producer-impl
wf-consumer-api
wf-consumer-impl
```

Now, let's develop each service step by step and understand the code.

 To save some space, I'll not show the package names and imports in each and every file. Refer to this book's GitHub account to get the full source code.

WF Reactive System – Producer API

In this section, we will perform the following steps to develop our Reactive System's Producer API (`wf-producer-api`) microservice:

1. Develop our Producer API model, as shown here:

```scala
case class WFMessage(city: String, temperature: String)

object WFMessage {
  implicit val format: Format[WFMessage] = Json.format[WFMessage]
}
```

2. Define the Producer WFService, as follows:

```scala
trait WFService extends Service{

  def wfTemperature(city: String, temperature:String):
   ServiceCall[WFMessage, Done]

  override final def descriptor: Descriptor = {
    import Service._
    named("wfproducer").withCalls(
     pathCall("/wf/:city/:temperature", wfTemperature _)
    ).withTopics(
      topic(WFService.TOPIC_NAME, wfTopic)
    ).withAutoAcl(true)
  }

  def wfTopic(): Topic[WFMessage]
```

```
    }

    object WFService  {
      val TOPIC_NAME = "wfTemparature"
    }
```

This service defines one endpoint, as illustrated here:

Endpoint URI	Associated function	Request	Response
`/wf/:city/:temperature`	`wfTemperature`	`WFMessage`	`Done`

If you observe the signature of `wfTemperature`, its service call takes `WFMessage` as an input and `Done` as an output. That means it's an HTTP `POST` request.

This service also defines one topic (`wfTemparature`) to post user-generated events.

WF Reactive System – Producer implementation

In this section, we will use the following steps to develop our Reactive System's Producer implementation (`wf-producer-impl`) microservice:

1. Create the Producer command(s), as shown here:

```
sealed trait WFCommand[R] extends ReplyType[R]

case class UseWFMessage(city: String, temperature: String)
 extends WFCommand[Done]

object UseWFMessage {
  implicit val format: Format[UseWFMessage] =
    Json.format[UseWFMessage]
}

case class WF(city: String, temperature: String) extends
 WFCommand[String]

object WF {
  implicit val format: Format[WF] = Json.format[WF]
}
```

2. Define an `EventTag` for our System Element(s), as follows:

```
object WFEventTag {
  val instance: AggregateEventTag[WFEvent] =
  AggregateEventTag[WFEvent]()
}
```

3. Define our System Event(s), as illustrated:

```
sealed trait WFEvent extends AggregateEvent[WFEvent] {
  override def aggregateTag: AggregateEventTagger[WFEvent] = {
    WFEventTag.instance
  }
}

case class WFChanged(city:String, temperature: String) extends
 WFEvent

object WFChanged {
  implicit val format: Format[WFChanged] = Json.format[WFChanged]
}
```

4. Define our System State(s), as depicted here:

```
case class WFState(city:String, temperature: String,
 timestamp: String)

object WFState {
  implicit val format: Format[WFState] = Json.format[WFState]
}
```

5. Define `JsonSerializerRegistry` for our objects:

```
object WFSerializerRegistry extends JsonSerializerRegistry {
  override def serializers: Seq[JsonSerializer[_]] = Seq(
    JsonSerializer[UseWFMessage],
    JsonSerializer[WF],
    JsonSerializer[WFChanged],
    JsonSerializer[WFState]
  )
}
```

6. Define our system Entity:

```
class WFEntity extends PersistentEntity {

  override type Command = WFCommand[_]
```

```
override type Event = WFEvent
override type State = WFState

override def initialState: WFState = WFState("None", "0",
 LocalDateTime.now.toString)

override def behavior: Behavior = {
  case WFState(city, temperature, _) =>
    Actions().onCommand[UseWFMessage, Done] {
      case (UseWFMessage(city,temperature), ctx, state) =>
       ctx.thenPersist(
        WFChanged(city,temperature)
       ) { _ =>
          ctx.reply(Done)
        }
    }.onReadOnlyCommand[WF, String] {
      case (WF(city, temperature), ctx, state) =>
       ctx.reply(s"$city, $temperature!")
    }.onEvent {
      case (WFChanged(city,temperature), state) =>
       WFState(city,temperature, LocalDateTime.now().toString)
    }
  }
}
```

7. Develop our system loader, as demonstrated here:

```
class WFLoader extends LagomApplicationLoader {

  override def load(context: LagomApplicationContext):
  LagomApplication =
    new WFApplication(context) {
      override def serviceLocator: ServiceLocator =
        NoServiceLocator
    }

  override def loadDevMode(context: LagomApplicationContext):
   LagomApplication =
    new WFApplication(context) with LagomDevModeComponents
}

abstract class WFApplication(context: LagomApplicationContext)
 extends WFComponents(context) with LagomKafkaComponents {

}

abstract class WFComponents(context: LagomApplicationContext)
```

```scala
extends LagomApplication(context) with
CassandraPersistenceComponents with AhcWSComponents {

  override lazy val lagomServer = LagomServer.forServices(
    bindService[WFService].to(wire[WFServiceImpl])
  )

  override lazy val jsonSerializerRegistry =
    WFSerializerRegistry

  persistentEntityRegistry.register(wire[WFEntity])
}
```

8. Provide the implementation for our `WFService`:

```scala
class WFServiceImpl(persistentEntityRegistry:
 PersistentEntityRegistry) extends WFService {

  override def wfTemperature(city: String, temperature:String):
    ServiceCall[WFMessage, Done] = ServiceCall { request =>
    val ref = persistentEntityRegistry.refFor[WFEntity](city)
    ref.ask(UseWFMessage(request.city, request.temperature))
  }

  override def wfTopic(): Topic[WFMessage] = {
    TopicProducer.singleStreamWithOffset {
      offset =>
      persistentEntityRegistry.eventStream(WFEventTag.instance,
        offset).map(ev => (convertEvent(ev), offset))
    }
  }

  private def convertEvent(wfEvent: EventStreamElement[WFEvent]):
   WFMessage = {
     wfEvent.event match {
       case WFChanged(city, temperature) => WFMessage(city,
       temperature)
     }
  }

}
```

9. Configure our WF system loader in the `applicaton.conf` file:

```
application.conf
play.application.loader = com.packt.publishing.wf.impl.WFLoader
```

It also has some default Kafka server configurations. Go through them once. Now move on to the Consumer side code walk-through.

WF Reactive System – Consumer API

In this section, we will perform the following steps to develop our Reactive System's Consumer API (`wf-consumer-api`) microservice:

1. Define the Consumer model, as shown here:

```
case class WeatherForcasting(city:String, temperature:String)

object WeatherForcasting {
  implicit val format: Format[WeatherForcasting] =
  Json.format[WeatherForcasting]
}
```

2. Define the Consumer Service (we will provide the implementation for this Service in the *Consumer Implementation* section):

```
trait WFConsumerService extends Service {

  override def descriptor: Descriptor = {
    import Service._

    named("wfconsumer").withCalls(
      restCall(Method.GET, "/api/wf", findTopTenWFData _),
      restCall(Method.GET, "/api/wf/one", findOneWFData _),
      restCall(Method.GET, "/api/wflatest", latestWF _)
    ).withAutoAcl(true)
  }

  def findTopTenWFData(): ServiceCall[NotUsed,
   Seq[WeatherForcasting]]

  def findOneWFData(): ServiceCall[NotUsed, WeatherForcasting]

  def latestWF(): ServiceCall[NotUsed, WeatherForcasting]

}
```

Here, to remove all confusion, we are using the `restCall` identifier directly. All endpoints serve HTTP `GET` request calls:

Endpoint URI	HTTP request method	Associated function	Purpose/usage
`/api/wf`	GET	`findTopTenWFData`	This endpoint is used to get the first 10 or top 10 WF data elements from the data store.
`/api/wf/one`	GET	`findOneWFData`	This endpoint is used to get the first WF data element from the data store.
`/api/wflatest`	GET	`latestWF`	This endpoint is used to get the latest WF data element from in- memory.

Let's provide implementation for these endpoints in the next section.

WF Reactive System – Consumer implementation

In this section, we will use the following steps to develop our Reactive System's Consumer implementation(`wf-consumer-impl`) microservice:

1. Define the WF Consumer's Model, as shown here:

```
case class WeatherForcasting(city:String, temperature:String)

object WeatherForcasting {
  implicit val format: Format[WeatherForcasting] =
    Json.format[WeatherForcasting]
}
```

2. Define the WF Consumer's command, as follows:

```
sealed trait WFCommand [T] extends ReplyType[T]

case class SaveNewWF(city:String, temperature: String) extends
 WFCommand[Done]

object SaveNewWF {
  implicit val formatter = Json.format[SaveNewWF]
}
```

3. Define the WF Consumer's `EventTag`, as depicted here:

```
object WFEventTag {
  val INSTANCE = AggregateEventTag[WFEvent]
}

sealed trait WFEvent extends AggregateEvent[WFEvent] {
  override def aggregateTag = WFEventTag.INSTANCE
}
```

4. Define the WF Consumer's event:

```
case class WFSaved(wf: WeatherForcasting) extends WFEvent

object WFSaved {
  implicit val formatter = Json.format[WFSaved]
}
```

5. Define the WF Consumer's state, as illustrated here:

```
case class WFState(city:String, temperature:String ,
 timeStamp: String)

object WFState {
  implicit val formatter = Json.format[WFState]
}
```

6. Define the WF Consumer's Persistence Entity, as demonstrated here:

```
class WFEntity extends PersistentEntity {

  override type Command = WFCommand[_]
  override type Event = WFEvent
  override type State = WFState

  override def initialState = WFState("None","0",
   LocalDateTime.now().toString)

  override def behavior: Behavior = {
    case WFState(city, temperature, _) =>
      Actions().onCommand[SaveNewWF, Done] {
        case (SaveNewWF(city, temperature), ctx, state) =>
          println(s"New WF message came to Lagom Kafka server:
           ${city} ${temperature}")
          val wf = WeatherForcasting(city,temperature)
          ctx.thenPersist(WFSaved(wf)) { msgSaved: WFSaved =>
           ctx.reply(Done)
```

```
        }
      }.onEvent {
        case (WFSaved(wf), state) =>
         println(s"FYI, New WF change event fired, which is converted
          into a Message.")
         WFState(city, temperature, LocalDateTime.now().toString)
      }
    }
  }
```

It defines the following three major components of the CQRS/ES architecture:

- **Command**: WFCommand
- **Event**: WFEvent
- **State**: WFState

It also defines our persistence entity behavior using `onCommand` (for Command operations) and `onEvent ()` for all WF events.

7. Define the WF Consumer's application loader, as shown here:

```
class WFConsumerLoader extends LagomApplicationLoader {

  override def load(context: LagomApplicationContext):
   LagomApplication =
    new WFConsumerApplication(context) {
      override def serviceLocator: ServiceLocator =
       NoServiceLocator
    }

  override def loadDevMode(context: LagomApplicationContext):
   LagomApplication =
   new WFConsumerApplication(context) with LagomDevModeComponents
  }

 abstract class WFConsumerApplication(context:
  LagomApplicationContext) extends LagomApplication(context)
  with CassandraPersistenceComponents with LagomKafkaComponents
  with AhcWSComponents {

    override lazy val lagomServer = LagomServer.forServices(
    bindService[WFConsumerService].to(wire[WFConsumerServiceImpl])
    )

    lazy val helloService = serviceClient.implement[WFService]
```

```scala
    lazy val messageRepository = wire[WFRepository]

    override lazy val jsonSerializerRegistry =
    WFConsumerSerializerRegistry

    persistentEntityRegistry.register(wire[WFEntity])

    readSide.register(wire[WFEventProcessor])
}
```

8. Define the WF Consumer's event processor, as depicted here:

```scala
class WFEventProcessor(cassandraReadSide: CassandraReadSide,
 cassandraSession: CassandraSession) (implicit ec:
 ExecutionContext) extends ReadSideProcessor[WFEvent] {

    private var insertWFStmt: PreparedStatement = _

    override def buildHandler(): ReadSideHandler[WFEvent] = {
      cassandraReadSide.builder[WFEvent]("message_offset")
        .setGlobalPrepare(createTable)
        .setPrepare { _ => prepareStatements }
        .setEventHandler[WFSaved](e => insertWFCreater(e.event.wf))
        .build()
    }

    override def aggregateTags: Set[AggregateEventTag[WFEvent]] =
     Set(WFEventTag.INSTANCE)

    private def createTable(): Future[Done] = {
      for {
        _ <- cassandraSession.executeCreateTable(
        """    CREATE TABLE IF NOT EXISTS weatherforecast (
                  city text,
                  temperature text,
                  insertion_time timestamp,
                  PRIMARY KEY (city, insertion_time)
                ) WITH CLUSTERING ORDER BY (insertion_time DESC)
          """)
      } yield Done
    }

    private def prepareStatements(): Future[Done] = {
      for {
        insert <- cassandraSession.prepare(
          """insert into weatherforecast (city,
          temperature   ,insertion_time) values(?,
```

```
              ? ,toTimestamp(now()))   """)
      } yield {
         insertWFStmt = insert
         Done
      }
   }

   private def insertWFCreater(wf: WeatherForcasting) = {
     Future.successful(List(
     insertWF(wf)
     ))
   }

   private def insertWF(wf: WeatherForcasting) = {
     insertWFStmt.bind(wf.city,wf.temperature)
   }

}
```

9. Define the WF Consumer's Repository, as follows:

```
private[impl] class WFRepository(cassandraSession:
  CassandraSession)(implicit ec: ExecutionContext) {

  def fetchWFData(limit: Int): Future[Seq[WeatherForcasting]] = {
    val wfQuery = "SELECT city,temperature FROM weatherforecast
     LIMIT ?"

    cassandraSession
     .selectAll(wfQuery, limit.asInstanceOf[AnyRef])
     .map { rows =>
        rows.map(row =>
         WeatherForcasting(row.getString("city"),
         row.getString("temperature")))
    }
  }

  def fetchOneWFData: Future[WeatherForcasting] = {
    val wfQuery = "SELECT city,temperature FROM weatherforecast"

    cassandraSession
     .selectOne(wfQuery)
     .map { row =>
        row match {
          case Some(wf) => WeatherForcasting(wf.getString("city"),
           wf.getString("temperature"))
          case None     => WeatherForcasting("None", "0")
```

```
          }
        }
      }

    }
```

10. Provide our WF Consumer API's service implementation, as demonstrated here:

```
class WFConsumerServiceImpl(registry: PersistentEntityRegistry,
  wfService: WFService, wfRepository: WFRepository)
  extends WFConsumerService {

    wfService.wfTopic
      .subscribe
      .atLeastOnce(
      Flow[WFMessage].map { wf =>
       putWFMessage(wf)
       Done
       }
      )

     var lastObservedMessage: WeatherForcasting = _

       private def putWFMessage(wfMessage: WFMessage) = {
         entityRef(wfMessage.city.toString,
           wfMessage.temperature.toString).ask(
           SaveNewWF(wfMessage.city, wfMessage.temperature))
         lastObservedMessage =
           WeatherForcasting(wfMessage.city,wfMessage.temperature)
       }

       override def findTopTenWFData(): ServiceCall[NotUsed,
        Seq[WeatherForcasting]] = {
        ServiceCall {
          req => wfRepository.fetchWFData(10)
        }
       }

       override def findOneWFData(): ServiceCall[NotUsed,
        WeatherForcasting] = {
        ServiceCall {
          req => wfRepository.fetchOneWFData
        }
       }

       override def latestWF(): ServiceCall[NotUsed,
        WeatherForcasting] = {
```

```
        ServiceCall {
          req => scala.concurrent.Future.successful(
          lastObservedMessage)
        }
      }

      private def entityRef(city: String, temperature:String) =
        registry.refFor[WFEntity](city)
    }
```

11. Configure our WF Consumer's system loader in the `applicaton.conf` file:

```
application.conf
play.application.loader =
  com.packt.publishing.wf.consumer.impl.WFConsumerLoader
```

It also has some default Kafka server configurations. Go through them once. Now move on to the Consumer side code walk-through.

We are done with our WF Reactive System's API and implementation parts. Now, it's time to develop our actual customer or user-facing frontend or `WebGateway` in the next section.

WF Reactive System – frontend

In this section, we will perform the following steps to develop our Reactive System's frontend (`wf-frontend`) microservice:

1. Define our WF data model and its form to capture data from end users:

```
case class WFForm(city: String, temperature: String)

object WFForm {
  val wfForm = Form(mapping(
    "city" -> nonEmptyText,
    "temperature" -> nonEmptyText
  )(WFForm.apply)(WFForm.unapply))
}
```

2. Define our WF Reactive System's `WebGateway` loader, as shown here:

```
abstract class WebGateway @Inject()(context: Context) extends
  BuiltInComponentsFromContext(context) with I18nComponents
  with AhcWSComponents with LagomServiceClientComponents {

  override lazy val serviceInfo: ServiceInfo = ServiceInfo(
    "wf-frontend",
     Map(
       "wf-frontend" -> immutable.Seq(ServiceAcl.forPathRegex(
       "(?!/api/).*"))
     )
  )
  override implicit lazy val executionContext: ExecutionContext =
   actorSystem.dispatcher
  override lazy val router = {
    val prefix = "/"
    wire[Routes]
  }

  lazy val wfService = serviceClient.implement[WFService]
  lazy val wfConsumerService =
   serviceClient.implement[WFConsumerService]
  lazy val wfController = wire[WFController]
  lazy val wfConsumerController = wire[WFConsumerController]
  lazy val assets = wire[Assets]
}

class WebGatewayLoader extends ApplicationLoader {
  override def load(context: Context): Application =
    context.environment.mode match {
      case Mode.Dev =>
      new WebGateway(context) with LagomDevModeComponents
      {}.application
      case _ =>
      new WebGateway(context) {
        override def serviceLocator = NoServiceLocator
      }.application
    }
}
```

3. Define our WF `WebGateway` controllers, as follows:

```
class WFController @Inject()(val messagesApi: MessagesApi,
  wfService: WFService, wfConsumerService: WFConsumerService)
   (implicit ec: ExecutionContext) extends
   WFAbstractController(messagesApi, wfService,
```

```scala
wfConsumerService) with I18nSupport {

  def show: Action[AnyContent] = Action.async {
    implicit request => Future(Ok(views.html.wf(wfForm)))
  }

  def changeMessage(): Action[AnyContent] = Action.async {
    implicit request => wfForm.bindFromRequest.fold(
    badForm => Future {
      BadRequest(views.html.wf(badForm))
    },
    validForm => {
      for {
        result <- wfService.wfTemperature(validForm.city,
          validForm.temperature).invoke(WFMessage(validForm.city,
          validForm.temperature))
      }
      yield {
        Ok("WeatherForecast saved to data store successfully.")
      }
    }
    )
  }

}

class WFConsumerController @Inject()(val messagesApi:
 MessagesApi, wfService: WFService, wfConsumerService:
WFConsumerService)(implicit ec: ExecutionContext)
 extends WFAbstractController(messagesApi, wfService,
wfConsumerService) with I18nSupport {

  def weather(): Action[AnyContent] = Action.async {
   implicit request =>
    wfConsumerService.findTopTenWFData().invoke().map {
      (result: Seq[WeatherForcasting]) => Ok(Json.toJson(result))
    }
  }

  def weatherOne(): Action[AnyContent] = Action.async { implicit
   request => wfConsumerService.findOneWFData().invoke().map {
     (result: WeatherForcasting) => Ok(Json.toJson(result))
    }
  }

  def latestWeather(): Action[AnyContent] =
   Action.async { implicit request =>
    wfConsumerService.latestWF().invoke().map {
```

```
        (result:WeatherForcasting) => Ok(Json.toJson(result))
      }
    }

  }
```

4. Define our WF `WebGateway` class's routings, as illustrated here:

```
GET    /assets/*file        controllers.Assets.at(path = "/public",
   file)

## WF Routes
GET    /weather             controllers.WFController.show()
POST   /changedWeather      controllers.WFController.changeMessage()

GET    /wf                  controllers.WFConsumerController.weather()
GET    /wf/one          controllers.WFConsumerController.weatherOne()
GET    /latestwf    controllers.WFConsumerController.latestWeather()
```

5. Configure our WF `WebGateway` class's loader in the `applicaton.conf` file, as shown here:

```
application.conf
play.application.loader = WebGatewayLoader
```

Testing the WF Reactive System

We have developed all five of our required microservices completely. If you feel that any component is missing, refer to this book's GitHub repository and get the full source code.

It's time to run our system and test it. As we know, Lagom Framework has a great feature, that is, the single SBT command to start all of our microservices.

Our system final project structure looks like the following screenshot:

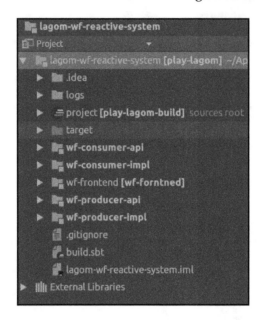

Execute the following command in our project folder:

```
lagom-wf-reactive-system$ sbt runAll
```

It starts all of our microservices and `WebGateway` and waits for client requests.

Access the WF Capture Data Form, as shown here:

Here, input the data, and click on the **Submit** button:

The data is submitted successfully:

Now, access the latest WF data from in-memory, as shown here:

Now, access the latest WF data from the data store, as follows:

Now access the top 10 WF data from the data store, as illustrated here:

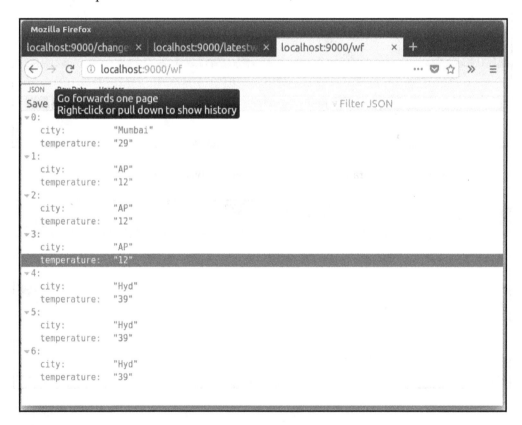

Summary

In this chapter, we introduced one of the modern and open source Reactive Platforms—Lagom Reactive Platform. It contains all the Reactive Technology stacks, such as Lagom Framework, Play, Scala, Akka Toolkit, and more.

We discussed Lagom Framework basics, and its internal components and building blocks to understand this platform well.

Then, we downloaded the Lagom Hello Service from the Lightbend Tech Hub and discussed each and every piece of code in detail. This gave us solid knowledge of Lagom Framework in order to develop our Reactive System.

Finally, we developed our Reactive System, the WF Reactive System, using the Lagom Framework Technology stack: Lagom Framework, Play Framework, Akka Toolkit, Akka Streams API, Lagom Persistence API, Cassandra, Kafka, Zookeeper, SBT, and IntelliJ IDE.

We tested our WF Reactive System very well using the web browser and some REST clients, such as Chrome POSTMAN, CURL Command, and more.

It's not possible to discuss every single concept of Lagom Framework and develop applications for all scenarios, as it's an ocean. It needs a separate book to go through all that in depth.

I hope this chapter gives you a very strong basic knowledge of Lagom Framework and provides a good start to dig into it.

We will cover some Reactive design principles and patterns in the upcoming chapters.

10
Testing Reactive Microservices

In this chapter, you will learn what **Test-Driven Development** (**TDD**) is, its importance, and you will learn how to unit test the components of our Scala-based Reactive web applications and Reactive microservices, using popular Scala testing frameworks.

I presume you are new to the TDD approach or know only some basics of TDD. So, initially, we will try to understand the TDD approach and the importance of TDD (unit testing) in developing web applications and microservices.

Unit testing means testing individual components of our application thoroughly. We should test each component separately and should test each and every line of code, to avoid most of the bugs. We have plenty of unit testing frameworks to test Java and Scala-based applications.

In this chapter, we will discuss the following:

- What is TDD and unit testing?
- The importance of the TDD approach
- How to unit test Scala components
- How to unit test Play Framework components
- How to unit test Akka Actors
- How to unit test Akka Stream components
- How to unit test Lagom Framework components
- What Code Coverage is and its importance
- An important Scala Code Coverage tool

Introduction to TDD

In this section, we will introduce you to a popular and very useful unit testing technique, that is, the TDD approach. Here, we will discuss only TDD theory concepts. From the next section onward, we will write unit tests for all of our Scala Reactive programming applications, one by one.

What is TDD?

Test-Driven Development (**TDD**) means *test first, code next*. This means, with the TDD approach, we first write the unit test before writing any code. Then, we execute that unit test; it will definitely fail (RED) because we have not written any code.

Next, we write the code to match that unit test (test case) and execute that test again; this time, it will pass (GREEN). Next, we write one more test case (unit test) for the same component, then write the code, and so on. Finally, once we finish writing all test cases and code, we finish the development of that component.

We can illustrate this approach with a diagram:

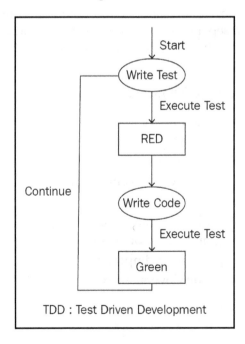

TDD is a unit testing technique in **Agile** methodology. As we write a test first, it is also known as the *Test First Development* approach.

As it is an iteration approach and allows changes of that component at any time, it suits the Agile process very well.

Code Coverage

Sometimes, we see some posts, tutorials, or tools for Code Coverage. It's good to understand this term, as it's related to unit tests.

Code Coverage refers to the number of source code lines that are tested, using unit tests. For instance, if we write unit tests to test each and every line of your source code, it means that you are maintaining 100% Code Coverage. It is also known as **Test Coverage**.

If we maintain better Code Coverage, it means that our source code is unit tested very well, and our source code contains fewer bugs. We will discuss one of the popular Code Coverage tools for Scala-based applications in the coming sections.

Benefits of TDD

The TDD approach gives us the following benefits in developing our software or applications in the Agile process:

- It is easy to accept the change
- It is easy to maintain and extend the components
- It is easy to identify bugs in the initial stages (development)
- There are fewer bugs because of 100% code coverage
- The quality is better, and the code is clean
- The interface Development is cleaner
- It is flexible to refactor code

 Don't confuse TDD with **Behavior-Driven Development** (BDD). We use BDD to write integration tests and TDD for unit tests; both are popular Agile methodologies.

As we need to discuss many new concepts, such as the Akka Toolkit, Akka Streams, the Play Framework, and the Lagom Framework, and develop our Reactive application, we have not written any unit tests in the previous chapters. This does not mean that we should write unit tests after developing our components.

We should start writing unit tests for each and every component from the beginning. We should start developing our application with unit tests. Make this practice a habit to develop clean and quality code.

Unit testing frameworks

We have many unit testing frameworks to test Play, Scala, and Akka-based applications. We can use the following frameworks:

- Spec2
- ScalaTest
- ScalaTest plus
- ScalaCheck
- ScalaMock
- Mokito
- Akka Toolkit's testing modules

In this chapter, we will use mainly ScalaTest, and its related frameworks to test our applications, and also Akka Toolkit's testing modules.

ScalaTest

ScalaTest is one of the popular unit testing frameworks for Scala-based projects. It is an open source, free software released under the Apache 2.0 license, developed by Bill Venners and Artima. It also supports the unit testing of Java-based applications.

It supports multiple testing styles, such as WordSpec, FlatSpec, FreeSpec, and PropSpec. We can choose the right spec to suit our project requirements.

ScalaTest's latest stable version is 3.0.4, and we can find its documentation at `http://doc.scalatest.org/3.0.1/#package`. Its official website is `www.scalatest.org`, and its source code is available at `https://github.com/scalatest/scalatest`.

If we want to use this library in our Scala-SBT-based applications, we should add the following dependency to the `build.sbt` or `project/Build.scala` file:

```
"org.scalatest" %% "scalatest" % "3.0.4" % "test"
```

ScalaTest Plus

ScalaTest Plus is also a unit testing framework. It is an extension of ScalaTest and integrates other libraries with ScalaTest to make it easier to test code using those libraries. The first such integration library is ScalaTest + Play, that is, `org.scalatestplus.play`.

We can find more details about this library at `http://www.scalatest.org/plus`, and its source is available at `https://github.com/playframework/scalatestplus-play`. As of now, its stable latest version is 3.1.2.

In simple words, ScalaTest + Play provides integration support between ScalaTest and the Play Framework.

```
Scale Test Plus ⇒ Scale Test +Play Framework
```

If we want to use this library in our Play Framework applications, we should add the following dependency to the `build.sbt` or `project/Build.scala` file:

```
"org.scalatestplus.play" %% "scalatestplus-play" % "3.1.2" % "test"
```

Benefits of ScalaTest

If we use the ScalaTest Framework to test our Scala-based applications, we will get the following benefits:

- A free and open source framework
- A product that is very flexible and easy to extend
- Highly productive
- It is easy to write and understand unit tests because we can write unit tests in a simple, human-readable format in the English language
- ScalaTest and ScalaTest Plus Frameworks are written in the Scala language

It's time to start writing unit tests for our Scala, Akka, Akka Streams, and Play Framework-based applications.

Unit testing Scala applications

In this section, we will discuss how to unit test Scala components using the ScalaTest unit testing framework. Most or all of the Scala-based applications use Case classes to represent their Data Models, so we should learn how to unit test Case classes.

Refer to the `scala-fp-app` project from `Chapter 2`, *Functional Scala,* GitHub repository. It contains the following Case class to represent our WF Reactive System data model:

```
package com.packt.publishing.caseclass
case class WeatherForecast (city: String, date: String, hour:
  String, temperature: String)
```

Perform the following steps to unit test `WeatherForecast` data model:

1. Write unit tests to test each and every data value of this data model using the ScalaTest unit testing framework.

2. Create a spec for our Data Model in the same package under the `/src/test/scala` folder:

```
package com.packt.publishing.caseclass

import org.scalatest.{WordSpec, Matchers}

class WeatherForecastSpec extends WordSpec with Matchers {

}
```

3. First, develop a function to create our Data Model with the available default values, as shown here:

```
private def createWeatherForecast(city: String = "London",
                                  date: String = "01/01/2018",
                                  hour: String = "10 AM",
                                  temperature: String = "6") =
          WeatherForecast(city, date, hour, temperature)
```

4. Write the first unit test to check all default values, as follows:

```
"WeatherForecast" should {
```

```
    "default values" in {
      createWeatherForecast().city shouldBe "London"
      createWeatherForecast().date shouldBe "01/01/2018"
      createWeatherForecast().hour shouldBe "10 AM"
      createWeatherForecast().temperature shouldBe "6"
    }
  }
}
```

5. Our final spec looks like this:

```
import org.scalatest.{WordSpec, Matchers}
class WeatherForecastSpec extends WordSpec with Matchers {
  private def createWeatherForecast(city: String = "London",
                               date: String = "01/01/2018",
                               hour: String = "10 AM",
                               temperature: String = "6") =
             WeatherForecast(city, date, hour, temperature)
  "WeatherForecast" should {

    "default values" in {
      createWeatherForecast().city shouldBe "London"
      createWeatherForecast().date shouldBe "01/01/2018"
      createWeatherForecast().hour shouldBe "10 AM"
      createWeatherForecast().temperature shouldBe "6"
    }

    "check city value" in {
      createWeatherForecast(city = "Hyderabad" ).city should
        not be "London"
      createWeatherForecast(city = "Hyderabad" ).city shouldBe
        "Hyderabad"
    }

    "check date value" in {
      createWeatherForecast(date = "06/04/2018" ).date shouldBe
        "06/04/2018"
    }

    "check hour value" in {
      createWeatherForecast(hour = "14" ).hour shouldBe "14"
    }

    "check city and temperature values" in {
      val wf = createWeatherForecast(city = "Hyderabad",
        temperature = "30" )
      wf.city shouldBe "Hyderabad"
      wf.temperature shouldBe "30"
```

```
            }

        }

    }
```

When we run this spec in the IntelliJ IDE, using the **Run WeatherForecastSpec** option, we will see the following results:

All five unit tests are executed successfully, which is why we see the GREEN bar.

Let's understand the preceding spec code in detail now:

Our `WeatherForecastSpec` extends `WordSpec` and `Matchers`, both are from the `ScalaTest` library.

The `WordSpec` component is useful to write unit tests in a human-readable form, as shown here:

```
"WeatherForecast" should {
    "default values" in {
    }
}
```

The `Matchers` component provides many asserting functions to unit test our components. For instance, it has the `shouldBe` and `should not be` functions:

```
"check city value" in {
   createWeatherForecast(city = "Hyderabad" ).city should not be
   "London"
   createWeatherForecast(city = "Hyderabad" ).city shouldBe
   "Hyderabad"
}
```

As discussed in the first section, ScalaTest not only has this `WordSpec`, but also has many other specs to test components in different ways. We can choose any one based on our project's requirements.

We can write the same spec using `FreeSpec`, as shown here:

```
package com.packt.publishing.caseclass

import org.scalatest.{FreeSpec, MustMatchers}

class WeatherForecastSpec2 extends FreeSpec with MustMatchers {

  private def createWeatherForecast(city: String = "London",
                                    date: String = "01/01/2018",
                                    hour: String = "10 AM",
                                    temperature: String = "6") =
    WeatherForecast(city, date, hour, temperature)

    "default values" in {
      val wf = createWeatherForecast()
      wf.city mustBe ("London")
      wf.date mustBe "01/01/2018"
      wf.hour mustBe "10 AM"
      wf.temperature mustBe "6"
    }

    "check city value" in {
      val wf = createWeatherForecast(city = "Hyderabad")
      wf.city must not be "London"
      wf.city mustBe "Hyderabad"
    }

    "check date value" in {
      val wf = createWeatherForecast(date = "06/04/2018")
      wf.date mustBe "06/04/2018"
    }

    "check hour value" in {
      val wf = createWeatherForecast(hour = "14")
      wf.hour mustBe "14"
    }

    "check city and temperature values" in {
      val wf = createWeatherForecast(city = "Hyderabad",
      temperature = "30")
      wf.city mustBe "Hyderabad"
      wf.temperature mustBe "30"
```

```
        }
    }
```

Try to experiment with other ScalaTest spec styles, and choose the right one to match your project requirements. Now let's move to test the Play Framework components.

Unit testing Play Framework components

In this section, we will discuss how to unit test Play Framework components, using ScalaTest and its associated ScalaTest Plus unit testing frameworks.

Test HelloWorld without using DI Controller

In this section, we are going to refer `play-scala-helloworld-app` Play Scala-based `HelloWorld` application available in the `Chapter-6` folder from the GitHub repository (`https://github.com/rposa-srp-book/srp-book-examples/tree/master/Chapter-6/play-scala-helloworld-app`) and write unit tests for its controller.

Perform the following steps to write unit tests for this application:

1. Add the following entry in the `build.sbt` file available in the root folder of this project:

   ```
   libraryDependencies ++= Seq(
     "org.scalatestplus.play" %% "scalatestplus-play" % "1.5.1" % Test
   )
   ```

   Here, we have configured the ScalaTest Plus unit testing framework in the Test scope. It provides all the required components to test Play Framework applications.

2. Execute the `sbt update` command to pull this library and add it to the `play-scala-helloworld-app` classpath.

3. Define a spec by extending the `PlaySpec` and `OneAppPerTest` components, as follows:

   ```
   import org.scalatestplus.play._
   import play.api.test.Helpers._
   import play.api.test._
   class HelloWorldNoDIControllerSpec extends PlaySpec with
   ```

```
OneAppPerTest {

}
```

Refer to the *Description* section to understand the use of the `PlaySpec` and `OneAppPerTest` components of the ScalaTest Plus unit testing framework.

4. Write a unit test to test the HelloWorld controller's routing:

```
"render the helloWorld page from Play Routings" in {
  val helloWorld = route(app, FakeRequest(GET,
    "/helloWorld")).get

  status(helloWorld) mustBe OK
  contentType(helloWorld) mustBe Some("text/html")
  contentAsString(helloWorld) must include ("Hello World Without
    DI")
}
```

Here, we are using the `route` function available in the `play.api.test.RouteInvokers` trait.

5. Complete the unit tests spec, as shown here:

```
class HelloWorldNoDIControllerSpec extends PlaySpec with
  OneAppPerTest {

  "HelloWorldNoDIController" should {

    "render the helloWorld page from Play Routings" in {
      val helloWorld = route(app, FakeRequest(GET,
        "/helloWorld")).get

      status(helloWorld) mustBe OK
      contentType(helloWorld) mustBe Some("text/html")
      contentAsString(helloWorld) must include ("Hello World
        Without DI")
    }

    "render the helloWorld page from Play application object" in {
      val controller =
        app.injector.instanceOf[HelloWorldNoDIController]
      val helloWorld =
        controller.helloWorld().apply(FakeRequest())

      status(helloWorld) mustBe OK
      contentType(helloWorld) mustBe Some("text/html")
```

```
        contentAsString(helloWorld) must include ("Hello World
          Without DI")
      }

    "render the helloWorld page by creating a new instance of
      controller" in {
        val controller = new HelloWorldNoDIController
        val helloWorld =
         controller.helloWorld().apply(FakeRequest())

        status(helloWorld) mustBe OK
        contentType(helloWorld) mustBe Some("text/html")
        contentAsString(helloWorld) must include ("Hello World
          Without DI")
      }

  }

}
```

Now let us understand the preceding Unit Test Spec step by step:

`PlaySpec` is a super Suite base class for Play tests with a combination of `WordSpec` and `MustMatchers`.

The class, `PlaySpec`, extends WordSpec with MustMatchers.

`OneAppPerTest` is a trait that provides a new Play Framework's Application instance for each unit test.

Like `OneAppPerTest`, ScalaTestPlus has many components, as shown here. Each one provides us with a specific functionality:

- `OneAppPerTest`: This provides a new application instance for each *test*
- `OneAppPerSuite`: This provides a new application instance per ScalaTest *Suite*
- `OneServerPerTest`: This provides a new aplication and running `TestServer` instance for each test executed in a ScalaTest *Suite*
- `OneServerPerSuite`: This provides a new application and running `TestServer` instance per ScalaTest *Suite*
- `OneBrowserPerTest`: This provides a new Selenium `WebDriver` instance for each test executed in a ScalaTest *Suite*
- `OneBrowserPerSuite`: This provides a new Selenium `WebDriver` instance per ScalaTest *Suite*

All the preceding Test suites are available in the `org.scalatestplus.play` package in the ScalaTestPlus unit testing framework:

`app` is defined in the `OneAppPerTest` trait, as shown here:

```
implicit final def app: Application = synchronized { appPerTest }
```

This `app` is an implicit method that returns the Play Framework's `Application` instance for the current test.

When we run this test, we will see the following output:

```
play-scala-helloworld-app$ sbt test
[info] HelloWorldNoDIControllerSpec:
[info] HelloWorldeNoDIController
[info] - should render the helloWorld page
[info] ScalaTest
[info] Run completed in 2 seconds, 615 milliseconds.
[info] Total number of tests run: 2
[info] Suites: completed 2, aborted 0
[info] Tests: succeeded 2, failed 0, canceled 0, ignored 0, pending 0
[info] All tests passed.
[info] Passed: Total 2, Failed 0, Errors 0, Passed 2
[success] Total time: 3 s, completed 31-Dec-2017 17:26:33
```

If we have more specs and want to execute only one spec at a time, we need use the `test-only` or `testOnly` SBT option, as shown here:

```
play-scala-helloworld-app$ sbt "test-only
controllers.HelloWorldNoDIControllerSpec"
```

We can execute the same commands by accessing the SBT console:

```
play-scala-helloworld-app$ sbt
```

Now it enters into the SBT console:

```
[play-scala-helloworld-app] $  testOnly
controllers.HelloWorldNoDIControllerSpec
```

This command is useful to execute only one Spec:

```
[play-scala-helloworld-app] $ test
```

This command is useful to execute all available specs in that project.

In the same way, test our `HelloWorld` Controller, which is implemented using Play Framework's **dependency injection (DI)** concept in the next section.

Test HelloWorld with DI Controller

In this section, we will refer to the `play-scala-helloworld-di-app` Play Scala-based `HelloWorld` application available in `Chapter 6`, *Extending Application with Play*, GitHub folder and write unit tests for our controller.

Perform the same steps that we discussed earlier to update the `build.sbt` file.

Complete the unit tests spec, as shown here:

```
package controllers
import org.scalatestplus.play._
import play.api.test.Helpers._
import play.api.test._
class HelloWorldDIControllerSpec extends PlaySpec with OneAppPerTest {
  "HelloWorldeDIController" should {
    "render the helloWorld page from Play Routings" in {
      val helloWorld = route(app, FakeRequest(GET, "/helloWorld")).get
       status(helloWorld) mustBe OK
       contentType(helloWorld) mustBe Some("text/html")
       contentAsString(helloWorld) must include ("Hello World With DI.")
    }
    "render the helloWorld page from Play application object" in {
      val controller = app.injector.instanceOf[HelloWorldDIController]
      val helloWorld = controller.helloWorld().apply(FakeRequest())
       status(helloWorld) mustBe OK
       contentType(helloWorld) mustBe Some("text/html")
       contentAsString(helloWorld) must include ("Hello World With DI.")
    }
    "render the helloWorld page by creating a new instance of
     controller" in {
      val controller = new HelloWorldDIController
      val helloWorld = controller.helloWorld().apply(FakeRequest())
      status(helloWorld) mustBe OK
      contentType(helloWorld) mustBe Some("text/html")
      contentAsString(helloWorld) must include ("Hello World With DI.")
    }
  }
}
```

Like the previous `HelloWorldNoDIControllerSpec`, it also defines the same kind of three unit tests. When we run this test, we will see the following output:

```
play-scala-helloworld-di-app$ sbt test
[info] HelloWorldDIControllerSpec:
[info] HelloWorldDIController
[info] - should render the helloWorld page from Play Routings
[info] - should render the helloWorld page from Play application object
[info] - should render the helloWorld page by creating a new instance of
controller
[info] ScalaTest
[info] Run completed in 3 seconds, 341 milliseconds.
[info] Total number of tests run: 3
[info] Suites: completed 1, aborted 0
[info] Tests: succeeded 3, failed 0, canceled 0, ignored 0, pending 0
[info] All tests passed.
[info] Passed: Total 3, Failed 0, Errors 0, Passed 3
[success] Total time: 4 s, completed 31-Dec-2017 17:55:56
```

Unit testing Akka Actors

In this section, we will discuss how to unit test Actors, using Akka Toolkit's testing modules. It is very tough to test Actor's asynchronous messaging and multi-threaded behavior without using these testing modules.

Akka Toolkit's testing modules

As we discussed in Chapter 4, *Building Reactive Applications with Akka*, Akka *extensions (or modules)* section, the Akka Toolkit has the following two modules for unit testing purposes:

```
actor-testkit
akka-stream-testkit
```

The `actor-testkit` module is useful to test Akka's Actors, and the `akka-stream-testkit` module is useful for testing the components of the Akka Stream's API.

In this section, we will discuss how to test Actors using the `actor-testkit` module, and in the next section, we will also discuss how to test the components of Akka Streams using the `akka-stream-testkit` module. In addition to Actor Testkit, we will use the ScalaTest unit testing framework.

As we know, we have developed a couple of Akka Actor's basic examples in `Chapter 4`, *Building Reactive Applications with Akka*. We will pick up a couple of projects from `Chapter 4`, *Building Reactive Applications with Akka* and write unit tests for them.

Testing HelloWorld Actor

In this section, we will write unit tests for Actors that are available in the `akka-scala-helloworld-app` application.

Perform the following tests to write unit tests for this Akka application:

1. Update `build.sbt` with the Testing Library dependencies.
2. To use the `Akka TestKit` module, we need to add the following line:

   ```
   "com.typesafe.akka" %% "akka-testkit" % "2.5.9" % "test"
   ```

3. To use the ScalaTest Framework, we need to add the following line:

   ```
   "org.scalatest" %% "scalatest" % "3.0.4" % "test"
   ```

4. Check out the full version of `build.sbt` from the `akka-scala-helloworld-app` at GitHub.
5. We use these two library dependencies only for unit testing purposes, we have added the test scope for them:

   Unit test HelloWorldActor:

   ```
   class HelloWorldActorSpec extends TestKit(system)
    with Matchers with WordSpecLike with BeforeAndAfterAll {

     "HelloWorld Actor" should {
        "pass on a HelloWorld message" in {
          val testProbe = TestProbe()
          val helloWorldActor =
           system.actorOf(Props[HelloWorldActor], "HelloWorldActor")
          EventFilter.info(message = "Hello World", occurrences = 1)
             .intercept(helloWorldActor ! HelloWorld)
        }
     }

     override def afterAll: Unit = {
       shutdown(system)
     }
   ```

```
    }

    object HelloWorldActorSpec {
      val system = {
        val loggerConfig = ConfigFactory.parseString("akka.loggers =
        [akka.testkit.TestEventListener]")
        ActorSystem("AkkaHelloWorld", loggerConfig)
      }
    }
```

We use the `akka.testkit.TestKit` of the ScalaTest Framework to test our Actors.

TestKit has everything to test our components. It contains `TestActorRef`, `LocalActorRef`, and `CallingThreadDispatcher`.

TestKit also contains `ActorSystem` with system. As our `HelloWorldActor` (Version 1, which is available at `com.packt.publishing.reactive.hello.actor` package name) is a Side-Effecting Actor, it just logs a statement and returns nothing. We should use `EventFilter` to intercept our `HelloWorldActor`'s log statement.

To enable Logging Events, we should enable `TestEventListener` and set our Actor System, as follows:

```
val loggerConfig = ConfigFactory.parseString("akka.loggers =
  [akka.testkit.TestEventListener]")
ActorSystem("AkkaHelloWorld", loggerConfig)
```

We use the `BeforeAndAfterAll` component, available in the ScalaTest Framework, to shut down our ActorSystem after executing our unit tests:

```
override def afterAll: Unit = {
  shutdown(system)
}
```

As our Actor does not return anything message, we use this assert—`TestProbe.expectNoMsg()`.

Unit testing HelloWorldActor (Version 2)

Now let's unit test our `HelloWorldActor` version 2 which is available
at `com.packt.publishing.reactive.hello.actor.v2` package name:

```
class HelloWorldActorSpec(actorSystem: ActorSystem) extends
 TestKit(actorSystem) with Matchers with WordSpecLike with
 BeforeAndAfterAll {

  def this() = this(ActorSystem("AkkaHelloWorld"))

  "HelloWorld Actor" should {
     "pass on a HelloWorld message" in {
       val testProbe = TestProbe()
       val helloWorldActor = system.actorOf(Props(new
        HelloWorldActor(testProbe.ref)), "HelloWorldActor")
       helloWorldActor ! HelloWorld
       testProbe.expectMsg(500 millis, HelloWorld)
     }
  }
  override def afterAll: Unit = {
    shutdown(system)
  }
}
```

Let us understand the preceding Test spec here:

- As our `HelloWorldActor` (Version 2) returns the `"HelloWorld"` message; we
  can assert this using the `TestProbe` component.
- The `TestProbe` component has many asserting messages, such as `expectMsg`,
  `expectNoMsg`, and `expectTerminated`.

Executing HelloWorld Actor unit tests

Now it's time to execute our two versions Actor's unit tests using the `sbt` command, as
follows:

```
akka-scala-helloworld-app$ sbt test
[INFO] [12/29/2017 18:50:28.122] [AkkaHelloWorld-akka.actor.default-
dispatcher-4] [akka://AkkaHelloWorld/user/HelloWorldActor] Hello World
[info] HelloWorldActorSpec:
[info] HelloWorld Actor
[info] - should pass on a HelloWorld message
[info] HelloWorldActorSpec:
```

```
[info] HelloWorld Actor
[info] - should pass on a HelloWorld message
[info] Run completed in 1 second, 58 milliseconds.
[info] Total number of tests run: 2
[info] Suites: completed 2, aborted 0
[info] Tests: succeeded 2, failed 0, canceled 0, ignored 0, pending 0
[info] All tests passed.
```

Unit testing Akka Streams

In this section, we will discuss how to unit test Akka Streams, using Akka Toolkit's testing modules.

As we discussed in the previous section, like the `actor-testkit` module for Akka's Actors, the `akka-stream-testkit` module is useful for testing the components of the Akka Stream's API. However, we can test Akka Stream's components, using the `actor-testkit` module, too.

As we discussed in Chapter 7, *Working with Reactive Streams*, Akka Streams have mainly the following three components:

- Source
- Flow
- Sink

We are going to unit test these three components in the coming sections. Please refer to this GitHub repository for the next two sub-sections: `https://github.com/rposa-srp-book/srp-book-examples/tree/master/Chapter-7/akka-streams-scala-helloworld-app`.

Uniting test Akka Streams, with Actor's Testkit

In this section, we will test three main components of the Akka Stream's API using Akka's `actor-testkit` Testing module.

Execute the following steps to test Akka Stream Components:

1. Update the existing libraries, dependencies in the `build.sbt` file with the following entry:

```
lazy val akkaVersion = "2.5.9"
"com.typesafe.akka" %% "akka-testkit" % akkaVersion % "test"
```

Write unit tests as shown here:

```scala
package com.packt.publishing.akka.streams.hello
import akka.actor.ActorSystem
import akka.stream.ActorMaterializer
import akka.stream.scaladsl.{Flow, Sink, Source}
import akka.testkit.{TestKit, TestProbe}
import org.scalatest.{BeforeAndAfterAll, MustMatchers,
 WordSpecLike}
import scala.concurrent.duration._

class AkkaStreamsHelloWorldSpec extends
 TestKit(ActorSystem("HelloWorldSystem")) with WordSpecLike with
 BeforeAndAfterAll with MustMatchers {

   override def afterAll: Unit = {
     system.terminate()
   }

   implicit val materializer = ActorMaterializer()

   "Akka Streams Components" should {

     "HelloWorld with 'Source >> Sink'" in {
       val helloWorldSource = Source.single("Akka Streams Hello
        World")
       val testProbe = TestProbe()
       val sink = Sink.actorRef(testProbe.ref, "Sent")

       val helloWorldGraph =  helloWorldSource.to(sink)
       helloWorldGraph.run()

       testProbe.expectMsg(500 millis, "Akka Streams Hello World")
       testProbe.expectMsg("Sent")
     }

     "HelloWorld with 'Source >> Flow >> Sink'" in {
       val helloWorldSource = Source.single("Akka Streams Hello
        World")
       val helloWorldFlow = Flow[String].map(str =>
        str.toUpperCase)

       val testProbe = TestProbe()
       val helloWorldSink = Sink.actorRef(testProbe.ref, "Sent")

       val helloWorldGraph =
        helloWorldSource.via(helloWorldFlow).to(helloWorldSink)
       helloWorldGraph.run()
```

```
        testProbe.expectMsg(500 millis, "AKKA STREAMS HELLO WORLD")
        testProbe.expectMsg("Sent")


    }


  }


}
```

Here, we have tested two flows—one from `Source` to `Sink`, and another from `Source` to `Flow` to `Sink`.

2. When we run the preceding Spec, using the `test-only` option, we will see the following results:

```
akka-streams-scala-helloworld-app$ sbt "test-only
com.packt.publishing.akka.streams.hello.AkkaStreamsHelloWorldSpec"
[info] AkkaStreamsHelloWorldSpec:
[info] Akka Streams Components
[info] - should HelloWorld with 'Source >> Sink'
[info] - should HelloWorld with 'Source >> Flow >> Sink'
[info] Run completed in 751 milliseconds.
[info] Total number of tests run: 2
[info] Suites: completed 1, aborted 0
[info] Tests: succeeded 2, failed 0, canceled 0, ignored 0, pending
0
[info] All tests passed.
```

Unit testing Akka Streams with Akka Stream's Testkit

In this section, we will test three main components of the Akka Streams API using Akka's `akka-stream-testkit` Testing module.

Akka Stream's Testkit module provides two main components to test the Akka Stream API:

- `TestSource`: This is useful to test the Sink component
- `TestSink`: This is useful to test the Source component

We will use these two Akka Stream Testkit components to write our unit tests now.

Execute the following steps to test Akka Stream Components:

1. Update the existing libraries, dependencies in the `build.sbt` file with the following entry:

```
lazy val akkaVersion = "2.5.9"
"com.typesafe.akka" %% "akka-stream-testkit" % akkaVersion % "test"
```

2. Write unit tests, as shown here:

```
package com.packt.publishing.akka.streams.hello

import akka.actor.ActorSystem
import akka.stream.ActorMaterializer
import akka.stream.scaladsl.{Keep, Sink, Source}
import akka.stream.testkit.scaladsl.{TestSink, TestSource}
import akka.testkit.{TestKit}
import org.scalatest.{BeforeAndAfterAll, MustMatchers,
WordSpecLike}

class AkkaStreamsHelloWorldSpec2 extends
TestKit(ActorSystem("HelloWorldSystem"))
              with WordSpecLike with BeforeAndAfterAll with
MustMatchers {

  override def afterAll: Unit = {
    system.terminate()
  }

  implicit val materializer = ActorMaterializer()

  "Akka Streams Components" should {

    "HelloWorld test Source" in {
      val helloWorldSource = Source.single("Akka Streams Hello
      World")

      helloWorldSource.runWith(TestSink.probe[String](system))
          .requestNext() mustBe "Akka Streams Hello World"

    }

    "HelloWorld test Sink'" in {
      val sink = Sink.cancelled

      TestSource.probe[String]
                        .toMat(sink)(Keep.left)
```

```
                              .run()
                              .expectCancellation()
            }

      }

   }
```

3. When we run the preceding spec, using the `test-only` option, we will see the following results:

```
akka-streams-scala-helloworld-app$ sbt "test-only
com.packt.publishing.akka.streams.hello.AkkaStreamsHelloWorldSpec"
[info] AkkaStreamsHelloWorldSpec2:
[info] Akka Streams Components
[info] - should HelloWorld test Source
[info] - should HelloWorld test Sink'
[info] Run completed in 816 milliseconds.
[info] Total number of tests run: 2
[info] Suites: completed 1, aborted 0
[info] Tests: succeeded 2, failed 0, canceled 0, ignored 0, pending
0
[info] All tests passed.
```

For more information about how to test Akka Stream's components, refer to the Akka Toolkit documentation at `https://doc.akka.io/docs/akka/current/stream/stream-testkit.html?language=scala`.

If you want to see the source code of these two Akka Toolkit Testkits, refer to the following GitHub repositories:

- `https://github.com/akka/akka/tree/master/akka-testkit`
- `https://github.com/akka/akka/tree/master/akka-stream-testkit`

Unit testing Lagom services

In this section, you will learn how to unit test Lagom Framework's microservices, using Akka Toolkit's Testing modules.

Lagom Framework provides the following two testing modules to unit test our Reactive microservices or Reactive web applications:

- `lagom-core-testkit`
- `lagom-scaladsl-testkit`

We will refer to the `lagom-scala-hello-service` project available under this chapter folder in the GitHub repository.

Perform the following steps to unit test the `lagom-scala-hello-service` components:

1. Add the following SBT plugin to the `/project/plugins.sbt` file:

   ```
   addSbtPlugin("com.lightbend.lagom" % "lagom-sbt-plugin" % "1.4.0-M3")
   ```

   The preceding Lagom's SBT plugin pulls not only the required Lagom libraries to develop a Reactive microservice, but also pulls the two previously mentioned Testing Module libraries, then set to our project's classpath.

2. Write a unit test to test our Hello Entity, as shown here:

   ```
   class LagomscalahelloserviceEntitySpec extends WordSpec with
    Matchers with BeforeAndAfterAll {
      private val system =
        ActorSystem("LagomscalahelloserviceEntitySpec",
         JsonSerializerRegistry.actorSystemSetupFor(
         LagomscalahelloserviceSerializerRegistry))

      override protected def afterAll(): Unit = {
        TestKit.shutdownActorSystem(system)
      }

      private def withTestDriver(block:
       PersistentEntityTestDriver[LagomscalahelloserviceCommand[_],
       LagomscalahelloserviceEvent, LagomscalahelloserviceState] =>
       Unit): Unit = {
         val driver = new PersistentEntityTestDriver(system,
          new LagomscalahelloserviceEntity,
          "lagom-scala-hello-service-1")
         block(driver)
         driver.getAllIssues should have size 0
      }

      "lagom-scala-hello-service entity" should {

        "say hello by default" in withTestDriver { driver =>
   ```

```
    val outcome = driver.run(Hello("Alice"))
    outcome.replies should contain only "Hello, Alice!"
  }

  "allow updating the greeting message" in withTestDriver {
    driver =>
      val outcome1 = driver.run(UseGreetingMessage("Hi"))
      outcome1.events should contain only
        GreetingMessageChanged("Hi")
      val outcome2 = driver.run(Hello("Alice"))
      outcome2.replies should contain only "Hi, Alice!"
  }

  }
}
```

Here, we mainly concentrate on the `PersistentEntityTestDriver` class:

- It is a testing utility to check whether our `PersistentEntity` emits expected events and side effects in response to incoming commands
- It also verifies that all the commands, events, replies, and states are serializable and it reports any such problems in the issues of the outcome.

3. Write a unit test to test our Hello Service, as shown here:

```
class LagomscalahelloserviceServiceSpec extends AsyncWordSpec
  with Matchers with BeforeAndAfterAll {
  private val server = ServiceTest.startServer(
    ServiceTest.defaultSetup.withCassandra(true)) { ctx =>
    new LagomscalahelloserviceApplication(ctx)
      with LocalServiceLocator
    }
    val client =
    server.serviceClient.implement[LagomscalahelloserviceService]
    override protected def afterAll() = server.stop()
    "lagom-scala-hello-service service" should {
      "say hello" in {
        client.hello("Alice").invoke().map { answer =>
          answer should ===("Hello, Alice!")
        }
      }
      "allow responding with a custom message" in {
        for {
          _ <- client.useGreeting("Bob").invoke(
            GreetingMessage("Hi"))
          answer <- client.hello("Bob").invoke()
```

```
            } yield {
              answer should ===("Hi, Bob!")
            }
          }
        }
      }
```

Here, we need to understand how `ServiceTest` works and is useful to test our `Service` component. It supports writing functional tests for one service.

The service is running in a server, and to in the test, you can interact with it using its service client, that is, calls to the service API.

The Code Coverage tool

In a previous section, we have already discussed what Code Coverage is, and the importance of this technique in writing unit tests.

If we maintain 100% Code Coverage, that is, if we unit test our code thoroughly, then we can avoid most of the bugs in the initial stage. So, how do we check our Code Coverage? In this section, we will discuss the Scoverage tool.

The SCoverage tool

SCoverage tool refers to the Scala Code Coverage Tool. It is an open source Code Coverage tool for Scala-based applications from the Apache Foundation.

Its plugins are available for the following build tools:

- maven
- sbt
- gradle

SBT SCoverage plugin

If you want to use this tool in our Scala-based SBT projects, add the following line of code in our project's `plugins.sbt`:

```
addSbtPlugin("org.scoverage" % "sbt-scoverage" % "1.5.1")
```

The `sbt-scoverage` is an SBT plugin that uses the `scoverage` Code Coverage library and performs checks and generates Code Coverage reports for us.

Once we are done with this step, then we can use the following command to check the project Code Coverage percentage:

```
$ sbt clean coverage test
```

We can find all the available plugins of the scoverage library at `https://github.com/scoverage` and the sbt-scoverage plugin's source code at `https://github.com/scoverage/sbt-scoverage`.

That's all about unit testing our Scala Reactive Programming applications. Here, we have discussed and implemented unit tests only for a couple of projects and leave rest of them intentionally. I advise you to write unit tests for the rest of the projects as your homework.

Summary

In this chapter, we discussed TDD basics and its benefits. It follows *Test First, Code Next* approach thats why it is also known as Test First Development.

We discussed ScalaTest and its associated ScalaTestPlus Unit Testing Framework. The ScalaTest Plus Framework is a useful library to unit test Play Framework components.

You learned how to test Scala Standalone projects, using the ScalaTest framework, how to test Akka Actors, using its Testing module, `akka-testkit`; and how to test Akka Streams components, using Akka Toolkits testing modules, `akka-testkit` and `akka-stream-testkit`.

We saw that the Lagom Framework provides two testing modules, `lagom-core-testkit` and `lagom-scaladsl-testkit`, to unit test its components.

Next, we talked about Scoverage, which is a Code Coverage tool for Scala-based applications and microservices. It supports three different plugins to support three popular build tools—SBT, Maven, and Gradle. By using this plugin, we can generate our Code Coverage report to know how many unit tests have been written for our components and which lines are required to write unit tests.

To become an expert in the TDD approach, write unit tests for the rest of this book's projects.

11
Managing Microservices in ConductR

In this chapter, we will discuss one of the important tools of Lagom Reactive Platform. It has two kinds of environments:

- The Lagom Production Environment
- The Lagom Development Environment

If we want to use the Production Environment, we need Lightbend's paid license. As it's just for experimental and educational purposes, we will use the Development Environment in this chapter.

Lagom Reactive Platform's Development Environment is ConductR sandbox. In this chapter, we will set up our ConductR Sandbox Local Development Environment and deploy our WF Reactive System into this environment and test it.

Refer to ConductR's documentations at `http://conductr.lightbend.com/docs/2.2.x/Home` for more information.

As of now, we have ConductR 2.2.x as the latest and the most stable version of ConductR.

In this chapter, you will learn the following concepts about ConductR:

- ConductR and its features
- Advantages of ConductR
- Components of ConductR
- How to install/set up ConductR
- How to convert our WF Reactive System to work with ConductR

- Bundle and its contents
- ConductR CLI commands
- Deploying and testing the WF Reactive System in the ConductR environment

Introduction to Lightbend's ConductR

In this section, we will discuss Lightbend's Development Environment, ConductR, and its basic elements, such as its features, benefits, architecture, and the major responsibilities of Lightbend's ConductR.

What is ConductR?

In Lightbend Reactive Platform, ConductR plays a very vital and important role.

ConductR is a Reactive Tool from Lightbend to manage Lightbend Reactive Platform in clustered environments. As it is Reactive by design, we will get all the benefits of Reactive.

In simple words, It is a **RAM** (**Reactive Application Manager**).

The Lightbend ConductR Sandbox is a developer environment. It is used as a preproduction or near-production environment for staging and debugging ConductR bundles. It is not suitable to use in our Production Environments.

The latest version of ConductR is 2.2.x.

Responsibilities of ConductR

The Lightbend ConductR tool is responsible for doing the following things in Lightbend Reactive Platform:

- Bundling Reactive applications
- Providing a Clustered Environment
- Deploying applications into the Clustered Environment
- Managing (start, stop, run, restart, and so on) Reactive applications in the Clustered Environment
- Locating Reactive services in a Clustered Environment

Advantages of ConductR

Lightbend's ConductR tool simplifies operations for Reactive Systems. It provides the following benefits:

- It automates Resilient and Elastic deployments easily
- It allows us to deploy cluster-ready, proxy-based production releases easily
- It instantiates isolated and redundant application instances
- It provides us dynamic discovery for *anywhere* services
- It has easy to understand and use ConductR commands

Components of ConductR

Lightbend ConductR has the following important components to fulfill its job easily. These are also known as the building blocks of ConductR:

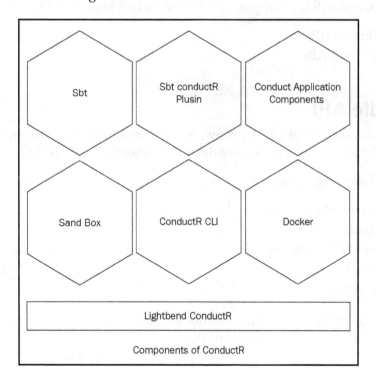

Sandbox is a local Development and Testing environment. It simulates the cluster environment locally.

The ConductR **CLI** (**Command-Line Interface**) is a set of commands that are useful to interact with the Lightbend ConductR environment. The `conduct` command is a ConductR CLI.

The ConductR CLI provides commands to load, start, stop, run, and unload (among other commands, bundles) to and from the ConductR environment. It provides the `logs` command to see log statements and the `events` command to view the event logs.

Docker is required to set up the Lightbend ConductR Sandbox environment locally. We will discuss all these components in detail in the coming sections.

ConductR APIs

The Lightbend ConductR tool supports the following two kinds of APIs:

- The Bundle API
- The Control API

The Bundle API

The ConductR Bundle API or Library provides a convenient Scala, Akka, and Play API over an underlying REST API. This document details the underlying REST API.

It supports the following services:

- Location lookup service
- List hosts service
- Receive hosts events service
- Find host service
- Status service

Refer to the ConductR Bundle API documentation at: `http://conductr.lightbend.com/docs/2.2.x/BundleAPI` for more information.

The Control API

The ConductR Control API or Library or Protocol is RESTful. It supports the following services:

- Loading a bundle and optionally its configuration
- Scaling a bundle, that is, starting it and possibly stopping it
- Unloading a bundle
- Querying a bundle state
- Receiving bundle state events
- Querying bundle configurations
- Querying bundle files
- Querying member states
- Querying agent states
- Querying logs by bundle
- Query events by bundle

Refer to the ConductRControl API documentation at: `http://conductr.lightbend.com/docs/2.2.x/ControlAPI` for more information.

Installing Lightbend ConductR

In this section, we will set up our local Lightbend ConductR environment to test our Reactive Microservices. We will discuss most of the setup steps for the Ubuntu Linux environment and check for similar options for other OS environments, such as Windows and Mac.

Prerequisites

The following are the prerequisites for installing the Conduct CLI tool:

- Oracle Java Runtime Environment 8 (JRE 8)
- Docker
- Python 3
- Pip 3

Before going through the ConductR setup, ensure that you set up this software first. We need to set up of Java JRE8.

We need a local Docker environment to install, deploy, and test our WF Reactive System with Lightbend's ContctR. Refer to the official Docker documentation to set up one of the flavors of Docker into your local system:

`https://www.docker.com/community-edition`

Go through your specific installation guide (for instance, if you are using Ubuntu, you can access its installation steps at `https://docs.docker.com/engine/installation/linux/docker-ce/ubuntu/#set-up-the-repository`) for more information.

To check your Docker setup, use the following command:

```
ram$ dockerps -a
```

You can check the Python version as well using the following command:

```
ram$ python --version
Python 2.7.12
```

If it's less than 3.x, perform the following steps to install Python 3:

1. If you are using Ubuntu 14.04 or 16.04, you can use the following:
   `https://launchpad.net/~jonathonf/+archive/ubuntu/python-3.6.`

   ```
   ram$ add-apt-repository ppa:jonathonf/python-3.6
   ram$ apt-get update
   ram$ apt-get install python3.6
   ```

2. Check the Python 3 version, as shown here:

   ```
   ram$ python3.6 --version
   Python 3.6.3
   ```

3. Even if you have other versions of Python 3, that is enough:

```
ram$ python3 --version
Python 3.5.2
```

4. We need Python's `pip3` tool to install our ConductR **CLI (Command Line Interface)**:

```
ram$ pip3 install conductr-cli
     pip3: command not found
ram$ pip3
```

5. The `pip3` program is currently not installed. You can install it by typing the following command:

apt install python3-pip

6. To install pip3, enter the following:

```
ram$ apt install python3-pip

ram$ pip3 --version
pip 8.1.1 from /usr/lib/python3/dist-packages (python 3.5)
```

We have now installed all the required prerequisites. It's time to jump to the ConductR CLI tool installation in our Ubuntu Environment.

Installing the ConductR CLI

Before installing the ConductR CLI, you need to register your details with Lightbend ConductR Developer:

1. Access the following URL to **Register, confirm your email and login**:

```
https://www.lightbend.com/product/conductr/developer
```

2. Select the **Terms and Conditions** checkbox and accept it.

3. Use the pip3 tool to install the ConductR CLI, as shown here:

```
ram$ pip3 install conductr-cli
Collecting conductr-cli
Downloading conductr-cli-1.2.25.tar.gz (212kB)
100%| 215kB2.1MB/s
. . . .
```

4. Running the `setup.py` file install for `conductr-cli` ... done

Here to save some space, I have provided only a few log statements from the ConductorR CLI installation step.

5. Once the installation is done successfully, we can execute a couple of basic commands to verify the installation process:

- To know the Sandbox version, enter the following:

```
ram$ sandbox version
1.2.25
Supported API version(s): 1, 2
```

- To run the Sandbox environment, enter the following:

```
ram:~$ sandbox run 2.1.12 -n 3 --feature visualization
|-------------------------------------------------|
| Starting ConductR |
|-------------------------------------------------|
Retrieving
https://dl.bintray.com/lightbend/generic/conductr-2.1.12-Linux-amd64.tg
z
[################################################] 100%
Retrieving
https://dl.bintray.com/lightbend/generic/conductr-agent-2.1.12-Linux-am
d64.tgz
[################################################] 100%
Retrieving
https://dl.bintray.com/typesafe/bundle/typesafe/continuous-delivery/2.1
.6-64affe9f9d126d31674f1408731b4e08232fbb4d557e34fe11daefeaa4d182ef/con
tinuous-
delivery-2.1.6-64affe9f9d126d31674f1408731b4e08232fbb4d557e34fe11daefea
a4d182ef.zip
[################################################] 100%
Loading bundle to ConductR..
[################################################] 100%
Bundle 64affe9f9d126d31674f1408731b4e08 is installed
```

```
Bundle loaded.
|-------------------------------------------------|
| Starting HAProxy |
|-------------------------------------------------|
Pulling docker image haproxy:1.5
Retrieving
https://dl.bintray.com/typesafe/bundle/typesafe/conductr-haproxy/2.1.10
-
e7de6590f3d23bcb0401498faae2486cb1306a6e9a360a182022d51a5c23d68a/conduc
tr-haproxy-2.1.10-
e7de6590f3d23bcb0401498faae2486cb1306a6e9a360a182022d51a5c23d68a.zip
[#################################################] 100%
Retrieving
https://dl.bintray.com/typesafe/bundle-configuration/typesafe/conductr-
haproxy-dev-
mode/2.1.0-92feca565e8cbe4a0e08b617829767f2c8a1a000212e14eb8b096175b3aa
b02e/conductr-haproxy-dev-
mode-2.1.0-92feca565e8cbe4a0e08b617829767f2c8a1a000212e14eb8b096175b3aa
b02e.zip
[#################################################] 100%
Loading bundle to ConductR..
[#################################################] 100%
Bundle
e7de6590f3d23bcb0401498faae2486c-92feca565e8cbe4a0e08b617829767f2 is
installed
Bundle loaded.
|-------------------------------------------------|
| Starting OCI-in-Docker support |
|-------------------------------------------------|
Pulling docker image lightbend-docker-registry.bintray.io/conductr/oci-
in-docker:0.1.0
|-------------------------------------------------|
| Starting logging feature based on eslite |
|-------------------------------------------------|
Deploying bundle eslite..
Retrieving
https://dl.bintray.com/typesafe/bundle/typesafe/eslite/2.1.4-920f4add9b
9eaf4ae4dda7342d39a6b9a21536902c364884b52f892434661f00/eslite-2.1.4-920
f4add9b9eaf4ae4dda7342d39a6b9a21536902c364884b52f892434661f00.zip
[#################################################] 100%
Loading bundle to ConductR..
[#################################################] 100%
Bundle 920f4add9b9eaf4ae4dda7342d39a6b9 is installed
|-------------------------------------------------|
| Summary |
|-------------------------------------------------|
|- - - - - - - - - - - - - - - - - - - - - - - - |
| ConductR |
```

```
|- - - - - - - - - - - - - - - - - - - - - - - - |
ConductR has been started:
core instance on 192.168.10.1
agent instances on 192.168.10.1, 192.168.10.2, 192.168.10.3
ConductR service locator has been started on:
192.168.10.1:9008
|- - - - - - - - - - - - - - - - - - - - - - - - |
| Proxy |
|- - - - - - - - - - - - - - - - - - - - - - - - |
HAProxy has been started
```

By default, your bundles are accessible on the following:

```
192.168.10.1:9000
```

ConductR Sandbox Visualizer

ConductR Sandbox Visualizer is a UI tool to determine the current state of the Sandbox (deployed in the ConductR Sandbox environment) in a graphically represented way.

When we start the Sandbox, it also loads and starts **The Visualizer,** as shown here:

```
|-------------------------------------------------|
| Starting visualization feature |
|-------------------------------------------------|
Deploying bundle visualizer..
Retrieving bundle..
Loading bundle from cache typesafe/bundle/visualizer
Resolving bundle typesafe/bundle/visualizer
Retrieving
https://dl.bintray.com/typesafe/bundle/typesafe/visualizer/2.1.0-cabaae
7cf37b1cf99b3861515cd5e77a16fa9638e225fa234929cc1d46dde937/visualizer-2
.1.0-
cabaae7cf37b1cf99b3861515cd5e77a16fa9638e225fa234929cc1d46dde937.zip
[###############################################] 100%
Loading bundle to ConductR..
[###############################################] 100%
Bundle loaded.
```

We can access the visualizer by
accessing `http://192.168.10.1:9008/services/visualizer`.

We can see the Visualizer UI, as shown here:

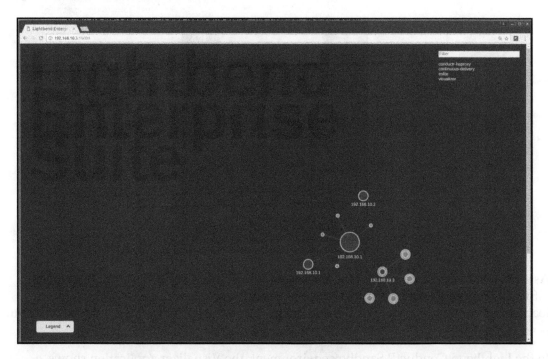

When we observe the Visualizer, we can see the following image in the top-right corner of its UI, which is currently deployed to the Sandbox environment (it may be just loaded but not running, or loaded and running services):

When we observe the left bottom corner of the Visualizer, we can see the following image:

As shown in the preceding diagram, the **Legend** is useful to know the Visualizer image information in more detail. For instance, the **Execution** circle represents the currently loaded and running service. The **Bundle** image represents the currently loaded service, but is not running.

In the Lightbend ConductR Sandbox environment, the Visualizer application shows ConductR nodes as small blue circles with the following extra information:

- It shows each Bundle's (a Component or Service) IP addresses next to them
- It shows green circles which denote **Bundle**
- It shows a spinning circle, meaning that a **Bundle** has started and is running without any issues

By default, ConductR's Visualizer application starts and runs only on one instance or one node. If we want it to start and run on more nodes, we need to start it by executing the following command:

```
conduct run --host 172.17.0.1 --scale 2 visualizer
```

Here, we are trying to run the Visualizer application on two nodes.

Note that we can find Lightbend's Lagom Framework SBT plugin's latest available version from their bintray at `https://bintray.com/lagom/sbt-plugin-releases/lagom-sbt-plugin`.

Understanding ConductR Sandbox information

We can run the `conduct info` command to see the currently deployed and running services in the Sandbox environment status, as shown here:

```
ram$ conduct info
Max ConductR agents: 1
ConductR Version(s): 2.1.*
Grants: conductr, cinnamon, akka-sbr
```

When we execute `conduct info` command, we can observe the following output from console:

ID	NAME	TAG	#REP	#STR	#RUN	ROLES
`64affe9`	continuous-delivery	2.1.6	1	0	1	continuous-delivery
`e7de659-92feca5`	conductr-haproxy	2.1.10	1	0	1	haproxy
`920f4ad`	eslite	2.1.4	1	0	1	elasticsearch
`cabaae7`	visualizer	2.1.10	1	0	1	web

Here, we will discuss the column usage of the `conduct info` command output, as shown here:

- `ID`: This represents the short hash of that service
- `NAME`: This is the name of the bundle, service, or microservice
- `TAG`: This is the version number of that bundle or microservice
- `#REP`: This represents the number of bundle replications available in ConductR Sandbox
- `#STR`: The represents the number of bundle instances that are starting in ConductR Sandbox
- `#RUN`: This represents the number of bundle instances that are running in ConductR Sandbox
- `ROLES`: This represents the role of the bundle, such as web, Cassandra, Elasticsearch and, so on

Preparing WF Reactive System for ConductR

As we know, we have developed a **WF (Weather Forecasting)** Reactive System in Chapter 9, *Reactive Microservices with Lagom*. We have tested it very well; it is working as expected. However, before deploying this kind of system to a Clustered Live (Production) System, we need to test it locally using a Cluster environment.

As we discussed, Lightbend Reactive Platform provides a Development Environment known as **ConductR Sandbox** for this kind of testing. We cannot deploy our Reactive System directly without any changes in this sandbox environment. We need to prepare with some minimal changes to our system to deploy it into Sandbox for Clustered Environment testing.

In this section, we will discuss the step-by-step process to prepare our WF Reactive System to make it compatible with the ConductR Environment. Even though these are very minimal changes, we should understand them very well.

ConductRSBT plugin

Like the SBT Play Framework plugin, we need to add the sbt-conductr plugin in the plugins.sbt file.

To use ConductR with our Reactive System, add the following sbt-conductr plugin to project/plugins.sbt:

```
addSbtPlugin("com.lightbend.conductr" % "sbt-conductr" % "2.3.5")
```

Now our plugins.sbt file looks like this:

```
// The Lagom plugin
addSbtPlugin("com.lightbend.lagom" % "lagom-sbt-plugin" % "1.3.0-RC2")
// The Lagom Conduct plugin
addSbtPlugin("com.lightbend.conductr" % "sbt-conductr" % "2.3.5")
```

When we add this plugin to our project, it will get the following libraries into its classpath:

- conductr-bundle-lib
- conductr-lib-common
- scala-conductr-bundle-lib
- scala-conductr-lib-common
- play25-conductr-bundle-lib

- `play25-conductr-lib-common`
- `akka24-conductr-bundle-lib`
- `akka24-conductr-lib-common`
- `lagom1-scala-conductr-bundle-lib`
- `java-conductr-lib-common`

This `sbt-conductr` plugin adds several commands to the SBT console, such as `install` and `bundle:dist`. We will use these commands in our Reactive system in the coming sections.

Mix ConductRApplicationComponents trait

In the next step, we need to mix the `ConductRApplicationComponents` trait into all our Reactive System's Loaders.

Mix it to `wf-consumer-impl` microservices' Loader, as shown here:

```
class WFConsumerLoader extends LagomApplicationLoader {

  override def load(context: LagomApplicationContext):
   LagomApplication  =
    new WFConsumerApplication(context) with
    ConductRApplicationComponents

  override defloadDevMode(context: LagomApplicationContext):
   LagomApplication = new WFConsumerApplication(context)
   with LagomDevModeComponents

  override defdescribeServices =
    List(readDescriptor[WFConsumerService])

}
```

Here, we have mixed this ConductR trait with our Consumer Application, as shown here:

new WFConsumerApplication(context) with ConductRApplicationComponents

Similarly, mix this trait to `wf-producer-impl` microservices Loader, as shown here:

```
class WFProducerLoader extends LagomApplicationLoader {
  override def load(context: LagomApplicationContext):
    LagomApplication = new WFProducerApplication(context) with
    ConductRApplicationComponents
```

```
override def loadDevMode(context: LagomApplicationContext):
 LagomApplication =  new WFProducerApplication(context) with
 LagomDevModeComponents

override def describeServices =
 List(readDescriptor[WFConsumerService])

}
```

Similarly, mix this trait with `wf-frontend` microservices' Loader, as shown here:

```
class WebGatewayLoader extends ApplicationLoader {
 override def load(context: Context): Application =
  context.environment.mode match {
   case Mode.Dev =>
   new WebGateway(context) with LagomDevModeComponents
   {}.application
   case _ =>
   (new WebGateway(context) with ConductRApplicationComponents {
     override lazy valcircuitBreakerMetricsProvider = new
     CircuitBreakerMetricsProviderImpl(actorSystem)
    }).application
  }
 }
}
```

Now our WF Reactive System is ready to deploy in a clustered ConductR Sandbox environment.

Deploying the WF Reactive System on ConductR

In this section, we will discuss how to start the ConductR Sandbox environment and how to bundle, load, and run our Reactive System components, such as `wf-producer-impl`, `wf-consumer-impl`, and `wf-frontend`.

Do we need to bundle and deploy only our `Impl` components into the ConductR Sandbox environment? How about the API components? The answer is yes, we need to deploy only `Impl` components into the ConductR Sandbox environment, but not the API components.

Starting ConductR Sandbox with multinodes

ConductR Sandbox runs the following command syntax:

```
sandbox run <SANDBOX_VERSION><FEATURES>
```

We have already discussed how to start Sandbox in the previous section, using the following command:

```
ram$ sandbox run 2.1.12 -n 3 --feature visualization
```

Let's understand the preceding command step by step:

1. The `sandbox run` command is used to start Sandbox.
2. The Sandbox version is `2.1.12`. This command interacts with Lightbend's bintray to download that sandbox version and starts it locally.
3. The `-n 3` specifies the number of nodes in that Sandbox Cluster environment.
4. The `--feature visualization` instruct Sandbox to bundle and deploy the Visualizer Reactive System into the ConductR Sandbox Environment.

When we observe the Sandbox logs, we can see the following log statements:

```
Starting ConductR core instance on 192.168.10.1..
Starting ConductR agent instance on 192.168.10.1..
Starting ConductR agent instance on 192.168.10.2..
Starting ConductR agent instance on 192.168.10.3..
```

This means our ConductR Sandbox has started on the three nodes that have these IP addresses.

Starting ConductR Sandbox with a single node

ConductR Sandbox runs the following command syntax:

```
sandbox run <SANDBOX_VERSION><FEATURES>
```

We have already discussed how to start Sandbox in the previous section, using the following command:

```
ram$ sudo sandbox run 2.1.12 -n 1 --feature visualization
```

Here, we start our Sandbox environment with only one available node in our cluster.

Bundle WF Reactive System components

In this section, we will discuss how to bundle our WF Reactive System components one by one using the ConductR Sandbox CLI.

Perform the following steps to bundle our components:

1. Open the SBT console in our `lagom-wf-reactive-system` project root folder:

```
rambabuposa@ram:~/Applications/lagom-wf-reactive-system$ sudo sbt
[sudo] password for rambabuposa:
[info] Loading project definition from /home/rambabuposa/Applications/lagom-wf-reactive-system/project
[info] Set current project to play-lagom (in build file:/home/rambabuposa/Applications/lagom-wf-reactive-system/)
>
```

2. Execute the `projects` command to list the available projects:

```
> projects
[info] In file:/home/rambabuposa/Applications/lagom-wf-reactive-system/
[info]      lagom-internal-meta-project-cassandra
[info]      lagom-internal-meta-project-kafka
[info]      lagom-internal-meta-project-service-locator
[info]    * play-lagom
[info]      wf-consumer-api
[info]      wf-consumer-impl
[info]      wf-forntned
[info]      wf-producer-api
[info]      wf-producer-impl
>
```

3. Execute the `bundle:dist` command to bundle or package our Reactive System components, as shown here:

```
>bundle:dist
....
[info] Bundle has been created: /home/rambabuposa/Applications/lagom-
wf-reactive-system/wf-frontend/target/bundle/wf-
forntned-1.0.0-8afb9230b7ed3b122e5434f80930aa7d9896f491b4a927febf182301
61481248.zip
[info] Packaging /home/rambabuposa/Applications/lagom-wf-reactive-
system/wf-producer-impl/target/scala-2.11/wf-producer-
```

```
impl_2.11-1.0.0.jar ...
[info] Done packaging.
23:51:31.571 [pool-5-thread-7] DEBUG c.l.l.i.api.tools.ServiceDetector
- Loading service discovery class:
com.packt.publishing.wf.impl.WFProducerLoader
[info] Main Scala API documentation successful.
[info] Packaging /home/rambabuposa/Applications/lagom-wf-reactive-
system/wf-producer-impl/target/scala-2.11/wf-producer-impl_2.11-1.0.0-
javadoc.jar ...
[info] Done packaging.
[info] Bundle has been created: /home/rambabuposa/Applications/lagom-
wf-reactive-system/wf-consumer-impl/target/bundle/wf-consumer-
impl-1.0.0-4c355f8488a9723c0d361369043cbc06c3e99ea68ba0dd46ea5bcc6611f1
3498.zip
[info] Bundle has been created: /home/rambabuposa/Applications/lagom-
wf-reactive-system/wf-producer-impl/target/bundle/wf-producer-
impl-1.0.0-6cef92710a4eb95cf8581c025c47199e5511e0a631560eee1d20be7afe54
dd77.zip
[success] Total time: 19 s, completed 04-Dec-2017 23:51:37
```

Here, to save space, I have provided only the required log statements. From here, we can
see that it has created three bundles:

- wf-
  frontend-1.0.0-8afb9230b7ed3b122e5434f80930aa7d9896f491b4a927fe
  bf18230161481248.zip

- wf-consumer-
  impl-1.0.0-4c355f8488a9723c0d361369043cbc06c3e99ea68ba0dd46ea5b
  cc6611f13498.zip

- wf-producer-
  impl-1.0.0-6cef92710a4eb95cf8581c025c47199e5511e0a631560eee1d20
  be7afe54dd77.zip

We can observe that bundles are created in the ZIP file format with some format. We will
discuss this format in depth in the next section.

Observing the WF Reactive System bundles

In the previous section, we created our WF Reactive System components bundles
successfully. In this section, we will look at what a bundle is and who creates them and how
to configure bundle information.

In Lightbend ConductR, the `sbt-conductr` SBT plugin provides another SBT plugin, `sbt-native-packager`, which is useful to create bundles. Bundles are ZIP files that are named by using the following syntax:

```
[Component Name]-[Version Number]-[Digest value].zip
```

Here, `Component Name` means `wf-frontend`, `wf-producer-impl`, and `wf-consumer-impl`.

The `Version Number` is as usual: 1.0.0, and the `Digest value` is a secure digest value.

In addition to the semantic name (such as `wf-frontend`), bundles are identified with a secure digest value, which is derived from their contents. When we change the component source code and re-bundle it, it will create a new digest value based on its new content.

Each bundle contains the following files:

- A bundle descriptor file
- A component's files

The source files, such as classes and properties, are related to the component under a directory named under the component's name/version combination.

We will discuss the Bundle descriptor in more detail in the next section.

ConductR Bundle descriptor

When we run ConductR Sandbox's `bundle:dist` command with SBT, it does the following things:

- Compiles all component classes
- Creates a Bundle descriptor
- Creates a Bundle ZIP file by following some naming convention (refer to the previous section for more information)

Here, the Bundle descriptor plays a very vital role. Each Bundle (or package, component, service, or microservice) should have a Bundle descriptor.

A Bundle descriptor is a flat text file with the name `bundle.conf`. We can observe the following information in a descriptor:

- Bundle format version number.
- Component version number.
- Component name and its description.
- An Akka cluster role that corresponds with the component. For instance, `web-server` and `web`.

Let's explore it in detail with one of our components or microservices' Bundle descriptor:

```
version             = "1"
name                = "wf-producer-impl"
compatibilityVersion = "1"
tags                = ["1.0.0"]
annotations         = {}
system              = "wf-producer-impl"
systemVersion       = "1"
nrOfCpus            = 0.1
memory              = 402653184
diskSpace           = 200000000
roles               = ["web"]
components = {
  wf-producer-impl = {
    description     = "wf-producer-impl"
    file-system-type = "universal"
    start-command   = ["wf-producer-impl/bin/wf-producer-impl", "-J-Xms134217728", "-J-Xmx134217728", "-Dplay.crypto.secret=77662d70726f64756365722d696d706c"]
    endpoints = {
      "akka-remote" = {
        bind-protocol = "tcp"
        bind-port    = 0
        services     = []
      }
    }
  }
}
```

Here, we can observe our `wf-producer-impl` microservice's bundle descriptor.

When we change the component source code and rebundle it, it will create a new digest value based on its new content. You can observe this with some of the changes to our `wf-producer-impl` microservice, as shown here:

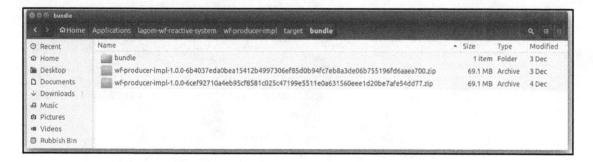

Here, I tried to update a few components and recreated the bundle. We can now observe the different bundle that is a new secure digest value.

Now its time to load and run our WF Reactive System's bundles into ConductR Sandbox's Development Environment.

Loading WF Reactive System bundles

In this section, we will load our previously created WF Reactive System's bundles into the ConductR Sandbox Environment.

Load wf-producer-impl

Execute the following steps to load the `wf-producer-impl` bundle into Sandbox:

1. `cd` to our project root directory:

   ```
   ram$ cd Applications/lagom-wf-reactive-system
   ```

2. Execute the `sbt` command to access the SBT console
3. Execute the `projects` command to see the available projects
4. Execute the `project wf-producer-impl` command to access this microservice

   ```
   > project wf-producer-impl
   [info] Set current project to wf-producer-impl (in build
   file:/home/rambabuposa/Applications/lagom-wf-reactive-system/)
   ```

5. Enter the `conduct load` command and press the *Tab* key on your keyboard. It will pick up the recently created bundle for that microservice, as shown here:

   ```
   > project wf-producer-impl
   [info] Set current project to wf-producer-impl (in build
   file:/home/rambabuposa/Applications/lagom-wf-reactive-system/)
   >
   > conduct load /home/rambabuposa/Applications/lagom-wf-reactive-
   system/wf-producer-impl/target/bundle/wf-producer-
   impl-1.0.0-6cef92710a4eb95cf8581c025c47199e5511e0a631560eee1d20be7a
   fe54dd77.zip
   Retrieving bundle..
   Resolving bundle using [uri_resolver]
   Loading bundle to ConductR..
   Bundle 6cef92710a4eb95cf8581c025c47199e is installed
   ```

```
Bundle loaded.
Start bundle with: conduct run 6cef927
Unload bundle with: conduct unload 6cef927
Print ConductR info with: conduct info
Print bundle info with: conduct info 6cef927
[success] Total time: 4 s, completed 05-Dec-2017 14:03:25
>
```

Now we have loaded our `wf-producer-impl` bundle into the ConductR Sandbox environment successfully. Go ahead and deploy the other two microservices in the same way.

Loading wf-consumer-impl

Now it's time to load the `wf-consumer-impl` bundle into Sandbox:

1. Execute the `project wf-producer-impl` command to access this microservice:

   ```
   > project wf-consumer-impl
   ```

2. Execute the `conduct load` command.

   Enter the `conduct load` command and press the *Tab* key. It will pick up the recently created bundle for that microservice:

   ```
   > conduct load /home/rambabuposa/Applications/lagom-wf-reactive-
   system/wf-consumer-impl/target/bundle/wf-consumer-
   impl-1.0.0-4c355f8488a9723c0d361369043cbc06c3e99ea68ba0dd46ea5bcc66
   11f13498.zip
   Retrieving bundle..
   Resolving bundle using [uri_resolver]
   Loading bundle to ConductR..
   Bundle 4c355f8488a9723c0d361369043cbc06 is installed
   Bundle loaded.
   Start bundle with: conduct run 4c355f8
   Unload bundle with: conduct unload 4c355f8
   Print ConductR info with: conduct info
   Print bundle info with: conduct info 4c355f8
   [success] Total time: 3 s, completed 05-Dec-2017 14:07:24
   ```

Now we have loaded our `wf-producer-impl` bundle into the ConductR Sandbox environment successfully. Go ahead and deploy the other two microservices in the same way.

Loading wf-frontend

Now it's time to load the `wf-frontend` bundle into Sandbox by performing the following steps:

1. Execute the `project wf-frontend` command to access this microservice:

   ```
   > project wf- frontend
   [wf-forntned] $
   ```

2. Execute the `conduct load` command. Enter the `conduct load` command and press the *Tab* key from your keyboard. It will pick up the recently created bundle for that microservice, as shown here:

   ```
   [wf-forntned] $ conduct load /home/rambabuposa/Applications/lagom-
   wf-reactive-system/wf-frontend/target/bundle/wf-
   forntned-1.0.0-8afb9230b7ed3b122e5434f80930aa7d9896f491b4a927febf18
   230161481248.zip
   Retrieving bundle..
   Resolving bundle using [uri_resolver]
   Loading bundle to ConductR..
   Bundle 8afb9230b7ed3b122e5434f80930aa7d is installed
   Bundle loaded.
   Start bundle with: conduct run 8afb923
   Unload bundle with: conduct unload 8afb923
   Print ConductR info with: conduct info
   Print bundle info with: conduct info 8afb923
   [success] Total time: 4 s, completed 05-Dec-2017 15:42:45
   [wf-forntned] $
   ```

We have successfully loaded all our `impl` and `frontend` microservice's bundles into the ConductR Sandbox environment. It's time to run all of them to use our WF Reactive System services.

Running and testing WF Reactive System bundles

In this section, we will run all our WF Reactive System bundles and test the application services.

1. To run `wf-producer-impl`, enter the following:

```
> project wf-producer-impl
[info] Set current project to wf-producer-impl (in build
file:/home/rambabuposa/Applications/lagom-wf-reactive-system/)
>
> conduct run wf-producer-impl
Bundle run request sent.
Bundle 2a4373013414028ac3f210cb5dd64429 waiting to reach expected
scale 1
Bundle 2a4373013414028ac3f210cb5dd64429 expected scale 1 is met
Stop bundle with: conduct stop 2a43730
Print ConductR info with: conduct info
Print bundle info with: conduct info 2a43730
[success] Total time: 11 s, completed 05-Dec-2017 23:53:20
>
```

2. To run `wf-consumer-impl`, enter the following:

```
> project wf-consumer-impl
[info] Set current project to wf-consumer-impl (in build
file:/home/rambabuposa/Applications/lagom-wf-reactive-system/)
>
> conduct run wf-consumer-impl
Bundle run request sent.
Bundle 67199e5e4e63c9444e617a7449961795 waiting to reach expected
scale 1
Bundle 67199e5e4e63c9444e617a7449961795 expected scale 1 is met
Stop bundle with: conduct stop 67199e5
Print ConductR info with: conduct info
Print bundle info with: conduct info 67199e5
[success] Total time: 11 s, completed 05-Dec-2017 23:57:40
>
```

3. To run `wf-frontend`, enter the following:

```
> project wf-forntned
[info] Set current project to wf-forntned (in build
file:/home/rambabuposa/Applications/lagom-wf-reactive-system/)
```

```
>
[wf-forntned] $ conduct run wf-forntned
Bundle run request sent.
Bundle 467064b9119e649d76bbf4b2d8165cfd waiting to reach expected
scale 1
Bundle 467064b9119e649d76bbf4b2d8165cfd expected scale 1 is met
Stop bundle with: conduct stop 467064b
Print ConductR info with: conduct info
Print bundle info with: conduct info 467064b
[success] Total time: 8 s, completed 05-Dec-2017 23:59:29
[wf-forntned] $
```

Now that we have successfully run all our required bundles, execute the following command to check all our bundles' statuses:

```
rambabuposa@ram:~$ conduct info
UNLICENSED - please use "conduct load-license" to use more agents.
Additional agents are freely available for registered users.
Licensed To: unknown
Max ConductR agents: 1
ConductR Version(s): 2.1.*
Grants: conductr, cinnamon, akka-sbr
```

4. When we run `conduct info` command now, we can observe the following output in the similar kind of table from console:

ID	NAME	TAG	#REP	#STR	#RUN	ROLES
67199e5	wf-consumer-impl	1.0.0	1	0	1	web
cabaae7	visualizer	2.1.0	1	0	1	web
2a43730	wf-producer-impl	1.0.0	1	0	1	web
64affe9	continuous-delivery	2.1.6	1	0	1	continuous-delivery
467064b	wf-forntned	1.0.0	1	0	1	web
e7de659-92feca5	conductr-haproxy	2.1.10	1	0	1	haproxy
a32763e	cassandra	-	1	0	1	cassandra

Now we can access our WF Reactive System services using the following URLs:

- http://192.168.10.1:9000/weather
- http://192.168.10.1:9000/latestwf

- `http://192.168.10.1:9000/wf`
- `http://192.168.10.1:9000/wf/one`

When we access these URLs in a web browser, they looks like similar to those in `Chapter 9`, *Reactive Microservices with Lagom*, only we need to change the URL from localhost to ConductR Docker IP addresses, as shown here:

To access our WF Reactive System we used the following URL from `Chapter 9`, *Reactive Microservices with Lagom*:

`http://localhost:9000/weather`

In the same way, we use the following URL to access the same system from ConductR Sandbox. The only difference is that we used the ConductR Docker IP address instead of `localhost`:

`http://192.168.10.1:9000/weather`

Here, input the data and click on the **Submit** button:

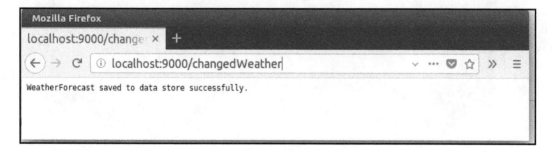

The data is submitted successfully:

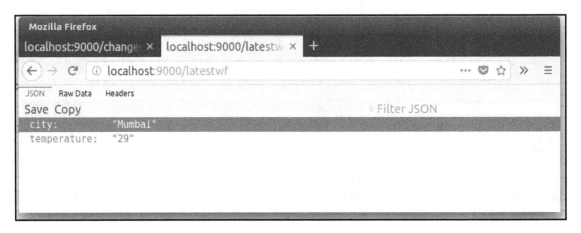

Now access the latest WF data from in-memory, as shown here:

Now access the latest WF data from the data store, as shown here:

Now access the top 10 WF data from the data store, as shown here:

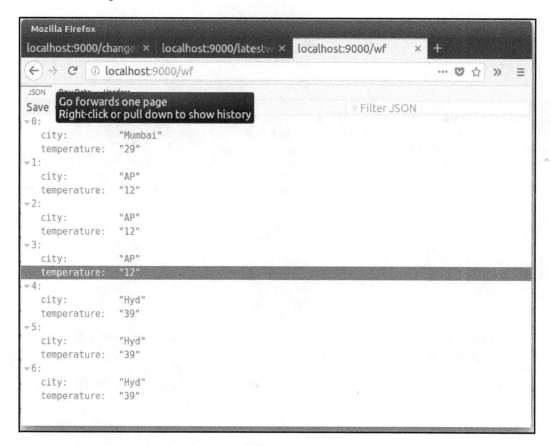

Useful ConductR commands

So far, we have discussed a couple of important and frequently used ConductR Sandbox commands. In this section, we will discuss some more useful ConductR Sandbox commands:

- To get some help about `sandbox` command, please use the following command:

```
ram$ sandbox -h
usage: sandbox [-h] {version,run,start,restart,stop,ps,logs} ...
```

The following `-h` or `--help` are optional arguments:

```
-h, --help show this help message and exit
```

- The following are Sandbox's useful commands:

```
{version,run,start,restart,stop,ps,logs}
```

To use one of the following sub-commands:

```
version      Print version
run (start) Run ConductR sandbox cluster
restart      Restart ConductR sandbox cluster
stop         Stop ConductR sandbox cluster
ps           List the pids for ConductR core and agent sandbox
processes
logs         Fetches the logs of ConductR core and agent processes
```

- To know the ConductR Sandbox version and its supported APIs, please use the following command:

```
ram$ sandbox version
1.2.25
Supported API version(s): 1, 2
ram$ conduct version
1.2.25
Supported API version(s): 1, 2
```

Here, `Supported API version(s): 1, 2` means this Sandbox or ConductR supports both API 1 and API 2.

- To run a Lagom's bundle in the ConductR Sandbox, please use the following command:

```
ram$ conduct run wf-producer-impl
```

Alternatively, you can run the following:

```
ram$ conduct run 2a43730
```

Here, `2a43730` is a short hash of the `wf-producer-impl` bundle. We can get it when we load it.

- To upload a Lagom's bundle into ConductR Sandbox, we need to use the following command:

```
ram$ conduct unload wf-producer-impl
```

We can execute all Sandbox commands by using bundle names, such as `wf-producer-impl`. However, sometimes, if we have more than one generated bundle locally at the same path, then we cannot execute most of the Sandbox commands using its name. If we do so, it will complain with an error saying that there is more than one bundle available with that name.

In this case, we should go with a short hash, as shown here:

```
ram$ conduct unload 2a43730
```

- To stop a running Lagom's bundle in ConductR Sandbox, we need to use the following command:

```
ram$ conduct stop wf-producer-impl
```

or we can also use the following:

```
ram$ conduct stop 2a43730
```

- To know the available events of a Lagom's bundle in ConductR Sandbox, we need to use the following command:

```
ram$ conduct events wf-producer-impl
```

or we can also use the following:

```
ram$ conduct events 2a43730
```

- To know the available logs of a Lagom's bundle in ConductR Sandbox, please use the following command:

```
ram$ conduct logs wf-producer-impl
```

or we can also use the following:

```
ram$ conduct logs 2a43730
```

By default, the `logs` command displays the latest 10 lines of log statements. If we want to see more logs, we should use the `-n` option, as shown here:

```
ram$ conduct logs -n 100 2a43730
```

This command displays the latest 100 log statements available in Sandbox.

- Use the `sandbox stop` command to stop the sandbox environment completely, as shown here. It stops all the currently running processes too:

```
ram$ sudo sandbox stop
|---------------------------------------------|
| Stopping HAProxy |
|---------------------------------------------|
sandbox-haproxy
HAProxy has been successfully stopped
|---------------------------------------------|
| Stopping ConductR |
|---------------------------------------------|
ConductR core pid 29913 stopped
ConductR agent pid 30010 stopped
ConductR agent pid 30016 stopped
ConductR agent pid 30009 stopped
ConductR has been successfully stopped
```

We can use the `conduct` command normally, as shown here:

```
ram$ conduct info
```

Alternatively, we can use it from the SBT console too, as shown here:

```
ram$ sbt
> conduct info
```

Refer to `Chapter 9`, *Reactive Microservices with Lagom* for screenshots of these URLs.

 In this chapter, we have installed and experimented with the Lightbend ConductR Sandbox free environment. If you want to test and use it in your live environment, please buy the license from Lightbend.

Summary

In this chapter, we learned about Lightbend's Development Environment—ConductR Sandbox. ConductR is a **RAM (Reactive Applications Manager)**. It provides a **CLI (Command-Line Interface)** to create our services bundles, and load and run those bundles in the Sandbox environment.

We discussed how to set up the local ConductR Sandbox environment and its main components.

Lightbend ConductR supports two kinds of APIs—the Bundle API and Control API.

We converted our WF Reactive System components to match the ConductR Sandbox environment, then created bundles and deployed them into Sandbox successfully. Finally, we tested our WF Reactive System.

In the next chapter, we are going to discuss the Reactive design principles, patterns, and some of the useful best practices.

12
Reactive Design Patterns and Best Practices

In this chapter, we will discuss the Reactive Design Principles, Design Patterns, and Best Practices we should know about in order to design and develop Reactive Systems (Reactive microservices or Reactive Web Applications).

In this chapter, these Reactive Design Patterns are investigated, and proven solutions to the commonly occurring problems in any Reactive microservices or applications or systems are provided.

We have already discussed what a Reactive Pattern is and how it solves common problems raised in non-Reactive Systems in Chapter 1, *Getting Started with Reactive and Functional Programming,* and a couple of Reactive Patterns in the previous chapters. For instance, we discussed the *Let-It-Crash Pattern* in Chapter 4, *Building Reactive Applications with Akka,* the *CQRS/ES Reactive Design Pattern* and the *Backpressure Pattern* in Chapter 7, *Working with Reactive Streams,* and so on.

As with **Object-Oriented Programming (OOP)** Design Patterns, Architectural and Integration Design Patterns, and **Functional Programming (FP)** Design Patterns, we need to learn Reactive Design Patterns to develop our Reactive Systems, which are reliable, Responsive, never fail, highly available, highly Scalable, high performing, and Resilient applications.

In this chapter, you will learn about the following Reactive Design Patterns and best practices:

- Let-it-crash Design Pattern
- Circuit Breaker Design Pattern
- Sharding Design Pattern
- Event Sourcing Pattern
- Event Streaming Pattern
- Active-Passive Replication Pattern
- Resource Management Design Patterns: Resource Loan and Resource Pool Patterns
- Message Flow Patterns: Request-Response, Tell and Ask Patterns
- Throttling Pattern
- Pull Pattern

In this chapter, we will discuss Reactive Design Patterns and best practices in theory with some useful code snippets. If you really want to know more about them and want to experiment and utilize those patterns in your projects, please refer to this chapter's GitHub location for full working examples.

Understanding Design Patterns

As we know, nowadays, we need to build Fault-Tolerant applications so that end users or customers don't feel frustrated using our application. We cannot write correct code to handle exceptions, errors, or faults and its a bit tough and not easy to do so.

It's not possible to develop a System or Application without it failing even once in its lifetime. New Systems may have more Faults (or Errors or Exceptions) and Legacy Systems may have less, but failures are common and it is expected in each and every System.

We should design and develop our Reactive Systems, Microservices, or Web Applications with failure in mind. As an **Object** is a first-class citizen in an Object-Oriented System, a **Function** is a first-class citizen in a Functional System, and a Fault-Handling Technique is a first-class citizen in a Reactive System.

In an Object-Oriented System, to handle Exceptions or Errors, we write lots of boilerplate defensive coding using `try...catch` blocks (the traditional approach). It's not possible to detect all error scenarios in advance and write Exception Handling for them, and it might seem tough to understand this approach.

The drawbacks of the traditional approach (`try...catch`) to handle Faults include:

- Lots of boilerplate code
- Fewer chances of finding all bugs
- Tough to cover all scenarios in advance
- Less readability; tough to understand, maintain, and extend the code
- No clear separation between actual Business Logic and Fault Handling Logic

This kind of `try...catch` or traditional approach is also known as **Defensive Programming**.

How to solve these problems? We should use some frameworks or tools available in the market to get Fault-Handling for free. Here, we will discuss Akka Toolkit's Fault-Handling Technique: Let-it-Crash.

Understanding Let-it-Crash

Let-it-Crash is a Reactive Model/Technique or Reactive Design Pattern used as a Fault-Handling Technique. It's the default Fault-Handling Technique in Akka Toolkit. Let-it-Crash eases the development of Fault-Tolerant applications easily.

Let-it-Crash means *Do your Business Logic (assigned Job). If something goes wrong, don't handle it. Just hand it over to someone to take the necessary action.* Akka Toolkit supports this technique using **Supervision**.

In simple words, Let-it-Crash = Do what you can do, let someone handle the Fault.

Supervision is a technique to organize the Akka Actors into a hierarchy that means creating a Parent-Child Relationship between Actors. In Akka terminology, the Parent Actor is known as a **Supervisor** and the Child Actor is known as a **Subordinate**.

When a Child Actor finds a Fault, it will escalate that to its Supervisor to take the necessary action. If its immediate Supervisor is able to handle that fault, that Supervisor handles that fault. Otherwise, the Supervisor will escalate the Fault to its Supervisor, and so on:

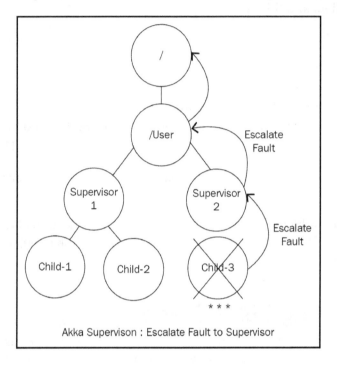

Akka Supervison : Escalate Fault to Supervisor

Here, if **Child-3** finds any fault, it will escalate that to its immediate Supervisor to handle.

The Supervisor does one of the following actions:

- **Restart**: The Supervisor Actor restarts the Child Actor to process the next messages.
- **Resume**: The Supervisor Actor resumes the same Child Actor to process the messages. That Child Actor ignores the previous crash or fault.
- **Stop**: The Supervisor Actor stops/terminates the Child Actor. It will no longer be available to process the messages.
- **Escalate**: If the Supervisor Actor doesn't know what to do with the fault, it will escalate the fault to its Parent (Supervisor) Actor.

When an Actor creates another Actor, that Actor automatically becomes the Supervisor Actor of that newly created Actor.

The main goal of Akka's Supervision is Clear Separation of Concerns; the Child Actor does the actual Business Logic and the Supervisor Actor does the actual Fault-Handling Logic.

 Refer to the *Akka Supervision* section in `Chapter 4`, *Building Reactive Applications with Akka,* for a better understanding and also refer to some code snippets and examples.

The Circuit Breaker pattern

In this section, we will discuss another popular and frequently used Reactive Design Pattern: the Circuit Breaker Design Pattern.

Understanding the Circuit Breaker pattern

A Circuit Breaker is one of the most popular and frequently used Reactive Design Patterns. It deals with our Reactive System Stability-related issues. It helps our Reactive System to deal with our System's dependency issues, such as down, crashed, slow performance, restart, and so on.

This Circuit Breaker component finds those dependency issues and stops the sending of further requests so that our system does not waste allocating resources, and also our end users immediately see some error message such as **System is unavailable, please try again later**.

The Circuit Breaker waits for a predefined amount of time and again tries to send one request to those dependencies (external system or components) and sees the results. If it receives a failure error again, then it waits for some time. If it receives the success response, then it sends the remaining requests to external systems. Then the end users will see the response.

With or without Circuit Breaker

As we know, every System (either Reactive or Non-Reactive) has some dependency with some external Systems or components. Here, components or external Systems are Data Stores, Filesystems, Servers, REST APIs, Web Sites, and so on:

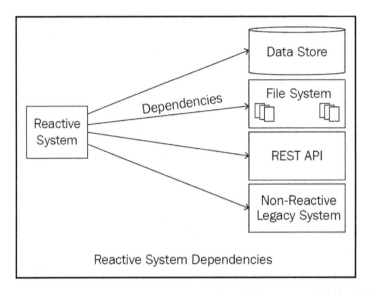

Reactive System Dependencies

As we discussed in the *Let-it-Crash design pattern* section, faults or errors are common in each and every component or system. We cannot expect such issues as component down, crashes, restarts, out of memory, and so on.

When end users interact with our Reactive System and our System in turn interacts with external Systems or components to serve the users, the External System or components may not be working as expected, or they may be down, or they may have crashed. In such a situation, our Reactive System end users wait for a long time. If they try again and again, or at the same time more users interact with our system for the same services or different services, they may see a lot of waiting time or timeouts.

Even though different users send requests to different services, they may face the same issue because our System allocates a lot of resources to them and may not able to serve the clients and release resources immediately to serve other user's requests.

Let's assume that our **Reactive System** is as shown here:

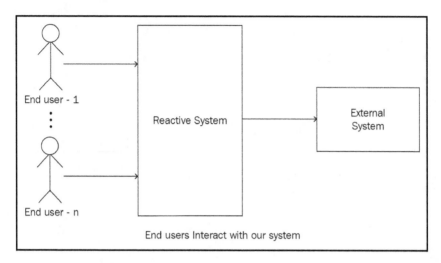

Imagine that the **External System** is down or has crashed, as shown in the following diagram:

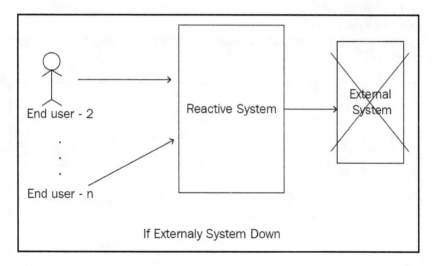

In that case, the whole flow goes down, as shown here:

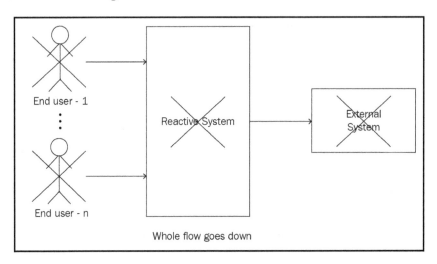

If our Reactive System uses the **Circuit Breaker** component, as shown in the following diagram, then end users will see some error page saying that our system has an issues and we should try again after some time. Then the user does not try again and again, so our system and external system will get some time to recover from that situation. If users interact with our system for other services that are up and running, they will get the response as expected:

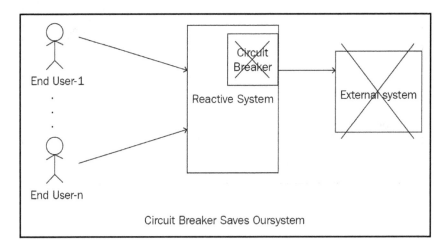

How a Circuit Breaker works

As shown in the preceding diagram, a **Circuit Breaker** component sits between our **Reactive System** and **External System** or Component. It works as a mediator to our **Reactive System**.

Our **Reactive System** sends end user requests to the **External System** through this component. We will discuss how a Circuit Breaker works with the help of its states or stages.

A Circuit Breaker component has the following three stages:

- Closed
- Open
- Half-Open

Observe the following diagram to understand how the Circuit Breaker works:

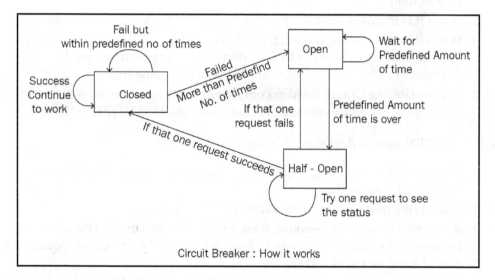

Circuit Breaker : How it works

Next, we will see how the Circuit Breaker components work.

Now, let us pick-up the Circuit Breaker's stages one by one and understand them very well.

Initially, the Circuit Breaker enters into a **CLOSED** state and waits for Client Requests.

In the **CLOSED** state, it does the following things:

1. It receives Client Requests and makes a call to the External Component or Service
2. If it succeeds and receives the response from that External Component, it will reset the failure count to 0 and send that Response back to our Reactive Service (the Circuit Breaker component owing service), which in turn sends that Response back to the Client (or end user)
3. If it fails to receive the response from that External Component, it will increment the failure count by one and check whether that count is greater than the predefined `failureThreshold`
4. If the `failureCount` is greater than the failureThreshold, then that Circuit Breaker component trips or enters into the **OPEN** state

In the **OPEN** state, it does the following things:

1. The Circuit Breaker component enters into this state when `failureCount` is greater than `failureThreshold`
2. When it is in this state, it does not make a call to the external component
3. When it is in this state, if the Client sends any requests to it through our Reactive System, it won't make a call to the external component; it just sends `CircuitBreakerOpenException` and waits for some time
4. In this state, the Circuit Breaker component waits for a predefined amount of time. Once that time expires, it will enter into the **HALF-OPEN** state

In the **HALF-OPEN** state, it does the following things:

1. The Circuit Breaker component enters into this state when it finishes the predefined waiting time.
2. It sends the first request to the external component.
3. If it receives a success response, then it will enter into the **CLOSED** state to process further Client Requests. Before picking up the first client request, it will reset the failure count to 0 again.
4. If it receives a failure response, then it will re-trip to the **OPEN** state and wait for a predefined amount of time.

Please refer to Akka Toolkit's CircuitBreaker Component implementation at `https://github.com/akka/akka/blob/master/akka-actor/src/main/scala/akka/pattern/CircuitBreaker.scala`.

The following are also known as Reactive Recovery Design Patterns:

- Let-it-Crash
- Circuit Breaker

The Sharding Pattern

Sharding means dividing a whole component into small and manageable parts and distributing them into different nodes of a cluster, so that that the whole component can be accessed at all times. It gives better performance and never fails. Let us assume, we design and develop our Reactive System by following this design pattern. Even if one of our system's portion or part fails, it will recover that functionality by using another portion from same node or a different node in that same cluster or different cluster.

Here, those small parts are known as **Shards**.

This principle is the same even in the Reactive World. In a Reactive System, we divide a big Domain Object into small partitions and distribute them into different nodes in the cluster so that we can access our Domain Object data without fail:

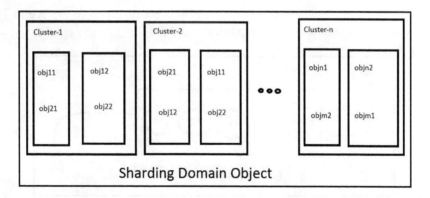

Sharding Domain Object

As shown in the preceding diagram, our Reactive System's Domain objects are distributed into different nodes in our cluster. There is no guaranteed order of those Shards. The Shards are distributed randomly.

The main goals of this Sharding technique are as follows:

- Scalability
- 100% availability
- Better performance

The Event Sourcing pattern

We have already discussed the **Event Sourcing** (**ES**) Reactive Design Pattern with **CQRS** (**Command Query Responsibility Segregation**) to store events to the WRITE side in a data store and retrieve those events from the READ side from a data store.

Refer to the CQRS/ES design Pattern section in `Chapter 7`, *Working with Reactive Streams*, to understand both the design patterns in depth.

The Event Streaming Pattern

We have already discussed what an Event Stream is and its usage in `Chapter 7`, *Working with Reactive Systems*. Please refer to that chapter for more details.

Like a Messaging Queue, which is useful to store Messages, an Event Stream is useful to store a Set of Events. In other words, we can say that an Event Stream is a sequence of events.

As we know, in a Reactive System, each User Action is represented as an Event. These events are stored in a data store, as shown here:

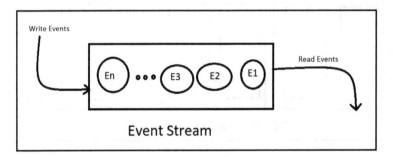

Let's look at the Cassandra Data store for a better understanding. We also used the same data store to store our **WF** (**Weather Forecasting**) Reactive System events.

In Cassandra, we store our System's sequence of Events into an Event Stream. It is known as a **Journal**. We use Akka Persistence and Lagom Framework's Persistence API to store or retrieve our System's events to/from the Journal.

We store each event into the Journal with a unique Persistence ID. This ID is useful to identify events uniquely for storing or retrieving them.

In Akka Toolkit, to store events into Cassandra's Event Stream, we use the Akka Persistence API, and to retrieve events from Cassandra's Event Stream, we use the Akka Persistence Query API.

The following are the main benefits of storing all events into a data store:

- We can create a history of existing Events
- We can generate reports
- We can analyze user actions performed in the past on our System
- We will get auditing for free

If we store all the events of a Persistence Entity into an Event Stream, we can maintain its state. If that entity crashes or restarts, we can recover that entity's State easily by playing all those events one by one.

 Both Event Sourcing and Event Streaming Reactive Design Patterns are useful when used in conjunction with the CQRS design pattern.

The Active-Passive Replication Pattern

What if some of our Reactive System Components fail to work due to a heavy load, or crash due to some issues? It does not give a good impression to the end users. Nowadays, every system should work normally and should be 100% available all the time, even if our System's critical components fail to work.

How to solve this problem? A proven solution is **Replication**.

The Replication technique allows us to distribute our Reactive System components into different Replicas across the clusters, so that our system is available all the time and supports fault-tolerance, high performance, high availability, and responsiveness.

In this section, we will discuss one of the important Reactive Replication Patterns: the **Active-Passive Replication Pattern**.

Observe the following Reactive System scenarios:

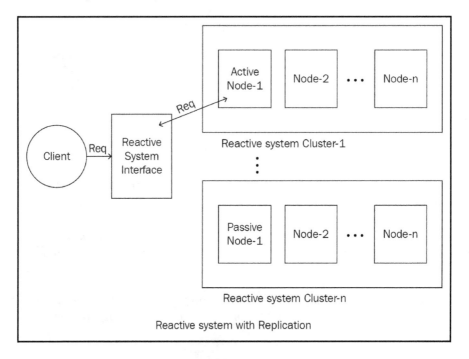

Here, one of our end clients or users sends a request to our Reactive System, and that request is received by Node-1 in our Reactive System Cluster.

Suppose that component fails to serve the Client Request; then our System should pick up another replica of the same component from the same cluster or a different cluster, from the same location or a different location, and assign that Client Request.

In this case, the previous Node-1 becomes a Passive Node and the newly assigned Node-1 will become an Active Node to serve the Client Request. This new Active Node will take the current System state and continue the execution of the computation logic and serve the results back to the end client, as shown here:

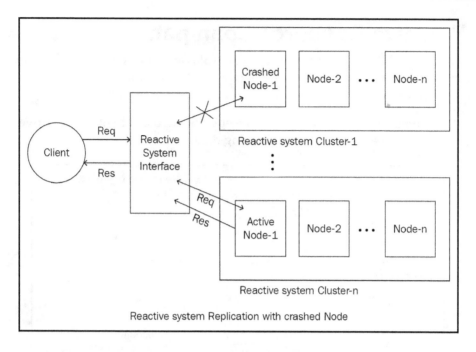

Reactive system Replication with crashed Node

The main goal of this Reactive Active-Passive Replication Pattern is that our Reactive System should allow only one component to be active at any given point in time to perform any modifications to avoid state inconsistency issues.

The Resource Management Design Patterns

As with other Systems, every Reactive System has a set of components to serve its services to the end clients. These components need a set of resources to help them or alleviate their functionality. Here, resources can be anything, such as an external system, external REST API, database, socket, and so on.

In order to utilize those resources efficiently and effectively by our Reactive System components, we should consider a set of Reactive Design patterns in the design and development of our systems.

In this section, we will discuss the following two important Resource Management Reactive Design Patterns:

- Resource Loan Pattern
- Resource Pool Pattern

The Reactive Resource Loan pattern

The Resource Loan Pattern is not new to Java or Scala developers. We have already used it in many applications to develop our non-Reactive System components, such as creating a database connection, creating a socket connection, creating a file, and so on.

In Reactive Systems, we also use the same concept, but we use it to utilize Reactive System resources effectively. Let's observe the following diagram:

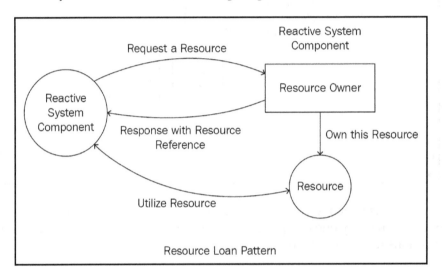

The Reactive Resource Loan Pattern works as follows:

1. In our Reactive System, one of our System components, which needs a resource to fulfill its computation task, sends a request (**Request a Resource)** to another System component, which owns that resource
2. The owning Resource checks that Resource's availability
3. If that Resource is available, it sends the Resource Reference as a Response (**Response with Resource Reference**)
4. Our End System Component submits its computation task to that Resource
5. The Resource performs and completes the computation task and sends the Results to that End System Component
6. The End System Component utilizes the Resource effectively and closes it

By observing this process, we can understand that it is similar to a database connection. However, we use it between Reactive System components.

The Reactive Resource Pool pattern

The Reactive Resource Pool pattern is similar to the previously discussed Resource Loan Pattern. Unlike the Resource Loan Pattern that deals with a single Resource, the Resource Pool pattern deals with a Pool or a set of Resources.

Yes, you are right. It's something similar to a Pool of Connection or Connection Pool, which we used in our Non-Reactive Systems or Legacy Systems. Let's observe the following diagram:

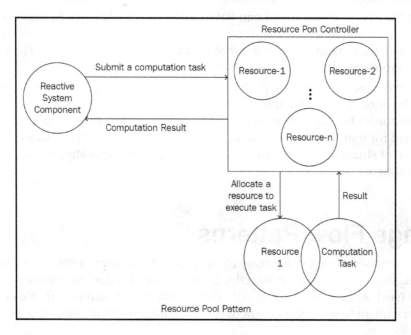

A Reactive Resource Pool Pattern works as follows:

1. In our Reactive System, one of our System Components, which needs a Resource to fulfill its computation task, sends a request (**Submit a Computation Task**) to another System Component which owns that Resource
2. The owning Resource checks the Resource availability in its **Pool of Resources**
3. If that Resource is available, it **Activates** that Resource
4. It sends the Resource Reference as a Response (**Response with Resource Reference**)

5. Our End System Component submits its computation task to that Resource
6. The Resource performs and completes the computation task and sends the Results to that End System Component
7. The End System Component utilizes the Resource effectively and closes it

The main differences between the two Reactive Resource Management Patterns are:

- The Reactive Resource Loan Pattern deals with only one Resource, whereas the Reactive Resource Pool Pattern deals with a Pool of Resources.
- In the Reactive Resource Loan Pattern, the Client (Reactive System component) who is going to utilize that Resource is responsible for taking care of shutting down, terminating, or closing that Resource once its job is over. The Owning Component of that Resource is not responsible for this.
- In the Reactive Resource Pool Pattern, the Client (Reactive System component) who is going to utilize that Resource is responsible for sending a message to the Resource Owning Component, saying that its task is fulfilled and that there is no need for that Resource anymore. Then, the Resource Owning Component takes care of shutting down, terminating, closing, or the activation/passivation of that Resource.

Message Flow Patterns

As we have discussed, Reactive Systems comprise a set of components. Each component may be a Reactive Microservice. A Reactive System may also depend on some external components (such as data store, REST API, filesystem, server, and so on). We need some common mechanism to communicate between the components to fulfill those components' jobs.

As per the Reactive Manifesto, the following are the four Reactive Design principles or characteristics of a Reactive System:

- Message-Driven
- Elasticity
- Resilience
- Responsiveness

Take a look at the following **Reactive Design Principles** diagram:

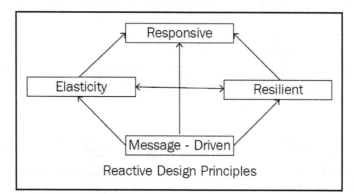

Reactive Design Principles

We can observe from the diagram that **Message - Driven** is the base principle for a Reactive System. This means that the **Message** is a basic building block or element to communicate with Reactive System components.

Yes, *Messaging* is a common technique in a Reactive System to communicate among its components. They communicate with each other by exchanging Messages.

Message Flow Reactive Design Patterns means *how messages flow between our Reactive System components, and how to control them*. These patterns are also known as **Communication Patterns**.

When a User interacts with a Reactive System, each User Action (User Request) is converted into an Event. This Event, in turn, converts into a Message. This Message is exchanged between the Reactive System component to perform computations or to retrieve data and serve the result as a response to the user, as shown here:

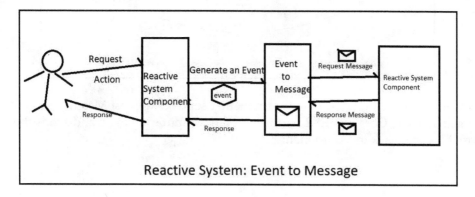

Reactive System: Event to Message

After observing the preceding diagram, we can understand that a Message is a basic building block of a Reactive System to communicate between its components to serve its clients' requests.

That's why it's very important to understand Message Flow Reactive Design Patterns. There are plenty of Message Flow Patterns, and it's not possible to discuss them in detail in a subsection. So, here, we cover only a couple of important and frequently used patterns.

The Request-Response Design Pattern

This is not a new design pattern. It is well known and the most familiar design pattern for Java developers. We already used this pattern in our Legacy/Non-Reactive Systems, which are implemented by using the Servlet API.

Servlets communicate with each other by sending HTTP Request and Response Objects.

In the same way, we use this Request/Response Reactive Design pattern in our Reactive Systems to communicate with its components by exchanging Request/Response Messages, as shown in the following diagram:

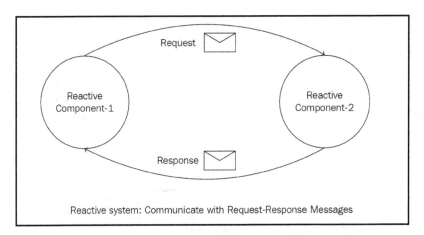

Reactive system: Communicate with Request-Response Messages

As shown in the preceding diagram, Component-1 sends a Request Message to Component-2. Then, Component-2 performs some computation logic and sends the Response Message back to Component-1.

Understanding the Reactive Design Pattern

A Tell Design Pattern means a Reactive component sends a request to another Reactive component and does not wait or look for that other component's Response. It just fires that Request message and forgets about it. This is why it is also known as **Fire-and-Forget Design Pattern**.

Akka Toolkit has implemented the same design pattern to send messages between its components (Actors). It has implemented this pattern as the function `tell`.

We can use this `tell` function to send a Message from one Actor to another, as shown here:

```
actorRef.tell(MyMessage)
```

We can also write the preceding code snippet in another format, as follows, by using one of the useful features of the Scala Programming Language:

```
actorRef tell MyMessage
```

Akka Toolkit also has a *Tell Operator* to perform the same job:

```
actorRef ! MyMessage
```

Here, the `!` symbol is a *Tell Operator*, which is Scala syntactic sugar to call that `tell` function.

Ask Reactive Design Pattern

In a Reactive System, one component asks or delegates its computation to another component by sending a Message and continues its further steps in an asynchronous way. Once the other component finishes that computation, it will send a response to the original component.

In simple words, one component delegates its request and asks another component to serve that request.

For instance, Akka Toolkit has implemented this Ask pattern as `akka.pattern.ask`. Like Tell, it also has a function `ask` and has an operator—? (Ask operator).

Let's implement an Akka application to demonstrate this Ask operator:

1. Develop a Data model, as shown here:

```
case object GetWeather
case class WeatherForecast(city:String, temperature:String)
```

2. Develop the WF (Weather Forecasting) Actor, as shown here:

```
class WFClient(wfTeller: ActorRef) extends Actor with ActorLogging {
  implicit val timeout: Timeout = 2.seconds

  def receive = {
    case GetWeather =>
      valwf = (wfTeller ? GetWeather)
      wf.onComplete{ wfValue =>
       log.info("Weather Forecast = " + wfValue)
      }
  }
}
```

Here, our `WFClient` Actor is using the Ask Operator (?) to delegate the `GetWeather` task to the `WFTeller` Actor, as shown here:

```
val wf = (wfTeller ? GetWeather)
```

Once it receives the response from `WFTeller`, it will process the WF and display `WFValue` to the console.

3. Develop the `WFTeller` Actor, as shown here:

```
class WFTeller extends Actor {
  def receive = {
    case GetWeather => sender() ! WeatherForecast("London", "12")
  }
}
```

Here, the `WFTeller` Actor is using Tell Operator (!) to send the `WeatherForecast` data back to the `WFClient` Actor.

4. Let's test our WF Actor logic using a Scala application, as shown here:

```
object AskPatternApp extends App{
  val system = ActorSystem("WFSystem")
  valwfTeller = system.actorOf(Props[WFTeller], "WFTeller")
  valclientActor = system.actorOf(Props(new WFClient(wfTeller)),
```

```
"WFClient")

        clientActor ! GetWeather
        Thread.sleep(1000)
        system.terminate()
    }
```

This example has demonstrated both the Tell and Ask operators.

The Throttling Pattern

The Throttling Reactive Pattern is a Reactive System's Flow control pattern. It is also known as the **Message Throttler**.

Our Reactive System has some external dependencies, such as the REST API. We want to make HTTP requests to that external REST API. The REST API has the following restrictions:

- It accepts only 10 requests per minute from an endpoint
- If it receives more than 10 requests in 1 minute, it will block the endpoint requests, or if we want to proceed, we need to pay some money

If we have this kind of restriction in our external components or systems, then it's good to use the Throttler.

A Throttler Design Pattern allows us to implement a component that sends requests to external components based on our configurations.

For instance, if we need a time-based Throttler to send requests to the preceding REST API, then we can configure how many requests we need to send and how much time we need to wait for the next request.

In this section, we are going to experiment with Akka Toolkit's `TimerBasedThrottler`. Akka Toolkit has a module or extension called **AkkaContrib**, which contains the following Timer-Based Throttler:

```
akka.contrib.throttle.TimerBasedThrottler
```

You can find this component source code at https://github.com/akka/akka/blob/master/akka-contrib/src/main/scala/akka/contrib/throttle/TimerBasedThrottler.scala.

Let's develop one application to test it:

```
class PrintActor extends Actor {
def receive = {
    case message ⇒println(message)
  }
}

object ThrottlerApp extends App{

val system = ActorSystem("WFSystem")
val printer = system.actorOf(Props[PrintActor])
  // The throttler for this example, setting the rate
valthrottler = system.actorOf(Props(classOf[TimerBasedThrottler],
    3 msgsPer5.second))
  // Set the target
throttler ! SetTarget(Some(printer))
  // These three messages will be sent to the target immediately
throttler ! "message-1"
throttler ! "message-2"
throttler ! "message-3"
  // These two will wait until a second has passed
throttler ! "message-4"
throttler ! "message-5"

Thread.sleep(10000)
system.terminate()
}
```

The Pull pattern

Like the Throttling Reactive Pattern, the Pull Reactive Pattern is also a Reactive System's Flow control pattern.

As we discussed in the *Backpressure* section in Chapter 7, *Working with Reactive Streams,* our Reactive Systems may have the following two flavors of Producers/Consumers:

- Faster Producer/Slow Consumer
- Slow Producer/Faster Consumer

In the Faster Producer/Slow Consumer scenario, Pull-based communication is suitable because the Consumer pulls its required amount of data from the Producer to avoid Buffer Overflow issues.

In the Slower Producer/Faster Consumer scenario, Push-based communication is suitable because the Producer pushes more amounts of data from the Producer to Consumer to avoid the Consumer's waiting time issues.

To solve this problem, Reactive Technologies use the *Backpressure* technique, which is a Flow Control mechanism. It uses the Push technique to solve the Slow Producer/Faster Consumer problem and the Pull technique to solve the Faster Producer/Slow Consumer problem.

For instance, the Akka Streams API uses backpressure with the dynamic push-pull technique to solve both of those problems.

We use the Pull Pattern for *Slow Consumer* to pull messages from a *Faster Producer*. In this approach, the Consumer sends a Request Message to the Producer specifying "The number of messages that the Consumer is expecting."

Then, the Producer sends a Response Messages with that number of Messages only. That's why in this technique, *Slow Consumer* does not face a *Buffer Overflow* issue.

Once the Consumer processes those messages, it will again ask the Producer for the next set of Messages, and so on. The Consumer sends the STOP message once it receives the required number of Messages.

Reactive System's best practices and tools

In this section, we will briefly discuss a couple of useful best practices and tools we need to consider in designing and developing Reactive Systems.

Tools

Use Akka Toolkit, Play Framework, and/or Lagom Framework to develop your Reactive Systems (Reactive Microservices or Reactive Web Applications) because they are Reactive by design.

Akka Toolkit supports Reactive Design Patterns by design. Play Framework is developed using Akka Toolkit under the hood. In the same way, Lagom Framework is developed by using Akka Toolkit and Play Framework under the hood.

Akka Toolkit supports the Akka Streams API (which implements Reactive Streams), for data streaming.

Useful best practices

Don't create the `Props` object each and every time we create an `Actor` object. It's good to provide the `Props` object in that Actor's companion object, as shown here:

Example-1:

```
class WFActor extends Actor {
    // receive function implementation
}

object WFActor {
defwfProps = Props[WFActor]
}
```

Example-2:

```
class WFActor(wfTeller: WFTeller) extends Actor {
    // receive function implementation
}

object WFActor {
defwfProps(database: Databse) = Props[WFActor] (classOf[WFActor], database)
}
```

Develop all of our Reactive System's component's functions using the **Future and Promise API** so that we can perform Reactive Asynchronous programming by default.

Prefer tell over ask with Akka Actors

As we know, we can use one of the following two approaches to send messages between Akka Actors:

- **Tell (!)**: It works in *Fire-and-Forget fashion*. Its a non-blocking and asynchronous approach.
- **Ask (?)**: It works in *Send-And-Receive-Future* fashion. It sends a message asynchronously and returns a Future representing a possible result.

There are performance implications of using ask since something needs to keep track of when it times out, there needs to be something that bridges a Promise into an ActorRef and it also needs to be reachable through remoting. So always prefer tell for performance, and only ask if you must.

 For more information refer to the Akka Toolkit documentation at `https:/` `/doc.akka.io/docs/akka/current//actors.html#send-messages`.

Don't sequentialize Futures

It's not a good practice the sequentialize the Future calls as shown in the following code snippet:

```
for{
  a <- obj1.getSomeThing()
  b <- obj2.getRest()
} yield(a, b)
```

Here, let's assume that both `obj1.getSomeThing()` and `obj1.getSomeThing()` make calls to external systems or remote Rest APIs and then return Futures. If we sequentialize them as shown in the preceding code snippet, we don't get benefits. Then our system will lose performance because we are not making those two calls parallel. To improve our system performance, we should use the following technique:

```
val aa = obj1.getSomeThing()
val bb = obj2.getRest()
for{
  a <- aa
  b <- bb
} yield(a, b)
```

Here we are making calls to those two external API parallel so that our system will gain lots of performance.

Summary

In this chapter, we have discussed Reactive Design Patterns. To develop Reactive systems, we should follow not just Reactive Frameworks and Tools, but also some Reactive Design Patterns and best practices to develop our Systems easily to make them highly available, highly Scalable, high performing, and Resilient. They even work under failure scenarios.

As we know, there are plenty of Reactive Design Patterns available. In this chapter, we discussed some of the important and useful Reactive Design Patterns. We have taken each design pattern and discussed it in detail with some suitable code snippets.

Reactive Systems should follow the *Reactive Manifesto* regarding the following four design principles:

- Message-Driven
- Elasticity
- Resilience
- Responsiveness

As we have discussed, a Message is a main or basic building block of Reactive Systems. Each User Action in a Reactive system generates an Event, which in turn is represented as a Message. These Messages are used to exchange information between our Reactive System components.

This is the last chapter of this book. I hope I have explained the Reactive World concepts very well and also given useful examples for each and every concept.

With this knowledge, please go through Lightbend's documentation and learn about a few more advanced concepts to become an expert in Lightbend's Reactive Platform.

Happy learning.

A
Scala Plugin for IntelliJ IDEA

In this section, we will discuss *how to set up Scala Plugin for IntelliJ IDEA IDE*. I will presume that you have already installed JDK 8, SBT, and IntelliJ IDE in your local filesystem.

If you don't have IntelliJ IDEA, you can download it at `https://www.jetbrains.com/idea/download`.

Understanding Scala Plugin

Scala Plugin is a plugin that is used to turn a normal IntelliJ IDEA into a convenient Scala development environment.

By default, IntelliJ IDEA does not come with Scala features. Scala Plugin adds Scala features means that we can create Scala/Play Projects, we can create Scala Applications, Scala worksheets, and more.

Scala Plugin contains the following technologies:

- Scala
- Play Framework
- SBT
- Scala.js

It supports three popular OS Environments: Windows, Mac, and Linux.

How to set up Scala Plugin for IntelliJ IDE

Perform the following steps to install Scala Plugin for IntelliJ IDE to develop our Scala-based projects:

1. Open IntelliJ IDE:

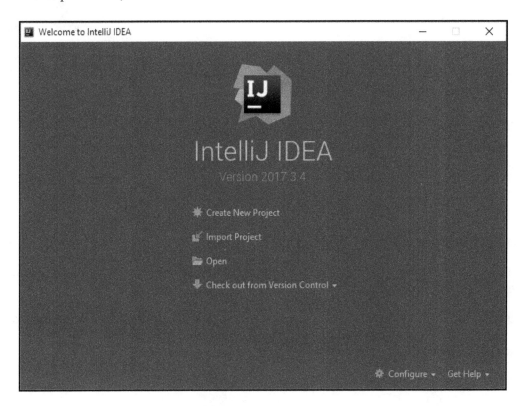

2. Go to **Configure** at the bottom right and click on the **Plugins** option available in the drop-down, as shown here:

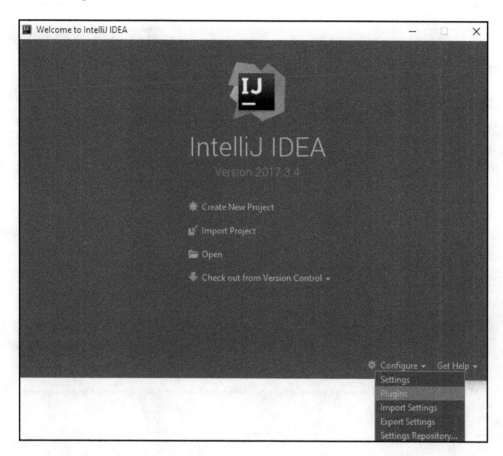

3. This opens the **Plugins** window as shown here:

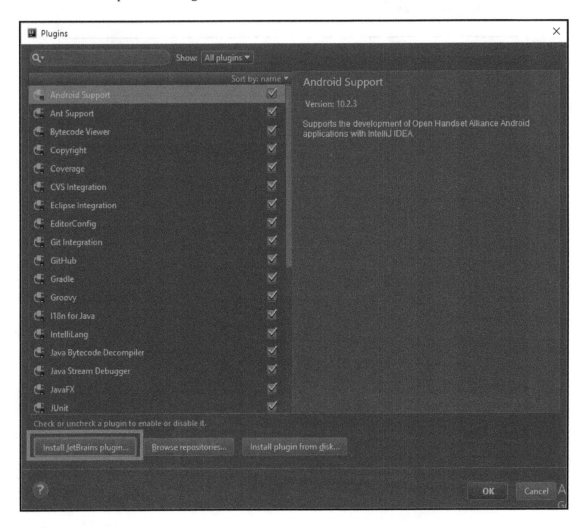

4. Now click on **InstallJetbrainsplugins**, as shown in the preceding screenshot.

5. Next, type the word `Scala` in the search bar to see the **ScalaPlugin**, as shown here:

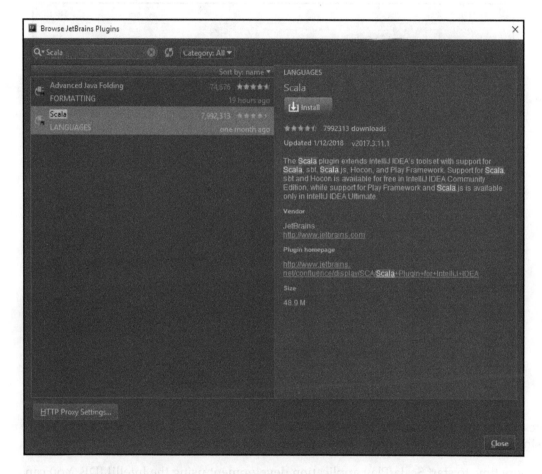

6. Click on the **Install** button to install Scala Plugin for IntelliJ IDEA.
7. Now restart IntelliJ IDEA to see that Scala Plugin features.

8. After we re-open IntelliJ IDEA, if we try to access **File** | **New Project** option, we will see **Scala** option in **New Project** window as shown in the following screenshot to create new Scala or Play Framework-based SBT projects:

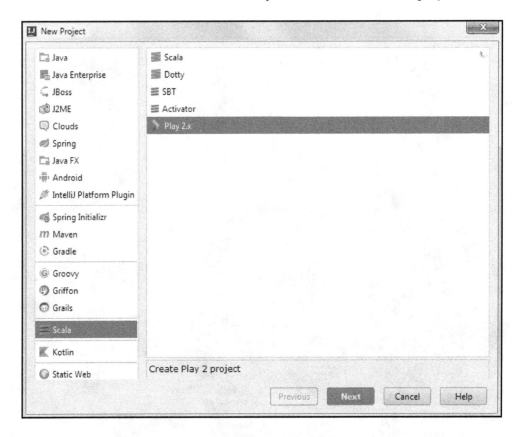

We can see the Play Framework option only in the IntelliJ IDEA Ultimate Edition. As we are using **CE** (**Community Edition**), we cannot see that option.

It's now time to start Scala/Play application development using the IntelliJ IDE. You can start developing some Scala/Play-based applications.

Summary

In this appendix, we saw what Scala Plugin is and covered the installation steps for Scala Plugin for IntelliJ.

B
Installing Robomongo

In this section, we will discuss what Robomongo is, how to set it up in Windows, Linux, and Mac environments, and how to use it.

What is Robomongo?

Robo 3T is a shell-centric, native, cross-platform management tool for MongoDB NoSQL data stores. It was formerly known as Robomongo.

At the time of writing this section, the latest version of Robo 3T is 1.1.1, which supports MongoDB 3.4. Its official website is `https://robomongo.org`.

Setting up Robomongo

We can download the latest version of Robomongo
from `https://robomongo.org/download`. When we click on the download link, we can
observe that it supports Windows, Linux, and Mac environments, as shown here:

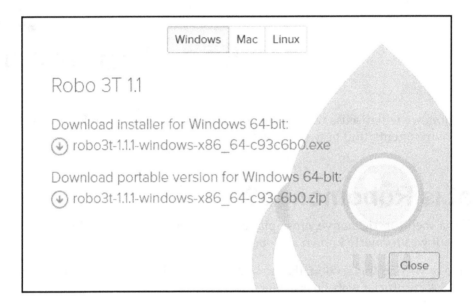

Here, we will discuss how to install Robo 3T in a Windows environment. It is almost similar
for all environments:

1. Download the latest version of Robomongo (for instance, Robo 3T 1.1) as a ZIP
   file. We will get the `robo3t-1.1.1-windows-x86_64-c93c6b0.zip` file.
2. Extract that Zip file to the required location in your filesystem.
3. Double-click on the **robo3t** application available at the Robo3T root folder,
   like `C:\robo3t-1.1.1-XXX`. This will open Robo 3T, as shown here:

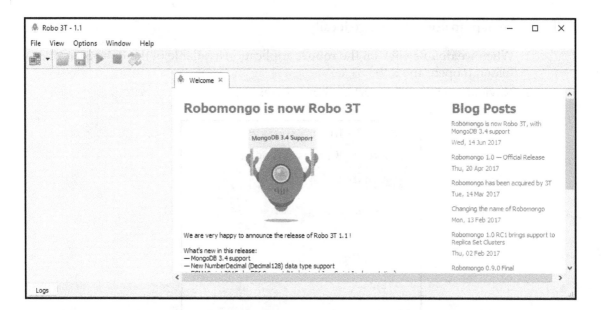

 We can find the Robo 3T source code at
`https://github.com/paralect/robomongo` repository.

How to use Robomongo?

In this section, we will discuss how to use Robo 3T installed in the Windows environment. Accessing Robo 3T is almost similar for all environments. Before performing the following steps, make sure that you have installed MongoDB locally and that it is up and running.

Follow these steps to use Robomongo locally:

1. When we double-click on the **robo3t** application available in the Robo 3T root folder, it opens the Robo 3T UI.
2. Navigate to **File** | **Connect** as shown here:

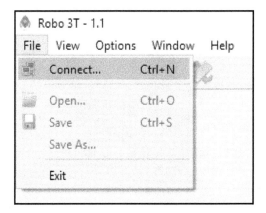

Alternatively, click on the **Connect** option directly available in the toolbar, as shown here:

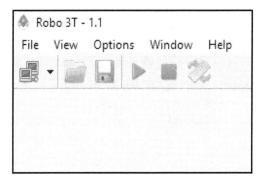

3. It will open the following diagram box to create new MongoDB connections:

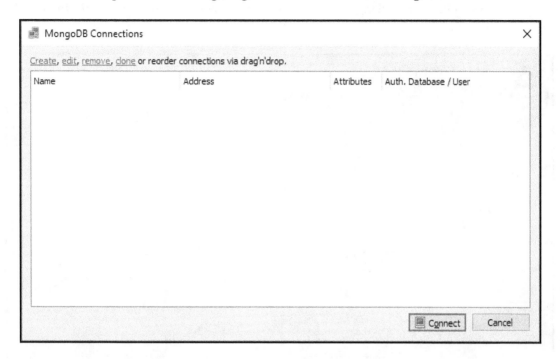

4. Click on the **Create** link available in the **MongoDB Connection** dialog box, as shown in the following screenshot, to create a connection to our local MongoDB data store:

5. It will open the **Connection Settings** dialog box. Use the default MongoDB configuration details. Just change the connection name as per your requirement, as shown in the following screenshot:

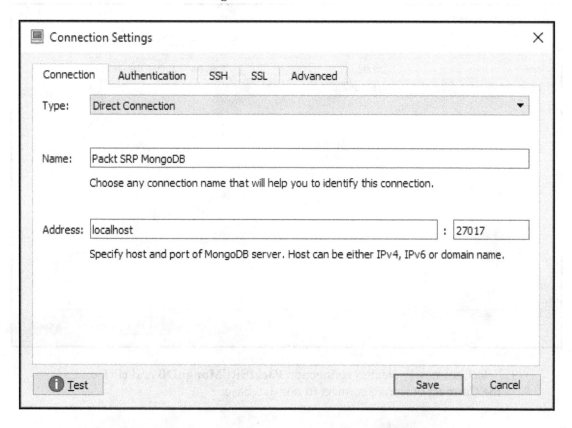

7. Here, our MongoDB connection is using the default configurations, for example, the hostname is `localhost` and the port number is `27017`.

8. Now, just click on the **Save** button. We can observe our newly created MongoDB connection, as shown in the following screenshot:

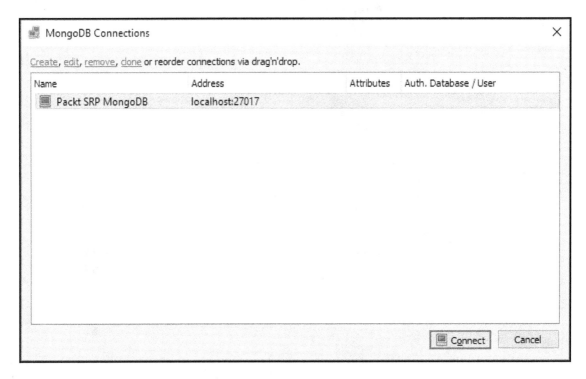

9. Select our newly created connection **PacktSRPMongoDB** and click on the **Connect** button to connect to our database:

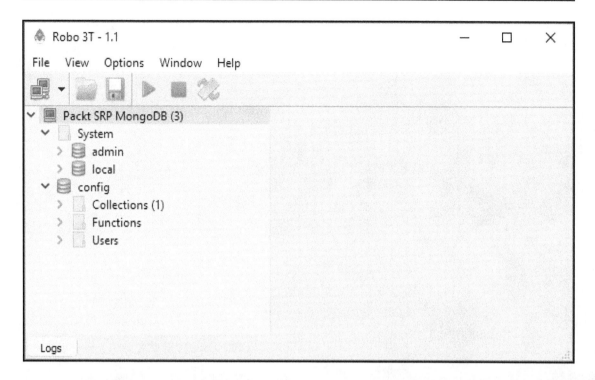

When it connects to our localhost MongoDB, it will show all the default databases and collections, as shown in the preceding screenshot.

Now onward, if we run any Play web application or Akka Persistence application that uses MongoDB as their data store, we can see our application's databases, collections, and data.

This knowledge is enough to use this Robo 3T or Robomongo GUI tool to run and see this book application's data stored in MongoDB.

Summary

In this appendix, we covered the installation steps of Robomongo, which can be installed on Windows, Mac, and Linux.

Other Books You May Enjoy

If you enjoyed this book, you may be interested in these other books by Packt:

Scala Microservices

Jatin Puri, Selvam Palanimalai

ISBN: 978-1-78646-934-2

- Learn the essentials behind Microservices, the advantages and perils associated with them
- Build low latency, high throughput applications using Play and Lagom
- Dive deeper with being asynchronous and understand the superiority it provides
- Model your complex domain data for scale and simplicity with CQRS and Event Sourcing
- Be resilient to failures by using message passing
- Look at best practices of version control workflow, testing, continuous integration and deployments
- Understand operating system level virtualization using Linux Containers. Docker is used to explain how containers work
- Automate your infrastructure with kubernetes

Learning Scala Programming
Vikash Sharma

ISBN: 978-1-78839-282-2

- Get to know the reasons for choosing Scala: its use and the advantages it provides over other languages
- Bring together functional and object-oriented programming constructs to make a manageable application
- Master basic to advanced Scala constructs
- Test your applications using advanced testing methodologies such as TDD
- Select preferred language constructs from the wide variety of constructs provided by Scala
- Make the transition from the object-oriented paradigm to the functional programming paradigm
- Write clean, concise, and powerful code with a functional mindset
- Create concurrent, scalable, and reactive applications utilizing the advantages of Scala

Leave a review - let other readers know what you think

Please share your thoughts on this book with others by leaving a review on the site that you bought it from. If you purchased the book from Amazon, please leave us an honest review on this book's Amazon page. This is vital so that other potential readers can see and use your unbiased opinion to make purchasing decisions, we can understand what our customers think about our products, and our authors can see your feedback on the title that they have worked with Packt to create. It will only take a few minutes of your time, but is valuable to other potential customers, our authors, and Packt. Thank you!

Index

www.ingramcontent.com/pod-product-compliance
Lightning Source LLC
Chambersburg PA
CBHW060637060326
40690CB00020B/4435

* 9 7 8 1 7 8 7 2 8 8 6 4 5 *